Letters from the Battle of Waterloo

Unpublished Correspondence by Allied Officers from the Siborne Papers

edited by
Gareth Glover

Greenhill Books

Letters from the Battle of Waterloo
Unpublished Correspondence by Allied Officers from the Siborne Papers

This paperback edition published in 2018 by
Greenhill Books, c/o Pen & Sword Books Ltd,
47 Church Street, Barnsley,
South Yorkshire, S70 2AS
www.greenhillbooks.com
contact@greenhillbooks.com

Publishing history
Letters from the Battle of Waterloo was first published in hardback in 2004 by Greenhill Books, London, under the title *Letters from Waterloo: The Unpublished Correspondence by Allied Officers from the Siborne Papers*. This 2018 paperback edition includes new introductory material by the author and a foreword by John Hussey.

ISBN: 978-1-78438-349-7

A CIP catalogue record for this book is available from the British Library.

Typeset by Palindrome in Garamond MT
Printed and bound by TJ International Ltd, Padstow

CONTENTS

Contents

PLAN OF THE BATTLE OF WATERLOO.

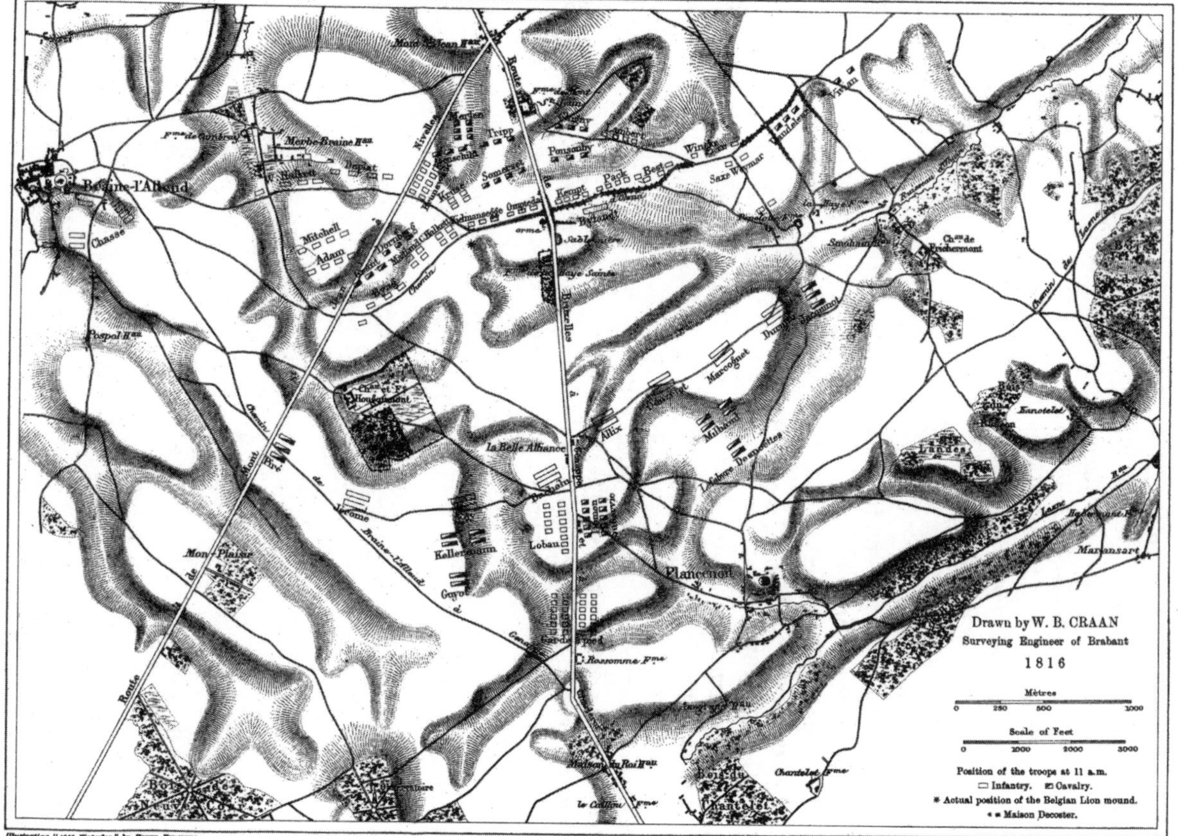

Illustrating "1815 Waterloo," by Henry Houssaye.

A & C. BLACK, LONDON.

W. & A. K. Johnston, Edinburgh & London

FOREWORD

It should go without saying that Waterloo was a great Allied victory, with contributions of varying importance by Wellington's British, Dutch, Belgian and German contingents and by Blücher's Prussian army. The results were 'sufficient for the glory of many such armies as the two great Allied armies engaged'. But the chance happening that Lieutenant William Siborne in 1830 was somewhat vaguely commissioned to prepare a plan and perhaps a model of the field led to unexpected consequences[1], and his assiduous collection of information from survivors resulted not only in a massive treasure trove of letters and two great models, but also in his famous *History*, first published in 1844. That *History* fixed indelibly in the minds of British readers the impression of a 'British victory', and it is not surprising that Prussian, Dutch and Belgian veterans – and even some in that superb component of Wellington's armies, the King's German Legion (KGL) – felt somewhat aggrieved.[2] As the century progressed, so various Continental historians – van Loben Sels, von Ollech and others – produced accounts relating to the achievements of their own people, as did, of course, the defeated French from their separate angle of vision.

By the beginning of the twentieth century not only were there major histories by French, Prussian, and Dutch-Belgian authors to round out the story as told by Siborne

---

1 William Siborne's hopeless lack of common sense or financial prudence led him progressively into the most appalling muddle, and his difficulties with the Horse Guards and the Treasury due to extravagance in a period of financial retrenchment were compounded by his own refusal to take advice or stick to such promises as he made to them. Using the evidence in the BL Siborne papers, I tried to make this clear in an article 'The Artistic Imperative and Government Procedures: Time, Taxpayers' Money, and Siborne's Large Waterloo Model', *First Empire*, No. 90, Sept/Oct 2006, pp. 9–16.

2 Comparing early works like John Booth's *The Battle of Waterloo, by a Near Observer*, the seventh edition of which came out in 1815, with several British works of the later 19th Century I am struck by the considerable space Booth gives to foreign reports, Allied and French. Wellington both in his 19 June 1815 Waterloo Despatch and his rather querulous 1842 Memorandum (from which the quotation in my first paragraph is taken) also explicitly praised his allies. That there was more than a 'British' aspect to the campaign was emphasised by Lt Colonel [later Maj. General] J Mitchell, *The Fall of Napoleon, an historical memoir*, 3 vols, 1845. His Book Four covers from Elba onwards and is an interesting early study of foreign sources, yet Colonel Charles Chesney, the next major British historian to present a more 'Allied' assessment in his *Waterloo Lectures* of 1868 made no reference to it. However, we should not forget that the first (if somewhat surprising) claim that it was the Prussian I Corps' attack at Smohain that 'decided the defeat of the enemy', was made by Blücher's chief of staff Gneisenau in his 20 June 1815 official report (see Booth, 7th ed., at p. 177).

and his many English successors, but there were also available several volumes of original documents.[3] Of these, the principal were Herbert Siborne's *Waterloo Letters* (London, 1891), a selection from his father William's large collection, the documents in Demetrius Boulger's *The Belgians at Waterloo* (London, 1901), and then the Prussian Julius von Pflugk-Harttung's great assemblage of German reports in *Belle-Alliance: Verbündetes Heer* (Berlin, 1915). Nothing comparable appeared for the rest of the century,[4] although specialist journals continued to print occasional fresh material from time to time. But *Belle-Alliance* was never translated into English, and *Waterloo Letters* comprised only 180 letters creamed from the Siborne collection and written by 123 English, Scottish, Welsh and Irish correspondents, but among whom only one served in the KGL and one with the separate Hanoverian contingent.

At this point, a young ex-Royal Navy officer now in full-time civilian employment decided that a further selection from the Siborne papers was essential. Living far from the British Library, and in addition to his employed work and family duties, Gareth Glover patiently transcribed a further 310 letters from 230 correspondents not used by Herbert Siborne, about 30 of them by German officers, some of whom wrote several letters (only to be too-often ignored by William). Thus, in comparison with Herbert's tally and purely British coverage the Glover additions were significant, and if the earlier editor skimmed much of the cream, Gareth's additional material was still of great value. Moreover, he added a further 29 letters in the collection that dealt with the making of the models and certain attempts by the Prussians to influence the layout of the troops on the models; plus a summary list of letters that were not judged worth printing.

Such a magnificent achievement required endless patience and skill in its creation and a massive command of detail right down to the colour of contingents' uniforms. The deciphering of scrawls was wearisome: ink was often faded, and the words sometimes only semi-legible. And it was all done in such spare time as this busy man could find.

When *Letters from Waterloo* was published in 2004 it was instantly recognized as a major work of scholarship. Some significant adjustments to the old story now became necessary and perhaps the most interesting was Gareth's revision to the account of Major Baring's defence of La Haye Sainte and the casualties suffered there. Praise was widespread: the historian Andrew Uffindell in *The Journal of the Society for Army Historical Research* termed it 'a gold mine' and in the *British Army Review*, I wrote that Waterloo scholars 'must all be eternally in his debt. "Gareth Glover, *Letters*" joins the select few among Waterloo books'.

But of course, that was not the end of the story, and since then Gareth's name has spread from a single book to a shelf of over a dozen major contributions (plus some 50 smaller ones), separate finds such as the Clinton correspondence – or James Stanhope's journals that hitherto only Fortescue seems to have studied. Moreover, there are the six important volumes of *The Waterloo Archive* (2010–14), which add many new Allied

3 Philippe de Meulenaere's comprehensive *Bibliographie Analytique des Témoinages Oculaires Imprimés de la Campagne de Waterloo* (Paris, 2004), lists and comments on virtually everything printed in French, English, Dutch and German between 1815 and 2003.

4 There were also anthologies of eyewitness accounts, and among them the outstanding *The Hundred Days*, compiled and edited by Antony Brett-James in 1968.

sources and include an English translation of virtually all Pflugk-Harttung's Belle-Alliance documents. In these works, the letters are presented in the same general sequence as Siborne's *Waterloo Letters* and Glover's *Letters from Waterloo*. Additionally, while two letters severely pruned by Herbert Siborne had been restored in *Letters*[5], there were other letters omitted in 2004 due to lack of space and because the writers had already been given considerable prominence by Herbert in 1891. This exclusion was a pity, so it is good to find that in some cases the omissions have been printed elsewhere by Gareth himself.[6]

In his new Preface Gareth speaks of the past few years as being 'a golden age' for Waterloo studies. That is a large claim to make but, if it is so, that is in no small part due to his own untiring and remarkable efforts. We all thank him for his work and pray that long may so-fruitful-a-quest continue.

JOHN HUSSEY

5 The pruned items WL, nos 76 and 84 appear in full in *Letters*, nos 63 and 73.

6 For example, Sir Hussey Vivian's important letter to Siborne of 14 February 1837 is now printed in *Waterloo Archive*, vol. IV, no. 3.

PREFACE

It has proven a very interesting, personal experience to revisit the publication of my first book, which was completed some fourteen years ago. The original foreword explained much of the reasoning behind my seeking to publish the remainder of the Siborne papers, but because some time has since passed, a few of my comments now require a little further explanation.

Waterloo: New Perspectives was published in 1993 by Hamilton Williams. It was this book, primarily, which had made such outlandish claims regarding William Siborne and the 'honesty' of his model, which caused me to seek out the truth for myself. This work contains a number of interesting and challenging concepts and ideas, but has since been proven to be less than scrupulous in the evidence provided to back up these assertions. Further claims circulating at the time regarding the true impact of the Prussian influence on the campaign and Wellington's perfidy further goaded me into action. That initial inspiration, to publish some of these various Napoleonic sources in their entirety, has continued to this very day, with over seventy publications now to my name and has also spawned a new generation of others to seek out and publish even more. This has led to great advances in our understanding of the campaign and the battles at every level and has completely altered our thinking on many aspects of the campaign.

Amongst these, I am very proud that my friend John Hussey, who encouraged and advised me in those early days, has agreed to write a foreword to this new edition and has finally published his own magnificent two-volume history of the Waterloo campaign,[1] which finally replaces William Siborne's *History* (long overdue) with a stunningly perceptive overview of the politics and grand strategy of the entire campaign of 1815 and comes thoroughly recommended by this author. I do not think it an overestimation to view the last decade, around the bicentennial of the campaign, as a 'Golden Age' of research on the battle of Waterloo and indeed the entire campaign that it encapsulates. I hope that this renewed interest will also enthuse a new generation with the same passion for the Napoleonic era and halt the downward spiral that has been all too evident for the last thirty years.

Anyone with even a passing interest in the history of the Waterloo campaign will probably know of the book *Waterloo Letters*, being a selection of the correspondence between Lieutenant William Siborne[2] and numerous participants of the battle of Waterloo, which was edited by his second son, Herbert Siborne, and published by Cassell in 1891.

1 *Waterloo: The Campaign of 1815*, by John Hussey (London, Greenhill Books, 2017).

2 The name appears to have been spelt without an 'e' until relatively recently. The Army lists of 1814 clearly show William and his father, Benjamin, as Siborn, however, I have used Siborne throughout as this is the spelling familiar today.

Preface

For many years I had been aware of the mass of further correspondence contained within the Siborne files, which had remained unpublished and virtually ignored in the British Library. I had wondered for hours about the contents of these unpublished letters. Who wrote them? What information did they contain? Did they provide any answers to the numerous inconsistencies and confusions that still remained over the exact sequence of events of that whirlwind campaign? For despite more books being published regarding Waterloo than any other battle in history, we still sought the definitive history of this campaign. I was propelled further by the virulent debate that had arisen over the previous decade among eminent scholars of the Waterloo campaign as to the honesty of the work of the Sibornes.

I became determined to view the letters for myself with the intention of establishing the facts. I initially sought access to the British Library manuscript department, where, following Herbert's death, the Siborne family had placed all the papers in six great folios. However, it proved extremely difficult to attend the Library regularly, living at such a distance, and therefore to gain the ready access to the files that I desired.

In 2001, I discovered the British Library website, listing all of the letters written to William Siborne in six folios – numbered in the Additional Manuscripts series 34703 through to 34708 inclusive (though the file numbering within is not straightforward and there are some problems[3]). From these lists I discovered that there were some 230 correspondents who had contributed a total of 310 letters but had not featured in *Waterloo Letters* at all.

It had been claimed that Herbert Siborne had sanitized the letters that he published in *Waterloo Letters* and completely ignored others that were at variance with the models and the *History of the War in France and Belgium* in 1815 produced by his father. I obtained photocopies of all the letters from correspondents that were omitted entirely by Herbert and that were therefore most likely to contain material that he wished to suppress. But I also obtained a selection of letters that he had published, to establish how he had edited them, how important were any omissions and whether they contained material he was desperate to hide.

The transcription of the letters proved a great deal more difficult than I had originally envisaged, as the writing was often feint, the handwriting execrable and dating poor. This led to long nights staring at some passages, desperately trying to work out that final word or phrase, followed by even more frustrating hours piecing together the information, which led finally to working out the true identification of officers or units mentioned in the texts. I spent many hundreds of hours preparing these transcriptions, working diligently to avoid errors. I am never foolhardy enough to claim that I have deciphered every letter perfectly, but I certainly did everything humanly possible to achieve the desired perfection.

From my initial reading of the first batch of letters I had received, it rapidly became clear to me that not only was there much evidence relating to the claims of these revisionist histories, but that there was a veritable treasure trove of both short and some

3 For example, the following files are listed in the folios in the British Library but proved impossible to find: Add MS 34705 fo. 20 denoted as by Best and Add MS 34705 fo. 37 Kuckuck.

very lengthy letters, containing much valuable information, some of which had not been brought to light in previous works regarding the campaign.

Students of the Peninsular and Waterloo campaigns like myself will readily recognize many famous names from Waterloo within the list of correspondents: Major Baring, famous for the heroic defence of La Haye Sainte; Lord Saltoun and George Bowles for that of Hougoumont; Edward Whinyates and Sergeant Daniel Dunnett of the rocket battery to name but a few. There are also many others who were famous themselves for their later writings, such as Robert Batty, Charles Cadell, Edward Cotton, John Gurwood, James Hope, Alexander Clark-Kennedy, William Leeke and Frederick Pattison. Their letters add further information to that published in their official memoirs.

This led me to the view that there were more than sufficient letters of real historical value to produce a second volume of Waterloo correspondence. These letters have, I believe, formed a new primary source of great value to serious students of the campaign, providing uncompromising evidence as to the guilt or innocence of William and Herbert Siborne. They are also a great, vibrant read for anyone remotely interested in military history, giving a real insight into what it was like to be there that day.

These letters – which describe so vividly the scenes that the correspondents witnessed in 1815 – were written between 1829 and 1845, some 15 to 30 years after the events described. However, those who casually dismiss them as the letters of old men with addled memories (as often happens with other memoirs of the period by some revisionist historians) need only look to the often very lucid memories of Second World War veterans in our own times. The horrors they describe are often seared into their memories and are as fresh as if they had occurred only the day before, sometimes forming the basis of nightmares to their dying day. Who, then, can say that such memories are just muddled ramblings? One must avoid blindly following them, making due allowance for the understandable mingling of events with time, but where descriptions from different sources can be compared the truth can eventually be verified.

The letters I included in this work do not account for all the unpublished letters in the files. Space restrictions have required me largely to dispense with publishing anything further from correspondents already published by Herbert, as they have already had their views voiced. Instead, I have concentrated on the mass of writers whose views have been silenced for 170 years or more. I have included a few letters that Herbert published but with huge tracts removed. These have been included for the further valuable information they contain and as an example of the kind of information Herbert omitted.

The letters in this book are reproduced in their entirety, with the exception of two letters where I have removed short paragraphs relating to the then current political situation, which is incomprehensible to us now. Where this occurred, I have clearly marked this omission and shown the missing text in a footnote. I avoided changing anything in the letters except for the spelling of names and places to agree with modern usage for consistency and understanding. In a few cases, where correspondents produced very long epistles with virtually no punctuation, I was forced to add a few commas or full stops where I deemed it vital to aid understanding. Capitalization was also reduced in an effort to achieve consistency. I also inserted the manuscript number of the start of each letter in the British Library for ease of reference to the original files. It should be noted that the British Library referencing system often causes gaps in the sequential numbering as even blank sheets and envelopes are numbered in the files and this can make it appear as though there are omissions, which is not actually the case.

The layout of the book largely follows that of the original publication by Herbert Siborne to ease cross-referencing by those who wish to utilise both volumes. The correspondent's letters are listed in order of the formation they belonged to at the time of Waterloo and their rank on that day. If letters were extremely short and contained nothing of historical interest, they have simply been listed in Appendix B, with a brief description of their contents for reference. I did, however, avoid using the side notes which litter Siborne's book, and which I find very distracting, but I inserted copious explanatory notes following each letter, for those who wish to read them and these have been updated in the light of new discoveries.

The illustrations and maps sent to William are included within their parent letters, my only contribution being to digitally remove staining and blemishes and adding clear labelling where necessary to improve clarity.

A number of the correspondents were from the King's German Legion or Hanoverian troops, who wrote to William Siborne in a rather archaic style of German and a few others in French. It should be remembered that more than three-quarters of the Allied armies engaged at Waterloo were of German or Dutch/Belgian extraction. I therefore arranged for the translation of all of these letters to allow these German allies their own voice at last. Indeed, their testimonies are some of the most interesting in this volume, often portraying very different views of incidents from those of their British allies.

I am aware that translation is not always a precise science. The meaning of a passage can be ascertained but there is always more than one way of phrasing that sentence. Some translators may vary a little in their interpretation of the wording of the sentence, but the meaning of the whole will be the same. I am not a linguist. To ensure accuracy I relied on the paid services of professional translators throughout and difficult sections were referred from one to the other for verification. Letters that have been translated are clearly marked to show the original language of the text. Those written in English are not annotated. I am, of course, responsible for any errors in the editorial comments and notes.

The works of William and Herbert Siborne have been variously described over the years: on the one hand as some of the most important military histories ever produced; on the other as the blatantly biased work of jingoistic bigots. Worse, William had recently been vilified as an historian who strayed from the path of truth, overstating the roles of his various benefactors in affecting the outcome of the battle as a reward for their gold. This dichotomy of opinion caused me to question where the truth lies, between these excessively divergent views. This book was, therefore, also designed to shine a beam of light through the fog of obfuscation shielding the protagonists from informed criticism and to open this debate to the public domain.

I hope that you find these letters to be as in interesting and informative as I have done.

HISTORICAL BACKGROUND

William Siborne was born in Greenwich on 18 October 1797, the only child of Captain Benjamin Siborne of His Majesty's 9th Regiment of Foot. Benjamin Siborne had served in the Walcheren Campaign and with Wellington's army in the Peninsula between 1810–14, being severely wounded at the Nivelle. At the culmination of the Peninsular War in 1814, he had recovered from his wounds and was well enough to sail with his regiment to Canada, to defend that country from encroachments in the war with the United States. However, soon after their arrival this war also ended.

On the news of Napoleon's escape from Elba, the regiment was rushed back to Europe but arrived too late to participate in the Waterloo Campaign. They found the army encamped near Paris and the regiment formed part of the army of occupation for the next two years. William only had his mother at hand for many of his childhood years, but he was extremely proud of his father, whose exploits in Spain were avidly read in his letters home. William grew up only knowing a country at war, but it was a period of unparalleled British military success both on land and sea, culminating in the stunning Battle of Waterloo.

During these years, the armed forces, particularly the army, had seen their social standing transformed. By 1812, army officers were much esteemed and highly desired as connubial partners, and every fashionable young man of substance wanted to be seen at all the gay soirees in a dashing uniform. William was no exception and at the age of 14, he joined the Royal Military College at Great Marlow, with which he later moved to its present home at Sandhurst. He was gazetted to the 2nd Battalion 9th Foot in 1814, serving at Chatham and Sheerness before being transferred to the 1st Battalion in August 1815. He proceeded to join his father with the 1st Battalion in France, and in the following November he became a lieutenant. William used his time in France to continue his military studies and was enthralled by the models of the great French victories on show in Paris.

With the reduction of the army in 1817, William and his father were to be separated again, this time forever. William, as a junior officer, was left to languish on the half-pay list for the next five years. His father meanwhile was ordered with the battalion to the West Indies, the graveyard of the army. Benjamin duly died on the island of St Vincent on 14 July 1819, apparently from the effects of his earlier wounds, but more likely from the ravages of one of the tropical diseases that regularly affected British regiments on these islands.

William was not idle during his enforced retirement and soon showed a penchant for topographical studies, publishing two works (in 1822 and 1827) on the use of topography in military operations, including the making of models. In 1824 William married Helen Aitken, the daughter of a Scottish colonel. In due course, the marriage produced two daughters and two sons, his second son, born in 1826, being Herbert Taylor Siborne, who later edited *Waterloo Letters*.[1]

He was reinstated to the army as a lieutenant in the 47th Foot in November 1824, the regiment being ordered to India and Burma. However, William had proven adept at administrative work and did not sail with the regiment, moving between various clerical appointments at home. Eventually, in 1826, he was appointed Assistant Military Secretary to the staff of Lieutenant General Sir George Murray, Commander-in-Chief in Ireland, and served in the same capacity to his successors – Sir John Byng, Sir Richard Hussey Vivian and Sir Edward Blaker – until 1843.

William came to the notice of General Lord Hill, the General Commanding-in-Chief, who in 1830 offered William financial support from the government to complete a topographical model of the field of Waterloo. William promptly sought and received a long leave and moved to Waterloo, living at the farm of La Haye Sainte for some eight months, while accurately surveying every square foot of the battlefield and obtaining crop information from the local farmers. It is often stated that William surveyed the battlefield before the Lion Mound was erected in honour of the Prince of Orange. This is clearly not correct, as the mound was constructed between 1824–26. William had surveyed the fields after the Allied ridge had been removed to furnish the earthen mound upon which the lion sculpture was placed and which dominates the site to this day. He therefore had to reconstruct the field to the best of his abilities from the memories of the local farmers.

During this period, William developed the original idea further and suggested that the model should include a representation of the troops with their positions at a given point in time, namely at approximately 7:15 pm at the height of the final attack of the French Imperial Guard.

Lord Hill seems to have agreed to this improvement and eventually allowed a circular letter (copied on pp 25–6) to be sent to all known surviving British and King's German Legion officers, requesting any information they could supply regarding their part in the battle and the other corps in their vicinity. He further requested descriptions of the crops in their location to ensure the accuracy of the model.

A large number of officers replied, and a lengthy correspondence ensued with certain key witnesses as William struggled to understand some aspects of the battle fully. However, things began to go badly awry. The Tory government had collapsed in November 1830 and the Whig prime minister, Earl Grey, had by 1833 ordered the patronage of the model to cease. The Treasury promptly informed William that they could no longer fund the project, as it was now clearly a commercial enterprise. They paid his costs to date but declined any further financial involvement in the business.

In one letter, William suggested that the Treasury might want the funds already advanced returned to them if the project was not continued. William was left with the dilemma of either abandoning the project and repaying the advances or completing it himself. He bravely determined to complete the work (he had little

1 There is some disagreement over how many children he had as a short family history in the National Army Museum by a Mr Henderson names three children: Herbert, Clara and Georgiana. However, the *DNB* entry, written largely by someone who knew his daughter Clara, states four children and she should know.

option financially), raised a loan of £500, a sizeable figure, and then sought further subsidies from those officers with whom he was corresponding. Some forwarded £10 or so, but others, such as Sir Richard Hussey Vivian, it is believed may have invested £1,000 into the scheme.

The model, costing £3,000, was built in Ireland in 39 sections and on completion shipped to England. The great model was finally exhibited to the public on 4 October 1838 at the Egyptian Hall, Piccadilly (unfortunately long-since demolished). The model was on a scale of 9 feet to the mile, and its overall dimensions were 27 feet 4 inches by 19 feet 8 inches wide, totalling some 420 square feet, with some 70,000 individual tin-lead alloy figures to denote the various troop formations.

The model was not the huge financial success that William had expected. An estimated 100,000 visitors each paying one shilling did visit, but the receipts failed to cover more than William's expenses from the public shows, and his investors failed to see any return on their loans. William suspected that the manager he had appointed to oversee the exhibition had embezzled him. It is unclear why William left the management of the exhibition to others. It seems inconceivable that he had any other more pressing commitments, as failure would financially ruin him. In 1843, William's tenure as Military Secretary finally ended and he moved to the Royal Military Asylum, London, as a Captain on half pay.

Despite the failure of the model as a financial investment, in 1844 William produced a second, smaller model, showing the armies in their positions at the time of Uxbridge's charge at around 2 pm. It is unclear how the finances were raised for this new project. The model was produced at a scale of 15 feet to 1 inch and measured 18 feet 7 inches by 7 feet 9 inches, constructed in ten sectional parts. The 7,000 figures were 1 inches high, with moveable arms and detachable armour, etc. This model was intended to be only one of six such smaller models representing the critical moments of the battle, which would be sited around the great model to help explain the various stages. The two models were displayed together at the Egyptian Hall on Christmas Eve 1845 with an entry fee of 2 shillings, but William failed to recoup much of his investment and the models were put into storage.

A Mr Evans, presumably a lessee, showed one of the models on the Continent. The model appeared in Berlin in 1848, and, from the description given by Chevalier Bunsen (Appendix A, letter 29), it seems that this was the second model. William finally found success in 1844 with the publication of the weighty two-volume *History of the War in France and Belgium* in 1815. This was based upon his correspondence over the previous fourteen years and led to a renewed flurry of letters to clarify contentious issues. This book was immediately acclaimed and became a financial success.

William remained in serious debt, however, and his final years were fully occupied in seeking redress from the Treasury for his expenses and losses on the model. He wrote numerous letters requesting that the new Tory government sanction the purchase of the models as important historical artefacts, but with no success.

Following the death of William on 13 June 1849 and his burial at Brompton Cemetery, his widow sought to clear his debts again by selling the models. A previous suggestion of William's to ask for subscriptions from the various Waterloo regiments came to fruition in 1851, when the first model was purchased for only £2,062 and presented to the Royal United Services Museum in Whitehall, where is was housed in what is now the Banqueting Hall.

William's younger son, Major-General Herbert Siborne, Royal Engineers, inherited all of William's various correspondence. Following the 75th anniversary celebrations of the battle in 1890 and the increased interest thereby regenerated in the period, Herbert published a selection of the letters written to his father by the surviving officers. This was published in 1891 entitled *Waterloo Letters*. The volume included a total of 180 letters from some 126 different correspondents, and proved an instant success, seeing many reprints to the present day. Following Herbert's death, William's correspondence was presented to the British Library, where it resides in the Manuscript Department, largely ignored until now.

The models today

Luckily both of Siborne's models have survived, but not completely unscathed. The first model, on the closure of the Royal United Services Museum in 1962, was stored in crates at Sandhurst and later at Aldershot. It was eventually offered to the National Army Museum when it opened in Chelsea in 1971. In 1975 the crates were opened and found to be in remarkably good condition. After some restoration work by the British Model Soldier Society and Bees Modelmakers, the model was placed on display at the museum, where it formed the centrepiece of the Waterloo room. Following a huge redevelopment of the National Army Museum recently, the model has received another makeover and has had a better lightshow added.

The second model has suffered a great deal more in its travels. On its return from the Continental tour of 1848, the model seems to have languished for many years in storage at an ironworks in Dublin. It briefly reappeared for the Irish International Exhibition in Dublin in 1907 and promptly disappeared again until rediscovered in the loft of a house in Cabinteely, County Dublin. The model was given to the Staff College at Camberley following repairs at the Tower of London in 1935. It returned to the Tower in 1937, having deteriorated badly, and was occasionally displayed there. In 1965 it was given to Dover Castle and was extensively refurbished in 1983–5, when it was discovered that the figures had deteriorated because of the fumes from the original adhesives used on the model. A special casing that extracts these corrosive fumes was produced to preserve the model. Recently, the model has been moved to the Royal Armouries Museum in Leeds, where it has been refurbished and remains on display.

Controversy

The models and subsequent history of the campaign by William Siborne have always been cloaked in controversy. From the very beginning, the first model was not without its critics, especially the Duke of Wellington and his friends. It is often remarked that the Duke of Wellington was wary of the model and declined visiting the exhibition to avoid the appearance of sanctioning it. Indeed, on seeing a plan of the model in 1840, Wellington wrote to Lady Wilton,

> 'No drawing or representation as a model can represent more than one moment of an action, but this model tends to represent the whole action: and every corps

> and individual of all the nations is represented in the position chosen by himself. The consequence is that the critical viewer of the model must believe that the whole of each army, without any reserve of any kind, was engaged at the moment supposed to be represented. This is not true of any one moment, or event or operation of this battle; and I was unwilling to give any sanction to the truth of such a representation in this model, which must have resulted from my visiting it, without protesting against such erroneous representation. This I could not bring myself to do on account; and I thought it best to avail myself of my absence from London, and of indisposition, never to visit at all'.[2]

Recently, however, a much more serious threat to the reputations of William and Herbert Siborne had emerged; claims were made that there was clear evidence to show that William's benefactors gained recompense for their investment by imposing upon him. It was claimed that these investors pressured William into placing their own corps wherever they felt they should be best positioned, to further their regiment's claim to the greatest honour in the defeat of the French Imperial Guard, sometimes against more weighty historical evidence. They further claimed that having allowed such alterations William then came under intense pressure from other aggrieved officers who disagreed with their corps' positioning on the model. These had allegedly found their units relegated to inferior positions to allow his benefactor's corps their required positions.

Further claims were made that William Siborne's history of the campaign was distorted to ensure it agreed with the previous models and that Herbert was therefore guilty of selective pruning to ensure that no part of the letters that he published later challenged his father's work.

This complete demolition of the works of the Siborne family intrigued me, as the evidence offered was noticeably thin, with little documentary source material. I was thus driven to seek the evidence to satisfy myself as to the truth regarding the claims, without having any preconceived ideas as to the guilt or innocence of the Sibornes.

Guilty or innocent?

The various controversies raised by the Duke of Wellington and more recently by revisionist historians, cast more than a cloud over Siborne's work and had been accepted by some eminent military historians; they can, however, now be answered dispassionately with established fact.

The claim that the investors exerted financial pressure to influence historical fact cannot stand. There is absolutely no evidence in any of the letters of financial incentives offered for 'adapting' the truth, either on the model or by altering the original correspondence to fall into line with Siborne's conjectures, as claimed. Indeed, the greatest sum (£1,000) was lent by Sir Hussey Vivian, who was involved in numerous altercations in the *United Services Journal* regarding the part his brigade took at Waterloo. Such a huge sum could have given Vivian great influence with William but there is absolutely no evidence, in fact, not even the suggestion, of coercion by Vivian, nor any sign of partiality

2 *Wellington and His Friends*, edited by Gerald, 7th Duke of Wellington (London, Macmillan Press, 1968, pp 133–4).

on the part of William. Vivian, as always, was not slow or shy in voicing his own opinions, but he does not appear to have swayed William into blindly following him.

It is true that William would not have dreamt of criticizing 'The Greatest Soldier of His Age', even when the duke's performance in the early hours of the campaign appears to have been a little below par. Nevertheless, he managed to do this despite taking the side of the Prussians with regard to their contribution to the final victory – against Wellington's wishes.

With regard to William's methods of establishing the facts of that fateful day, his comparison of the numerous references available to extract the most likely course of events is only to be applauded. His comments show clearly his understanding of the dangers inherent in such work and he clearly states his main aim is 'accuracy not effect' (Appendix A, letter 3). No evidence has ever been produced, beyond vague unsubstantiated innuendo, to refute his working methods and integrity, and there is certainly no evidence that he suppressed unwelcome evidence. Modern historians may not now agree with all his conclusions, but his errors do not signify any intent to mislead. William generally avoided any serious bias in his narrative (barring his negation of the Dutch/Belgian contribution); in fact a much heavier bias has been very evident in some of the more modern 'revisionist' histories of the battle.

No one has yet achieved the 'perfect' history of the Waterloo Campaign, although John Hussey has come very close. William certainly did not reach that goal, but he must be highly commended for going to such lengths to produce a near masterpiece while many of the main characters were still alive and so vociferous in their own defence. A similar complaint is made against Napier (who wrote a history of the Peninsular War) for similar reasons.

It was claimed in evidence by Hamilton Williams that Major Macready, who had complained bitterly of the incorrect positioning of the 30th Regiment on the model and their movements as given in the history of the campaign, had maintained a protracted correspondence with William and was finally appeased in the reprint of the book, as the 30th Regiment's movements were altered to conform exactly with Macready's statements. This proves nothing beyond the fact that William, although embarrassed by the affair, was quite prepared to update his work in the light of new evidence. There have always been historians prepared to maintain their position at all costs despite overwhelming evidence against their claims. William avoided this trap.

Indeed, no greater compliment to the excellence of William Siborne's work can be given than that of Sir James Shaw Kennedy when he states that 'Captain Siborne's account of the campaign has very great merit. I doubt if, as to any other battle, there were ever a greater number of facts brought together, or more care, industry, and fidelity displayed in their collection; so that all other accounts of the battle, to be correct, must, for the great portion of the details, borrow from Siborne, as he had access to sources of information that no historian following can have.'[3]

Similarly, the oft-quoted complaints raised against the model by the Duke of Wellington and his friends denotes a remarkable turnaround in the duke's views, as in

3 Sir James Shaw Kennedy, *Notes on the Battle of Waterloo* (London, John Murray, 1865; reprinted Staplehurst, Spellmount, 2003, p. 51).

1836 Wellington had praised the topography William had produced.[4] However, the Duke of Wellington had reasons of his own to cast doubt on the veracity of the model. He certainly had no wish to see the Prussian forces portrayed so heavily engaged with the French around Plançenoit at the time of 'the crisis', as this would diminish his victory. Evidence for his reasons comes from his friend Lord Fitzroy Somerset, who states that those 'who see the work will deduce from it that the result of the battle was not so much owing to British valour, and the great generalship of the chief of the English army, as to the flank movements of the Prussians' (see letter 16, Appendix A). As further proof of this, only when William became desperate to sell the model and being aware of the reason for the duke's disapproval, did he finally offer to move the Prussian formations on the model once the government had bought it (see letter 20, Appendix A), but it was deemed too late to alter it.

It is also untrue that senior Headquarters personnel were not consulted regarding the model, as many corresponded with William regarding their memories. Even the Duke of Wellington appeared to have some discussion with William regarding the model, indicating a readiness to meet him if he came to London, which William unfortunately declined on the grounds of expense (see letters 12 and 13, Appendix A).

Again, no solid evidence was provided to back claims that William Siborne raised the level of subscription requested in a cynical ploy to gain further incentives. Still extant in the files (printed in Appendix A) are the letters that passed between William and Horseguards regarding raising a subscription to complete the model and later, to purchase the model for the country. These letters clearly establish that the subscription was officially sanctioned through Lord Fitzroy Somerset's department and that they were fully involved in the detailed aspects of its organization. It is clear that William saw the payments simply as a loan, for he had no reason to doubt that his project would be anything less than a glorious triumph. The only thing that William appears guilty of in the letters is a supreme confidence in his own abilities and an ardent desire to see his name 'in lights' – an understandable yet unattractive trait, but nothing more than that.

The cost of the project (£3,000) was a very serious investment and should be put into perspective: at this time the Quartermaster General's Department had an annual budget of just under £6,000 and the Quartermaster General himself was paid £1,384 per annum plus £500 for allowances! It has been shown in Mitchell & Deane's *Abstract of British Historical Statistics* (p. 396) that during the years 1831–5 inclusive, the Whig government reduced overall spending on the army and ordnance by some 18 per cent. It is therefore not totally surprising that the administration saw this project as a prime one for cost cutting. William's decision to forge ahead, taking out hefty loans despite having a young family to support, indicates a man on a mission, but unfortunately without the financial acumen to make a success of it.

It was again claimed that William Siborne was unable to read the correspondence written in German and that he could not afford a translator, hence ignoring their evidence in his history. This is a gross distortion, as William quite clearly carried on a prolonged correspondence with German sources regarding the accuracy of his account of their actions. Baron Bunsen of the Prussian Staff mentions William's ability to read

4 *Supplementary Dispatches, Correspondence and Memoranda* . . ., 15 vols (London, John Murray, 1853–72, vol. X, p. 513).

and write German very well and Colonel Wagner of the Prussian Staff extols the accuracy of his description of the fighting around Plançenoit. William also tried to gain information from the French side but was, understandably, met with a stony silence, apart from a short note from Count Lobau.

If William is to be criticized, it must be for his serious failure to procure any substantial information from the Dutch/Belgian contingent. The reason for this is not readily apparent, the Dutch/Belgian troops were certainly a very sizeable contingent in the Allied army and there were (and still are) a number of questions regarding the actions of various Dutch/Belgian units during the battle. The failure to correspond with some of the key figures such as Perponcher and Chassé is inexcusable and led directly to the negation of any achievements of the Dutch/Belgian troops in the battle by virtually all British histories since.

William's History of the campaign suffers from the same problem as most histories that were published in the jingoistic Victorian era; namely a subjugation of all foreign claims to any of the laurels heaped upon the victors of Waterloo. The failures of some foreign units are undoubtedly used to destroy the reputation of complete national contingents, whereas the failures of British units are whitewashed. Quite rightly therefore, many of William's statements are being reappraised in a more enlightened era.

It is, however, an undoubted fact that no truly honest history of any major event has ever been written during the lifetime of the primary actors in that drama. Too many reputations are at risk for an honest appraisal of each person's role. Wellington himself agreed that this was the reason that no true history of the battle would appear in his own lifetime. William's attempt must be looked upon in this light and so huge conspiracy theories seem very questionable, indeed implausible.

Claims that his son Herbert omitted paragraphs from letters that were at variance with his father's History were backed up by little actual evidence, apart from reference being made to one missing paragraph in a Ietter by Captain Mountstevens. This one example is far from proving a massive distortion of history as a fact. In reference to the original letter, it has been shown that the missing sentence (not paragraph) is merely omitted to avoid offending Dutch/Belgian readers rather than hiding controversial facts.[5]

It is clear to me, having checked a number of original letters with the published versions, that Herbert did omit many paragraphs from letters, some of which led to the omission of important historical information (see Letters 63 and 73 in this volume for examples), but none of the omissions indicates any attempt by Herbert to cover up controversial facts; they merely show a very erratic editing style.

It is also true that Herbert did not print a single letter from any of the German officers in *Waterloo Letters*, but in his case it is not clear whether he was actually able to read the German texts well.[6] This cannot excuse the omission of many major texts by the German contingent as their exclusion from the book did tilt the balance of the text

5 The words of the missing passage were published by D. S. Mill in 'Waterloo: New Perspectives and the Siborne manuscripts', *First Empire Magazine* edition 26, pp. 37–8. It read: 'Rather an absurdity, by the way, to suppose *Les braves Belges* would have been there when they had legs to carry them off.'

6 Herbert had been sent to Germany for his education for one year, but annotations on some of the letters, incorrectly identifying the correspondent and views expressed within the texts, lead me to question how proficient he actually was in the language.

hopelessly towards the British view. However the criticism has not taken account of the time in which he was publishing, Victorian Britain demanded to read of a British victory and nothing else.

These omissions and the editing out of large sections of some major letters are both reprehensible and unfortunate but there is certainly no evidence of malicious intent. No terrible fact that destroys reputations or theories has been encountered in my reappraisal of the letters.

One reason for my publishing this correspondence was to discuss these controversies, but more especially, I believed that these letters add further important eyewitness statements to the sum of material already available. Each letter forms a new brick in the construction of that 'perfect' history of those four fateful days in June 1815, which every military historian aspires to. Indeed, some aspects of the Campaign that have often brushed aside in previous histories are brought fully into the light. These include the rarely mentioned diversion of desperately needed reinforcements from Quatre Bras to guard the Mons-Brussels road, the KGL involvement in the repulse of d'Erlon's attack, the inflated losses at La Haye Sainte and a great deal of further evidence on the 'crisis' and the great advance that immediately followed it, to mention but a few.

ACKNOWLEDGEMENTS

With a work such as this numerous people have been enlisted to give of their time in searching out answers to the multitude of questions raised by the letters. I have to thank therefore a great number of people for their time and patience in aiding my efforts.

I must of course start by thanking the staff of the reproductions office at the British Library who supplied the thousand or more copies I requested of the various Siborne manuscripts and cheerfully answered my numerous queries regarding further files mentioned in the letters. I must particularly thank Stephen Roper, Malcolm Marjoram and Lora Afric for their help in this time-consuming business.

I am also extremely grateful to the staff of the National Army Museum in London for their help in providing invaluable information and supplying copies of articles on numerous matters. I must particularly mention Sara Jones (Department of Weapons, Equipment and Vehicles) for much information on the models, Jonathan Grewcock (Archive Department) for copies of numerous articles and Christina La Torre (Picture Library). Further thanks must go to John Montgomery, Librarian at the Royal United Services Institute for Defence Studies, for supplying invaluable information on the second Siborne model.

I have a multitude of people to thank for their unstinting efforts to help translate the large number of letters in French and particularly the archaic German, which proved so difficult. I must thank Kenneth Kronenburg of Cambridge, Massachusetts and Doctor Peter Hohn of the Förderverein Altenzentrum Ansgar, Hamburg for their professional help with the translation. A willing band of volunteers have also worked on the letters and I must particularly thank the following for their tireless efforts: my old friend Gwyn Prosser for actively enquiring throughout Yorkshire for German translators and leading me to James Bowen and Boris Erchenbrecher who have helped greatly with some of the German and the old French.

There are many others, too many to list, who have been extremely helpful in aiding the completion of this work by providing information when requested, and to whom I offer my thanks. I must also thank Philip Haythornthwaite for reading the full text, suggesting a few corrections and providing further valuable information on individuals and controversial issues which I have incorporated in the notes. His help and encouragement in the early days were of great benefit to me.

Last, but by no means least, I must record my grateful thanks to Mr Desider Golten who, once introduced to my project, has been an untiring enthusiast. Without his support and practical help it is quite possible that this project may have floundered and I will be eternally grateful for his encouragement and advice.

GARETH GLOVER
CARDIFF

LIST OF ABBREVIATIONS: MEDALS AND ORDERS

BWM	British Waterloo Medal
CB	Companion of the Order of the Bath
GCB	Knight Grand Cross of the Order of the Bath
GCH	Knight Grand Cross of the Order of Hanover
GCMG	Knight Grand Cross of the Order of St Michael and St George
HeGL1	Hessian Order of the Gold Lion
HeIH	Hessian Order of the Iron Helmet
HeM	Hessian Medal for Campaigns
HGO 1	Hanoverian Guelphic Order 1st Class
HGO 2	Hanoverian Guelphic Order 2nd Class
HGO 3	Hanoverian Guelphic Order 3rd Class
HM	Hanseatic Medal for Campaign 1813–14
HWC	Hanoverian King William's Cross
KCB	Knight Commander of the Order of the Bath
KCH	Knight Commander of Hanover
KCMG	Knight Commander of St Michael & St George
KG	Knight of the Order of the Garter
KMB	Knight of Maximilian of Bavaria
KMT	Knight of Maria Theresa of Austria
KT	Knight of the Order of the Thistle
KH	Knight of Hanover
KTS	Knight of the Tower and Sword of Portugal
KStA	Russian Knight of St Anne
KStG	Russian Knight of St George
KStV	Russian Knight of St Vladimir
KW	Netherlands Knight of Wilhelm
NWO3	Netherlands Military Order of William 3rd Class
PrIO	Prussian Order of St John of Jerusalem
PrMOM	Prussian Order of Military Merit
PTS	Portuguese Order of the Sword and Tower
RANO	Russian Order of Alexander Nevsky
RM	Russian Medal for Campaigns
RPM	Russian Medal for Capture of Paris
RTM	Russian Medal for the Turkish Campaign
RStAO3	Russian Order of St Andrew 3rd Class
RStGO1	Russian Order of St George 1st Class
RStVO4	Russian Order of St Vladimir 4th Class
SwOS	Swedish Order of the Sword

CIRCULAR LETTER TO SURVIVING WATERLOO OFFICERS

Dublin

Sir

Having for some time past been occupied in constructing a model of the field and battle of Waterloo, upon a scale sufficiently large to admit of the most faithful representation of that memorable action; and the General Commanding-in-Chief having, with the utmost kindness, and with a view to insure to the undertaking the greatest possible accuracy, granted me permission to apply for such information as I may conceive desirable and necessary, to the several officers who, from the commands which they held, or from the circumstances in which they were placed on that occasion, may be considered likely to afford it: I have accordingly the honour to request you will have the goodness to reply to the following queries, as far as your recollection and the circumstances of your position at the time will admit.

What was the particular formation of the ____________ at the moment (about 7 pm) when the French Imperial Guards, advancing to attack the right of the British forces, reached the crest of our position?

What was the formation of that part of the enemy's forces immediately in front of the ____________?

Would you have the goodness to trace these formations, according to the best of your recollection, upon the accompanying plan?

On examining the plan you will find that I have marked with a pencil, on the different fields in and near which the ____________ was generally posted throughout the 18th of June, the nature of the crops which, it is presumed, from the information afforded me by the farmers residing on the spot, they respectively contained on that day. Have you any doubts as to the correctness of such information, and if so, in what particular? Considering the extremely devastated and trodden-down appearance of all kinds of vegetation at the period of the crisis of the battle, it is more with reference to the existence of ploughed or fallow land that I ask this question.

I shall feel very much obliged by your affording me, in addition to the information already solicited, any remarks which you may consider likely to conduce to the accuracy and fidelity of the model, as regards the positions, movements, and formations of the contending armies, not only at the precise moment of action selected for representation, but also during the day. Hints concerning the tracks of the French columns which passed near the ____________ either in advancing or retreating; details of the different attacks made or sustained by the ____________, as also remarks upon the general appearance presented by that part of the field of battle nearest to the

____________, with the addition of any little circumstances which, in your opinion, ought not to be overlooked in a work of this kind, will be most acceptable. It is only by such means as these that I shall be enabled to ensure the accuracy of the model in every particular, and, with the aid of an explanatory memoir, to lay before the public a complete and satisfactory exposition of this ever memorable battle.

In concluding, I take the liberty of earnestly entreating that you will not allow yourself to be deterred from giving the requested information by any fear of committing mistakes: which, indeed, considering the period that has elapsed since the battle took place, are not only most excusable, but almost unavoidable. If officers will, however, but favour me with their remarks and opinions, freely and without reserve, I trust that, by fairly weighing and comparing the data thus afforded me, I shall be enabled to deduce a most faithful and authentic record of the battle, the surest means of imparting to the model that extreme accuracy which, in a work of this nature, not dependent, like a pictorial representation, on effect for its excellence, must always constitute its real value.

I have the honour to be, Sir, your most obedient, humble servant,

W SIBORNE
LIEUT-ASSIST MIL SEC.

THE GENERAL STAFF

No. 1 Major, the Comte de Sales, Sardinian attaché to Lord Wellington[1]

Thorens, Kingdom of Sardinia, 19 December 1842

ADD MS 34707, FO 528

Original in French

Sir,

I have received the letter which you have done me the honour of writing from Dublin on the 6th of this month and in which you appeal to my memories of a particular circumstance which is of interest to you from the battle of Waterloo.

On this memorable day, upon which I was, in effect, at all times in the Duke of Wellington's retinue, I can affirm in addition that, during the period to which you refer in your letter, I found myself as the only one of the officers in his retinue, accompanying him for half an hour.

I subsequently had to inform an officer who was asking me for information, that I could not speak English, but I do not remember at all what it was that he wanted to know nor his name or to whom he was sending this message.[2]

I can only reply to confirm the fact that you appear to want to establish that the Duke of Wellington was to be found towards the most advanced positions of his army at the moment he gave the order to attack, and yes, all the corps were just in front.

The movement to attack was made so quickly and with such fervour, the Duke being at all times towards the front, that, upon arriving at the position which had just been abandoned by the French troops, he had to give me the order to call a halt to the firing of a Prussian battery which was continuing to fire in this direction without realizing that the balls were falling upon the English troops.

It was as a commissioned officer of His Majesty the King of Sardinia, positioned with the English army in the general vicinity of the Duke of Wellington, that I took part in the campaign of 1815, and my rank was that of major of cavalry.

It is with great honour in regard of this information that I remain your very humble and obedient servant.

DE SALES

1 The Comte de Sales served with Wellington's personal suite and remained close to him throughout the battle. He eventually became His Excellency, Lieutenant General Comte Paul François de Sales, the Sardinian ambassador at Paris.

2 This confirms the statement of Major T. Hunter Blair, 91st Regiment, Brigade Major to Adam's brigade, published in Siborne's *Waterloo Letters* (number 121). It is evident that it was he who met with de Sales.

No. 2 Lieutenant Henry Webster, 9th Light Dragoons, Extra Aide de Camp to HRH The Prince of Orange[1]

31 Upper Brook Street, London, 20 September 1836

ADD MS 34706, FO 161

Written to Lieutenant Colonel Augustus Cuyler[2]

My dear Cuyler

I have received your obliging letter, containing Mr Siborne's memorandum and in answer to his question regarding the spot where the Prince of Orange[3] was stationed at the moment he was wounded at the battle of Waterloo. I should say, as far as I can recollect, that he was on the left of Sir C. Halkett's brigade.[4]

Your account of Mr Siborne's model is very interesting and [I] hope he may succeed in getting all the information he requires to accomplish so arduous and useful an undertaking, which you properly call 'national'.

Believe me, my dear Cuyler, yours very sincerely

H WEBSTER

---

1 Henry Webster joined the 9th Dragoons on 27 March 1810 and was slightly wounded at Vittoria where he served as an extra ADC to Major General Brisbane. It was he who carried Constant-Rebecque's despatch to the Prince of Orange from Braine-le-Comte to the Duke of Richmond's ball at Brussels on 15 June: a remarkable ride in the dark. He was made KW for Waterloo. Afterwards he became Lieutenant Colonel Henry Vassall Webster KTS and went on the half-pay list in 1826. He killed himself in a fit of insanity on 19 April 1847.

2 Lieutenant Colonel August Cuyler had served at Waterloo as an extra ADC to Major General Cooke, his letter is published in this volume (number 94). He seems to have been instrumental in gleaning information for Siborne from ex-officers of the Staff at Waterloo.

3 General His Royal Highness the Prince of Orange was the son and heir of King William I of the Netherlands. He had served on Wellington's Staff in Spain from 1811 and commanded the I Corps at Waterloo where he was wounded. He succeeded as King William II in 1843 only to die in 1849. The position where the Prince of Orange was wounded as described in the letter corresponds with the site of the Lion Mound.

4 Sir Colin Halkett KCB was the founder of the King's German Legion. He joined the army in 1803 as a lieutenant colonel in the 2nd Light Battalion KGL serving in Hanover, the Baltic and the Peninsula in 1808–13 (during this period he also served in the Walcheren expedition in 1809), receiving a Gold Cross with bars for Albuera, Salamanca, Vittoria and the Nive. While commanding the 5th Brigade at Waterloo, he had four horses shot beneath him and was eventually severely wounded himself. He had three letters (numbers 135–7) published by Siborne in *Waterloo Letters*. Afterwards he was made GCB, GCH, Colonel-in-Chief of the 31st Foot, Governor of Jersey and later Commander-in-Chief at Bombay. Eventually he became the Governor of Chelsea Hospital where he died on 24 September 1856.

No. 3 Major R. Egerton, 34th Foot, Aide de Camp to Lieutenant General Lord Hill[1]

Eaton Banks, Tarporley, 7 October 1845[2]

ADD MS 34708, FO 214

Dear Siborne,

I have been reading your *History of the Waterloo Campaign* with that deep interest the subject merits, and as I know your aim is to be correct even in the most minute particulars, I venture to mention a trifling error which concerns myself in particular and which I have no doubt you will be so good as to rectify when a third edition of your book is called for.[3]

In appendix no. 10 of the 2nd volume, in the list of the officers present you put down Lt Colonel C. Hill as ADC to his brother, Lord Hill. I had the honour of being First ADC to his Lordship in that campaign, Lt Colonel Clement Hill[4] being with his regiment, the Royal Horse Guards Blue, in which corps you have *also* inserted his name.

I may here mention a little anecdote *confidentially* to you, which I do not wish to go further, for as the subject has never been alluded to by Sir Thomas Reynell[5] in our subsequent intercourse, I should be sorry to occasion one moment's pain or annoyance to so old and distinguished an officer.

On the advance of the 52nd Regiment, as described at page 177 of your second volume, I perceived that Sir T. Reynell had faced the 71st to the right about.[6] What was his object in doing so I have never been able to discover, but at this most critical moment of the battle, it appeared to me of vital importance that we should show as good a front as possible. I therefore rode up to Sir Thomas, told him that the Duke had ordered a general advance of the line and requested he would follow the movement of the 52nd, which was immediately done without the slightest delay or hesitation, and the 71st advanced as stated by you at page 179.

I shall be anxious to know whether you have ever heard the foregoing circumstance from any other quarter.

I was in town lately, when it was my intention to have seen you for the purpose of talking these matters over, but the weather was so wretched that I was glad to get back to the country.

Pray remember me to your commandant who is an old friend of mine, and believe me, dear Siborne, extremely yours

R EGERTON

---

1 As a subaltern Richard Egerton served in North America with the 29th Foot and in South America with the 89th Foot. He then served with the 2nd Battalion 34th Foot in the Peninsula from 1809. In 1812 he served as an ADC to Lord Hill and served as such throughout the remainder of the Peninsular and Waterloo campaigns. He received a General Service Medal with eight bars for Busaco, Albuera, Vittoria, Pyrenees, Nivelle, Nive, Orthes and Toulouse. He went on half pay in 1819. Lord Hill as General Officer Commanding-in-Chief chose him as his first ADC and private secretary in 1828. He received the CB and became Colonel-in-Chief of the 46th Foot. He died at Eaton Banks on 21 November 1854.

2 The villages of Eaton and Tarporley in Cheshire are about 5 miles to the east of Chester.

3 Egerton was shown as first ADC in the third edition, but both Siborne and Dalton have persisted in showing Clement Hill acting as an ADC at Waterloo, despite his own statement of service, written in 1829 stating 'The regiment having arrived in that country in May, I gave up my staff appointment and joined my own troop, and was present with it at the battle of Waterloo'.

4 Lieutenant Colonel Clement Hill, brother to Lord Hill, had joined the Royal Horse Guards as a cornet in 1805. In 1808 he joined the army in Portugal as an ADC to his brother, in which position he served throughout the Peninsular campaign. He was slightly wounded at the passage of the Douro at Oporto, and sent home by Lord Wellington with the dispatches

after the action of Arroyo-del-Molino in 1811, for which he was raised to the rank of brevet major. He again carried the dispatches home after the Nive, for which he received his brevet lieutenant colonelcy. He was severely wounded at Waterloo when his leg was pinned to his horse by a sword. Afterwards, as a major general, he commanded the forces at Madras. He then became equerry to HRH The Duchess of Kent. He died on 10 December 1842 at Hardwick Grange. His letter was published by Siborne (number 28).

5 Lieutenant Colonel Thomas Reynell joined the army as an ensign in 1793 and served in Holland in 1795, in Minorca, Malta, Egypt and the Peninsular campaign. He commanded the 71st Highland Regiment at Waterloo and was wounded. He received the KCB and became Colonel of the 87th Regiment and Lieutenant General in 1837. His letter was published by Siborne (number 125).

6 That is, he had turned the regiment to face the rear, possibly preparatory to retreat.

No. 4 Colonel Sir John Elley, KCB, Royal Horse Guards, Deputy Adjutant General[1]

No address or date[2]

ADD MS 34706, FO 413

Written by Lieutenant Colonel Stovin

Private

My dear Siborne,

I have had a long interview with Sir J. Elley – he is getting very prosey and much of self. At the period of the battle which you will show – he was wounded in 4 places and very exhausted from loss of blood – but he will look over the plan and questions and let me have both such observations that he finds himself competent to make. I wish *you* could see him and hear him for though prolix – [he] is always clear.

Of the Quatre Bras affair he gave me a clear history. He was desired by Lord Anglesey to take the Household brigade and Heavies to the rear[3] and take up position to cover the retirement of the Light cavalry – he first moved them in line on each side the road – but from observation, finding that the Light cavalry would soon be pushed up the road, he removed the Household brigade into column of ½ squadrons *à cheval* and the heavy brigade into column on the left of the road.

The enemy pushed the light cavalry back as had been foreseen and they passed to the left of the Household brigade who then formed squadrons and filled the road and drove back the French through Genappe. The guns behind the Household opened on the enemy as soon as the Light cavalry had got clear. After clearing them over the bridge the Household brigade retired slowly under cover of skirmishers on either side of the road (furnished from the *heavy* brigade) who had been in reserve and thus the whole got into the lines of Waterloo.

I send you Elley's own sketch[4] of the thing and as near as I can what he said – but he was averse to put it on paper himself for reasons which I would say – but cannot write.

The Queen holds a Levee this day week and the day after I go to Southampton.

Ever yours

J STOVIN[5]

1 Elley had joined the army as a common soldier and rose through the ranks. He commanded

the cavalry rearguard at Talavera and was slightly wounded at Salamanca. He was seriously wounded at Waterloo. He was on the staff from 1807 to 1819, when he resumed command of the Horse Guards. He was made KCB, KCH and KMT. Afterwards he became Lieutenant General and Colonel-in-Chief of the 7th Hussars and later MP for Windsor. He died on 23 January 1839 at Cholderton Lodge near Amesbury.

2 The date of this letter is implied by the reference to the Queen: it must be between June 1837 when Victoria ascended the throne and Elley's death in January 1839.

3 This refers to the movement of retirement from Quatre Bras to the position at Waterloo on 17 June 1815, as the cavlary arrived too late to participate in the action of the 16th.

4 This sketch has not survived.

5 See the letter of Lieutenant Colonel Stovin in this volume (number 16).

No. 5 Lieutenant Colonel Lord Greenock, Permanent Assistant Quartermaster General to the Cavalry[1]

Edinburgh, 28 May [1837?][2]

ADD MS 34706, FO 429

Written by M. Moore

My dear Sir

Yours of the 20th instant was delayed by the heavy fall of snow and only reached me two days ago. I immediately communicated with Lord Greenock who required I would excuse his not replying to your former letter ere this, but that in fact he had been unwilling to send any information that could not be authenticated by documents, as he sees in recent publications how much of correspondence and paper that is occasioned by giving the impressions of different persons on the same events. I have managed to give you his own words as relating to those parts of the battle of Waterloo which he remembers.

Lord Greenock's recollections at the distance of 22 years are not sufficiently accurate to enable him to answer with confidence Lt Siborne's questions. He cannot take upon himself to say how the cavalry was formed previously to the commencement of the action, there having been no general order given on that head. This therefore was left entirely to General Officer's commanding brigades and probably they may have offered in this respect. To the best of his recollection however, those Lord Greenock saw were in contiguous columns at close order. Lord Greenock was on the left of the road when the 1st charge took place. He was crossing the road at the moment the 2nd Life Guards were coming down it in the manner Lt Siborne describes, and he accompanied that regiment until he found Lord E. Somerset[3] and the 1st Life Guards and Blues. He therefore did not see the commencement of this charge by the regiments on the right of the road, but understood that the enemy was here located considerably beyond the crest of the position[4] and therefore they might have been in line when they first met the enemy. Mr Siborne is right in supposing with reference to the Belgian cavalry that he alluded to the same occasion as described by Lord Anglesey and also in respect to the spot where Lord A.[5] received his wound!

I have now given you all the information I received from Lord Greenock and it only remains for me to wish you well off with your arduous task. Please remember me most kindly to Sir Guy and Lady Campbell,[6] and believe me my dear Sir

Most truly yours

M MOORE[7]

1 Charles Murray Cathcart, Lord Greenock, joined the army as a second lieutenant in 1799 and served in Holland, Naples, Walcheren and the Peninsula and was severely wounded at the Pyrenees. He received a General Service Medal with bars for Barrosa, Salamanca and Vittoria. Afterwards made GCB, General and Colonel-in-Chief of the 1st Dragoon Guards. He succeeded his father as 2nd Earl Cathcart in 1843. Later, he was Governor of Edinburgh castle, then Commander of the Forces and Governor General in North America. He died at St Leonard's on 16 July 1859. A previous letter of his was published by Siborne (number 7).

2 The letter has no year, but it clearly states that it was 22 years since the scenes of Waterloo.

3 Major General Lord Edward Somerset commanded the 1st Cavalry Brigade including the Life Guards at Waterloo.

4 That is, still in the valley between the contending armies.

5 Lieutenant General the Earl of Uxbridge commanded all the Allied cavalry at Waterloo. He was wounded in the right knee in the final advance and his leg, which was amputated later, and buried under a tree! He became Marquis of Anglesey on 23 June 1815 and eventually attained the rank of field marshal in 1846, and was made KG, GCB and GCH. He died on 29 April 1854 and is buried at Lichfield Cathedral. His letters were published by Siborne (numbers 3–6).

6 Brevet Lieutenant Colonel Sir Guy Campbell CB of the 6th Foot, a son of Sir Colin Campbell, had joined the army as an ensign in 1794. He served as an assistant adjutant-general at Waterloo. Afterwards he went on the half-pay list in 1816 but eventually became a major general. He died at Kingstown, Ireland on 25 January 1849.

7 There is no record of an M. Moore at Waterloo nor in the army lists; most likely he was secretary to Lord Greenock.

No. 6 From the same

Edinburgh, 20 October 1840

ADD MS 34707, FO 203

Lord Greenock presents his compliments to Mr Siborne and in reply to his note of the 14th July begs to acquaint him that according to his recollection of the positions of the different brigades of cavalry at Waterloo the only portion of the Allied cavalry that passed *by our right* of Hougoumont at the period of the great and final advance of the army was Sir C. Grant's Brigade[1] which had been stationed and operating upon our extreme right in that direction during the whole day. Lord Greenock is not aware to his present recollection of any other portion of the Allied cavalry having been specially detached in that direction, with reference to the movements of *Pire's* brigade of Light cavalry,[2] although he can not take upon himself to state positively that this was not the case, as their fate might very possibly have either escaped his observation at the time, or his memory after the lapse of so many years.

[UNSIGNED]

1 The 5th Cavalry Brigade of Major General Sir Colquhoun Grant, consisting of the 7th and 15th Hussars and the 2nd Hussars KGL.

2 General de Division Comte Hippolyte Marie Guillaume Piré, who commanded the 2nd Cavalry Division of Reille's II Corps. This division was stationed on the extreme left of the French army throughout the day, near Hougoumont.

Letter no. 7

No. 7 From the same
Edinburgh, 8 September 1842

ADD MS 34707, FO 412

My dear Sir,

My brother Colonel G. Cathcart[1] having forwarded to me your letter to him dated the 1st August last, with a request that I would answer as far as it might be in my power to furnish, the questions it contained.

I take the earliest opportunity after the bustle and hurry consequent upon the Queen's[2] visit to Edinburgh to comply with his desire, premising that I feel the greatest diffidence in speaking at this distance of time concerning facts which are to become the subject of history, from my own recollection, unless assisted by official documents or any memoranda of my own, made at the time; for although by our impression respecting the general march of the events as they occurred in the course of the highly interesting period to which you refer is sufficiently vivid, I am not so sure that my recollection of all the details respecting dates and places is so much to be relied on.

It fortunately happens however that among the papers in my possession, which I have carefully examined in the hope of finding any that might assist your labours, I have been able to lay my hands upon a complete series of the *original* orders for the movements of the army in which those of the cavalry are included on the advance to Paris, commencing from the 23rd of June, and extending to the 7th of July on which day the troops took up their quarters in the environs of Paris and the Duke of Wellington established his headquarters in that city, the headquarters of the cavalry being on that day at Malmaison.

The orders are wanting for the few days that intervened between the 18th and 23rd of June, but the cavalry did not move from the position they took up at the close of the battle of Waterloo until the 20th, on which day the cavalry headquarters moved to Thieu, near Mons, the cavalry occupying the advanced villages towards Binch.

On the 21st they were moved to Malplaquet where I think we halted the next day, on the 23rd the cavalry headquarters were at Croix, to which place the first order of that date which is headed Maroilles was forwarded; all the subsequent movements are clearly detailed in the documents which I will be much obliged to you to take great care of and to return them to me as soon as you have quite done with them, as they are curious and valuable from being originals.

With respect to the exact position of the 1st Light Battalion of the King's German Legion[3] at the period of the conflict to which you refer, I can give no positive information, but I am inclined to agree with those who doubt their having been on the spot specified when the first charge of the cuirassiers took place, for I have no recollection of having seen them at that moment, although I accompanied Lord Edward Somerset's brigade down the Genappe road. At that time, they were not only driving the French cuirassiers before them, but there were also many of them riding individually on our flank and even mixed with our troops endeavouring to make their escape, before we came to the hollow way in question, which is a proof that the cuirassiers must have passed across it before they came into contact with the Household Cavalry.

The new model you are now constructing will be highly interesting and I shall look forward with much interest to the appearance of your history, to which I shall be most happy to be a subscriber.

Believe me with best wishes for the success of your present undertaking.

Very faithfully yours

GREENOCK

---

1 Lieutenant the Honourable George Cathcart, 6th Dragoon Guards, served at Waterloo as one of Wellington's extra aides de camp. He had joined the army as a cornet in 1810 and served in Germany 1813–14 as an ADC to Lord Cathcart at the Allied Headquarters. He was present at many of the great battles of this campaign including Lutzen, Bautzen, Dresden and Leipzig. He was Lieutenant Colonel of the 1st Dragoon Guards at the time of the letter. He eventually became a lieutenant general and commanded the forces at the Cape of Good Hope. He commanded the 4th Division in the Crimea and fell at the battle of Inkerman. He was awarded the GCB.

2 Queen Victoria.

3 This obviously refers to a recurring theme in Siborne's letters; did the 1st Light Battalion KGL cross the Brussels road to aid the repulse of D'Erlon's attack? Greenock's answer concurs with that given by other British correspondents in this series of letters that they did not. The letters from officers of the 1st Light Battalion are equally adamant that they did. See their letters (letters 147–62 below). On balance it would seem that the 1st Light Battalion did support the defeat of the attack.

No. 8 From the same

Edinburgh, 14 September 1842

ADD MS 34707, FO 418

Note in Greenock's handwriting squeezed into the top of the letter

Particulars with sufficient accuracy to enable me to speak with any certainty respecting them. Alava[1] I think, wore his hat fore and aft but I am inclined to believe that Pozzo di Borgo[2] and Müffling[3] wore square to the front. Baron Vincent[4] would also have worn his hat *square*.

Yours very truly

GREENOCK

Dear Captain Siborne

I have received a letter this morning from Colonel Gurwood[5] who is very anxious that I should furnish him with all the documents and papers relative to the Waterloo campaign and appears on enquiry that the book in which the memoranda of movements were inserted contains no entries of those subsequent to the 13th of June until the 6th of July, which very much increases the value of those which I recently sent to you. I have informed Gurwood in reply, that I had forwarded all the documents I could find relative to the period referred to by him to you, but as it appears that the Duke of Wellington is himself desirous of inspecting them for some purpose of his own, he had my full permission to apply to you either for a *sight* of the *originals*, or for *copies* of them as might be found most convenient.

As you inform me that being now exclusively occupied with your new model, the publication of your history must be deferred until February, you might be able to share the original documents for a short time without inconvenience if Gurwood should write to you for them; requesting that he would take care of them and return them to you.

I can easily account for the blank interval you notice in the series of memoranda between the 30th June and the 6th of July, for after the cavalry took up their quarters in the neighbourhood of Paris, while the headquarters of the army were at Gonesse and those of the cavalry at the Chateau du Roissy, they remained for the most part stationary and therefore no general memoranda of movements were circulated during that period or until the cavalry were put in movement on the 7th of July, to cross the Seine at Argenteuil and take up quarters to the south of Paris, when Sir J. Vandeleur's[6] headquarters were transferred to Malmaison.

If any orders relative to the Duke's disposition on the 1st and 2nd of July in connection with Blücher's movement of the right towards the left bank of the Seine, to the General commanding the cavalry, then they must have been conveyed in *private* communications to Sir John Vandeleur which did not pass through my hands.

I can easily understand the importance of the information you ask for, however trivial it might appear, but I regret that either my recollection does not serve, or that my attention was too much occupied otherwise at the time that I do remember and probably did not notice the particulars.

[UNSIGNED]

---

1 Lieutenant General Miguel de Alava, the Spanish military representative. Interestingly, he was one of a very few who were present at both Waterloo and Trafalgar.
2 Lieutenant General Count Carlo Andrea Pozzo di Borgo, the Russian military representative.
3 Major General Philipp Friedrich Carl Ferdinand Freiherr von Müffling, the Prussian military representative.
4 Field Marshal Baron de Vincent, the Austrian military representative.
5 Captain John Gurwood of the 10th Hussars, who edited the Duke of Wellington's dispatches. His letters are published in this volume (numbers 54–6).
6 Major General Sir John Vandeleur commanded the 4th Cavalry Brigade throughout the Waterloo campaign. His letters were published by Siborne (numbers 51 & 52).

No. 9 From the same
Edinburgh, 16 September 1842

ADD MS 34707, FO 421

My dear Sir,

I have again had a strict search through my papers in the hope of finding more of the memoranda issued by Sir C. Broke Vere[1] for the movement of the army during its advance to Paris but I am sorry to say without success, with the exception of the one herewith enclosed dated Nivelles 19th June 1815, which contains the order for the march and quartering of the cavalry on the 20th, being the first movement made by the cavalry after the battle of the 18th.

There is now only one other wanting to complete the series up to the 30th June viz. that received at Thieu directing the march on the 21st to Malplaquet.

The result of this further examination proving the absence of all official documents of this description between the 30th of June when the Army arrived before Paris and the 7th of July, when it crossed to the left bank of the Seine, confirming me in the belief I before expressed, that no general movement of the cavalry took place during that interval. No circular memoranda or other information that passed through my hands were issued from the Quartermaster General's office or headquarters, which were then at Gonesse within that period.

Sir John Vandeleur who I believe resides in Dublin may however be able to inform you better on this subject.

The memorandum now transmitted should be added to the other documents which are already in your possession.[2]

Believe me, very faithfully yours

GREENOCK

1 Lieutenant Colonel Sir Charles Broke, Permanent Assistant Quartermaster General, became Acting Deputy Quartermaster General on 19 June, due to the mortal wounding of De Lancey. He had joined the army in 1796 as a cornet and served at the Helder, Hanover, South America and the Peninsula, for which he received a General Service Medal with bars for Albuera, Badajoz, Salamanca, Vittoria, Pyrenees, Nivelle, Nive, Orthes and Toulouse. He took on the additional surname Vere in 1822 and eventually became a major general.

2 These memoranda no longer exist in the files and were presumably returned; however the information of the daily movements they provided are clearly reproduced in Siborne's *History*.

No. 10 From the same
Edinburgh, 21 September 1842

ADD MS 34707, FO 423

My dear Sir,

In my last letter[1] in which I transmitted to you the original regimental record of the headquarters of the cavalry for the movement of the army on 20th June 1815, in its advance to Paris, I told you that the Duke of Wellington being desirous for some purpose of his own to refer to the orders by which the movements of that period were regulated, had caused search to be made in the books at the Quartermaster General's office for copies of them, but none had been found and that no entries had been made of any of these orders between the 15th of June and the 7th of July, before learning however that I had preserved so many of the original documents in question. His Grace expressed a wish through Colonel Gurwood that I would send them to London for his inspection, but this communication did not reach me until some days after I had forwarded them to you. I lost no time in making this circumstance known to Colonel Gurwood, from whom I received a letter this morning in which he requests that I will ask you to forward to him as soon as possible *all* the papers of the above description which I lately sent to you, that they may be shown to the Duke, after which they shall be returned to you without delay. As they will not be required for a longer period than a week or ten days it is hoped that you will be able to spare them for that time without inconvenience, and I have the less scruple in complying with Colonel Gurwood's request as you lately informed me that being so much engaged at present in completing your model you have been obliged to postpone the publication of your history, for which these papers are principally required. I will accordingly esteem it a favour if you will *immediately* on the receipt hereof, transmit the whole of these papers to Colonel Gurwood whose address is no. 70 Lowndes Square, London, requesting that the receipt of them may be duly acknowledged to you, to whom they are to be carefully returned.

Believe me always, very faithfully yours

GREENOCK

---

1 Siborne was obviously being tardy in providing the papers to the Duke of Wellington, who wanted them as material for his memorandum of 4 October 1842 in reply to Clausewitz's claims.

No. 11 Major The Honourable George Lionel Dawson, 1st Dragoon Guards, Assistant Quartermaster General[1]

30 July [1835?][2]

ADD MS 34705, FO 319

My dear Cuyler[3]

I met Flahaut[4] yesterday at dinner at Lord Grey's and in talking over the content of your letter – you know he was one of Napoleon's aides de camp at Waterloo, it was strange to find how much we had both forgotten of the details that you still wish for.

However, we came to the conclusion that the Imperial Guards had blue trousers, and the line grey – you must recollect that the French almost invariably fight in greatcoats – the line grey, the Guard blue. The Guards had grenadier caps with no ornament on – the Grenadiers of the line shakoes with red tape around the crown – and two stripes on each side thus –

(the shako is too high) you see I was not born to be an artist, to which you will say that I can hardly write.

I hope this information will give satisfaction – I wish you joy on the new appointment and conclude it is a good one.

Your humble servant

DAMER[5]

---

1 He originally joined the army as a cornet in 1806. He is recorded as being wounded at Waterloo. Promoted brevet lieutenant colonel on 4 December 1815 and appointed CB, he was placed on half pay on 17 August 1820. He died on 14 April 1856.

2 The year is not stated, but it would appear to date from around 1835.

3 See note 2 of Rooke's letter printed in this volume (number 95).

4 General August Charles Joseph, Comte de Flahaut de la Billarderie, Imperial ADC.

5 Dawson assumed the additional surname of Damer on 14 March 1829.

King's German Legion Staff

No. 12 Captain Lewis Benne[1]
Hanover, 5 March 1835

ADD MS 34705, FO 13

My dear Sir,

Your notes of the 7th and 21st February came duly to my hands likewise *all* the packets with plans and letters. Although I have not written to you I may conscientiously assure you I have not been idle in regard to your undertaking – but 'till within the last few days I remained in a despairing situation as to my ultimate success. For, not withstanding my having received some *very good* sketches for your purpose – I considered them far too incomplete to be of any material use.

The *great event* lays too far back and the officers have quite forgotten it. Others are not to be got out of their ease to reply. Under these circumstances I became quite disheartened, which I regretted the more as the KGL, in unison with the Hanoverians, had so eminent a share in the battle as the returns of their losses amply prove.

At last I recollected that about 10 years ago, the Prussian government applied most diligently to the Duke of Cambridge to put them in possession of every particular respecting the battle of Waterloo. Upon which His R.H.[2] directed that all materials should be collected and the most intelligent officers of the Staff employed for constructing a military map showing the formations and positions not only of each corps but also of the *whole army* at *about noon* and again at *about 7 pm* of the 18th June. Many officers were called together of the different corps and examined upon the subject of the formation and position of their respective corps during that day and the result proved most satisfactory – and I this day have read the flattering letter which His R.H. received from Berlin[3] acknowledging the receipt of the plan and thanking him in the highest terms for so complete and accurate a work.

As this plan is the *very thing* you want – The same has been requested back *as a loan* from Prussia by the Director of our Military Academy and the whole will then be laid down in *your own plan*, according to the scale given under it, by that same *very clever* captain[4] of our General Staff officers who shared in the compilation of the plan alluded to.

I am very happy in being thus enabled to hold out to you the best of hope for ultimate success – but I must add that about six weeks will necessarily elapse before the plan can be completed – but you may rely on my endeavours that not a moment shall be lost in setting to the task as soon as the plan arrives from Berlin.

I hesitate sending you the information I have got in hand for fear of misleading you – but I will keep all till the plan is finished and then send you the whole at once.

Some years back I compiled returns both of the KG Legion and the Hanoverian subsidual troops showing the brigades, corps, commanding officers by name, effective strength in the battle and the losses they sustained near Waterloo, which our most gracious King and others found very interesting. I willingly would send you copies thereof, but as you appear not to be in want of *such* information it is useless to make the offer. These returns, with many others of mine, will be published in the 2nd vol. of Beamish's *History of the KGL.*[5] If you have read the 1st vol. you will have seen a good deal of my work.

I shall inform you now and then of the progress of the plan and in the meantime beg to remain,

My dear Sir, your very obedient humble servant
L BENNE KH, CAPTAIN AND BREVET MAJOR LATE K G LEGION

---

1 Listed as John Frederick Lewis Benne, no. 6 in Beamish, but clearly only uses the name Lewis Benne in his letters. He had joined the KGL as a cadet and served in Hanover and the Baltic. He became a captain on 8 August 1815 and afterwards went on half pay at Hanover. He received the HGO3.

2 His Royal Highness, Field Marshal The Duke of Cambridge KG, GCB, GCMG, GCH, seventh son of King George III, administered Hanover for the crown. He was also Colonel of the Coldstream Guards.

3 Capital of Prussia at that time.

4 This probably refers to Captain Brandis, whose own letter is included in this volume (number 167).

5 Volume 1 was published in 1832, volume 2 in 1837. Unfortunately only the returns for the KGL were published. This book remains the primary source of information on this corps.

No. 13 From the same
Hanover, 17 August 1835

ADD MS 34705, FO 321

My dear Sir,
The plans of the battle of Waterloo alluded to in my former communications were completed some time since but on their being submitted for inspection and approval to the heads of our Staff, the opinions differed so materially upon their *entire* correctness that it was determined not to part with them for your use for fear of subjecting the compiler to disputes or other unpleasantness. Every one of our General and Staff officers however allows that Captain William von Brandis[1] has performed a very clever *[sic]* task and that he bestowed infinite labour upon the compilation of the positions and movements of the several corps at different periods of the day of 18th June 1815.

Captain Brandis made use of all official reports rendered on account of the King's German Legion, Hanoverian and Brunswick troops and next of *all* the works, written on the battle of Waterloo, particularly the French – and although he may be well borne out by the information he *thus obtained* – yet his work cannot be considered as resting on unquestionable authority and official documents.

Feeling very disappointed at my expectations remaining unrealised – I requested, *as a particular favour*, that the plans might be given to me on the condition that they *were not* to be considered as resting upon authentic and official sources – this has been agreed to and I find great pleasure in sending you.[2]

As you, no doubt, will have the means in your power for correcting this compilation you may render it most valuable and if you would be pleased to favour us hereafter with your corrections and lay them down in your own plans we shall feel much obliged.

Captain Brandis experienced great difficulty in tracing the positions of the *Corps* of *the* British army – for instance where was *the* British Reserve Artillery? – where the 13th Light Dragoons? Are the movements of the brigades of Mitchell and Lambert correct?

In short we wish to be favoured with similar plans from you as you now receive from us in order that at least we may have the *British army* correct on each of the five plans.

I further send you herewith such information respecting the King's German Legion and Hanoverian troops as may be considered correct *after* an elapse of so many years and the imperfect reports we prepared upon the subject.[3]

And lastly I forward to you the sketches[4] I collected from different officers of the KG Legion – of which however I only send you *such* as I conceive of some value – all the rest I have destroyed. The narrative given by the gallant veteran, Major General Charles Best,[5] you will find highly interesting.

Now, my dear Sir, having furthered your wishes as far as I was able, I must call your attention to what I have before observed respecting the five plans and in wishing you every success in your undertaking I beg to remain,

My dear Sir, yours most faithfully

L BENNE

---

1 Captain William von Brandis, an ensign in the 3rd Line Battalion KGL at Waterloo, numbered 498 in Beamish. He died at Imbsen, near Dransfeld, in Hanover on 29 March 1830.

2 I have omitted a long list of enclosures; these generally do not appear to be extant, although Jacobi's letter is itemized in the section dealing with letters I did not feel were worthy of printing. The omitted section reads:

1, A letter from Major Jacobi [Aide Quartermaster General of the Hanoverian Army and First Teacher at the Military Academy] dated 21st July 1835 stating in positive terms that the placement of the troops in the plans is not to be considered as being grounded upon authentic information, particularly with regard to the Hanoverians and King's German Legion.

2, The Legende of the battle of Waterloo on the 18th June 1815 and explanation of the plans.

3, Plan No. I. Showing the first emplacement with *Ordre de Bataille* of the two armies and the commencement of the battle from ½ past 11 to near 2 o'clock in the afternoon.

4, Plan No. II. Showing the engagements and movements from 2 to 4 o'clock pm.

5, Plan No. III. Ditto from 4 to 7 pm.

6, Plan No. IV. Ditto from 7 to 8 pm.

7, Plan No. V. Ditto from 8 to 9.

3 I have omitted a further list of enclosures; this reads:

Viz

A A letter to me of 26th June 1835 from Major and Aide Q. M. Gen Jacobi.

B A statement of the different corps of the King's German Legion and Hanoverian troops – their dispositions at 7 o'clock in the evening with a short exposition of their exploits during the day.

C Your plan of the field of Waterloo in which the corps of the Legion and the Hanoverian troops have been entered.

4 These sketches refer to descriptions of the battle written by various officers and are therefore published under their own names.

5 He commanded the 4th Hanoverian Brigade. His letter is published in this volume (number 194).

Letter no. 14

No. 14 From the same
Hanover, 2 April 1838

ADD MS 34706, FO 462

My dear Sir,
I have to acknowledge the receipt of your letter of the 12th instant and I send you herewith some notices from myself and Captain Fricke[1] respecting the 1st and 2nd Light Dragoons KGL as I could not conveniently ask General Dörnberg[2] for the same who lives very retired at a great distance from here.

The enquiry at Darmstadt will be pursued – but in regard to the other point I fear all *labour* is lost. I have now still a clue, but it seems the people are not disposed to answer the call upon them.

I believe that I have mentioned to you before that I prepared a great return of the Hanoverian subsidual corps employed at Waterloo and which contains every particular you seem to be in want of. This return of which I have only one copy left and which costs me a great deal of labour without any reward, I will lend you on condition that you do return it to me undamaged – and as I am under orders to proceed to London by the 8th or 9th of this month, I will bring it with me and deliver it to our friend Lindsay for being forwarded to you and through whom I shall expect it back when you have used it. You may rely on its correctness and I give you my full permission to publish it in your work,[3] but in that case you must state that I am the compiler and my name must be under it.

Waterloo has been a source of much labour for me without any benefit whatsoever – even of the history of the Legion for which I have furnished the principal part. I have been obliged to pay for my copy whereas it costs me, besides my own labour, full £20 for hire of a clerk out of my pocket.[4]

In regard to your returning thanks in the preface of your work I suggest to say: 'Trifling assistance has been rendered by Major Lewis Benne, KH, formerly Brigade Major of the King's German Legion and through his intercession by Lieut. Colonel Jacobi, Major Ch Heise, Captain Brandis[5] and many other officers of the Hanoverian Army and the K G Legion as well as of the Brunswick and Nassau Corps.'

I wish you may succeed in the completion of your work by next June and that you may gain a full consideration of your great labour. A few days ago we had a short notice of it in the Hamburg papers.

I remain, my dear Sir, yours most faithfully

L S BENNE

[Notes supplied by Benne with this letter:]

Quarters of the *1st Light Dragoons* King's German Legion

25th January 1815	Mons, Jemappes, Nimi, Cuimes, Guaregnon, Hornu & Wasmes
25th February	do do do do do Baudiere, Ghlien
25th March	do do ____________ St Symphorien
25th April	Malines {The regiment had at this time been formed into 4 squadrons, the 9th and 10th troops having been divided among the other eight – three captains are in the 2nd and three in the 3rd squadron}
25th May	do
25th June	Bivouac – Cammersuriel {*effective present & fit for duty on this date: 5 captains, 4*

lieutenants, 5 cornets, 1 regimental quartermaster, 1 surgeon, 2 assistant surgeons, 1 veterinary surgeon, 1 troop quartermaster, 39 sergeants, 8 trumpeters, 15 farriers, 21 corporals, 260 other ranks, 344 troop horses} (Captain Hans von Hattorf commanding.)[6]

1st Light Dragoons

25th January 1815	Tournay
25th February	do
25th March	do
25th April	Brussels – the 10 trooops had been formed into 8 or 4 squadrons
25th May	Malines
25th June	Bivouac – Bellenglise – France – *{fit for duty: 26 officers, 1 troop quartermaster, 23 sergeants, 8 trumpeters, 330 rank and file, and 369 horses}* (Colonel von Jonquiers commanding.)[7]

NB On the 16th June the regiments marched from Malines into bivouac near Quatre Bras, in front of the enemy and moved after the battle of the 18th with the army into France.

Hanover had *no* engineers in 1815 – and of the engineers of the KG Legion *none* were at Waterloo.

L S BENNE

---

1 Adjutant William Fricke of the 1st Dragoons KGL, numbered 121 in Beamish. He had served in the Legion since 1804, serving in Hanover, the Peninsula and southern France. He is recorded as having been severely wounded at Waterloo. Later a captain on half pay at Celle in Hanover. His letters are published in this volume (numbers 37–8).

2 William von Dörnberg, Colonel Commandant of the 1st Dragoons and commanding the 3rd Cavalry Brigade at Waterloo, numbered 86 in Beamish. He was previously Colonel Commandant of the Brunswick Hussars from 1809 and served in northern Germany and Holland. He was severely wounded at Waterloo. Afterwards a lieutenant general on the retired list and Ambassador at St Petersburg. His awards were HGO1, CB, RANO, RStAO1, RStGO3, HeGL1, PrMoM, NWO3, HEIH, BWM, RM, RPM, RTM, HM, HeM.

3 Siborne's preface merely thanks the various officers of the KGL that had helped him; there is no particular mention of Benne by name. The returns on pages 573 to 575 in Siborne's *History of the Waterloo Campaign* are credited to Benne in a footnote to each return.

4 A clear plea for funds, something Siborne also lacked.

5 All of these officers' letters are printed under their own name. Benne obviously helped Siborne a great deal in his quest for information from the German officers.

6 See p. 68, note 2. I believe that Benne is correct in stating that von Hattorf commanded the regiment only after Waterloo, as Colonel von Dörnberg was detached commanding the 3rd Cavalry Brigade; and Lieutenant Colonel von Bülow and Majors von Reizenstein and von Sichart are all recorded as having been severely wounded at Waterloo.

7 Beamish no. 127 is recorded as being slightly wounded at Waterloo. Colonel von Veltheim was obviously not with the regiment, hence Jonquières commanded.

No. 15 Lieutenant Lewis Henry Von Sichart [1]

Hanover, 10 July 1836

ADD MS 34706, FO 90

Original in German

With regard to the request by Lieutenant Siborne for information regarding an event during the battle of Waterloo, I have the honour to respond as follows to Your

Excellency in the name of Colonel Jacobi.

According to information from inquiries of several officers of the late 1st Dragoon Regiment KGL, *absolutely no* attack occurred at the battle of Waterloo involving this regiment at the time that the commanding officer of the artillery battery reported;[2] however, it is very probable that the following facts are based on the story told by the officer mentioned.

The 1st Dragoon Regiment was, as recounted in the earlier report, in column at first, but then in line. While this first attack was undertaken while in line, a corps of French cavalry (about one squadron strong) suddenly appeared at its left flank while the regiment was in the process of making its way towards the slope. The then Major von Reizenstein,[3] realizing the danger of being taken in the flank by them, threw himself with a corps of his regiment, which he quickly detached from the left wing and formed up, and stood against this enemy corps and repelled it. However, the 1st Dragoon Regiment and the enemy cavalry then charged each other with such vehemence that both corps broke through each others lines – at least partially – and were scattered pell-mell among each other. A number of officers of the 1st Dragoon Regiment were wounded in the encounter, and among these was one who was wounded in the south during the chase of the retreating portion of the enemy corps, when he was stabbed by an enemy infantryman – proof that both enemy corps must have broken through each other.

Thus, since a breakthrough of each of the corps must have taken place, and because the direction of the flank attack corresponded to the direction which the artillery officer detailed both in his description as well as that taken by the French corps on the plan, it is therefore probable that what is being described here is based upon the story told by the aforementioned officer – except that in this case, doubt must be raised over whether the skirmish took place *exactly* where indicated on the plan.[4]

The letter from Lieutenant Siborne is being returned in the enclosure.

Most respectfully yours, Your Excellency

L V SICHART,
CAPTAIN OF THE GENERAL STAFF

---

1 Lewis Henry von Sichart was an officer of the 2nd Line Battalion KGL but attached to the Staff. He is listed as number 453 in Beamish. He only joined the corps in 1814, serving in the Netherlands and in the Waterloo campaign. Afterwards he was a captain in the 4th Hanoverian Line Battalion but was placed on half pay in 1816.

2 This almost certainly refers to the statement by Captain Mercer of G Troop RHA in Siborne's *Waterloo Letters*, letter 89, p. 216, regarding a German and French cavalry regiment charging right through each other.

3 Major Augustus von Reizenstein of the 1st Dragoons KGL is listed as number 88 in Beamish. He joined the corps in 1804 and had served in Hanover, the Peninsula in 1812–14 and the Netherlands. He was severely wounded at Waterloo but made a lieutenant colonel on that date. CB, BWM and HGO2, he died as a brevet colonel in command of the Hanoverian Garde du Corps at Celle in Hanover on 6 November 1830.

4 The plan appears to be no longer extant.

THE CAVALRY

No. 16 Lieutenant Colonel Frederick Stovin[1]

No address or date

ADD MS 34704 FO 151

(Not at Waterloo)

My dear Siborne

You require advice on a delicate subject – any conflicting statements between the *two*[2] in question, brought under the view of *either*, might be attended by very disagreeable results, and therefore as you received the one you are about to acknowledge – *before* the other – it will be most wise and prudent not to notice any discrepancy of their respective views – and to write as if you seem not in possession of the *last* received. That the Light cavalry did *not* support the *heavies* is beyond dispute – *why* was not made manifest – but in *conversation* with Lord A.[3] he distinctly stated that in the morning he had told all the Commanders of cavalry there, as it might be impossible to send orders on every occasion 'the general object was always to support movements in their front.'

That there was a deficiency is clear – depend on it, the subject is one you and I ought not if possible, to be touched – I could *tell* you more than I wish to write – and after what I *have* written you will see the propensity of this merits delicate caution.

Think about my comments.

Ever yours

F STOVIN

As this must rest a day in London I send it through Lindsay.

---

1 Frederick Stovin joined the 52nd Regiment as an ensign in 1800 and served at Ferrol. He transferred to the 28th Foot in 1803 and served in Hanover, Copenhagen, Sweden, Corunna, Walcheren. He served in the Peninsula, including Ciudad Rodrigo, Badajoz, Salamanca, Vittoria, Pyrenees, Nivelle, Orthes and Toulouse and became an ADC to Sir Thomas Picton. He served at New Orleans where he was wounded, therefore missing Waterloo. He was made KCB and KCMG. He was placed on half pay in 1829 and eventually became a major general in 1841.

2 This letter obviously refers to counter claims by two senior officers, regarding the support or otherwise of the light cavalry once the great charge of the heavy cavalry against D'Erlon's Corps had foundered. The persons are not identified, but Sir John Vandeleur or Sir Hussey Vivian is the most likely candidate in the defence of the light cavalry, hence the latter's extensive correspondence with officers of his brigade, published in this work. His antagonist is not known but Lord Anglesey or Sir George Elley is the most likely.

3 Lord Anglesey, Commander of the Allied cavalry at Waterloo.

1st Cavalry Brigade

The 1st Life Guards

No. 17 Lieutenant George Randall[1]

Tooting, 7 December 1834

ADD MS 34704 FO 20

Sir,
In reply to the first question; what was the particular formation of the 1st Life Guards, as far as my recollection and circumstances will admit, the 1st Life Guards were in *line*.

The brigade charged in line about (eleven am).

In reply to the second, what was the formation of enemy forces in front of Life Guards. In *Line*

Having made every enquiry I believe I am correct the Life Guards were in line the whole of the 18th. The last charge was made about (5 or 6 pm). I am extremely sorry I cannot point out the spot on the plan.

I have the honour to be Sir your most obedient servant

GEORGE RANDALL HP [HALF-PAY]

---

1 Promoted to captain on 18 June 1815. He received a General Service Medal with one bar for Vittoria. He went on half pay on 13 October 1825.

The 2nd Life Guards

No. 18 Major The Honourable Edward P. Lygon[1]

St James Square, 11 September 1839

ADD MS 34707 FO 126

Major General Lygon presents his compliments to Mr Siborne and begs to forward him the enclosed papers. If there is any other point Major General Lygon can be of service to Mr Siborne again, he will most readily communicate with him.

[UNSIGNED]

Memorandum on the remark made by Lord Edward Somerset respecting the movement

Sir Hussey Vivian in July 1836 says 'Whether the attack of Ponsonby's brigade[2] preceded that of Lord Edward Somerset's,[3] is a question I have lately heard discussed and decided in the affirmative, that is that it *did* precede it.'

Lord Anglesey[4] says 'I had come at speed from towards the right upon seeing this advance, and as I passed the Household Brigade, I ordered it to wheel into line, and passing over the road to Sir William Ponsonby, I ordered him to form and charge in line with the former brigade, which I instantly put in motion. These two brigades carried all before their front.'

Quartermaster McDowell[5] and a private of 6th Dragoons say the brigade charged in line, the Inniskillings being the centre regiment.[6]

Sir James Kempt[7] says the charge of cavalry was upon an infantry column to his left and that not a single cavalryman co-operated with his brigade.

(Extract from you about 2 guns on knoll has been sent to Kincaid[8])

Lord Greenock conceives that the enemy's cavalry had penetrated considerably beyond the crest of the position (on the right of the knoll) and that therefore the Household Brigade might have been in line when they first met the enemy. Refer this point to Captain Waymouth.[9]

---

1 Major the Honourable Edward Pindar Lygon had joined the army as a cornet in 1803 and served in the Peninsula from 1812, receiving the General Service Medal with a bar for Vittoria. He commanded the two squadrons of the 2nd Life Guards at Waterloo. He was made CB and KStV. Afterwards he was Inspector General of Cavalry, General and Colonel-in-Chief of the 13th Light Dragoons. He died on 11 November 1860.

2 The 2nd (Union) Brigade of cavalry.

3 The 1st (Household) Brigade of cavalry.

4 Lord Anglesey was then Lieutenant General the Earl of Uxbridge, who commanded all the cavalry at Waterloo.

5 McDowell of the Inniskilling Dragoons received a severe sabre cut to the head but survived. The Waterloo Medal Roll states that Frederick McDowell was a corporal in Captain Madox's Troop at Waterloo. It would appear from Hart that he became a quartermaster in 1829.

6 This statement seems to confirm that the Union Brigade charged in line and therefore without a reserve. This was possibly a major factor in their losses as they retired following the charge. However it must be stated that others have claimed that there was a reserve.

7 He commanded the 8th Brigade of Infantry; he claims in a letter published by Siborne (number 148) that he defeated the French column directed against his brigade without the aid of the cavalry charge.

8 First Lieutenant John Kincaid, Adjutant of the 1st Battalion 95th Rifles. Presumably this refers to the questions also put to the members of Whinyates' Troop, as Siborne endeavoured to discover whose guns they were on the knoll. Siborne printed Kincaid's letter (number 161) and further correspondence from members of Whinyates' Troop were published by Siborne (numbers 83–8). Further letters from members of this troop are published in this volume (numbers 72–80).

9 Lieutenant Samuel Waymouth of the 2nd Life Guards. His letters were printed by Siborne (numbers 19–25). A map that accompanied the letters but was not published by Siborne, is now printed in this volume as letter number 20.

No. 19 Lieutenant William Elliott[1]

London, 24 January 1835

ADD MS 34704 FO 199

Sir,

As far as my recollection serves me at this distant period, the situation of the 2nd Life Guards on the morning of the 18th was in a wheat field, (as I perfectly recollect gathering some wheat sheaves not ripe to rub my horse down as I thought it would refresh him after standing all night in a mizzling rain) about 100 yards from the Brussels road, and nearly in a line of what we then designated the Farm House,[2] and situated on the left side of the road from Brussels. Opposite to the entrance gateway to the farm yard and house stood a small brick building and an old tree standing close to it, I mention this as you say you have been on the spot, you will at once recognise, the farmhouse I am speaking of, and which was some distance in the advance of the village of Waterloo. While I was in the act of rubbing my horse down, I received an order with a party of the regiment to take possession of the head of the road, which was at the farm house, for the purpose of keeping it clear from any kind of stoppage, and where I remained during the day – you will therefore perceive I was not in a situation to answer the enquiries of your printed circular which I should have been most happy to have done. I cannot with satisfaction to myself trace on your map the spot the regiment stood when I left it, but I am certain it was a wheat field from the circumstances I have stated, namely, rubbing my horse down with some wheat sheaves.

As the farm house occupies so much of this letter I take leave here to mention a circumstance, which at the time was considered a good joke – the mistress of the farm house as a place of safety ascended into the attic with all her stock of poultry, and remained there during the day.

Sir, your humble servant

W ELLIOTT, CAPT HP [HALF-PAY] 11TH FOOT

---

1 Elliot had served in the Peninsula and received a General Service Medal with bars for Vittoria and Toulouse. He received a Waterloo medal and is recorded as being the acting paymaster at the time. Promoted to captain on 14 April 1818, he was transferred to the 17th Foot on 20 January 1821 and later to the 11th Foot and half pay in 1824. He died on 18 February 1866.

2 The farm of Mont St Jean.

No. 20 Lieutenant Samuel Waymouth[1]

The map overleaf belongs to letter number 19 in Siborne's *Waterloo Letters*, but was omitted.

Point X apparently marks the position where the fleeing cuirassiers became congested and lost a great many casualties to the pursuing Life Guards. He also mentions that here French *chasseurs* lining the banks of the road brought down many Life Guards in their turn.

The depiction of the Duke of Cumberland's hussars near Mont St Jean is in agreement with evidence from others.

---

1 Waymouth was severely wounded and taken prisoner in a charge against the cuirassiers. He became a lieutenant in the 88th Foot in 1825 and went on half pay. He retired as a lieutenant colonel in 1841. He died as a colonel on 26 December 1863.

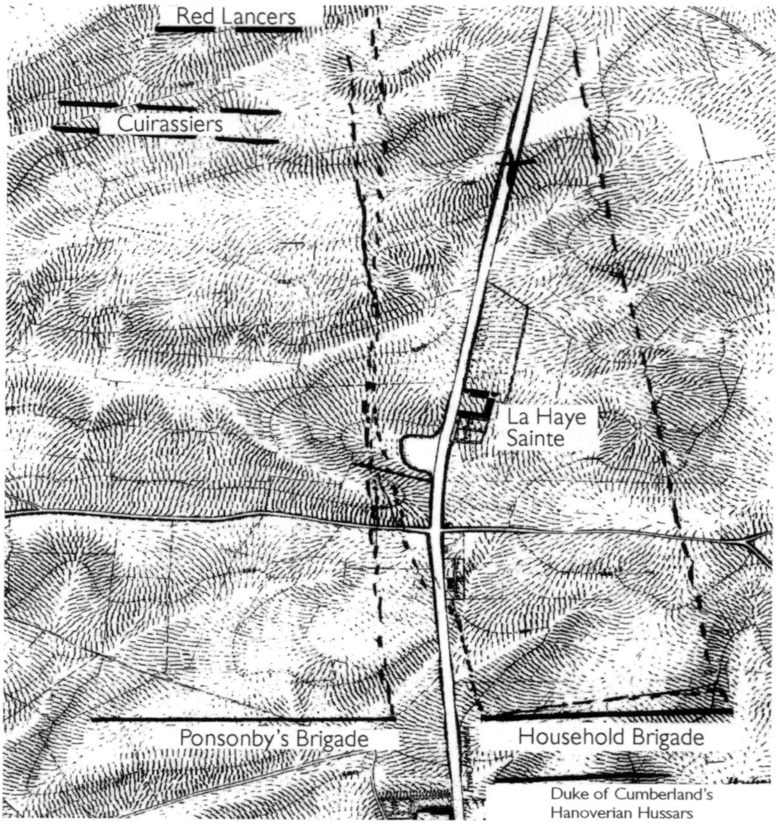

No. 21 Cornet Thomas Marten[1]

Glasgow, 20 July 1840

ADD MS 34707, FO 179

My dear Siborne,

I have been so occupied the last few days from having recently joined the regiment that it has not been in my power to reply to your questions, but I shall now be most happy to give you all the information I can of the first and principal charge of the Household Brigade at Waterloo, which although a very young serrefile[2] at the time, I feel have a perfect recollection of, at least as far as related to my own regiment the 2nd Lifeguards.

To commence then – I should say that it was about 1 o'clock, when we were called upon to advance from our position, in rear of the right centre, to charge a body of cuirassiers – but I never saw them until we had crossed the road near La Haye Sainte – and just beyond where the 95th Rifles were, and there it was *our* first *collision* took place – and not on the crest of the hill as you suppose. It is not improbable however that the other regiments of the brigade might have there met the French cavalry – but we, having the farm in front of us – were obliged I imagine to bring up our right shoulders and descend the hill by the left of it, and in doing this, as you observe, we met with many difficulties in the way of broken ground, banks and such – but you ask me if any of our men proceeded along the road to this point. I should say certainly not, and I would think I cannot be mistaken in this because I was somewhere about the left centre, and I believe we had only two squadrons. I must therefore have remarked it if they had – and now for the charge itself. Just after we had crossed the road (as I have said before) we came in contact with a line of cavalry either cuirassiers or carabineers,[3] I cannot remember which, but they had all cuirasses. A pause here took place and I then beheld plenty of single combats around me. We then progressed onwards shortly falling in with a small party of lancers, who appeared to have been broken by some other force of ours and it was either just before or about this period that we were in the midst of French infantry, who appeared widely disbursed all around, many of whom had thrown themselves down flat on the ground and were apparently dead, but these gents I afterwards saw get up and fire after us. From this scene we pursued our broken course a little further on, *but still in the low ground*, or base of the French hill, and their finding no force to oppose, our people I suppose thought it best to take the shortest way back, over to the left of our position, and in doing this got behind our infantry (who rose and cheered us). We passed a regiment of our light dragoons advancing to the crest in column (it was said the 23rd, at the time), we then crossed the road just in front of Mont St Jean and collecting the remains of our scattered squadrons in front of an orchard, again advanced to our original position in rear of the infantry. This I think is all that can be said of that charge.

You ask me if your remarks of the acts of regiments are pretty correct, I cannot help thinking you have made *us* the *2nd* descend into the road *rather too near* where the cross-roads are, but this you will be the better judge of, from having seen so much of the ground thereabouts, and so soon after the action. I know that we had a good deal of broken ground where we crossed and my impression is, *that* it was nearer La Haye Sainte, than where you have marked it.

I wish you every success in your fine undertaking, and am very glad to hear you are about to publish a history of that war, a copy of which I shall certainly peruse on its coming out. If I can add any more to your already numerous sources of information I can only say, I shall have much pleasure in doing it, and believe me to remain.

Very faithfully yours

T MARTEN

---

1 He joined the regiment as a cornet in 1813 and served through to the end of the Peninsular war, receiving a General Service Medal with one bar for Toulouse. He became Lieutenant Colonel of the Royal Dragoons in 1835. Afterwards he was a Major General and Colonel-in-Chief of the 6th Dragoons and made KH. Two other letters by this officer were published in *Waterloo Letters* (numbers 26 & 27).

2 This term used in all his letters is not recorded in military glossaries of the time, but appears in *Light Infantry Out-posts* by F. de Brack pp 170–1, printed in English in 1876 (recently republished by Ken Trotman, 2002). It appears to be an alternative word for a subaltern or NCO who formed behind the two lines of troopers, rather than the senior officers who led the lines.

3 Although both types of cavalry wore a cuirass front and rear, they were quite different, the cuirassiers' uniforms being blue with cuirass of iron, the carabiniers' being white with cuirass of burnished brass (officers copper) that looked like gold. The unit Marten describes

were most certainly cuirassiers, as the two regiments of carabiniers formed part of Kellermann's cavalry corps which stood behind Jerome's division facing Hougoumont. They only came into action later that afternoon, during the great cavalry attack on the Allied centre.

No. 22 From the same
Glasgow, 29 July 1840

ADD MS 34707, FO 181

My dear Siborne,
I have read the different accounts you have sent me with much interest and attention and am extremely surprised to find that the French cuirassiers never during the day advanced to the charge on their right of the Brussels road. I am now quite satisfied that what you state must have been the case. Regarding that what I, as a serrefile in rear of some very big men, thought a force advancing upon us, were evidently those cuirassiers who had been pursued and overtaken by us and who then turned round, (as I before observed) and stood single combats.

I should now imagine the case to have been with us, that on being ordered up in line to meet the cuirassiers who were advancing from the other side of the hill, the moment we reached the crest, the French turned about (at least those in our front) and made the best of their way down the hollow road to the plain across and where, the 95th describe them, we certainly never came into collision *before* the time I stated, just after we passed the right of the Rifles and I well remember seeing them. General E. Lygon[1] might have been able to say how near we approached to those cuirassiers on the hill and before they turned about. I could not see from being behind so many tall men, all the comments you have received from the rifle officers depend upon it, are quite correct, for they must, from standing still, have seen and know more of what passed than *we*, who had to pick over ground as we advanced.

I have read Kincaid's book[2] and an excellent account he gives of all. I myself must have crossed the road between the sand pit and Rifles, the latter I perfectly remember seeing, and almost certain I beheld the *pit*. Also there was very bad ground where I described before crossing the road.

You ask me if I saw Lord Anglesey in front of *us* in this advance. I do not remember that I did, but saw him ride down in front of our line I think shortly *before*.

I hope you will now be able to make out most satisfactorily all our relative positions and truly glad shall I be to hear that you have been some day amply repaid for all your labours and ingenuity.

I return you the papers with many thanks for their perusal and remain my dear Siborne.

Very faithfully yours

T MARTEN
LT COL ROYAL DRAGOONS

---

1 See his letter is published above (number 18).

2 First Lieutenant John Kincaid of the 1st Battalion, the 95th Foot, wrote his memoirs in two books, *Adventures in the Rifle Brigade* published in 1830 and *Random Shots from a Rifleman* which followed in 1835; it is unclear to which he refers here.

Letter no. 23

No. 23 From William Siborne[1] to Cornet Thomas Marten
Dublin, 2 September 1841

ADD MS 34707, FO 284

My dear Colonel,

I find it so extremely difficult to clear up the question whether the *German* rifles were in front of our line on the *left* of the chaussee at the time of your first charge, that I hope you will kindly forgive my asking whether you can tax your memory any further respecting *the* rifles you saw.

The 95th were upon *high ground* their right resting on the steep bank which falls into the chaussee.[2] The rifles of the KGL were in the hollow or dip in *front*, about where I have placed them. The Wavres road immediately in front of the 95th was partially lined with a straggling hedge.

You are supposed to have taken the direction of the line *a-b* in your charge. The Germans say that while they were in the dip or hollow between the Wavres road and the little hedge with three trees in it (near the sandpit) *British* cavalry advanced and they spread out to let them pass to the front.

Perhaps these little circumstances may tend to refresh your recollections.

Allow me at the same time to ask you another question. Do you think your regiment came at all into collision with the cuirassiers before you crossed the chaussee? for I feel *pretty certain* that *no* French cavalry advanced on the *left* of the road.

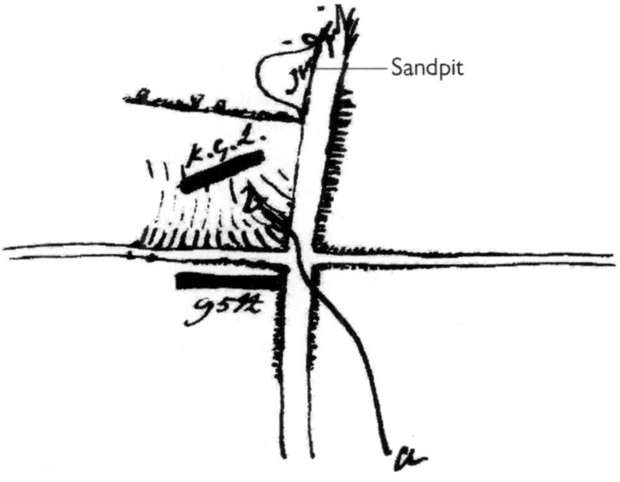

Pray [be] compassionate [with] me in my difficulties, and believe me very truly yours.

W SIBORNE

---

1 I have chosen to print this letter as the only extant example of a request from William Siborne for further clarification in the files. There is a clear explanation of the circumstances as William sees them and a genuine request for help in confirming whether his conjectures are correct or not. There is absolutely no evidence of coercion of any kind being used to force the correspondent into agreeing with his views as has been claimed by others; rather an open and frank request for help to establish the truth.

2 This comment confirms that aging officers did not imagine the high banks and hollow way

many years later as some historians have recently stated. It should be remembered that William Siborne had spent a year on the field just after the Lion Mound was constructed and was therefore perfectly sure of the ground he described. The earth removed from the crest of the ridge to construct the mound must have been collected from this side of the crossroads as well, for certainly there is not the merest trace of the hollow way now.

No. 24 Cornet Thomas Marten
Beverley, 6 September 1841

ADD MS 34707, FO 286

My dear Siborne,
Your letter of the 2nd has been forwarded me here and I lose no time in answering your questions, though I am sorry to say I cannot solve your difficulty as to whether the rifles you have placed in the *fore* ground were *Germans* or *not*. I am very positive however that I saw a body of riflemen somewhere *about the* spot you have marked and I always fancied they were the 95th, but passing over that ground as quickly as we could gave me no opportunity of scrutinizing them much.

The track you have laid down as our advance, may be the exact one, but my impression is that we descended to the chaussee *just beyond* the Wavres road, but if you remember the ground *about there* you will be able to judge of the spot when I tell you, that where my part of the regiment went down the slope, the ground was exceedingly hard and broken, as to require some caution, until we reached the road. However I am sure you have *very nearly* if not quite hit the precise spot, and I have no doubt that if they were German at all, we were the people they made way for at that moment.

Now with regard to the collision, since you state from all your information, that you are pretty certain that no French cavalry advanced at this period of the day against our *left* centre. I am inclined to believe that which Waymouth[1] says you suggested to him, viz. that the cuirassiers we came into collision with were *part* of the line that had advanced by the *French left* of La Haye Sainte to attack our brigade and who had endeavoured to escape by crossing the chaussee near the rifles, and it was probably this circumstance that induced us to bring up our right shoulders in pursuit of them as I am *sure no collision* took place on the *rising ground*. For although a serrefile I must have seen it if it had, for I was close up to the rear rank, but very soon after crossing the chaussee I found myself in the middle of cuirassiers *broke and fighting* with our men in single combats.

After a short pause there we passed on to a broken body of French infantry, part of which I have often before told you, *sham'd dead* and *afterwards rose and fired upon us*, (I mean as we travelled onwards).

To revert however to the rifles, I remember meeting Kincaid and others of the 95th in Paris after the battle and they all certainly gave us to understand that *they were the riflemen* whom made way for us on the occasion alluded to. Of course you have their version of it and this it is perhaps that has made it so conflicting. I hope we shall soon see now the result of your exertion in this interesting business, and that it may well compensate you for all your troubles and expense in completing, is the sincere wish of myself.

Yours truly

TM

1 Lieutenant Samuel Waymouth of the regiment, see his letters published by Siborne (numbers 19–25).

No. 25 Cornet Alexander McInnes[1]
Ufford, near Woodbridge, Suffolk, 4 December 1834

ADD MS 34704, FO 3

Sir,

I received your letter of the 27th instant and should have replied to the several queries therein contained sooner, but have, in very many changes of residence since the year 1815, unfortunately mislaid a journal kept during that campaign in which I had entered some memoranda respecting the movements of the Household Brigade of cavalry on the 18th of June. I have searched everywhere for the journal without success, and must therefore trust to my memory for the little information which I may now be able to give you.

To your first question I am sorry to say that I cannot give any positive answer. On the evening of the 17th the 2nd Regiment of Life Guards bivouacked in the lower part of the field on the opposite side of the road to the farm of Mont St Jean, and near a part where the road was raised above the level of the field. On the following morning (the 18th) the brigade was formed, I think, in close column of squadrons in the upper part of the same field with the road leading from Brussels to Genappe on the left, and almost opposite the farm of Mont St Jean where I have made the pencil mark on the map.[2] In this position we remained until we made our first charge, which was against French cuirassiers, I believe of the Imperial Guard; and after this, to the best of my recollection, we reformed on, or very near our original position. Some time after this we were again ordered to charge some description of cavalry, but whether cuirassiers I cannot say, as they did not allow us to get sufficiently near them, having fled in disorder on seeing us again advancing. After this I think we again formed on our original ground, but whether in squadrons or in one line I cannot now remember. We remained here till the Grand Advance of the line about 7 o'clock in the evening.

Your second question I cannot answer, being unfortunately very near-sighted and unable to distinguish anything very accurately unless very near objects. For the same reason I cannot answer your last question. No French troops passed near us while we were in position, and when we were engaged my attention was directed to keeping with my own squadron. As far as my recollection now serves me, we had the great road from Brussels to Genappe on our left during the whole of our movements.

In regard to the crops on the different fields I think you are correct. I know that the field in which we bivouacked on the 17th and formed on the 18th, was both barley and wheat: but the others were much trampled on before we advanced to our first charge. The field in which I bivouacked with the remnant of the brigade at 10 o'clock on the evening of the 18th and which was part of the French position, had been a barley field.

I regret that from my having mislaid my journal and from the period that has elapsed since the battle, as well as my deficiency of sight, I am now able to give you so little information. There are however, still some officers of the 2nd Regiment of Life Guards, who may be able to give you more, viz. Col. E.P Lygon[3] now in the regiment; Captain Samuel Waymouth,[4] who was then a lieutenant and was taken prisoner; Major Martin[5] of the Royal Dragoons, now at Brighton, and Captain Elliott[6] now residing in

Seymour Place, Montague Square, London.
I am, Sir, your most obedient servant

ALEXANDER NICHOLSON[7]
LATE 2ND LIFE GUARDS

1 He joined the 2nd Lifeguards as a cornet on 7 June 1809, serving in the Peninsula but resigned his commission in 1813. He was commissioned a cornet again in the same regiment on 16 June 1814 and became a lieutenant in 1818 but again retired from the army in 1822. He received a General Service Medal with one bar for Vittoria and a Waterloo medal. He died on 9 February 1862 at Ufford. There is a well-known portrait of this officer by Reinagle.
2 The plan referred to does not appear to be extant.
3 Major Edward P. Lygon had commanded the two squadrons of the regiment present at Waterloo.
4 Lieutenant Samuel Waymouth, see his letters published by Siborne (numbers 19–26).
5 Probably Cornet Thomas Marten whose letters appear in this volume (numbers 21–4).
6 Lieutenant William Elliott, see his letter published in this volume (number 19).
7 Alexander McInnes assumed the name and arms of Nicholson by royal licence in 1821.

The Royal Horse Guards

No. 26 Captain William Robert Clayton[1]
Harleyford, near Marlow, 9 November 1834

ADD MS 34703, FO 201

Sir,

In reply to your letter of the 29th instant which I had the honour to receive from you, I beg to inform you that the Royal Horse Guards formed a part of the Household Brigade, consisting of the 1st and 2nd Regiments of Life Guards, to which the 1st Dragoon Guards, of 8 troops, were attached – and this brigade occupied ground, nearly in the centre of the British army. The infantry of the enemy, in our immediate front, was generally formed in squares, supported by cuirassiers.

The 57th Regiment (I believe)[2] and the Dutch infantry[3] were formed principally in squares in our position, the steady fire of this infantry from these squares were well directed against the cuirassiers in their repeated and formidable advances on our brigade, and were to an extent in point of executions (which many persons who ignorantly and absurdly imagine that a cuirassier is almost invulnerable could not believe), this of course tended to weaken the advance of the heavy columns of cavalry, which were constantly directed against our immediate position. Towards the close of the day, however, after the repeated charges made and sustained of the cuirassiers, we charged the squares of infantry, from whose fire we also suffered considerably.

The nature of the crops, as far as my recollection will extend, is correctly stated in your plan. The ground having however been occupied by troops, during the evening of the proceeding day, and during the night when torrents of rain fell, the ground presented a surface of mud; and which, soon after the commencement of the action became so deep, on that part of the ground on which we moved, as to render it very difficult, when advancing to the charge, to push our horses into a trot.

The artillery of the centre suffered severely in officers, men and horses generally either killed or disabled, and the wheels of the guns shot away. This of course, rendered the advance of the masses of cavalry which were pounced upon and charged, as less difficult, their charges being more effectively covered by their guns – the precipitate and disorderly retreat of the Belgian cavalry[4] through our column (which were intended as our support) checked our formation, in our endeavour to recover from the effects of the previous attacks.

I have endeavoured, as far as my time which is much occupied, will admit of, to adhere to points especially requested in your letter; I shall be happy however to give you any further information in my powers if you should require it, and to subscribe to your work. Your letter having been addressed to me at Messr. Coutts, which is not my bankers, a delay has been necessarily occasioned in receiving it, this I trust will provide my excuse for the apparent inattention in not having returned this letter earlier.

As you will probably require it, my address is,

Lt Colonel Sir William Robert Clayton Bart: MP
Harleyford
Marlow

I have the honour to be Sir your obedient servant

WILLIAM ROBERT CLAYTON LT COL
MAGISTRATE & DEPUTY LIEUT OF COUNTY OF BUCKINGHAM

NB [In the same hand] – The British Light Dragoon horse when in marching order on service carries on an average 18 stone. The Heavy Dragoon horse 22 stone and it is in marching order of course, that cavalry on service generally go into action – I am confident, that when the additional weight on a horse of a cuirass, and the encumbrance and inconvenience to the soldiers, making him less active, are taken into account; when we are aware also, that it is quite useless as a protection to the man, when exposed to shot, shell, or point blank musketry – the head throat and legs being unprotected and exposed also to the sure points of a *good* swordsman, I must think that we have unadvisedly copied the French in this respect and rendered both man and horse less effective[5] in the ordinary course of warfare as the immense number of cuirassiers dead on the field prove this.

---

1 He joined the army as a cornet in 1804 and as a captain accompanied the regiment to the Peninsula in 1812. He commanded a squadron at Vittoria and the Pyrenees and received the General Service Medal with one bar for Vittoria, having had his claim for a bar for Toulouse disallowed. He went on half pay in 1826 and succeeded as 5th Bart in 1834. He attained the rank of Major General in 1851 and died in 1866.

2 This clearly is a mistake as the 57th were not at Waterloo.

3 This would be the Nassau Brigade of Major General von Kruse.

4 This must refer to the Dutch/Belgian carabineers of Major General Trip's heavy brigade, which reputedly left the field. The other Dutch/Belgian cavalry appears to have stood firm and suffered severe losses, but the carabineer brigade suffered relatively minor casualties, possibly backing up this claim.

5 This refers to the issuing of cuirasses to the Lifeguards and Horseguards following Waterloo, in emulation of the famed cuirassiers, and which they wear to this day on ceremonial duties.

2nd Cavalry Brigade

The 1st or Royal Dragoons

No. 27 Lieutenant Colonel Arthur Benjamin Clifton[1]

Brighton, 22 December 1834

ADD MS 34704, FO 73

Sir,

Agreeably to your request, I herewith send you such information, which at this distant period comes, in these my recollections of the movements etc. of the Royal Dragoons at the battle of Waterloo on the 18th of June 1815.

In the morning of that day, the Royal Dragoons being in brigade with the Scots Greys and Enniskillen Dragoons *[sic]* were positioned in 2 lines on the British left of La Haye Sainte in the rear of Picton's division, and near to the great road leading to Brussels. And opposite, were the enemy consisting of the whole of Count D'Erlon's corps of infantry, which corps had *[sic]* and the enemy about 2 o'clock advanced in three close columns, under cover of their artillery, and had reached the crest of the British position, where there is a little crossroad with two low hedges, leading apparently towards Frasnes.

At this moment the brigade received orders to charge, which was instantly obeyed in the most gallant fashion, and I need not now tell you that the result of that charge, was of the most brilliant nature, having rushed past numbers, taking from them two eagles and colours and making upwards of 2,000 prisoners including about 40 officers.

Shortly after that most gallant charge Lieutenant Colonel Dawson,[2] a staff officer came galloping to us with the most pressing order for the Royal Dragoons and brigade to move to the other side of the road, and we took up the position which the Household Brigade of cavalry had before occupied opposite to which, were both cavalry and infantry of the enemy, in which formation we remained amid the most galling and destructive fire, until the termination of the action, which reduced our numbers in so great a degree, that on the British army advancing, we were linked to the Household Brigade who appeared to have suffered as much as ourselves.

With regard to the crops on the ground, as far as my observation and recollection, I believe to be totally correct.

I regret that I cannot furnish you with a more detailed account, but have sent you the leading features of the countryside near the Royal Dragoons on that day, which statement corresponds with the report I made to His Grace the Duke of Wellington as senior officer of the 2nd Brigade of cavalry at the termination of the action.[3]

I have the honour to be, Sir, your obedient servant

ARTHUR CLIFTON

1 He joined the Army as a cornet in 1794 and served in the Peninsula, receiving a General Service Medal with two bars for Fuentes d'Onoro and Vittoria. He became a General and Colonel-in-Chief of the 17th Lancers and died on 7 March 1869.

2 Major the Honourable George Lionel Dawson, 1st Dragoon Guards, acted as an Assistant Quartermaster General at Waterloo. Dalton indicates that he was wounded during the battle. He died on 14 April 1856.

3 On the death of Sir William Ponsonby, Lieutenant Colonel Clifton took command of the 2nd Cavalry Brigade as senior officer.

No. 28 Major Philip Dorville[1]

Clacton, 15 November 1834

ADD MS 34703, FO 231

Sir,

My being absent from home must excuse my not having attended to the letter you favoured me with respecting the battle of Waterloo, and in reply to it I beg to acquaint you the Royal Dragoons, in Sir William Ponsonby's brigade, made the charge in which our lamented General fell nearly at the commencement of the day. We suffered as you are well aware very great loss in that charge. Afterwards we collected behind a wood, where we were rallied a short time and then were brought forward again to the front and suffered with the brigade, for a *long* time under a most destructive fire. On occasions to our front were French cavalry and as far as I can recollect on their left some infantry, on our side fronted by some Belgian infantry, and the Blues.

At the period you mention about 7 pm the heavy cavalry and the Royal Dragoons amongst the rest were to the most part reduced to a small number, so much so that several of the regiments were formed in one indiscriminate squadron; in front of them some of the most distinguished officers of the different brigades. The heavy cavalry being at that period of the day so much reduced, the light under General Vandeleur and Vivian were brought forward and formed up with the heavy, they were relieved by the Prussians.[2] In respect to giving you information as to particular situations, nature of ground and such, I should be most happy to do so but the period is so distant, I would not give it with any degree of conviction, further than the ground we charged over was a beautiful slope, and capital for the purpose, and being exceedingly taken up throughout the day with the regiment I might not notice those particulars so much as might be wished, and indeed my forte does not at best lay much in that way. After the death of General Ponsonby, Colonel Straton[3] took the command of the brigade, who being wounded was succeeded by Colonel Clifton[4] and which period which remained, the Royal Dragoons fell to my command.

I beg to return the plan[5] sent such as probably it may be useful to you, so I transmit for further information.

I have the honour to be, Sir, your most obedient little servant

PHILIP DORVILLE

1 He joined the regiment as a cornet in 1794 and served as an ADC in Moore's campaign in the Peninsula, receiving a General Service Medal with bars for Sahagun, Benevente and Fuentes d'Onoro. At Waterloo Colonel Dorville commanded the two squadrons of the 1st Dragoons, 'which rushed into the second column of the enemy, consisting of about 4,000

men, and after a desperate fight returned with a French Eagle (the 105th)'. In this charge, Col Dorville had his scabbard shot away and a bullet passed through the breast of his coat without striking him. He also had three horses shot beneath him. Made a CB for Waterloo, he retired on half pay on 8 March 1827. He died on 10 November in the same year.

2 On the appearance of the Prussians at Ohain near the left wing, Vandeleur and Vivian moved their brigades to shore up the centre behind La Haye Sainte.

3 This name is an anachronistic error. Lieutenant Colonel Muter, commanding the 6th (Inniskilling) Dragoons took command of the brigade on the death of Ponsonby. He took the name of Straton in 1816 to succeed to his aunt's property at Kirkside, Montrose. He became a Lieutenant General and Colonel-in-Chief of 6th Dragoons, and was awarded CB and KCH. He died on 23 October 1840. His letters were published by Siborne (numbers 43 & 44).

4 See his letter published in this volume (number 27).

5 This plan appears to be no longer extant.

No. 29 Captain Paul Phipps[1]

Bartley Manor House[2]

ADD MS 34704, FO 141

Sir,

I have in reply to your letter of March 16th to say, that the Royal Dragoons bivouacked on a spot of ground, somewhere marked by you in pencil; that they charged about one o'clock in the day from the exact place I have pencilled, having the great Brussels road immediately on their right, being the right regiment of Sir W. Ponsonby's brigade which charged Count D'Erlon's Corps of infantry and which captured two French eagles, several pieces of artillery, and many prisoners. The Royal Dragoons secured one of the eagles, after which the regiment reformed and crossed the high road to Brussels to assist Lord Edward Somerset's brigade to support the columns of British and German infantry which were stationed on the centre right of the position.

The formation of the Royal Dragoons about 7 o'clock pm was two weak squadrons, and the enemy immediately in their front were cavalry supported by their Lt. Infantry. These are the few statements of the formations of the Royal Dragoons, which I can now remember after a lapse of nearly 20 years, the corps suffered great loss on that day both in officers and men, which the returns will have readily acquainted you with.[3]

I have the honour to be, Sir, your obedient humble servant

P PHIPPS

LIEUTENANT COLONEL UNATTACHED

Sir W. Ponsonby's brigade consisted of the Royals, Scots Greys, and Inniskilling Dragoons, the Greys were in support and in the *rear* of the other two regiments[4] when they charged Count D'Erlon's corps of infantry.

1 He received a General Service Medal with bars for Fuentes d'Onoro, Vittoria and Toulouse. After he became a lieutenant colonel on half pay and KH. He died on 22 November 1858.

2 This village lies a few miles west of Southampton.

3 Siborne shows losses of 4 officers, 85 men and 161 horses killed; 9 officers, 88 men and 35 horses wounded and 1 officer and 9 men missing.

4 This is an issue upon which it is very difficult to establish the facts. Many of the statements concur with his view, but just as many others state that this brigade charged without a reserve and from which cause most of the losses occurred. It seems impossible to reconcile the opposite views.

The 2nd or Scots Greys

No. 30 Lieutenant John Mills[1]
London, 13 November 1834

ADD MS 34703, FO 223

Sir,
As far as my recollection serves me, I have traced upon your sketch of the fields of Waterloo, the different positions occupied by the 2nd Brigade of cavalry during the action of the 18th of June. I can speak to the accuracy of the pencilled statement of crops growing in the fields, over which the Greys passed.

Where I marked with red on the plan,[2] shows the clover field where the Greys bivouacked on the night of the 17th.

CC position of the 2nd Brigade prior to the first charge and extent of the charge into the enemy's line, in which two eagles and 2,000 men were captured.

+ Small wood where the brigade re-formed after the charge.

DD New position of the brigade in the afternoon and up to the period of the advance of the whole army.

Opposed to the brigade were the artillery and infantry of the enemy the cuirassiers occasionally menacing, but never charging it. On the flanks of the brigade were squares of our allied infantry.

I have to apologise for this hasty and I fear inferior first sketch and at the same time to offer my best wishes for the success of your undertaking.

Very faithfully, yours

JOHN MILLS
LT COLONEL (LATE MAJOR, GREYS)

P.S. The effective strength of the 2nd Brigade never really exceeded 1,200 men. The position marked DD, they were considerably below that number.

---

1 Dalton shows him as being wounded at Waterloo and promoted to Captain on 19 July 1815. No further information has been found regarding this officer.

2 Unfortunately the plan these points refer to cannot be found.

No. 31 Major Frederick Clarke[1]
Ballincollig,[2] 14 June 1839

ADD MS 34707, FO 72

(Not at Waterloo)

My dear Siborne
I take this opportunity of thanking you for the information you were good enough to

furnish me with at Colin's[3] the other day.

I have been talking over with Crawford[4] the subject of your note to him. He seems perfectly clear and decided on one point, viz. that at *no* period prior to the charge of the heavy brigade of Ponsonby, were the Royals and Inniskillings in *front* of the Greys. He remembers the Greys, some time before they charged, being ordered to advance a little, so as to be more under the crest of the rising ground in their front, and be thus hidden from the range of the French artillery, which had considerably annoyed them and caused some loss. He also remembers that they then stood in a hollow, precisely as you have placed them, but his impression is that by this forward movement, they were something in advance of the other regiments of the brigade. They were in line at this time, but afterwards wheeled 'half squadrons to the right' thus forming an open column to the right. Subsequently they received a sudden order to wheel again 'left into line' and attack immediately; (This coincides with your Inniskilling account)[5] they complied with the order, and advanced *straight to their front*, almost immediately meeting the 92nd retiring somewhat confusedly.[6] They passed these, cleared the hedge in their front, and about 60 paces from it encountered the French columns, who poured in a most destructive fire, as they rapidly formed themselves into three squares. The first and nearest square had not time to complete their formation, and the Greys charged through it. The passing of the hedge had considerably broken the regularity of the Grey's line, and given the Frenchmen time very nearly to form their squares. They all however gave way to the impetuosity of the cavalry attack, and the Greys went through and through, passing a considerable way to their rear.

Crawford, in addition to the foregoing details, states his perfect recollection that there was no appearance whatever of any wounded *Dragoons* or horses in their front as they advanced on the French. It is indeed evident that these columns could not have received any previous charge of cavalry about that time, when you consider their steady formation and their ample and destructive fire, nor is it possible that advance of either Royals or Inniskillings could have taken place any *time* previous to this without the Greys being aware of it. Crawford is perfectly satisfied that the columns attacked by the Greys were fresh and unshaken battalions. Is it probable that this regiment would have attracted the observation and called forth the remark of Napoleon,[7] had the Grey horses been merely a supporting line? Colonel Hankin[8] was taken to the rear sometime prior to the charge, and Crawford observing several men supporting him, rode to the rear to enquire the extent of his injuries.

Anyone else might have *looked back*, and observed the same thing. I remember some years ago being in a brigade with two other regiments near London and charging in echelon of regiments: I was a boy[9] at the time, but perfectly recollect a remark being made that this was in imitation of a charge made by a cavalry brigade at Waterloo. Could it have been the case in the charge in question? My own impression from what I can collect is that the whole brigade wheeled into line and advanced at the same time, but that the hedge in front of the Greys may have somewhat checked their progress *bodily*, and created an impression in the Inniskillings that they were to the rear. Will this in any way help the difficulty. I presume there were more columns of the French than one, and the Royals and Greys may have charged distinct though contiguous bodies. Pardon the officiousness of my observations and believe me

Very sincerely yours

FREDERICK F CLARKE

1 This officer appears to be the son of Major Isaac Blake Clarke who was second in command of the regiment at Waterloo and was wounded. His father was promoted Lieutenant Colonel of the regiment on 20 July 1815 as Lieutenant Colonel Hamilton had been killed at Waterloo. He however retired from the regiment in 1821, possibly because of his wounds and died on the Isle of Thanet in 1850. Little is known of the junior Major Clarke.
2 Ballincollig is approximately 3 miles west of Cork.
3 I cannot identify this person.
4 Probably Regimental Sergeant Major William Crawford of Captain Barnard's troop as there were no officers of this name in the regiment. Siborne prints a letter from him in *Waterloo Letters* (no. 42) and states that he was a cornet at Waterloo. However the return of the regiment quoted in Dalton (p. 258) shows clearly that he was promoted cornet and adjutant on 17 August 1815. He is also shown as a Sergeant Major in the *Waterloo Medal Roll.* He eventually became Paymaster to the Scots Greys.
5 This refers to the letters of Lieutenant General Sir Joseph Straton of the Inniskillings, published by Siborne (numbers 43 & 44; see also below, p. 65, note 4). On p. 84 he describes looking back at the fallen Lieutenant Colonel Hankin of the Greys, this is obviously what Clarke refers to here.
6 This indicates clearly that the infantry were breaking when the cavalry charged.
7 Napoleon reputedly remarked of the Greys' charge, 'Those terrible grey horses, how they fight!' Quoted from p. 210 of Albert Nofi's *The Waterloo Campaign.*
8 Major Thomas Pate Hankin was knighted in 1816. He became Lieutenant Colonel of the regiment in 1821 (When the post became vacant on Clarke's resignation), but died at Norwich cavalry barracks in 1825.
9 This indicates the youth of this officer at this event commemorating Waterloo, probably then serving as a cornet, hence his description of himself as a 'boy'. This would make it highly likely that he was a son of Major Clarke.

No. 32 From the same
Upper Montenotte, Cork, 3 August 1839

ADD MS 34707, FO 103

My dear Siborne
I was unable to do anything about your paper of questions and answers when I received it, Colonel Wyndham[1] being then absent. I quitted Ballincollig before his return, and left the papers with Crawford, requesting him to engage the Colonel's attention to them on his return. I only yesterday discovered that they were still without any reply having been sent to you, which I very much regret. I have spoken to the Colonel and he promises to communicate with you tomorrow.

He thinks the Greys encountered *two* columns – one *at* the hedge, and another some way down the hill, the latter however being considerably the strongest, and also that they took their prisoners from the last.

I am really very sorry that your questions should have remained so long without being answered, but I really conclude that they had been soon after Wyndham's return to Ballincollig.

I am writing in great haste and must request you to excuse brevity.

Believe me always, faithfully yours

FREDERICK CLARKE

---

1 Charles Wyndham joined the regiment as a cornet in 1813 and had risen to the rank of lieutenant at Waterloo where he received two severe wounds. He became Lieutenant Colonel of the regiment and Keeper of the Crown Jewels at the Tower of London, where he died on 15 February 1872. His letters are published in Siborne's *Waterloo Letters* (numbers 40 & 41) where the month is guessed at as April or May. As letter 40 is likely to be the one promised in the above letter, it would have to have been written in August.

The 6th or Inniskilling Dragoons

No. 33 Captain Thomas Macky[1]
Clifton, 20 March 1835

ADD MS 34705, FO 81

Sir,

So long a period having elapsed since the action of June 1815, I can not pretend to much accuracy but believe the 6th Dragoons, at 7 o'clock pm, was about the position marked by me[2] in pencil on the right of the road from Brussels to Genappe a little to the rear and the left of a square of infantry with light facings, probably the 52nd Regiment.[3]

The 6th Dragoons not occupying more space than described, being no more than two thirds of a squadron from casualties incident to a cavalry regiment by a file being rendered ineffectual either by man or horse killed or wounded and a full troop escorting prisoners to the rear.[4]

The formation of the enemy's forces in front I could not describe from the dense smoke and being then a supernumerary in rear of the regiment.

That part of the field marked by you with the nature of the crops was the ground on which the regiment was formed; deployed and advanced the earlier period of the day; but, I am impressed with the idea there were more oats about a foot high, and that the crop (immediately past the road from Wavres, and charged) marked by you as *clover* was rye, about the usual height at that period of the year.

What was fallow or ploughed ground I have not the least recollection of.

The position of the 6th Dragoons as marked was taken some time after the 1st and effectual charge when the brigade was moved to the right of the road, the Greys being a little in front and to the left – the Royal Dragoons in rear of the 6th. I regret having no useful information to communicate or being able to give any opinions that might tend to the accuracy of your plan from being only in command of a half squadron in the action and having so little opportunity compared to any staff officers of making observations.

Lieutenant Colonel Madox[5] was commanding the 6th Dragoons and who commanded the regiment at the period you request information on would be more competent to give it.

I have the honour to be, Sir, your most obedient humble servant

THOS MACKY

BREVET MAJOR

---

1 His surname is clearly spelt Macky in the letter and the *Waterloo Medal Roll*, yet Dalton spells it Mackay; I have followed the letter for its spelling. Macky joined the army as a cornet in 1803; he became a brevet major in 1821, and went on half pay in 1825. Little else is known about him.

2 This plan appears to be no longer extant.

3 The identification of the infantry regiment must be a mistake as the 52nd were on the right of the line near Hougoumont rather than near the crossroads as described here.

4 This jumbled sentence perhaps needs some clarification. The regiment had sent one of its six troops to the rear escorting prisoners, the remaining troops had lost approximately half of their number killed or wounded. As the regiment started the battle with 396 men, the situation described would leave the regiment with approximately 160 men in line at this time.

5 Henry Madox joined as a cornet in 1800; he was a senior captain at Waterloo and would have gained the command after his seniors, Lieutenant Colonel Muter and Major Miller, had both been wounded. He was promoted major on 18 June 1815 and eventually rose to Lieutenant Colonel and KH. He retired on half pay in 1838.

No. 34 Lieutenant Theophilus Biddulph[1]

Southampton, 23 November 1834

ADD MS 34703, FO 325

Sir,

In compliance with your request I have marked on the plan,[2] which I have had the honour to receive from you, the positions of the 6th Dragoons on the 18th June 1815. In the position to the right to the best of my recollection the regiment was drawn up in line and was opposed to squares of French Infantry with cavalry in cuirasses intervening. I have no reason to doubt the accuracy of the state of the crops which you have marked on the field to the left where the regiment in line was previously placed and from whence it charged upon the squares of French infantry with artillery intervening marked in its front. Not being on the field more than half an hour before the commencement of the battle I had no opportunity of observing the positions of the armies, and not having visited it since. Hence after a lapse of so many years, the positions I have marked must be very far from correct and I regret that I have not better information in furtherance of the object you have in view.

I have the honour to remain, Sir, your obedient humble servant

T BIDDULPH CAPTAIN

HALF PAY 6TH DRAGOONS

---

1 Biddulph served in Captain Macky's troop and was promoted to captain on 14 September 1815. He was placed on half pay on 25 March 1816. Little else is known about this officer.

2 This plan appears to be no longer extant.

No. 35 Lieutenant John Linton[1]
Stirtloe, 2 May 1835

ADD MS 34705, FO 239

Sir

I was not at home when your circular of the 16th of March arrived here. In reply to your note of the 27th instant on the same subject, I beg to say that it is not in my power to give you any accurate information which could be of any assistance to you in the formation of your model. The time is long gone by, and I then held a very subordinate situation in the Sixth Dragoons. At the period of the day which the model is intended to represent the regiment was very weak in the field, as in addition to the severe loss the brigade had suffered, half of the effectives[2] of the Inniskillings had been sent to Brussels with prisoners.

I have the honour to be your most obedient servant

JOHN LINTON LT COLONEL

---

1 He joined the regiment as a cornet in 1808 and was a major of the regiment from 1825 to 1830, when he retired on the half-pay list as a lieutenant colonel. Little else is known of this officer.

2 This statement indicates that some three troops were detached to escort prisoners to Brussels, rather than the one stated by Captain Macky in his letter (number 33).

No. 36 Lieutenant Colonel Jeremiah Ratcliffe[1]
Caher, 14 March 1839

ADD MS 34707, FO 17

(Not at Waterloo)

My Dear Sir,

Our Quartermaster Mr Mc Dowell,[2] and a private now stationed here, tell me that the brigade charged in line on the occasion you mention, the Inniskillings being the centre regiment.

They are the only individuals now in the regiment (except one who is at Kilkenny) who were present at Waterloo. They both seem quite positive that the whole of the 3 regiments were in one line at the moment of the charge.[3]

I do not know Sir J. Straton's[4] address, but I should think the agents of his regiment or Colonel Pratt, will be able to inform you about it.

If there are any questions you wish to ask of our Quartermaster relative to the battle of Waterloo, I am sure he will be glad to communicate anything he knows.

Believe me, my dear Sir, very faithfully yours

J RATCLIFFE

---

1 He joined as a cornet in 1811and served in the Peninsula at Salamanca, Vittoria, Pyrenees and Toulouse. He became a lieutenant colonel in 1838 and went on half pay, and was made KH.

2 Frederick McDowell served as a corporal in Captain Madox's troop at Waterloo where he received a severe sabre cut.

3 This statement confirms that the three regiments charged D'Erlon's columns without

forming a reserve; this is claimed to be a major cause of their subsequent losses.

4 Lt Colonel Joseph Muter, who commanded the regiment at Waterloo, changed his surname to Straton in 1816. His letters were published by Siborne (numbers 43 & 44).

3rd Cavalry Brigade
The 1st Light Dragoons KGL

No. 37 Lieutenant and adjutant William Fricke[1]
Celle, near Hanover, 16 March 1835

ADD MS 34705, FO 69

Original in German

With regard to Your Excellency's letter of 15 January of this year from Dublin to Captain H. Hattorf,[2] which was forwarded to me by Captain Benne. I humbly respond according to my best recollection that on 18 June 1815 at the battle of Waterloo, the 1st Light Dragoon Regiment of the King's German Legion consisted of four squadrons and that it constantly stayed in a formation of column of squadrons, both when in position and when charging.

The regiment had spent the night to the right of and not far from Mont St Jean and left this place at about 7 o'clock in the morning and marched a distance forwards to the right, through a clover field and awaited further orders.

Toward 9 o'clock, the regiment marched into position, where the 2nd Light Dragoons and the 23rd Light Dragoons had been formed into a brigade.[3] The brigade ground was a low-lying clover field.

Towards midday the 23rd and the 2nd Regiment received orders to take positions elsewhere, and so the 1st Regiment occupied the brigade ground by itself. From 11 o'clock on, we were subjected to enemy fire, until finally at about 1 o'clock an oncoming column of cuirassiers was attacked and repulsed by us. Hardly had the regiment reached the brigade ground again, when a second column of cuirassiers made a rapid charge. We met this one just as quickly as the previous one, and between 1 and 2:30 there followed four charges. I believe that these charges were carried out by the 2nd, 3rd, 8th, and 11th French Cuirassier Regiments.[4] During the third charge, we were attacked on our left flank by a group of grenadiers on horseback.[5]

On this memorable day, the 1st Light Dragoon Regiment KGL attacked enemy cavalry a total of nine times, whereby the enemy were prevented from forming a breakthrough three times.[6]

I mentioned earlier that the brigade ground assigned to us was low-lying. An elevation in front of us hindered us completely from taking note of the positions taken by the French army, because we were unable to see it, except when we charged, but such a moment was not suitable for taking notes.

I have noted with red numbers the positions of the troops immediately surrounding our regiment on the enclosed plan. The following is a more detailed elucidation:

No. 35	– KGL 2nd Light Battalion	**2nd KGL Brigade**
No. 1	– KGL 8th Line Battalion	Lt Colonel Ompteda,
No. 2	– KGL 5th Line Battalion	Lt Col. Baring commander of La Haye
No. 3	– KGL 1st Light Battalion	Saint.
No. 4	– Nassau 1st Regiment	General Kruse
No. 5	– Nassau 2nd Regiment	
No. 6	– Nassau 3rd Regiment	
No. 7	– Landwehr Batt. Luneberg	**1st Hanoverian Brigade**
No. 8	– 1st Batt. Duke of York's	Major General Count Kielmannsegge
No. 9	– Landwehr Batt. Grubenhagen	
No.10	– Landwehr Batt. Verden	
No.11	– Chasseurs von Spërken[7]	
No.12	– Landwehr Batt. Bremen	
No.13	– KGL Artillery[8]	**Divisional Artillery**
No.14	– English Horse Artillery[9]	
No.15	– English Guards Blue	**1st Cavalry Brigade**
No.16	– English 1st Life Guards	Major General Lord Edward Somerset
No.17	– English 2nd Life Guards	
No.18	– English 1st Dragoon Guards	
No.19	– KGL 2nd Light Dragoons	**3rd Cavalry Brigade**
No.20	– KGL 1st Light Dragoons	Major General Sir W. Dörnberg
No.21	– English 23rd Light Dragoons	
No.22	– KGL 3rd Hussars	**7th Cavalry Brigade**
No.23	– English 13th Light Dragoons	Col. F. Arenschildt
No. 24	– English 15th Hussars	**5th Cavalry Brigade**
No. 25	– English 7th Hussars	Major General Sir C. Grant
No. 26	– Hanover Cumberland Hussars	
No. 27	– Dutch 4th Dragoon Regiment	**2nd Brigade**
No. 28	– Belgian 8th Hussars	Maj. Gen. Ghigny
No. 29	– Belgian 5th Light Dragoons	**1st Brigade**
No. 30	– Dutch 6th Hussars	Maj.Gen.Van Merlen
No. 31	– Dutch 1st Carabiniers	**1st Heavy Brigade**
No. 32	– Belgian 2nd Carabiniers	Maj.Gen. Trip
No. 33	– Belgian 3rd Carabiniers	
No. 34	– In the vicinity of which most of the four charges took place.	

Because I was wounded in the fourth charge and was brought from the battlefield to Brussels, my report about the matter ends here.

The Major Lieutenant von Uslar of the 2nd Regiment[10] from Osnabrück, who remained unharmed with the regiment until the end of the battle could perhaps give you

Letter no. 37

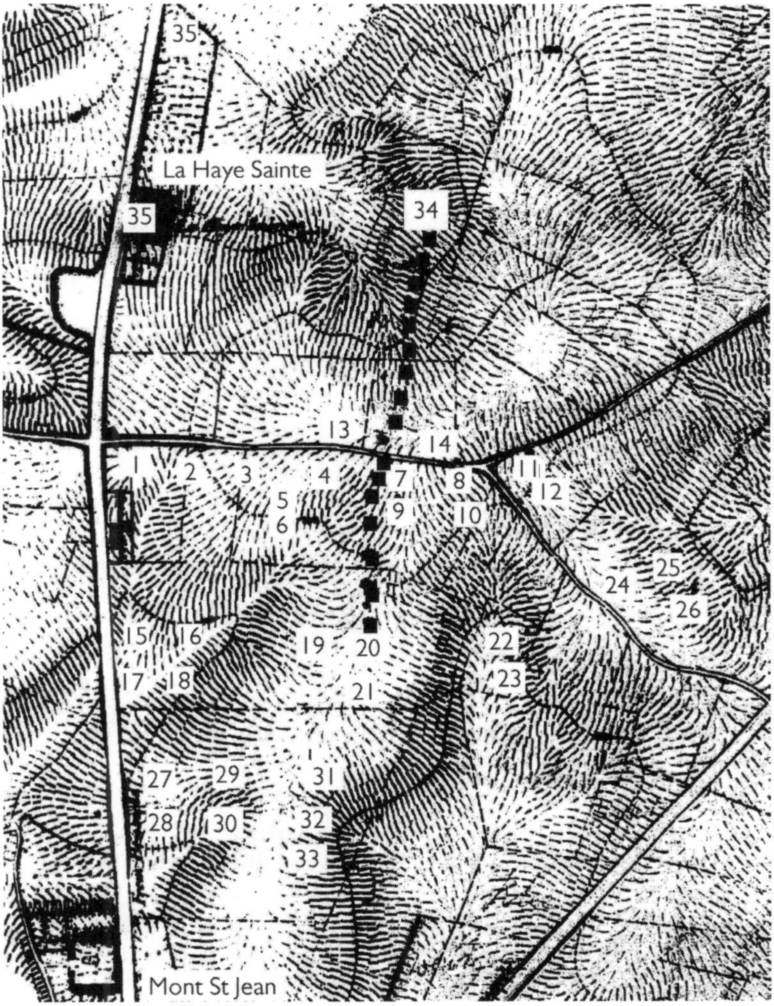

sufficient information. I must beg you excuse me if my description is faulty, to which a 20-year gap contributes greatly, and as such…

WM FRICKE
CAPTAIN, LATE ADJUTANT
1ST LIGHT DRAGOONS KGL

On the 18th June 1815 in the battle of Waterloo:

	Officers	*Sergeants*	*Corporals*	*Trumpeters*	*Privates*	*Officers Horses*	*Troop Horses*
Killed	4	3	3	1	23	12	53
Wounded	12	7	15	1	67	5	95
Total	16	10	18	2	90	17	148

1 William Fricke, numbered 121 in Beamish. He joined the Legion in 1805, serving in Hanover, the Peninsula from 1812–14, then Holland. He was severely wounded at Waterloo. Afterwards, he was promoted to Captain but went on half pay in 1816.
2 Captain Hans von Hattorf of the 1st Dragoons, numbered 90 in Beamish. He joined the Legion in 1804, serving in Hanover 1805, the Peninsula 1812–14 and Holland. He received the HGO2, PrIO and the HWC. He afterwards became a colonel on the Hanoverian Staff.
3 3rd Cavalry Brigade.
4 These were in the brigades of Donop and Guiton, forming part of Kellermann's 3rd Cavalry Corps, stationed in front of Hougoumont.
5 This must refer to the *grenadiers a cheval* of Guyot's cavalry division, who followed the cuirassiers into the charges on the Allied centre.
6 The 1st KGL Dragoons were heavily involved in the counter charges launched against the disorganized French cavalry as they cleared the infantry squares. They helped to drive them back over the crest numerous times. Historians often overlook these successful actions of the Allied cavalry.
7 The brigade included two companies of Field Jäger under the command of Captain von Reden, it would seem that the Jäger unit was named the 'Chasseurs von Spërken'.
8 Captain Cleeves' 1st KGL Foot Artillery Battery.
9 Major W. Lloyd's Royal Horse Artillery Troop.
10 Captain Frederick von Uslar of the 1st Dragoons KGL, numbered 91 in Beamish. He joined the Corps in 1804, serving in Hanover, the Peninsula and southern France. He was slightly wounded at Majalahonda in 1812. He received a Gold Medal for Vittoria, HGO3, and HWC. Later, he became Colonel of the 2nd Hanoverian Regiment of Dragoons.

No. 38 From the same
Undated

ADD MS 34706, FO 464

Original answer in German

Extract of a letter to Major L. Benne from Lieut. Siborne dated Dublin 12th March 1838:

'Could you possibly ascertain for me whether at the *commencement* of hostilities in 1815, the 1st and 2nd Light Dragoons KGL were on outpost duty along the *frontier* between *Mons and Tournay* and if so, whether General von Dörnberg received, in the evening of the 15th June, any dispatch from the Duke of Wellington *requiring* information as to any hostile demonstrations in his front. The other regiment of the brigade, the 23rd Light Dragoons, was, I have reason to believe, at Goike near the Dender.'

Answer

On the 17 March 1815 the 1st Dragoon Regiment was at Mons and received the following general order: 'General Order – Headquarters – Brussels – 17 March 1815: The army will immediately prepare to take the field.'

From 23 March, daily pickets and outposts were deployed on the French border in the direction of Maubeuge.

On 4 April the regiment marched from Mons to Leuze, on the 23rd to Grammont, on the 24th to Alost, on the 25th to Malines, on the 26th to Berghen near Antwerp (here was stationed the other regiment of the Light Dragoons and their equipment)

On the 5th May to Malines and vicinity.

On 16 June at 5 o'clock in the morning came the order to move towards Genappe – the regiment rested at Quatre Bras on cultivated land. The 17th mixed up in the retreat of the army with the rear guard.

On the night of the 17th into the 18th June Captain Sichart[1] and his squadron were sent out on patrol. The regiment stayed the night not far from Mont St Jean.

On 15 June we were totally unworried at Malines, if any orders were received by General von Dörnberg on this day is unknown to me.[2]

The regiment, as said before, received an order on the 16th at 5 o'clock in the morning to proceed.

The above is from Captain Fricke, late adjutant 1st Light Dragoon Regiment K G Legion, now confined to his bed by illness.

L BENNE

1 Captain Philip von Sichart, numbered 89 in Beamish. He joined the Legion in 1806, serving in southern France in 1813–14 and the Waterloo campaign. He was severely wounded at Waterloo. He received a General Service Medal with a bar for Toulouse and was made HGO3. Later brevet colonel on half pay, at Osnabruck. He died on 23 August 1836.

2 Major General Dörnberg commanded the 3rd Cavalry Brigade. However from his own account of the Waterloo campaign (recently published by John Hussey in *First Empire* magazine, number 73) it is clear that he had been detached on the frontier to undertake intelligence duties and was therefore in no position to supply orders to the brigade. He states that he sent a message from Mons on the 15th and rode out to the Dutch outposts before riding for Brussels at 4 am on the 16th and reporting to Wellington. He was sent to order Picton's Division to move on from Waterloo to Quatre Bras. He then accompanied Wellington on his visit to the Ligny battlefield and was present at the meeting with Blücher, and subsequently joined his brigade resuming command.

The 2nd Light Dragoons KGL

No. 39 Captain William Seeger[1]

Leer,[2] 6 February 1835

ADD MS 34704, FO 221

Original in German
Written to Captain Benne

Your Honours,

I have the honour to reply to your kind letter of the 30th of this month and say that I can respond to the request of Lieutenant and Assistant Military Secretary Wm. Siborne only in so far that I enclose in the attachment a copy of a report. This concerns the participation of the 2nd Light Dragoon Regiment of the former King's German Legion in the battle of Waterloo on the 18 June 1815 that was undertaken at the request of the King's General Command as stated in the documents of 24 November 1824.

I mentioned then and I repeat it again now that on the day of the battle of Waterloo I was acting as 2nd Captain on the wing of the squadron and so did not have the opportunity to note everything very carefully as to what was happening around me and give a reason why this or that move of the regiment was necessary or how perhaps the commander of the regiment should have acted. I have therefore not marked the various positions of the regiment on the plans of the battlefield (which I have the honour to enclose) but I hope that Lieutenant Siborne will be in a position to fill in these from my report.[3]

Colonel Friedrichs[4] and Captain A. Poten[5] who on the day of the battle of Waterloo acted the former as a major and the latter as a lieutenant in the 2nd Light Dragoon Regiment will be in a position to give clearer details in this matter.

Respectfully I have the honour, your obedient servant

WM SEEGER

---

1 William Seeger, numbered 135 in Beamish, joined the Legion in 1806, serving in the Peninsula in 1813–14 and the Waterloo campaign. Awarded HGO3 and became a brevet lieutenant colonel on half pay.

2 Leer is just to the south of Emden in north Germany.

3 This report appears as letter number 40.

4 Major Augustus Freidrichs, numbered 128 in Beamish, joined the Legion in 1803. He served in Hanover in 1805, the Baltic in 1807, Sicily in 1809, the Peninsula in 1810–14 and the Waterloo campaign. Made CB, HGO3, he received the Gold Medal for Toulouse. He later became a brevet colonel on the retired list at Hameln.

5 Captain Augustus Poten, numbered 138 in Beamish, joined the Legion in 1806. He served in Hanover in 1805, the Peninsula in 1812–14 and the Waterloo campaign. He received a General Service Medal with three bars for Salamanca, Vittoria and Toulouse. He was slightly wounded at Majalahonda in 1812 and was made HGO3 and HWC.

No. 40 From the same

Leer, 5 February 1835

ADD MS 34704, FO 222

Original in German

Report

Regarding the role played by the late 2nd Light Dragoon Regiment of the King's German Legion at the battle of Waterloo on 18 June 1815.

The above-mentioned regiment under the command of the then Major General von Jonquières[1] was until 15 June 1815 billeted near Mechelen.[2]

On the night of the 15th to the 16th of that same month [the regiment] received orders to march with the utmost dispatch because hostilities had already begun. The regiment marched on the 16th of June, passed through Brussels and arrived toward evening at Quatre Bras, where it bivouacked for the night hard on the right of the chaussee.

On the 17th, the regiment, along with the rest of the English cavalry, covered the retreat of the allied infantry and artillery.

Towards 5 o'clock in the afternoon, the brigade arrived at Mont St. Jean. From this place, the left wing division of the regiment charged from Hougoumont and Mont Plaisir[3] a part of the French cavalry advanced guard, meeting with great success. This division was under the command of the then Lieutnant von Hugo.[4]

Letter no. 40

The battle of Waterloo

On 18 June 1815, the day of the battle of Waterloo, the 2nd Light Dragoon Regiment KGL along with the 1st Light Dragoon Regiment of this Legion joined the 3rd British Cavalry Brigade under the command of Major General von Dörnberg. As far as I can remember, the 23rd English Light Dragoon Regiment belonging to the brigade only rejoined the brigade on 19 June.[5]

On the other hand, I believe the Hanoverian Hussar Regiment under the Duke of Cumberland was also under the command of Major General von Dörnberg on 18 June 1815.[6]

These regiments spent the night from 17 to 18 June in bivouac at the angle which is formed by the chaussee to Genappe and Nivelle and Mont St Jean, not far from the Mont St Jean farm.

On 18 June at approximately 10 o'clock in the morning, when the French army attacked the English army at the position taken at Mont St Jean just in front of Waterloo, Dörnberg's brigade remained in regimental columns of companies behind the artillery and the infantry, which occupied the rise of the Hougoumont position from La Haye Sainte as far as the chaussee to Genappe. At the beginning, both Light Dragoon Regiments, stood behind the rise not far from Hougoumont. The Duke of Cumberland's Hussar Regiment stood to the left, to the side of the brigade above the angle formed by the two chaussees. Other cavalry brigades were there as well, and others to the right stood on the other side of the chaussee to Nivelle. However, I do not know which brigades these were.

Both light dragoon regiments after a short time switched the direction of their columns to the right, and as a result found themselves in a column of squadrons, not far from the right wing.

Both regiments suffered some losses of men and horses in this position behind the rise as a result of enemy artillery.

At approximately 4 o'clock in the afternoon, the 2nd Light Dragoon Regiment was ordered from this position to Braine l'Alleud by the cavalry general, the Earl of Uxbridge, and led there by chief adjutant, Captain von Strenuwitz,[7] in order, as I believe, to attack the left wing of the enemy cavalry, when Grant's English brigade on our right wing mounted a frontal attack on the enemy cavalry.

However, this attack did not succeed, perhaps because it repeatedly gave rise to enemy attacks against the centre of the position, so that Grant's brigade[8] had to march there to reinforce it; after the 2nd Light Dragoon Regiment had been held in column for approximately one hour at Braine l'Alleud, and after receiving news from patrols that had been dispatched, that the enemy cavalry on the left were removed as well as the cavalry on the side of the right wing from their previous position, and the commander of the above mentioned 2nd Light Dragoon Regiment was then ordered back to the old position with his regiment.

During the march there, it was fired at heavily by an enemy battery of the left wing, and suffered the loss of several horses. The regiment marched behind the position approximately half way between Hougoumont and Mont St Jean, with the chaussee to Nivelle in front of it then marched for a short time across the chaussee, where Belgian cavalry were also emplaced. It then again took up almost the same emplacement which it had taken before it was ordered to Braine l'Alleud. It was stopped there at approximately 7 o'clock in the evening. Soon thereafter the adjutant of the commanding general came bounding over the rise and delivered an order from the commander to hurry up and march over the rise. The regiment advanced immediately and broke off into squadrons in divisions in order to get up the rise through the intervals between the artillery, and to clear the infantry squares. The regiment was then quickly reformed. At this moment we saw the entire Allied cavalry marching forward, and the enemy cavalry charging.

In front of us, at approximately 800 to 1,000 paces, there were approximately six to eight squadrons of enemy chasseurs and cuirassiers, the latter from the left wing. Their front spread significantly beyond the right wing of the regiment. But because – I think it was a Hussar brigade that was marching in the direction of Genappe – was noted at a certain distance off to the left of our cavalry, the regiment charged along with friendly cavalry that was in front of us, to approximately 100 paces distance. The enemy seemed to want to contain us and received us with fairly heavy carbine fire.

The regiment then broke clean through the enemy, and our cavalry fell upon them and took several prisoners. It pursued the enemy perhaps a little too vigorously, because the enemy cavalry still threatened our right flanks.

Because of this, the commander of the regiment therefore found it necessary to give up for the moment the pursuit of the enemy, and to give the signal to reassemble the regiment. At this time he was wounded by a cavalry bullet. Major Friedrichs quickly reassembled the regiment, and in spite of the contusion he had received the commander continued to lead the regiment until they were approximately a half an hour from Genappe, where the enemy was in the process of a full retreat after leaving his artillery in the area. The regiment bivouacked the night from 18 to 19 June on the field on this side of Genappe, and continued to march on 19 June with the English army, and thus entered France.

According to the lists compiled by the adjutant of the regiment, regimental losses on 17 and 18 June were:

On 17 June:

Missing	2 rank-and-file	2 (KGL) horses
Wounded	2 rank-and-file	1 (KGL) horse

On 18 June:

Deaths	2 officers, 18 rank-and-file	30 KGL horses, 6 officers' horses
Wounded	5 officers, 6 [sergeants?], 43 rank-and-file	35 KGL horses
Missing	"	20 KGL horses, 1 officer's horse

Names of the officers killed on 18 June:

1. Captain von Bülow[9]
2. Cornet Drangmeister[10]

Wounded:

1. Lt. Col. von Jonquières slightly
2. Lt. Col. von Maydel[11] slightly

3. Captain von Harling[12] severely
4. Lieut. Ritter[13] severely
5. Lieut. Lorentz[14] severely

WM SEEGER
LT COL, RET
PREVIOUSLY CAPTAIN 2ND LIGHT DRAGOONS
KING'S GERMAN LEGION

---

1 Lieutenant Colonel Charles Frederick de Jonquières, numbered 127 in Beamish. He joined the Legion in 1804, serving in the Peninsula in 1812. He was slightly wounded at Waterloo. He received a Gold Medal for Salamanca and was made CB, HGO3. He died as a major general, retired, at Plate, near Lüchow in Hanover, on 12 October 1831.

2 Mechelen is on the great road from Brussels to Antwerp.

3 An estate lying to the south-east of Hougoumont.

4 Lieutenant Brandano Henry Frederick William Ludolphus von Hugo, numbered 140 in Beamish. He joined the Legion in 1806, serving in the Peninsula in 1812–14. He was slightly wounded at Venta del Poco (lance wound to sword arm) in 1812. He received a General Service Medal with three bars for Salamanca, Vittoria and Toulouse. He became a captain, half pay, retired at Harburg.

5 This is a mistake, the 23rd were certainly part of the brigade at Waterloo.

6 The Duke of Cumberland's hussars were at Waterloo, despite the rest of the Hanoverian cavalry brigade being posted at Hal. Therefore the Cumberland hussars were attached to Dörnberg's brigade. The Cumberland hussars are infamous for refusing to charge and fleeing the battle en masse.

7 Captain Anthony von Strenuwitz, 2nd Hussars KGL was an Aide de Camp to Major General Alten. He is numbered 219 in Beamish, where he is mistakenly shown as Steeruwitz. He joined the Legion in 1810 and served in the Peninsula from 1810–13.

8 Grant's 5th Hussar Brigade formed the left wing of the allied army.

9 Captain Friedrich von Bülow, numbered 805 in Beamish. He joined the Legion in 1806, serving in the Peninsula in 1812–14.

10 Cornet Henry Drangmeister, numbered 815 in Beamish. He joined the Legion in 1812, serving in the Peninsula in 1812–14.

11 Lieutenant Colonel Charles von Maydell, numbered 248 in Beamish. He is listed by Beamish as from the 3rd Hussars, but Seeger clearly indicates that he served with the 2nd Light Dragoons at Waterloo. He joined the Legion in 1803, serving in Hanover 1805 and the Peninsula in 1812–14. He was slightly wounded at Venta del Poco in 1812 and the retreat from Burgos, and again at Waterloo. He later left the army and settled at Bordeaux.

12 Captain Christian Theodore Leopold George von Harling, numbered 136 in Beamish. He joined the Legion in 1806, serving in the Peninsula in 1813–14. He died at Hanover on 7 November 1823.

13 Lieutenant Hermann Heinrich Conrad Ritter, numbered 144 in Beamish. He joined the Legion in 1812, serving in the Peninsula in 1812–14.

14 He is shown as Cornet Ferdinand August Lorentz, numbered 152 in Beamish. He joined the Legion in 1814. He received a General Service Medal with a bar for Toulouse. He died at Detmold on 2 October 1831, as a brevet captain, retired list.

4th Cavalry Brigade

The 11th Light Dragoons

No. 41 Lieutenant George Sicker[1]
Ipswich, 26 December 1834

ADD MS 34704, FO 102

Sir
As far as I can recollect on the evening of the 18th June about 7 pm the 11th Dragoons were formed in line in rear of the Foot Guards, about 120 yards from the Brussels road leading to Genappe. On the enemy, retiring after their last attack, the eleventh formed open column of divisions and went in pursuit, I think the pencil marks in the plan[2] seems pretty correct.

I am, Sir, your obedient servant

G SICKER
LIEUT. HALF PAY 23RD DRAGOONS

1 He went on half pay on 30 July 1818. Appointed a Knight of Windsor, he died on 17 January 1848. Little else is known about this officer.
2 This plan appears to be no longer extant.

No. 42 Cornet Henry Bullock[1]
Maidenhead, Berkshire, 15 March 1835

ADD MS 34705, FO 65

Sir
I should have replied earlier to your enquiries (of the 24th December) but having left some plans and memorandum relating to the battle of Waterloo in London which I have not yet been able to get at. I was unwilling to do so till they arrived, but as it may be a week or two before I get them I will no longer delay acknowledging the receipt of your letter. I can however answer your 1st question viz. 'What was the formation of the 11th Light Dragoons at 7 p.m. on the 18th June 1815.'

The 11th Light Dragoons were in line (3 squadrons) about 50 yards on the right of what I should say was the crest of the position, on which a regiment of Hanoverian Infantry was posted and driven back soon with my regiment, which soon after led the advance supported by the 12th and 16th Dragoons (Sir John Vandeleur's brigade) and Sir H. Vivian's in our rear.

I have the honour to be, Sir

HENRY W BULLOCK MAJOR
CAPTAIN 1ST GUARDS

1 He joined the regiment in 1813 and was appointed a captain in 1st Lifeguards on 26 December 1821. He became a major in 1831 and went on half pay in the 60th Foot in 1837. He died at Bury St Edmunds on 9 July 1855.

No. 43 From the same
Maidenhead, 20 April 1835

ADD MS 34705, FO 171

Sir

I enclose the plan of the field of Waterloo and have marked in red ink where the 11th Lt. Dragoons were posted in different parts of the 18th June. You will see they were on the left of *La Haye Sainte* till 5 or 6 o'clock pm, when we were moved to the right of that farm, (about 500 yards) to support the infantry – 2 squares of which were driven back by the French in their last attack on our position, our Field officers assisted the officers of the square nearest us to make it front, which they succeeded in doing, this was just before our advance, as the Duke of Wellington came up to Colonel Sleigh[1] and said, 'That's right, tell them the French are retiring.'

Sir John Vandeleur's brigade led the advance supported by Sir H. Vivian's. At the end of the field near where we halted for the night we charged some columns of infantry that were masked by some of their cavalry, who retreated and left the infantry to receive us, many of whom we took prisoners, it being nearly dark, we were ordered to give the pursuit up to the Prussians who were advancing on the high road.

I have the honour to be, etc., etc., etc.

J W BULLOCK MAJOR
CAPTAIN 1ST LIFE GUARDS

---

1 Lieutenant Colonel James Wallace Sleigh, commanding officer of the 11th Light Dragoons. He joined the army as a cornet in 1795 serving in Flanders and rising to captain by 1798. He served in the Scheldt in 1799 and the Peninsula in 1811–12, receiving a General Service Medal with a bar for Salamanca. Towards the close of Waterloo, he commanded the 4th Brigade. Afterwards General Sir J. Sleigh, KCB and KMB and Colonel-in-Chief of the 9th Lancers. He died at Hanworth House, Middlesex, on 5 February 1865. His letters were published by Siborne (numbers 53 & 54).

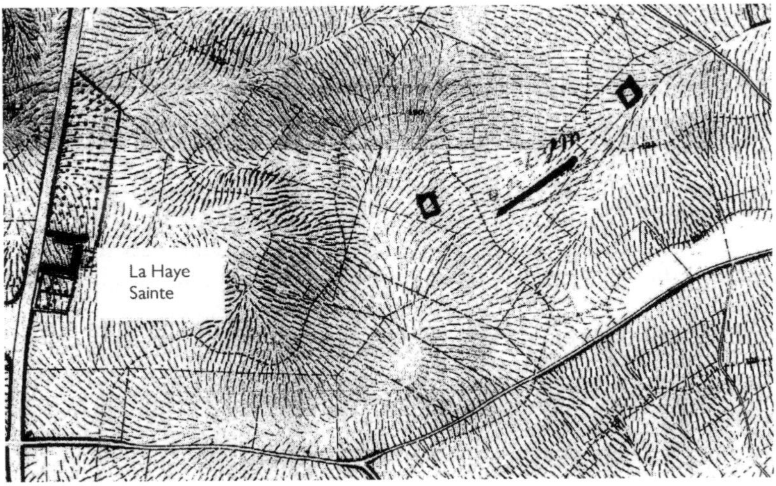

The 12th Light Dragoons

No. 44 Captain Samson Stawell[1]

Cavalry Barracks, 11 August 1836

ADD MS 34706, FO 132

Lt Colonel Stawell presents his compliments to Mr Siborne and begs to state in reply to his note of the 2nd instant that to the best of his recollection the brigade when halted and formed in several near the Nivelles road, stood *in line* thus, 11th on the right, 12th left and 16th in the centre.

Lt Colonel Stawell's absence for some days from the regiment has caused the delay in replying to Mr Siborne's note.

[UNSIGNED]

1 He joined the army as a cornet in 1801. He served in Walcheren and the Peninsula in 1811–14, including the sieges of Ciudad Rodrigo and Badajoz, the cavalry affair of La Rena, the bridge of Almaraz, Vittoria, San Sebastian and in southern France. He received a General Service Medal with three bars, for Vittoria, Nivelle and the Nive. He was promoted to brevet major on 18 June 1815 and became a colonel in 1838. He died on 21 August 1849.

The 16th Light Dragoons

No. 45 Lieutenant Colonel James Hay[1]

Lamberton Park, Mayford,[2] 20 December 1834

ADD MS 34704, FO 65

Sir,

I herewith return the plan of the field of Waterloo with remarks of Major Luard[3] who was acting as Adjutant to the 16th Dragoons on the day of the battle. I consider him the most competent person of my acquaintance (now alive) who was in the action, to give the desired information, being not only a very intelligent officer, but a very superior draughtsman.

For my own part I am unable to give any information on the subject having been wounded severely early in the action, and never afterwards having had an opportunity of going over the ground.

The 11th and 12th Lt. Dragoons having been brigaded with the 16th – many officers of these regiments who were in the action, by giving you their view of it would enable you to compare it with the recollections of Major Luard whose letter on the subject I think it as well to enclose you herewith.[4] Have the goodness to return it to me undercover to the Honourable Mr Justice Moore, Henrietta Street – when you have done with it.

I have the honour to be, Sir, your obedient servant

JAMES HAY

1 Hay joined the army as a cornet in 1795 serving in the Peninsula, France and Belgium. He received a General Service Medal with three bars, for Talavera, Fuentes d'Onoro and

Nivelles, he also received a commanding officer's Gold medal for Vittoria with a bar for the Nive. He was so severely wounded at Waterloo that he could not be moved from the field for eight days. Afterwards Lieutenant General, CB and Colonel-in-Chief of the 79th Highlanders. He died on 25 February 1854.

2 The place name appears to be Mayford, which is near Woking in Surrey.

3 John Luard was a lieutenant at the time of Waterloo. He joined the 4th Light Dragoons as a cornet in 1809 having previously served in the Royal Navy from 1802–7. He served in the Peninsula and received a General Service Medal with three bars for Albuera, Salamanca and Toulouse. Afterwards he became a major and brevet lieutenant colonel of the 21st Foot. He died in 1875. A biography of John Luard was published by J. Lunt, entitled *Scarlet Lancer,* in 1964.

4 This refers to Luard's letter published by Siborne (number 61).

No. 46 Lieutenant George Baker[1]

No date

ADD MS 34708, FO 295

Question 1. In what manner did the 16th Light Dragoons support Sir Wm. Ponsonby's heavy brigade? Was Vandeleur's brigade put in motion simultaneously with, or subsequently to, Sir Wm. Ponsonby's advance?

Answer. Vandeleur's brigade was brought forward in the early part of the 18th for the purpose of supporting (or rather saving and bringing off the remains of) Ponsonby's heavy brigade, at that time broken and dispersed by a too forward movement after their charge.

Question 2. When the 16th *advanced over the brow* of the hill, what were the circumstances that presented themselves to their view at that moment? Was the heavy brigade in the act of charging the *leading* columns of the enemy's infantry, or had it already passed these; and charged their *supporting* columns lower down the slope?

Answer. When the 16th, as centre regiment of the brigade, was passing the hedge, the heavy brigade was as above stated completely *éparpillé*[2] having never stopped to reform after their first gallant and successful charge upon the leading columns of the enemy's infantry, and being at that moment cut up in every direction by the enemy dragoons and lancers.

Question 3. Did the 16th charge cavalry or infantry?

Answer. In the morning the 16th were only engaged with cavalry – Lancers and Dragoons.

Question 4. On the first advance of Vandeleur's brigade it is understood that the 12th Light Dragoons were detached and moved a considerable distance down the slope, where they formed the left of the brigade. When that regiment subsequently made its charge, did any of the 16th accompany it on its immediate right? Sir *Frederick* Ponsonby informed me that he was inclined to think that a *portion* of the 16th did join in the charge made by his regiment, but added that he was uncertain on this point....

Answer. In the advance of Vandeleur's brigade with the object stated in No. 1, they moved forward from their supporting ground in the rear of the extreme left, in column of half squadrons (or divisions I do not remember which) left in front, the 12th of course leading; on clearing the road and hedge, and having passed the infantry which opened out with this view, they were in the act of forming line, of two attacking and one supporting regiments, to disengage and bring off the heavy brigade, when Hay,[3] I think, was wounded. The 12th had already formed and were moving on, the 16th were in the act of forming on their immediate right when this occurred (as my impression is) from a stray shot of some awkward Hanoverian or Belgian on our right rear. Certain it is however that at that moment the regiment was not under any close fire of the enemy's infantry and as the ball went clear through him, it could not have been a spent shot. However this may be, the effect from the command being momentarily paralysed, threw the direction of the squadrons for a short time upon the squadron officers, and the fact is, I believe, as Ponsonby has stated it, that the left squadron accompanied the 12th in their charge, the right and centre squadrons being engaged with bodies of cavalry more to the right and supported by the 11th Dragoons. These two squadrons never advanced beyond the hollow, though their skirmishers (which by the way I remember I commanded) were thrown on the other side of it and continued to occupy the line of the hollow for some time after the body of the brigade was again reformed and withdrawn over the hill.

Question 5. On advancing over the brow of the hill, did the brigade pass through any infantry – Hanoverian or Dutch – and if so, how was this infantry *formed*, and in what *manner* did the brigade pass through it?

Answer. In advancing over the brow, the brigade passed through some Hanoverian or Dutch infantry (I do not remember which, they having both red jackets[4]) formed *in line*; a company fell back and opened out and we passed through in open column of divisions or half squadrons.

---

1 Baker joined the army as a cornet in 1809 and served in the Peninsula and received a General Service Medal with two bars for Fuentes d'Onor and Salamanca (slightly wounded). He became a colonel on the half-pay list and died on 22 December 1859.

2 Scattered.

3 Lieutenant Colonel James Hay commanding the 16th Light Dragoons was severely wounded. His letter is published in this volume (number 45).

4 If these troops were dressed in red it is almost certain they were Hanoverian troops as the Dutch/Belgian troops wore green or blue.

Letter no. 47

5th Cavalry Brigade

The 7th Hussars

No. 47 Assistant Surgeon Robert Alexander Chermside[1]

Paris, 8 June 1835

ADD MS 34705, FO 281

Dear Sir

I regret extremely to learn, by an indirect communication from the Honourable Colonel Thorn,[2] that you have not yet received any information from either of the Marshals, Soult[3] or Lobau.[4] I am of opinion that a communication for you has miscarried. I can only assure you that I called at least five different times on Marshal Soult, ascertained the time of his return to Paris; left the various parcels addressed to him myself, and was in hopes that you had long since heard something satisfactory. Marshal Soult did not remain many days at Paris, he was, as you are, perhaps, aware, in political affairs etc. etc.

I did not fail to try to obtain answers to your different queries from Generals de Flahaut[5] and Exelmans[6] but they either could not or would not furnish the information desired.

I am surprised that Marshal Lobau has not communicated with you, as he appeared disposed to do anything in his power, indeed said so to myself. With Marshal Soult I never could obtain an interview. I sincerely wish I could, in any way, be of use to you. Could you come here for a week or so, I think you might be able to extract something from Marshal Lobau or others. I believe General de Flahaut will soon accompany his family to Brighton whither they are going very soon for sea bathing.

In haste I am, dear Sir, yours very sincerely,

R A CHERNSIDE

---

1 He had served with the 7th in Southern France, receiving a General Service Medal with two bars for the Nive and Toulouse. He went on the half pay list immediately after Waterloo. He held the post of Surgeon to the British Embassy in Paris at the time of this letter.

2 Almost certainly Lieutenant Colonel Nathaniel Thorn (spelt Thorne in the Military General Service Roll), he became CB, KH and Assistant Quartermaster General. Having joined the army in 1802, he served with the 3rd Foot or as an ADC. He received a General Service Medal with nine bars for Talavera, Busaco, Albuera, Vittoria, Pyrenees, Nivelle, Nive, Orthes and Toulouse. He was slightly wounded at the Nive. He also served at Plattsburg in North America. He became Colonel of the 3rd Foot in 1854.

3 Marshal Nicholas Jean de Dieu Soult acted as Chief of Staff to the French Army of the North. At the time of the letter he had just completed his first term as Minister of War.

4 Marshal Georges Mouton, Comte de Lobau had commanded the VI Corps at Waterloo. He was wounded and taken prisoner at Plançenoit. He died in 1838 when an old wound reopened.

5 Flahaut was Aide de Camp to Napoleon at Waterloo.

6 General Rémy Joseph Isidore Exelmans commanded the II Reserve Cavalry Corps at Waterloo.

No. 48 Private Edward Cotton[1]
Mont St Jean, Waterloo, 7 September 1845

ADD MS 34708, FO 208

Sir

No doubt you have received Martin Nisbet's[2] letter by this as he gave it to Monsieur Meline a fortnight ago tomorrow, if not, the following is the replies to your questions.

No part of the field or villages of Sombreff or Ligny[3] can be seen from Quatre Bras. The church spire and mill of Marbais can be seen from Quatre Bras, but no portion of the village.

The height of Marbais and Brie are so elevated as to prevent the field of Ligny being seen from Quatre Bras. A few houses called little Marbais can be seen from Quatre Bras along the Namur road on high ground, about a league distant. No trees has grown up *[sic]* since 1815 between Quatre Bras and Ligny, but the wood of Delhutte has been cut down.

I am pleased to hear you expect a third edition of your work soon. Please be so good as to put my regiment and present situation to my name in the list of subscribers, as in the first it is put from the 18th Hussars, an error of Mr Longman[4] to whom I remitted my subscription money.

I am, Sir, your most obedient

EDWARD COTTON
LATE SERGT MAJOR 7TH HUSSARS
GUIDE AT WATERLOO

---

1 Cotton had served in southern France, receiving a General Service Medal with two bars, for Orthes and Toulouse. He served with his regiment at Waterloo, having his horse killed beneath him by a cannon ball. He later owned a hotel on the battlefield with a small museum and acted as a guide to the many visitors. He later wrote a history of the battle entitled *A Voice from Waterloo*. He died on 24 June 1849 and is interred in the crypt of the British Monument at Evere cemetery, Brussels.

2 I have been unable to identify this person, although the way in which Cotton mentions him, he is likely to have been a fellow soldier. His name however does not appear at all in the Waterloo Medal Roll and Cotton unfortunately does not mention him in his work.

3 The site of the battle of Ligny between the Prussians and the main French army fought on 16th June, while Wellington's Allied forces met Ney's force at Quatre Bras. It has sometimes been stated that Wellington could clearly see the French overthrowing the Prussians from his position at Quatre Bras. This letter confirms that Wellington could not see what was occurring at Ligny.

4 Mr Longman of the London publishers Longman, Rees, Orme, Brown and Green of Paternoster Row.

Letter nos 49–50

6th Cavalry Brigade

The 10th Hussars

No. 49 Lieutenant Colonel George A. Quentin[1]

Kew, 20 August 1835

ADD MS 34705, FO 326

In answer to the questions you have done me the honour to send me respecting the position of the 10th hussars *at the moment* when the French Imperial Guards had reached the crest of our position, I have to inform you that having been wounded about the time the regiment arrived at the station where it was formed in support of the infantry engaged near the farm of La Haye Sainte, I am not able to give you such correct information as I would wish, but I should conceive that the 10th Hussars were *at that moment* either moving in open column from the left to the station before mentioned, or were already formed in support of the infantry.

With respect to the nature of the crops, it is very probable they were such as you have stated them to be in the plan, but they were so much trodden down that it is impossible to be quite accurate in respect to them, nor does my recollection serve one at this distance of time, to state with any degree of accuracy the positions, movements or formation generally of the contending armies.

I have the honour to be, Sir, your obedient humble servant,

G QUENTIN
M GENERAL

---

1 Originally from Gottingen, he had served five years in the Garde du Corps of Hanover before joining 10th Hussars in 1793. He served with Moore in the Peninsula and received a commanding officer's Gold medal for Sahagun with a bar for Benevente. Hart's Army List for 1840 states that he received a medal with clasp for Orthes and Toulouse. He was severely wounded at Waterloo. He became CB, KCH, ADC to George IV and Crown Equerry to Queen Victoria. He died in London on 7 December 1851 aged 92. Much controversy surrounds this officer, as at the culmination of the Peninsular war, the regimental officers drew up a petition for the removal of their Commanding Officer (Quentin) on the grounds of cowardice. In the ensuing court martial he was exonerated, but his officers were reprimanded and forced to resign. A number of officers from other regiments were then hurriedly drafted in to fill the gaps.

No. 50 Lieutenant Colonel Lord Robert William Manners[1]

London, 19 January 1830

ADD MS 34703, FO 120

My dear Sir Hussey[2]

I am glad you approve generally of my account of what occurred,[3] and as the 10th were concerned, at Waterloo, and the days preceding, and I am obliged to you for your corrections.

I must in the first place confess that my omission of so important a feature in our retreat on the 17th as that of passing the Dyle by so narrow a defile,[4] and under the circumstances you mention was a great oversight. Your remarks have called it to my memory: you formed us on the opposite bank, and though I have an imperfect recollection of your dismounting part of the 10th it was, I conclude, for the defence of the bridge, if the enemy had thought not to endeavour to force it.

You were quite right[5] as to the period of Quentin's[6] being wounded: it was to form we crossed the road, or at any rate before you had formed up in rear of the infantry. With regard to the movement to the rear after being so formed, certainly the impression left on my mind was that it took place at the time the Brunswickers fell back, and I supposed your object in adopting that course was to give them greater space and better opportunity for rallying, and recovering their order: but I dare say your explanation of it is the correct one, and that it was done with a view of sheltering us from fire, because I am aware that you had attended particularly to that circumstance during the day, both on the left and during our progress towards the centre which was all along more or less exposed to the enemy's fire, in some places to a very great degree, and the avoiding of which, as well as I recollect, very awkward ground, struck me and others as so admirably managed by you. I was afraid I might be in error with respect to the names of some of the villages, and towns, as well as the direction of some of the roads, for the recollection of which I am indebted to Hayter-Smith[7], who had taken notes, for I have no good map.[8]

Yours most truly

R MANNERS

---

1 He was the third son of Charles, 4th Duke of Rutland and brother to Charles Henry Somerset Manners, Lieutenant Colonel of the 3rd Dragoons. The careers of these two brothers has been mixed up by Dalton and Burks's *Peerage*. Charles served with the 10th Hussars as a Major at Sahagun and Benevente but transferred to the 3rd Dragoons as a Lietenant Colonel in 1812. Robert had previously been Lieutenant Colonel of the 23rd Light Dragoons but was transferred into the 10th Hussars in November 1814 as one of the replacements following the Quentin trial (see footnote 1 letter 49 above). He died on 15 November 1835.

2 This letter although in the files, was written before Siborne launched his quest. The letter is written to his brigade commander, Major General Sir Hussey Vivian, who collated his own information and certainly forwarded other similar correspondence to Siborne.

3 This account unfortunately does not appear in the files.

4 The 10th in Vivian's brigade formed part of the left wing in the retreat and passed the river at the little bridge of Thuy.

5 This paragraph now leaps to a description of the latter period of the battle of Waterloo.

6 Lieutenant Colonel George Quentin, commanded the 10th Hussars, but having been wounded, Manners took command.

7 Lieutenant William Slayter Smith, 10th Hussars.

8 The rest of the letter is not concerned with Waterloo. I reproduce it here for the sake of completeness: 'I don't believe a word about any change of ministry. Some ten days ago it was positively asserted in the Standard, but it turned out to be a hoax of Chas Grant's upon Sir R. Inglis whom he met in the street, and the latter posted off to the Standard office and gave it as gospel. What horrid weather, the thermometer here last night was 14. I heard of another run 18 miles [away?] end last Saturday week with [Foljambes?] hounds which is still farther north than ours.'

Letter no. 51

No. 51 From the same
Leicester, 13 November 1834

ADD MS 34703, FO 219

Sir,

In answer to your communication in reference to the particular formation of the 10th Hussars in the battle of Waterloo (about 7 pm) I beg to inform you, that according to the best of my recollection, they were either marching in open column from the left of the line, to the centre, or having reached that station, were formed in support of a battalion of the Brunswick troops, which was warmly engaged with the enemy near the farm of La Haye Sainte (also Lieut. Siborne, occupied by the French) but I cannot take upon myself to say, what was the exact formation of the troops of the enemy engaged with the Brunswickers. I have therefore traced on the accompanying plan, the movement of the regiment to the centre, and their formation (when arrived) in rear of the Brunswickers.

On the advance of the British army against the enemy's line at the close of the action, the 10th Hussars were wheeled round the flank of the infantry in their immediate front by Sir Hussey Vivian (commanding the brigade) and led by him to the charge. They first encountered a mixed body of the enemy's cavalry, consisting of Cuirassiers, Lancers and Hussars of the Guard, which they dispersed. They afterwards made other charges against various bodies of the enemy, and particularly one by a squadron of the regiment under the Honourable the Major Howard,[1] who was unfortunately killed against a square of infantry.

With regard to the nature of the crops on the different fields near which the 10th Hussars were posted, I have no means of giving a correct opinion, because they were so completely trodden down, that as well as my recollection serves, the entire ground

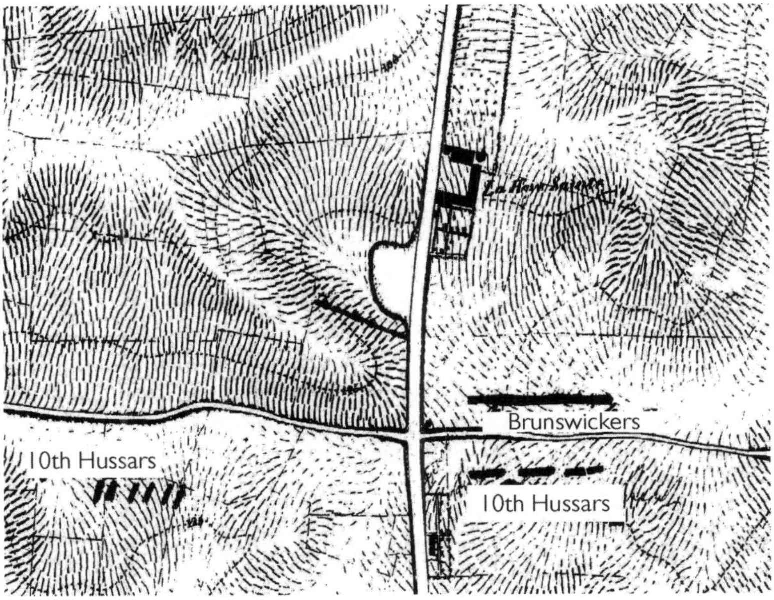

presented the appearance of a field of mud, owing to the incessant rain which had fallen the night before, nor can I pretend to give you any information to be relied upon, with regard to the formations, positions, and movements of the contending armies during the day.

I have the honour to be, Sir, your most faithful & obedient servant

ROBERT MANNERS

1 Major the Honourable Frederick Howard, 3rd son of Frederick, 5th Earl of Carlisle was initially buried at Waterloo. Major Howard's remains were removed to Streatham where he was re-interred on 3 August 1815. In 1879 his remains were moved again to the family mausoleum at Castle Howard, Yorkshire.

No. 52 Captain Thomas William Taylor[1]

Ogwell House, Newton Abbot, 8 March 1836

ADD MS 34706, FO 60

There are many points contained in the questions proposed by you to Sir Hussey Vivian and Colonel Murray[2] on which I can give no information.

No.1 I remember when we were formed in line on the crest of the hill on the left of our position with our right to a low hedge that was at right angles to the Namur road. A battery annoyed us much for several rounds and the shot striking the ground first before and just going over my squadron. I remarked to Major Howard I wished they would find something else to fire at – in a little time they changed their direction – but this was early in the day – and not the time alluded to I think.

When we were directed above the hollow way more to the right, than the above marked position, there was a considerable cannonade and many cannon shots flying over us, but I did not know what battery they came from.

No. 2 In what I described in the paper before sent,[3] of a regiment of Brunswickers (I supposed them to be such from their dark uniform) being about to pass between two of our squadrons to the rear. When I stated Captain Shakespear[4] (and as I still think) Sir Hussey Vivian spoke to them and cheered them to advance – I did not mean to say that our line was forced, but the French were evidently pushing much, and the fire was very heavy. I saw their men through the smoke apparently not 50 paces from our infantry and our regiment was in line close behind the infantry. Captain Gurwood,[5] my right half squadron officer was shot in the knee at this time – so I believe was Major Wood[6] – our horses were wounded more than men – though they suffered too, but from the effects of that fire – there were many horses that had two or three balls in them, and the first day of the march[7] our farriers and veterinary surgeon were constantly cutting them out. Now whereabouts in the field this heavy fire was I do not know, from not having been on the field since, and having had no previous knowledge of it – but I know it was soon after we came out from behind a knoll to our left having passed through a coppice at the back of the ridge.

After the enemy were driven back here, and our support was not more required, we wheeled half squadrons to the right and went on more to the right of the position.

No. 3 I do not know anything about Lord Anglesey at that time – I should say there

Letter no. 52

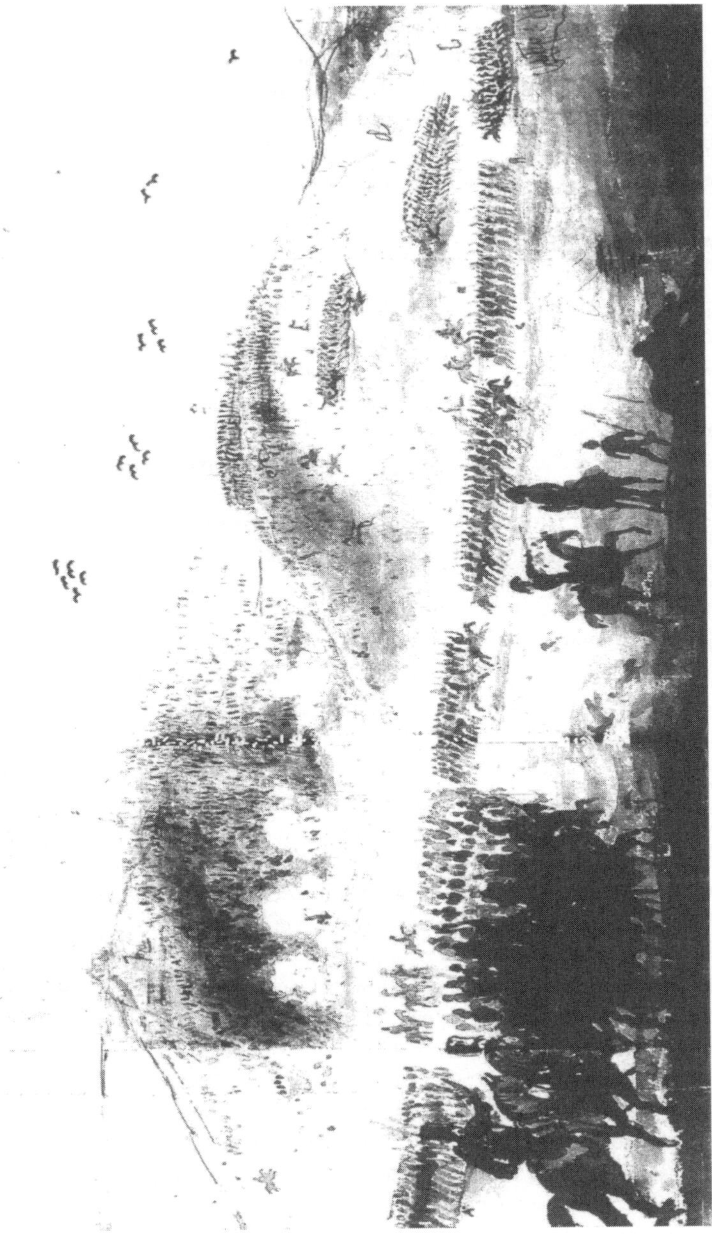

Taylor's sketch of the final advance of the cavalry, looking towards La Belle Alliance. His letter refers to the sets of birds shown in the illustration.

was rather musketry than grape on us when in line – and no round shots from the sound.

No. 4 I do not remember seeing any deserted batteries when we were advancing to the charge. I think there were some cannon firing from the lower part of the slopes, which the French army was already [abandoning?] in confusion. V[iz]: sketch but I cannot place them exactly.

No. 5 The first guns I saw of the enemy taken were to the best of my knowledge of the ground under the five birds [in the illustration] on the slope of the 2nd hill a little above a road, where there were several in returning from pursuit, our men were sabring a man by one of the guns and on my reconnoitring, they said he had come from under the gun and fired at them after they had passed.

Questions to Colonel Murray[8]

No. 1 I do not know where or when that was.

No. 2 I do not know.

No. 3 I do not know where they were.

No. 4 The troops I saw were as I have said above in a dark dress and looked like Brunswickers, they did not retire through the squadron intervals, but turned about and advanced again with other battalions to the left in a general rally, drums rolling: Lieutenant Duperier[9] at the same time urging forward some troops of the same description corroborates my accounts. It was probably another battalion of the same force.

No. 5 I do not remember passing any guns of ours or the French, after we passed the battery that was firing until we saw some guns *firing from* the slope –V [iz] sketch. [The illustration appears here in the letter]

After we had passed the battery that was firing on the enemy and advanced at a gallop and bringing our left shoulders forward, formed nominally a line (without a hitch) but really echelon, the scene of the French army in confusion crowding up the hill, some guns and a few muskets firing to protect their retreat, some cavalry formed on an advanced knoll to our right at first, appeared from our change of direction in front. The sun giving a lurid sort of glare, all made such a picturesque battle piece that I have after wished I could paint it, I can still shut my eyes and see it – and have made an attempt just to sketch it in a sort of hieroglyphic in sepia – and really I should say *it does* give me an idea of it, and may not be uninteresting to one as you are. I do not know where Belle Alliance would be, I suppose to the hill above the left smoke, about. You may be able to complete and make more correct the outline of the ground.

The brigade was in ½ squadrons – but that that would take time and space, so I have contented myself with divisions or a few in front – surrounding the ½ squadron on the extreme right are the enclosures near Hougoumont.

One bird the party of the 23rd Dragoons or Germans, coming round our right squadron. I never saw them pass before the brigade. The first I saw of them were just as here represented, they might not be the same as Captain Banner's.[10]

Two birds the French lancers *white with red facings*, which gallantly charged down the hill on the 23rd though they saw our brigade coming on – and I think cheered their advance.

I remember Captain Shakespear declaring to me his seeing one of the lancers giving two or three pulls to get his lance out of one of our dragoons he had struck – our right squadron came in upon the lancers, and sent them off.

Three birds some green dragoons in helmets who charged to support the lancers and came upon our right squadron. My squadron, the centre of the 10th under the *4 birds* came in on the dragoons, and there a mixture of lancers, dragoons and hussars – they turned of course in flight –. When we were advancing I saw a body of cavalry on the crest of that slope with so much red about them, I thought at first they were the Life Guards and wondered how they came there. I have numbered them with red – these evidently were the carabiniers Captain Banner had been fighting. What became of them, whether they charged to support the dragoons, or set off – I do not know, I saw no more of them. According to my idea the 10th proceeded from the hill and over it into a hollow between it and the next hill, there the French squares according to my idea, was formed, in charging which I suppose Major Howard was killed. I did not see the charge – as I followed Lord Robert Manners with some of the regiment up the slope over a road and above the road we saw the guns I mention under the *five birds*. No attempt at defending them was made, they were in fact captured by us, but we passed on and charged some infantry rallied, and cavalry behind them on the crest of that hill about 60 or 70 yards from the brow. They broke and were pursued a little way – our horses were very much blown by this time – so we collected the men and returned to join the rest. Some of the 18th passed me, darted down a slope beyond that hill, and up another steep hill with a square of infantry at the top – and were repulsed, as was natural, from the circumstance that I do not think there were more than 30. The hill was very steep and pointed, the square on the apex. General Vandeleur's brigade was then coming on and when we were reformed and advancing towards the observatory,[11] we met some of them coming back with many prisoners, and in the dark we passed places where numbers seemed to have thrown down their arms by the sound of the horses feet treading on them.

I have taken no copy of any of the papers you sent me which I return herewith and have no desire to enter any description on the subjects. I have told you all I can remember as it appears to me now. I should have mentioned that in the sketch I have sent, some infantry in columns which I saw advancing on our left and some Staff Officers which I believe to [have] been the Duke of Wellington and who I understood anticipated our advance.

The space in front of the slope the enemy are retiring up is perhaps too great.

As anything relating to your work may be interesting I enclose some lines written in 1822 when I was by myself in a transport (not a *practical* one) cruising to Ireland with the regiment, which you may keep or burn, the first part pretty closely coincides with the sketch. Lieutenant Gunning[12] according to the account of my own servant, formerly my batman, who died this year, was killed later, in charging the square. I understood [from] the Adjutant he saw him fall in our advance and particularly described his instant death; he was shot through the heart.

I have the honour to be Sir your humble servant

T W TAYLOR

PS

As we were crossing the road above the French square and below the guns we took – I saw a battalion in red a good way to our left coming along the road. I heard they were Hanoverians which I believe Sir H.V.[13] expected to cooperate in attacking the square – but Colonel Arnold 16th Lancers[14] – then Lieutenant, told me afterwards they declined – they perhaps were the Hanoverian Militia.

I take the liberty of mentioning that I saw an exhibition at the coronation in Regents Park 5 or 6 years ago, which they were pleased to call *Panstereomachia*. It was a model of the field of Poitiers and the figures were beautifully done, perhaps you saw it, but if not, I mention it because the people that executed the figures might be of use to you if you could find them out.

---

1 He joined the army as a cornet in 1804 and served at the capture of Java in 1811, for which he received a General Service Medal. He was made a brevet lieutenant colonel for Waterloo and CB. Afterwards he became a major general, Lieutenant Governor of the Royal Military College at Sandhurst and Colonel-in-Chief of the 17th Lancers. He died at Haccombe in Devon on 8 January 1854. His letters to his family during the Waterloo campaign were recently republished in facsimile by Ken Trotman as Military Monograph number 4, 2002.

2 Lieutenant Colonel The Honourable Henry Murray, who commanded the 18th Hussars. See his letter in this volume (number 63).

3 This refers to his previous letter of some length, printed by Siborne (number 75).

4 Captain Arthur Shakespear, see his letter (number 57).

5 Captain John Gurwood, see his letters (numbers 54–56).

6 Captain Charles Wood, he went on the half pay list in 1821. He is not recorded as wounded by Dalton.

7 On the march to Paris, following the victory.

8 The questions posed seem to be different to those posed to Vivian, but it is not clear what they were.

9 Lieutenant Henry Duperier, 18th Hussars, see his letter (number 64–65).

10 Lieutenant John Banner of the 23rd Light Dragoons, his letters were published by Siborne (number 47 & 48). Later he was a Captain in the 93rd Highlanders. He became heavily embroiled in the argument with Gawler over the 'Crisis', writing frequently to the United Services Magazine. He died on 24 December 1837.

11 A wooden platform standing behind the French lines. Some sources claim the French built it the night before the battle, but this is highly unlikely. Drawings of the structure following the battle show it to be quite substantial, furthermore the French had never used such a structure before and there is no mention of its construction in the numerous memoirs. A more plausible explanation is that it was a tower built to aid the surveying of the area, which had been ordered by the new King of the combined Kingdom of Belgium and Holland. See the discussion on this subject in the *Journal of the Friends of the Waterloo Committee* vol. 23 number 2.

12 This refers to Lieutenant George Orlando Gunning. Dalton omits to show him as having been killed.

13 Sir Hussey Vivian.

14 Lieutenant Robert Arnold, in 1809 he was an Ensign in the 4th Foot, in 1812 he transferred as a Lieutenant to the 16th Light Dragoons and was wounded at Badajoz (severely) and Vittoria (slightly). He went on half pay at the end of the war in 1814. He joined the 10th Hussars before Waterloo, where he was wounded. Later in 1826 he became a Lieutenant Colonel in the 16th Light Dragoons. He died on 20 August 1839.

No. 53 From the same

Bishops Teignton, Teignmouth, 8 September[1]

ADD MS 34706, FO 155

Sir,

In reply to your note of August 11th I am afraid I can give you but little additional

Letter no. 53

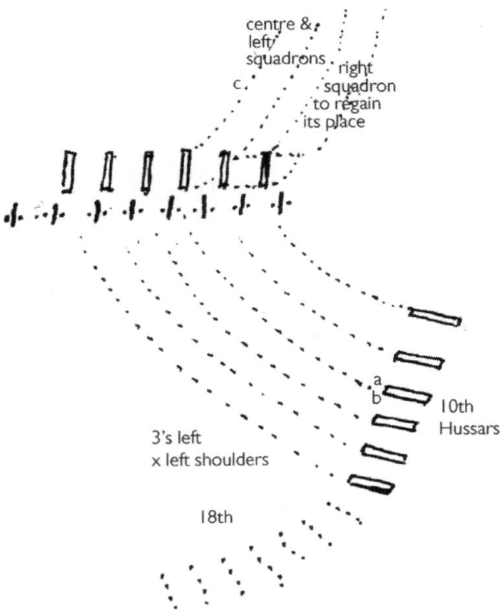

information. I have taken the liberty to mark three passages – A, B & C in your letter to Sir Hussey Vivian.

With regard to A – it all agrees perfectly with my recollection.

B agrees with my recollection – I should say the position of the brigade at the time of the repulse of the enemy was more to the right than in the plan No. 1 – and as you say with the head advanced to the right beyond the right gun of the battery, and with right shoulders more brought up – at least the leading regiments.

My post was at **a** – Lt. Hodgson[2] at **b** – when he had his horse killed by a shot under my horse's neck.

I think the rear of the brigade did not cover, but was more away towards the left.

After having wheeled upon passing the guns (which were English, for I spoke to and was answered by the bombadier at one gun) when stated one gun was fired, so that the shot ranged close in front of the horses near of one of my half squadrons.

Advanced at **c** –gallop bringing up right shoulders – a little way on at **c** a Staff officer met us, I am pretty sure Colonel, afterwards Sir Felton Hervey,[3] and said 'Come along, come along.' I said 'Our right squadron is left behind by the guns' and he appeared to gallop on to them, they soon came up on our right at a splitting pace and took their place at the head.[4]

C – I can now say nothing as to our Captain Banner's squadron[5] having no recollection of seeing it, it being clear that what I described in the sketch, was the leading squadron of the 2nd German LD[6] – the right squadron of the 10th probably concealed the rest of the regiments from me and prevented me observing more than the leading squadrons or ½ squadron. They came just between our right squadron and Hougoumont *ferme* – as it is said Captain Banner crossed the front of the 10th, it was probably in rear of the 10th.

I am sorry that I can give no information as to the Dutch troops you mention and mark in the plan 3[7] as we were right in front, my post was of course on the left, so probably I had the column between me and them, and one was more able to look to the left or front than to the rear. I remember seeing Lord Anglesey and Staff and what appeared little more than a squadron of heavy cavalry, which I understood to be the remains of the Household Brigade – but really, I was so intent on my own business I did not think much of looking about, and then there was so much fog and smoke, there was not much to be seen, till we got to the front upon guns advancing to the charge when the scene described in the sketch lighted up by a gleam of evening lights – struck me forcibly – as I never saw the ground before or since then galloping over it I [little think I] am qualified to find the sketch has any semblance to the local features.

I think I have a slight recollection of the Light Brigade cheering.

Where Captain Banner found Sir Hussey forming the 18th I think must have been after our charge. When he was preparing to attack a square formed in a hollow – in which attack I conclude Major Howard was killed, but am not certain – as Lt Robert Manners led some of the regiment on up a hill to some guns which were taken, to attack some infantry rallied in line with cavalry behind them, which opened a fire on us – but ran when we charged.

I am sorry I can be of no more assistance, and also that I have been so long in answering your letter but I have been unable to find time.

I remain Sir your humble servant

T W TAYLOR
LT COL

---

1 Probably written in 1836.
2 Lieutenant Ellis Hodgson became a captain in 1820 and went on the half-pay list in 1821.
3 Colonel Felton Hervey, 14th Light Dragoons, was on the Staff at Waterloo as an Assistant Quartermaster General. He lost his right arm at Oporto and nearly lost his leg at Fuentes d'Onoro, but a thick book in his saddle pocket deflected the cannon ball, which struck his horse. He received a gold medal for Salamanca. After Waterloo he was appointed as an aide de camp to Wellington, which post he held throughout the occupation of France. He was created a baronet in 1818; afterwards he became Colonel Sir Felton Elwell Hervey-Bathurst Bart. He left a brief account of the campaign, published in *The Nineteenth Century* magazine, March 1893. He died in 1819.
4 That is, head of the regiment.
5 Lt John Banner of the 23rd Light Dragoons, 3rd Cavalry Brigade of Major General Dörnberg.
6 The 2nd Light Dragoons, KGL, also formed part of the 3rd Cavalry Brigade.
7 I cannot discover this mark on the plan.

No. 54 Captain John Gurwood[1]
Portsmouth, 22 February 1835

ADD MS 34706, FO 443

My dear Sir,

I am quite ashamed at not having replied to your communication relative to your very interesting work. You are mistaken with regard to my having been on the Staff at the battle of Waterloo, as I was serving with my regiment, the Xth Hussars at that battle.

With respect to the position of the Xth and the brigade in which I served commanded by Sir Hussey Vivian, I cannot refer you to better authority than the Commander of the Forces in Ireland. I have however taken the liberty to forward your communication to an old friend of mine, W. Slayter Smith of the Yorkshire Hussars, but Lieutenant in the Xth at that battle. And as a corroborative testimony of Sir Hussey Vivian you cannot have a better authority as I know his memory to be of the most correct.

I wish you every success in your enquiries, that your labours may be satisfactory in this very national undertaking, and I congratulate you on having completed the most essential part of it. The position of the troops at the hour you mention is of little importance in comparison with the ground, and cannot display the merit of particular corps.

Very sincerely yours

J GURWOOD

---

1 He joined the 52nd Regiment in 1808 and served in the Peninsula, being severely wounded in a skirmish in 1811. As a subaltern he commanded the forlorn hope at Ciudad Rodrigo where he received a severe wound on his head but still took the Governor General Barrie prisoner, whose sword was presented to him by Wellington. He joined the 10th Hussars in 1814. He is listed by Dalton as being Aide de Camp to Sir Henry Clinton at Waterloo, but he evidently fell out with him and he did duty with his regiment. Dalton does record him as being severely wounded in the knee at Waterloo. Afterwards he was CB and Colonel and Deputy Lieutenant of the Tower. He died at Brighton on 27 December 1845 by his own hand and is buried at the Tower. Dalton mistakenly states the year as 1843.

No. 55 From the same
Paris, 23 March 1838

ADD MS 34706, FO 460

My dear Sir

Sir H. Vivian forwarded to me here your letter of the 17th March. On my return to London I shall probably be able to answer some of your questions, but as I hope to be able to complete the 12th volume[1] in July or August next with the Waterloo campaign (I will finish the XIth next month) it may be as well for you to wait for the whole of the correspondence, which you will have as it comes from the press. I have read all of it, but at the present moment I do not see [much] about the points adverted to in your queries. The particulars would be best ascertained, that is the orders of movement etc, from the registers of the QMG's[2] department, which of course were never mislaid, even at the unfortunate moment of Colonel De Lancey's[3] death. I should think Colonel Freeth[4] might give you some hint where these are to be found. I recollect the account of the passing of the Sambre at Charleroi having arrived at Bruxelles about dinner time[5] on the 15th, for I was then at HQ, but I was too much occupied with the organisation of the ball at the Duke of Richmond's to recollect much about what else was to take place that night, further than that I heard everything was to move at daylight. These particulars I fear will not be shown in his Grace's papers. I will however [go] carefully back over them on my arrival at Apsley House[6] after the 15th April and let you know. The enquiry as to the interview between the Duke and Prince Blücher on the 16th or 17th[4] I can make of His Grace, but I believe no such meeting took place.

Believe me very faithfully yours

J GURWOOD

1 Gurwood became Wellington's Private Secretary and was the editor of *The Duke of Wellington's Dispatches 1799–1815*, published between 1834 and 1839. Volume 12 covered the period of the Waterloo campaign and the subsequent period of occupation in France.
2 The Quartermaster General's office, among whose responsibilities was the transmission of orders to the various corps.
3 Colonel Sir William Howe De Lancey KCB, Deputy Quartermaster General, was severely wounded at Waterloo when the wind of a cannon ball detached his ribs from his backbone, he died ten days later. His final days are recorded by his young wife who remained by his side throughout, in the very poignant *A Week at Waterloo in 1815*, published in 1906.
4 Lieutenant Colonel James Freeth KH had joined the army as an ensign in1806. He served in the Peninsula, receiving a General Service Medal with eight bars for Fuentes d'Onoro, Ciudad Rodrigo, Badajoz, Salamanca, Vittoria, Pyrenees, Nivelle and Nive. He was placed on half pay in 1830 but continued to work as an Assistant Quartermaster General.
5 The time when Wellington received notification of the commencement of the French invasion by the Prussians has been the cause of much debate. Some claim that a message must have been received by mid morning although there is no definite evidence to this effect, while others including Gurwood maintain that the first intimation was received at dinnertime, which was between 4 and 5 pm on 15 June. All of the evidence available now heavily weighs towards the fact that Wellington was unaware of events at Charleroi until 5 pm.
6 Apsley House is still the London residence of the current Duke of Wellington and retains the simple address, No. 1, London.
7 There are on record two very separate conversations recorded by guests at dinner parties with the Duke of Wellington. In both they claim that he described sneaking away from his quarters at Waterloo on the night of 17 June to meet Blücher secretly, to confirm their plans for the following day. However, this scenario remains *very* unlikely and is very probably a myth.

No. 56 From the same
70 Lowndes Square, 6 May 1842

ADD MS 34707, FO 359

My dear Sir,

I have looked over the Duke of Wellington's papers for the enquiry respecting the date of the proclamation from Malplaquet.[1] I find the enclosed copy of it is my own handwriting.

This is not however satisfactory, as to the exact date. In compiling the Despatches, I placed in their regular order, all that I had printed, and I cannot tell where I obtained the English and French Proclamation dated Malplaquet. It is evident from the docket on the back that I have somewhere found the English one, and that I explained it by that which I enclose. It is evident therefore that it is not a misprint by me. Of course I never presumed to alter anything, particularly a date. The proclamations were not put up with his General correspondence which most is still separate in bundles marked 'To' and 'From' and I have no recollection where I found this one. A copy of the *Moniteur*[2] however will supply the date, and I am not quite sure whether I did not go to the British Museum for this copy. I regret that my explanation will be so little satisfactory.

Faithfully yours

J GURWOOD

1 This refers to the Proclamation in French dated 22 June 1815, printed on pp 494 and 495, vol. 12 of Gurwood's *The Duke of Wellington's Dispatches.*

2 The newspaper *Le Moniteur* was the official mouthpiece of the French Government.

No. 57 Captain Arthur Shakespear[1]

Boxsell Court, Wotton-under-Edge, 20 September 1835[2]

ADD MS 34706, FO 482

To Sir Hussey Vivian

Dear Sir Hussey

Living as I do in the 'back settlements', Major Gawler's crisis and your reply, never reached me until Hesse[3] of the 18th came to see me. I have however carefully read both. Major Gawler is wrong in many points. I perfectly recollect our forming in line, upon being taken to the right of St Jean, and that the 18th [on the] left, was close upon the chaussee. It is not likely that any one present at that time, should forget it, for a heavier fire I don't believe any troops ever stood under. You will remember, that the roar was so great, though close together, we could not make ourselves understood, but by Holloa'ing.

I feel honoured by your mentioning me as being attached to your Staff, and more particularly, upon our endeavouring to rally the 'White shako's' *[sic]*.[4] The 10th and 18th stood at closed intervals. The rapid movement we made off the position, renders it impossible that the 52nd could keep the ground, as stated,[5] we must have been upon them, or they have been in the rear of those French troops, who's heads we saw through the smoke, so close to us, but who *never crossed the summit!* I have them in my eye at this moment.

If I remember right, we went in a hard canter down the hill, our charges were also rapid, nor did we halt a moment, until we came suddenly upon *the square.* I was with that squadron, trying to form, when you came up. I perfectly recollect what passed as to whether we should charge, and I am *positive* the red coats[6] who made their appearance, were directly *behind* us about 100 yards, and not in a situation to fire upon *'another face of the same square'*. They were coming down upon our rear, which mainly decided you to charge.

I maintain, that, that charge was not *attempted*, but most gallantly executed, and had it's effect – though the square did not instantly disperse and the cavalry were not beat off, as Major Gawler states. I deny that we came up, *'to the support of the 71st'*, we were down the hill, and scoured the plain, to be free of any other troops.

What do the Guards say to this statement, because if true, the 52nd take all credit from them – as Major Gawler's says, they charged across their front!

I think Sir, your reply is excellent, but not severe enough – which is bad enough, but his arrogating for the 52nd all the glory of the crisis, deserves severe handling. Those who served under you, will feel thankful for the part you have taken, in defending the brigade – and indeed other regiments, entitled to share the honour of the day.

I am delighted to be roused, and will always maintain, that no troops stood under a heavier fire than we did on position, that our movements were rapid, and successful, and led on most gallantly!

If you think my knowledge of the circumstances, can be of service in speaking to the correctness of the reply[7] – write me what I shall say, and I will send it to the editor. In considering this business over, I have naturally been led to the many happy days passed with you, when I had no claim to your consideration.

I go back to 1810 in Dublin! And then to Abbeville where the 'pates' *de foie gras* 'used to create so much fear'. Do you remember the morning of the 19th at Ailincourt [?] I can see you in your shirt now!

Allow me to congratulate you upon the marriages that have taken place in your family. May you live to enjoy your laurels, and may I have the pleasure of once more shaking you by the hand.

For I shall ever be most sincerely yours

ARTHUR SHAKESPEAR

---

1 He was actually listed as a supernumerary officer in the Waterloo Medal Roll. Placed on half pay in 1818, he died in 1845.

2 Wotton-under-Edge is approximately 8 miles south west of Stroud.

3 Lieutenant Charles Hesse, 18th Hussars, who was believed to be a natural son of the Duke of York, was wounded at Waterloo. Afterwards he joined the Staff Corps in 1816 and he was killed in a duel with Count Léon, a natural son of Napoleon.

4 The 1st Nassau Regiment wore white shako covers at Waterloo. I must thank Erwin Muilwijk for bringing this to my attention.

5 Lieutenant Gawler of the 52nd Regiment; later, as a Lieutenant Colonel, he had claimed in articles published in the *United Service Journal* in 1833 that the 52nd Regiment swept across the field before any other unit and therefore swung the victory. The cavalry claim to have charged before the 52nd came up. He joined the Army as an Ensign in 1810, serving in the Peninsula in 1811–14 at Badajoz, Vittoria, Nivelle, San Munos (wounded in neck) Orthes and Toulouse (wounded by musket ball below right knee). He went on half pay in 1834 and in 1840 was serving in the Government of South Australia. A letter of his is published by Siborne (number 124).

6 A battalion of what is usually described as Hanoverian infantry.

7 This refers to the strong reply by Sir Hussey Vivian in the United Services Magazine repudiating the claims of Gawler for the 52nd Regiment at Waterloo. Gawler and Vivian seem to have both agreed a text published in the *United Service Journal* in 1835.

No. 58 Lieutenant William Slayter Smith[1]
8 March 1835

ADD MS 34705, FO 23

Memorandum of the movements of the 10th Royal Hussars on 18 June 1815

When the advance of the Prussians became obvious, and our left[2] beyond all danger of being turned, Sir Hussey Vivian marched his brigade towards the centre of our position.

We first crossed a bye lane which led from the Wavre road to Mont St Jean, and connects the latter place with Papelotte and the adjoining hamlets, and then passed in rear of a pond and halted us exposed to fire.

We continued our route crossing the road leading from Genappe to Brussels just below Mont St Jean and found ourselves between 6 and 7 o'clock in the centre of the position in rear of the road leading from Nivelles to Wavre about the point where it is intersected by that from Braine l'Alleud. There we found the Household Brigade strangely mixed and reduced to a handful of men and a square of the Foot Guards now lying on the ground, but soon rose after our approach.

When the Duke ordered the line to advance we were in the reverse of the crest in a Column of half squadrons* right in front. At this moment Sir Hussey was ordered by Lord Anglesey to charge with his brigade, who begged that he might gain the crest of the hill, and at least first see his enemy.

The Tenth formed line on its leading half squadron† as it went up the ascent, and on reaching the crest of the position were exposed to a destructive fire of artillery, but instantly charged a motley though strong body of cavalry composed of cuirassiers, lancers, hussars and dragoons, which were much hurt and driven back upon some squares of the Imperial Guard, one of which was either disorganised by this retrograde movement of their own cavalry or by the attack of our infantry, or fire of artillery, and presented a fair opportunity of being destroyed before which Sir Hussey directed Major Howard to form the squadrons as quickly as possible and charge, but by that time the square had resumed its course and Major Howard commanding, orders imparted, charged, lost to life and had [the] leading squadrons considerably damaged. I understood from Lt. Arnold‡ who charged with three squadrons and was badly wounded, that the square was penetrated and severely cut up.

The right and centre squadrons continued pressing the cavalry and driving the artillerymen from their guns, ultimately fell in with a body of cuirassiers§ which still retained some order. These had as much the appearance of British troops from the quantity of red they wore, that they were really confusing. The mistake however was soon rectified and they were dispersed.

Sir Hussey now ordered us to halt and to re-assemble our scattered men, whilst the 18th Hussars charged, which they did on our right in admirable style in an open column of squadrons threading the sinuations of the valley between the original positions of the two armies towards La Belle Alliance.

Towards 9 o'clock the Tenth again advanced and fell upon a mass of French infantry rather beyond La Belle Alliance, who threw themselves on our mercy and claimed protection against the Prussian troops which were now mixing fast with ours on the centre and right of the French position.

Between 9 and 10 o'clock the Duke of Wellington and Marshal Blücher met at La Belle Alliance¶, when the latter took upon himself the further pursuit of the French army.

I never saw any thing of the 1st German Hussars‖ till the 18th charged when I observed them in line to the right of their original position of the Tenth when that regiment formed line and charged. I state they were between the two regiments and ready to support either.

Major General Vandeleur's brigade had made a similar ascent to our right and we mixed with them late in the evening intercepting the discomfited troops of the enemy.

Notes in same hand

* In the plan I have put 1 squadron to seem to all, as I presume the position is merely required.

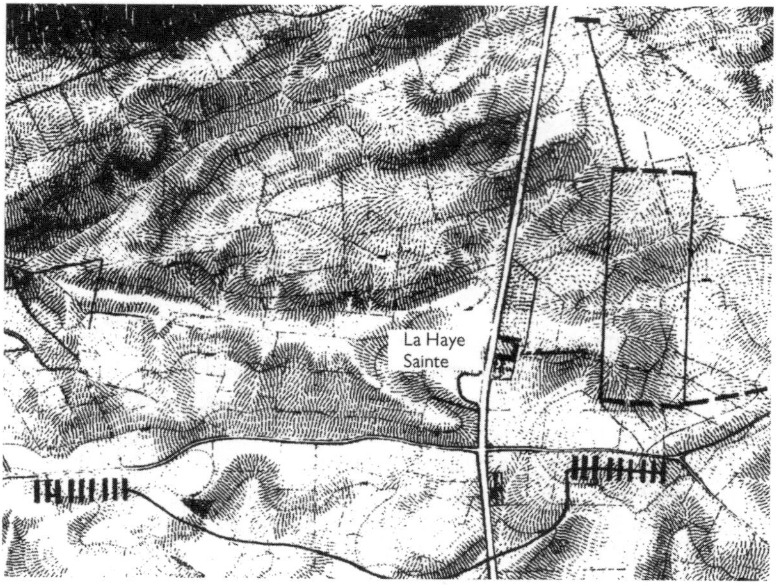

† I am not sure that we did not first form squadrons.
‡ Now Lieutenant Colonel of the 16th Lancers.
§ I afterwards understand that they were part of a regiment of carabineers.
¶ I saw them meet and shake hands.
|| I forget whether the regiment was composed of 3 or 4 squadrons.

---

1 He joined the army as an ensign in the 2nd Garrison Battalion in 1806 and rose to the rank of Lieutenant by 1808. He transferred to the 13th Light Dragoons and was severely wounded at Campo Mayor in 1811. He transferred to the 10th Hussars in 1814 and transferred again to the 1st Life Guards in 1819 but in the same year transferred to the 72nd Foot and retired on half pay as his wound still bothered him. He became Adjutant to the Yorkshire Hussar Yeomanry.

2 The left flank of the Allied Army was now covered by the near approach of the Prussian I Corps, allowing troops to be pulled in to bolster the weakened centre.

No. 59 From the same

The Castle,[1] 25 March 1843

ADD MS 34708, FO 68

My dear Sir

I *took* Lauriston close to the town of Nesle[2] at the tail of a column of French Gendarmes, and so mixed up were we with the French troops, that several deserters took us for French Hussars, and delivered themselves up to us accordingly. The details of the circumstances are interesting enough especially my interview with the Duke when I carried Lauriston to him, who considered him as a *prisoner*.[3]

If I could see you ten minutes I could put you into the possession of the facts of the case and I shall return to England on Tuesday, I will endeavour to see you on Sunday or tomorrow, or I will send you the details from England where I can refer to my notes, but five minutes conversation would determine the weight of my information on this point.

I remain, my dear Sir, yours very faithfully

W SLAYTER SMITH

---

1 Dublin Castle, the Headquarters of the British Army in Ireland.

2 Slayter Smith captured General Lauriston, Aide de Camp to Napoleon, in his carriage on the evening of 26 June. See the footnote, p. 465 of Siborne's *History of the Waterloo Campaign* for more details.

3 Lauriston indicated that he had wanted to defect and make his peace with his King, but Wellington felt that as he had been captured when trying to flee, which meant that he could only be regarded as a prisoner of war.

No. 60 From the same

Kirkham Abbey, Whitwell, Yorkshire, 9 April 1843

ADD MS 34708, FO 77

My dear Sir

I have to offer you many apologies for not having sent these 'notes' sooner, but on my return home (to Green Boyd, Ripon), I found I had so much business to get through in a given time, that I really could not conveniently attend to any thing else. I came here yesterday to find Mr. Smith, who has been on a visit here to some friends during my stay in Ireland, and I had only just time tonight before Friday to copy the notes in question, which of course you will use and quibble as will best suit your interesting history. For your own amusement I could not refrain sending you the conversations I had with the Duke in the autumn of 1827. I think the journal (for I have not your letter with me), states that I took the General on the 28th of June, but in my notes I find the circumstance under the heading of the 26th,[1] and so I have left it there, but I presume it is not one of the least of a historian's difficulties to reconcile these anachronisms.

My notes are very rough, which I trust you will excuse and should you require any explanatory items, have the kindness to address me at Green Boyd, Ripon, Yorkshire.

I remain, my dear Sir, yours very faithfully

W SLAYTER SMITH

I am very sorry not to have seen you at Lady Blakeney's[2] on the 27th.

The following anecdote may perhaps be interesting as it bears upon the capture of General Lauriston

On the 6th October 1827, I met the Duke of Wellington at dinner at Studley Hall near Ripon (Lord Lawrence's) after having escorted him through the town with a squadron of the Yorkshire Hussar Yeomanry. After dinner the Duke spoke to me of my taking Lauriston, the French General, a few days after the battle of Waterloo. The Duke said 'When you brought him in, a Frenchman* whom Fouché had sent to me to treat for a capitulation was in the room, who was so alarmed at hearing that Lauriston was at the door, that he begged to know how he might escape without being recognised. I told him there was but one door and one window, and to take his choice. He preferred the door and escaped by getting behind my back. I remember the whole circumstance perfectly well' added the Duke, 'It was on the night of the siege of Peronne, I sent Lauriston to the King and it was a serious difference to him, having been taken prisoner, instead of joining the King as a Volunteer.'

* Whom in passing I took to be his Master of the Horse.

---

1 It was on the evening of 26 June.

2 Wife of the Right Honourable Sir E. Blakeney, KCB, GCH,. Commander of the troops in Ireland and Colonel of the 7th Regiment of Foot. He was at the capture of Martinique and was a Peninsula veteran, being severely wounded at Albuera and Badajoz. He received a Gold Cross for Martinique with bars for Albuera, Badajoz, Vittoria and the Pyrenees. Eventually be became a Field Marshal and Governor of Chelsea Hospital. He died in 1868.

No. 61 Lieutenant Anthony Bacon[1]
1841

ADD MS 34707, FO 332

Sir,

I have not replied to yours of the 19th before, being unwilling to intrude upon your time which you say is much occupied. I will however take an early opportunity of calling upon you, and since you have such high authority for the supposed mistake of the leading half squadron of the 10th.

I cannot expect you to adopt my version of it, of which I am as positive as though it only took place yesterday, and on this subject I shall propose addressing a letter to you through the medium of the *U. S. Journal*[2] or any other periodical publication, so that at least my testimony may be upon record, as well as Lord Vivian's, and indeed it is a duty I owe to Arnold,[3] one of my earliest and dearest friends.

I shall besides make it my business to find out the officer, if living, who was upon the *left* of the guns we wheeled through. So much as I saw of Vivian in after years, and so often as we talked over the Waterloo day, he never mentioned to me the circumstance as he viewed it, or I think I could easily have convinced him of his erroneous impression, and that the confusion which called forth his anger was just afterwards in my half squadron as I have mentioned; Hardmann[4] the Adjutant if living is mad, or he could have corroborated my statement, but such was the thickness of the smoke that I know of no one else who can. The officers with the half squadrons in the rear could not see at that moment what was going on in their front, of this I am very sure, for I could not see the leading half squadron until I had regained my last interval, then all at once we burst from the darkness of a London November fog into a bright sunshine.

The order was then given 'Front form squadrons', *our horses were very tired, and the ground was very deep, and the leading half squadron instead of slackening, increased its pace to a gallop*, so that it was with great difficulty I came up into line with my half squadron, and certainly not well formed; in short our charge was en *'debandade'*.[5] Of the rear of the column, I cannot speak, but if those squadrons came up in echelon, it must have been upon our right, and thus we perhaps attacked with our right squadrons inverted. I only throw out this hint as worth enquiry to account for the right squadron being upon the left of the rest of the regiment; as you say 'you cannot bring us to the left of the other squadrons across their front.' Their direction was probably changed to the right, when we were charged in flank.

The charge of the German light dragoons which you describe at a later period of the day is precisely what took place upon our right front before we charged, the French dragoons waited for them as I have described, and received them with a volley of carbines,[6] the lancers do not carry those arms; the German line was checked by the fire, and we passed them before we came up with the troops in our front, I could point them out in your model as I did when I saw it some years since, to an inch.

I can mention two circumstances which recall this very vividly to my recollection, Arnold who was leading the squadron was attacked by an officer and soldier of the cuirassiers and I got up to him and took one of his opponents from him, and it was at that moment, we were charged on our right flank by a body of cuirassiers, and all was confusion, in the midst of which a trooper upon a grey horse, reined his horse short up, and holding up his sword called to the men to form upon him, and to him was due the merit of the squadron being so quickly reformed, he was afterwards killed in Howard's charge, or he would have been rewarded. After this period we do not agree as to the *locale*, and I am still in the same state of perfect conviction. I have a letter from Lord George Lennox[7] who says his memory is not very good, but that his impression is that I am right, *and that I may make use of his name in any correspondence I may deem necessary*. I will endeavour to find out the *exact point* where Maitland's brigade of Guards struck into the Charleroi road, and no doubt there are some survivors among them who saw our charge on *their* left front.

We were halted for a few minutes upon the edge of the road before we crossed it, and then it was that Gunning[8] was killed. I saw him fall in the rear of my half squadron, one of the men calling my attention to him. You are perfectly right in your statement that he was killed just before Howard's charge, but as to the spot, your informants and myself differ very widely. I send you a very rough sort of a plan of the advance of Vivian's brigade, should you think it worth while to compare it with other information. Vivian's is no doubt very high authority, and it may be deemed presumptuous in me to differ from it, but I have seen a great deal of cavalry operations, far more than fell to the lot of my master (Lord Vivian), and from experience know how easy it is for, a commander to be mistaken in minutiae, though not in the general operations of the force under his orders, most particularly when circumstances or inclination lead him to conduct attacks in person.

I am well aware of the difficulties attending the description of any field of battle, and that you have chosen is perhaps surrounded by more than most others, on account of the improbability of distinguishing anything that passed beyond your own immediate position on account of the columns of smoke that hung over the field during the whole day.

The conflicting accounts you have received must no doubt be numerous, and the selection a most difficult task. I will do myself the pleasure of calling on you as soon as I can bring sufficient evidence of Howard's charge having been on our left of the road;

that fact established, I have little fear but that my statement will be received as authority with regard to the alleged blunder of our leading half squadron.

I have the honour to be Sir your most obedient servant

ANTHONY BACON

Annotations to the diagram

A Advance of Vivian's brigade in open column of half squadrons.
B Cuirassiers and other cavalry attacked by 10th.
C Advance of 1st Hussars after the charge of the 10th & before Howard charged.
D German light dragoons.
E French dragoons.
F Right squadron of 10th reformed.
G Right squadron of 10th halted to let 18th pass.
H 18th Hussars.
J Cuirassiers who charged the right squadron of the 10th.
K French cavalry before the charge.
L French cavalry.
M Imperial Guards
N Advance of General Maitland's brigade of Guards about the spot where I met them.
O French cavalry.
P Hanoverians who refused to come to Howard's assistance.
Q The cross is about the spot where I met the Duke attended by Lord G. Lennox only.
R Right squadron 10th.
S Imperial Guards. The column formed in square before Howard charged.
T Imperial Guards. The column which fired into the 18th as they crossed the road.
U About the position of the centre and left squadrons of the 10th if they followed up the enemy's cavalry at the time. Vivian made use of the 18th and halted the right squadron of the 10th.

---

1 Bacon was severely wounded in the last charge led by Major Howard and lay all night on the battlefield. He was appointed a captain in the 13th Light Dragoons in 1818 and a Major in the 17th Dragoons in 1825. He retired from the British service in 1827. He served in the Portuguese army from 1832–3 as Colonel Commandant of their cavalry. Afterwards General Anthony Bacon KTS, he died on 2 July 1864.

2 *United Service Journal.*

3 Lieutenant Robert Arnold, afterwards Lieutenant Colonel 16th Light Dragoons. He died on 20 August 1839.

4 Lieutenant Samuel Hardman, Adjutant, went on half pay in 1816 and died on 25 November 1855. It would appear he left the army due to mental health problems.

5 French for 'helter skelter'.

6 A short musket issued to some forms of cavalry, it was notoriously inaccurate however it seems to have been used here to good effect.

7 Lord George Lennox of the 9th Light Dragoons, Aide de Camp to Lord Wellington, son of the Duke of Richmond of ball fame. His father the Duke and youngest brother, Lord William Pitt Lennox, visited the field in civilian clothing while the battle raged and were noted in numerous memoirs of that day. The Duke of Richmond remained in civilian clothes as although a full General, he recognized his lack of campaign experience (having

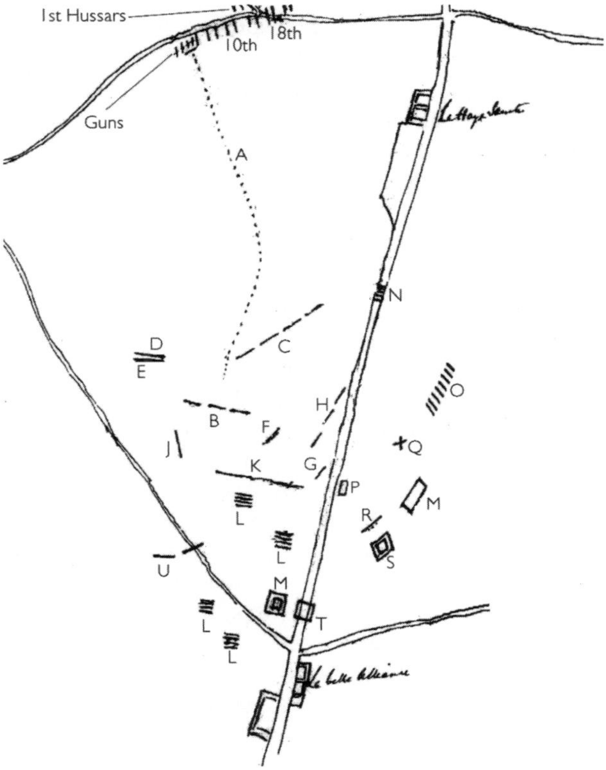

been Lord Lieutenant of Ireland 1807–13). Had he been in uniform his rank would have placed him second only to Wellington himself as the senior British officer present. Lord George's eldest brother, Captain the Earl of March of the 52nd Foot, also served at Waterloo as an extra ADC to the Prince of Orange. Lord George joined the army as a cornet in 1811 and served in the Peninsula, receiving a General Service Medal with six bars for Vittoria, Pyrenees, Nivelle, Nive, Orthes and Toulouse. He became MP for West Sussex between 1832–41 and Gentleman of the Bedchamber to Prince Albert. He died in 1873.

8 As already recorded he is not listed among the killed by Dalton, but this letter corroborates the statement of Captain Taylor above.

No. 62 From the same[1]
No date

ADD MS 34708, FO 162

I have read your first edition of the history of the battle of Waterloo with the greatest interest, and as you say in your preface, you will be glad to receive any *'well authenticated information from eye witnesses'*. I venture to call your attention to some parts, which appear to me to be erroneous.

I of course in common with others can only speak of what took place in the immediate positions occupied by the brigade in which I served, and at times only of the squadron to which I was attached, the right squadron of the 10th Hussars.

1 In the first place, where you have done me the honour of mentioning my name, you have made a mistake in the individual, I never was in the 23rd Dragoons, but retired from the British service as Senior Major of the 17th Lancers in 1827, and subsequently entered the Portuguese army, and commanded the cavalry during the War of Liberation.

2 You have omitted to mention the long halt of a large portion of the cavalry at Grammont on the morning of the 16th, our brigade with others was halted there for some hours, and at length on moving to the front we were ordered to throw away our corn,[2] and move upon Enghien, Nivelles and Quatre Bras at the trot. We arrived on the ground in open column of squadrons about sunset, the head of the column close upon the Charleroi road, our right resting on the Nivelles road, thus opening the wood of Bossu. A few shot were fired at us from the enemy's batteries, but without effect; had it not been for this halt, notwithstanding we did not march till the morning of the 16th, much of the cavalry could have been at Quatre Bras by 2 o'clock. The halt was not in accordance with the Duke's orders (appendix 14 & 15 vol. 1 of your work[3]). According to the first order, all the cavalry should have been at Ninove, Lord Anglesey's head-quarters on the night of the 15th and the second order which must have reached Ninove before 12 o'clock that night would have put the whole cavalry on the field at Quatre Bras before the action commenced.[4]

3 The patrol, which escorted Sir Alexander Gordon[5] on the morning of the 17th, was as you state commanded by Captain Grey.[6] The French *vidette* on the height above Ligny was not seen by our patrol until we arrived on the rising ground opposite the height on which he was posted, and when we first discovered him, our party was not seen by *him*. There appeared to be a dismounted sentry at the door of a house in the bottom, and I was ordered with a party to patrol up to it, whilst Captain Grey remained with the larger portion of his troop, concealed from the enemy by the side of the road, it was on my party moving on, that the vidette began circling and fired his carbine, the party in the house between us immediately fell back on the high road. I was recalled, a few cavalry galloped up to the videttes on the height, but did not advance. We then retired till we came to a cross road, which a peasant informed us was the Prussian line of retreat.[7] Captain Grey remained on the high road with directions to watch the enemy's movements, and fall leisurely back to the regiment, whilst Sir A. Gordon took me with a small escort on the track of the Prussians, whose rearguard of cavalry we came up with, formed in a close column on the side of a hill, and in right front of a village, about which I remember there was a good deal of water and marshy ground, which from the distance from the high road I take to be either Mellery or Gentinnes as laid down in your map. After communicating with them we returned to Quatre Bras by some cross roads and rejoined the regiment at the same time, a little before 9 o'clock, with Captain Grey who had not been followed by the enemy.[8]

4 The heavy rain commenced immediately before our retreat, the 18th Hussars relieved our skirmishers and the circumstance of the rain preventing their using their

carbines, and that they attacked the enemy's skirmishers with their swords is fresh on my memory, as also the sudden cessation of the shelling which began to be rather unpleasant. The cavalry was at that time formed in three lines, not two, the light dragoons forming the centre line.

Vandeleur's stupidity very nearly compromised Vivian's brigade; he never was fit for the command of cavalry, as all those who like myself served in his brigade in the Peninsula will have some recollection of: he was always at variance with Frederick Ponsonby who commanded the 12th and always making some blunder. The above is of little further importance, than showing that the Duke had communicated with the Prussian vanguard on the morning on the 17th. All that passed with our brigade in covering the retreat of our left column is exceedingly correct.

5 On the morning of the 18th about an hour and a half before the battle commenced a curious circumstance took place in front of our brigade. A French lancer rode up to the left squadron of our line to within 20 yards of our men, turned his horse leisurely to the left and rode down the whole line till he came to Vandeleur's brigade, when he turned off towards the French position, and stretching into a gallop regained his corps without a shot being fired at him; he was at first supposed to be a deserter, and when his true character was seen, in place of a shot he received a cheer from some of our men for his extreme boldness. I can add my testimony as to the correctness of the hour when the Prussian skirmishers first appeared on our left, it was certainly an hour before Napoleon threw back his right flank, that change of position I suppose must have been preparatory to the march of the 6th Corps;[9] we did not see these troops leave their ground for we were shortly afterwards moved to our right. The exact period of the arrival of the Prussians has, I know, been the subject of much dispute, and I am glad to find your statement agrees with what the officers and men of Vivian's brigade could not well be mistaken in, for in our position we were free from the smoke that covered the field upon our right, and could distinctly see all that passed on the French right, our own left.

Colonel Percy passed us on the morning of the 18th on his way to the Prussian headquarters, and returned before the action commenced, telling us that the Prussian corps of General Bülow[10] was on its march to join us.

After forming upon the plateau in the right rear of La Haye Sainte, and upon the right of the remnant of Lord Edward Somerset's and Ponsonby's brigades, we were exposed to a murderous fire; Colonel Quentin, Captains Grey, Gurwood and Wood[11] were quickly wounded and our men and horses fell fast. Lord Robert Manners who had hitherto commanded the right squadron, took command of the regiment. Lieutenant Arnold succeeded to the command of the right squadron (Captain Grey being wounded) and I took Arnold's place in command of the 2nd half squadron, all this passed in a much shorter space of time than I have taken to write it – the Captain of the 2nd Troop was not present in the action. I am very particular in this on account of a mistake you state to have occurred in the leading half squadron shortly afterwards; a confusion there was, but it occurred in a very different manner, and arose from a different cause to that you describe as I will presently explain, and as it is calculated to cast a slur upon the late Lt. Colonel Arnold, one of the best officers present on that eventful day, one of my dearest friends, and one of the last officers in the British army likely to have made such a blunder, I deem it imperative on me to enter into an explanation of the facts, which will I am sure be corroborated by the officer of artillery who caused the confusion, if he is still living, for he cannot but remember the circumstance.

The smoke was so thick at this period that I could not see further than a few file from the right of our centre squadron, therefore did not see the Nassau troops giving way, but a column of the Brunswick infantry was stopped [going] to the rear, bent upon the interval between our right and centre squadrons; Lt. Arnold rode out upon their right flank with myself, and I have no doubt the officers of our centre squadron did the same upon the left, when the column faced about, and marched to the front. At that moment my first horse was shot and I was scarcely remounted before Vivian rode up and ordered the advance in line, and subsequent wheel of half squadrons to the right as you describe. What was passing in our front, was impossible to tell, for we could not see ten yards from us, but the shower of musket balls coming from the dense columns of smoke told of a formidable enemy close to us.

I now come to the wheel by half squadrons through the battery you describe as commanded by Captain Napier.[12] I must premise by reminding you that it is *the squadron officer, not the half squadron leader* of the *leading half squadron* who gives the word of command to the latter, Lt. Arnold had halted in front of the guns with his horse's head towards them, and as I came up with the 2nd half squadron to the pivot, one of the guns was fired directly between Arnold's horse's head and mine, and some others through the leading half squadron while in the act of wheeling, which threw it into confusion, and the hearty damn you state as coming from Vivian, came from Arnold to the artillery officer. Arnold desired me to halt after completing the wheel with my half squadron, while he reformed the leading half squadron (Captain Grey's troop in which both he and myself served) which was done in less than a minute, for the men were only scattered by the fire from our own guns, and did not wheel to the right by a mistake of their own or their officer, besides Vivian had gone to the front after ordering the wheel to the left, as it was impossible from that position, on account of the smoke, to direct the advance of our column. The account has been jumbled by your informants with what took place immediately afterwards, and before we got clear of the smoke. I should say we inclined considerably to our left after passing these guns, and subsequently a little to the right on descending from our position. Just after we moved off from our guns to the front, a shell burst in front of my half squadron doing some mischief, and my second horse was shot, I was consequently obliged to dismount a hussar, and the second half squadron being without an officer lost its interval, and was in some confusion. Lt Hardman, the Adjutant came (with *a hearty damn* I have no doubt) from the General, and met me mounted on a troop horse coming up with the half squadron at a gallop to regain the lost interval. I mention this because I think it must have been jumbled with the affair of the leading half squadron by those who cannot speak to the fact like myself, and I most certainly assert that no wheel to the right or rear was made, but that the confusion took place exactly as I have above described, and this circumstance I trust you will set right in your second edition in justice to Arnold, who was too old and tried a soldier to make such a blunder. We were in the 16th together in the Peninsula, and although he was well known, and his memory cherished, by all old soldiers of the Duke's army, still by others, who knew not his worth, a censure may be cast where it never was deserved.

From this point I shall be very minute because your account does not agree with the movements of our brigade as they appeared to me.

I had scarcely regained my position in the column when the order *'front form squadrons'* was repeated. From the pace of the leading half squadron it was with difficulty I got up to it. In going up we saw the German light dragoons charge, not in column, but in line, and not lancers but dragoons who received them with a fire of carbines, which did not appear to do much mischief, but it checked the charge, and the circumstance of these dragoons being formed on (what in Wiltshire and the lower parts of Berkshire is called) a linshot, (so the name is pronounced, a turf bank dividing the corn tracts in the open country) gave them a decided advantage, and they appeared as if determined on resistance; of them we saw no more, for we were ordered to charge the cavalry in our front which was rather thrown back from the dragoons which the Germans had charged and these were principally cuirassiers mixed with lancers and dragoons; they did not wait to receive us, but went about when we were close upon them. After we had pursued them about 200 yards, a body of cuirassiers charged our right squadron on its right flank, and forced us to the left, this was the attack of cuirassiers you mention, it certainly did not take place before we attacked, or I must have seen it, being in command of the 2nd half squadron. On being charged in the way mentioned, we must have been carried 100 yards or more to our left before we reformed, which we did, our right being brought very much forward from our original direction so that had we continued a direct march from that point, we should have passed La Belle Alliance on our right flank. The cuirassiers that charged us took that direction, and we again became pursuers. It must have been at that moment that our centre and left squadrons passed our right flank and got among the enemy's cavalry, for we saw no more of them. We had just come close upon the Charleroi road when Vivian rode up and said *'halt 10th and let the 18th come up'*. Major Howard came up to us at that time and of course took the command, Gunning also came with him, he asked me where his troop was, I had scarcely told him he had better remain with us when he was shot. When we halted, there was a heavy *column* of the Imperial Guards on the opposite side of the road, marching in a diagonal direction towards La Belle Alliance inclining to the right, and on its left flank was a large number of mounted officers, on the high road and close to La Belle Alliance was another *column*, and on our right of the road, and on our right flank which was thrown back about a quarter distance, was a *square* of the Imperial Guard behind which some cavalry was reforming. The 18th Hussars came up upon our left and the 1st German Hussars were advancing in the same direction, their right thrown forward, and about 300 yards in our rear. We were then far in advance of any of our troops, and Vivian sent to request Vandeleur would support him, and we afterwards heard that the answer brought back, was, that he was Vivian's senior officer and he would receive no orders from him. The 18th were formed towards the column I have mentioned, and advanced in a beautiful line across the road to charge, as they crossed the high road, a heavy fire was poured into their right flank from the column formed on the high road. At that moment some cavalry appeared in the left front of the

18th, they rode furiously into them thereby changing their former direction rather to the left, the 18th had hitherto been lookers on, and I never saw men so bent upon destruction as they were when let loose. Vivian rode after the 18th at full speed *first desiring Howard* to form the 10th and charge the column in his front, the column however in the mean time had nearly gained the top of the hill had formed square, for they could see the advance not only of the German Hussars, but of Vandeleur's, and Grant's brigades, and other cavalry. Howard advanced at a trot, and when we got within I should say 150 yards or less of them, Arnold seeing a battalion cloaked in red, had come up close on our rear and on our left of the high road *persuaded Howard* to halt, and let him go for the infantry to fire into the square before he charged. It proved to be a Hanoverian battalion and the officer in command refused to come to our assistance – Arnold gave him the order in Vivian's name – but he still refused saying that he did not care for General Vivian, that he was not his General, and his force was not sufficient to attack that square; Arnold finding neither threat nor persuasion of any avail returned to us and we immediately charged, they reserved their fire till we were close upon them, and the havoc was frightful. Howard, Arnold and myself rode close together in front of the squadron, and were all hit about the same moment, and it was *the right squadron* of the regiment reinforced by some men who had probably got forward in our first charge from the other troops and were carried away in the melee when we were charged in flank by the cuirassiers. When we inclined to the right before our first charge, the centre and left squadron would naturally have followed the movement, and the right squadron being charged; as it was, would have uncovered the front of the centre squadron, and then it was that they must have come upon the cavalry as you describe, they never passed us on our left, but I can no more speak to what the other squadrons were doing at that period, than any officer or man with them can say what we were about. I have said this much to show you that it was the right squadron with a few men of other troops which was with Major Howard when he was killed and not some stragglers collected there, it was his command after Lord R. Manners succeeded to the command of the regiment, and he had no opportunity of joining us before, besides it would have been very odd if Arnold and myself should have lost his squadrons; the men of my own troop were with me, and that is conclusive to the question of the squadron.

That our charge was on the left of the road and up the hill towards the French right of La Belle Alliance I give you the following as corroborative evidence.

On my way to the rear after being wounded I came upon the Duke attended, it is true, *by one officer only*, but that officer was *Lord George Lennox*, for he rode up to me and directed me the way to La Haye Sainte where I should probably find a surgeon. The Duke was not 200 yards in the rear of our squadron at this time, and about half that distance from the high road; when I got to the road, I turned to my right, and made [out] Maitland's brigade of Guards marching along it, I passed on their left flank, at this time I could scarcely sit upon my horse, and I cannot readily forget Colonel Gunthorpe[13] who was with other officers at the head of the column sending a man to lead my horse, I remember passing La Haye Sainte, and soon afterwards being joined by Arnold and several wounded men of the regiment, after which I became senseless, I can remember nothing till I was put into my gig with Colonel Quentin the following morning. Had our charge been on our right of the high road I must have turned to my left on reaching the high road, and not to the right, in this I cannot be mistaken.

[UNSIGNED]

---

1 The narrative is not dated nor signed, however it is recorded as being written by Bacon in the British Library Catalogue and the handwriting appears to match his earlier letter.

2 While on the march it was sensible to carry a sack of corn or a bundle of hay, as supplies could not be guaranteed, but when going into action these supplies would be discarded as a dangerous encumbrance.

3 This refers to Siborne's *History of the Waterloo Campaign*, which was originally published in two volumes. Appendix 14 refers to the initial order sent around 6 pm on the 15th, for the cavalry to form up at Ninove; while Appendix 15 refers to the follow up order of 10 pm on the 15th, ordering the cavalry to Enghien as soon as possible. They however do not include orders to move on to Quatre Bras as Bacon infers.

4 As to the question of when it was possible for the cavalry to arrive at Quatre Bras, let us look at the situation. An order made out at 5 pm had to be written for each brigade commander and could not be sent much before 7 pm; from Brussels it could realistically travel the 16 miles to Ninove in three hours. Orders would therefore be with the various brigades, ordering them to form up at Ninove by 10 pm and with individual regiments by 11 pm. It must be stated however that many corps report not receiving orders before 2/3 am. The second order could not have been received before 2/3 am., and if a night march had been attempted (always a haphazard venture), the cavalry could have marched the 12 miles to Enghien by 6 am, even allowing for their slow progress at night. Had this happened exactly to plan, then the cavalry would be within approximately 25 miles (across difficult roads) from Quatre Bras, no more than a six-hour journey including rest periods. The contention that the cavalry could have been at Quatre Bras by 2 pm is therefore theoretically possible. However in actuality, the cavalry and attached horse artillery does not appear to have been raised until 3 am, possibly to avoid a night march, and marched at 5 am, arriving at Enghien only at 9 am. Here they awaited orders until 12 am, therefore not reaching the battlefield until approximately 8 pm because of the congestion on the roads. Had the orders been received at Enghien on arrival, it was still possible for the cavalry to have arrived at Quatre Bras by approximately 5 pm when the battle still raged and although much fatigued, could have been very useful in assisting the counter offensive launched by Wellington, to regain the ground lost earlier in the day.

5 The Honourable Lieutenant Colonel Sir Alexander Gordon, 3rd Foot Guards, on the Staff as Aide de Camp to Lord Wellington. He joined the Guards in 1806 and had served in the Peninsula as an ADC, carrying home the Ciudad Rodrigo dispatch and being severely wounded at the Pyrenees. He died the night of 18 June in Wellington's quarters, of wounds received at Waterloo.

6 Captain John Grey of the 10th, afterwards Lieutenant Colonel of the Scots Greys. He died at Sidmouth on 21 December 1843.

7 The fact that the peasant so clearly indicated the route of retreat of the Prussians is illuminating. The French failed miserably to obtain any information of the retreat, indicating their failure to send patrols out in this direction. Napoleon only ordered patrols to the East, in the direction that *he* was convinced they had retired.

8 Bacon states that they reported to Wellington at 9 am, however most other sources state that Gordon returned about 7.30 am.

9 The French VI Corps commanded by the Comte de Lobau was held in reserve until being moved to form a flank guard on the French right to meet the challenge from the Prussian forces as they arrived.

10 General Friedrich Wilhelm Bülow von Dennewitz commanding the Prussian IV Corps which fought bitterly for control of Plançenoit to the rear of the French right flank.

11 Captain Charles Wood had joined the 10th in November 1814. He had previously served in the Peninsula with the 52nd Foot as a Deputy Assistant Adjutant General, being slightly wounded at Busaco. He was afterwards placed on half pay on 5 April 1821. Bacon states that he was wounded and is listed as such in the *London Gazette* of 1 July 1815, Dalton omits to show him as wounded.

12 Second Captain Charles Napier of Bolton's battery of foot artillery, who had only just assumed command following the death of Captain Samuel Bolton during the attack of the Imperial Guard. He became a brevet major in 1819, but retired from the Army by selling his commission in 1827. He died at Lisburn, Ireland on 20 June 1849. It is also conceivable that command had devolved upon First Lieutenant George Pringle at this period, as soon after the defeat of the Guard, Napier received eight wounds from a shell burst. This confusion might explain the rash act of firing through friendly troops so censured by Bacon.

13 Lieutenant and Captain J. Gunthorpe, 1st Foot Guards, Major of Brigade to Major General Maitland's 1st Brigade of Guards. He served in the Peninsula and received a General Service Medal with three bars for Corunna, Nivelle and Nive. He was promoted to lieutenant colonel in the army in 1821. He retired from the army in 1833.

The 18th Hussars

No. 63 Lieutenant Colonel, The Honourable Henry Murray[1]

Wimbledon, 27 December 1834

ADD MS 34704, FO 106

This letter was originally published in Siborne's Waterloo Letters (number 76), but is incorrectly dated as 1835. A great deal of the letter was omitted by Siborne including copious notes. The complete letter had been entered here; the text left out by Siborne is printed in italics. Murray's annotations are marked by [A, B,] etc., to represent his manuscript symbols.

Sir,

Being absent from home, to which I returned only a few days ago, it has not been in my power to send you sooner the answer requested by the letter with which you honoured me.

In the published account of Sir Hussey Vivian, all I know of the 6th Brigade of cavalry at Waterloo is detailed.

That I could aid a work undertaken with so much zeal and labour, and deserving much respect and encouragement as yours would really be a pleasure to me; but after a minute, careful and repeated examination of General Vivian's letters, and those of Major Gawler and Sir Thomas Reynell[2] and comparison of them with my own less perfect recollection and memoranda, I have not been able to ascertain anything new or interesting.

To send you loose conjecture or uncertain incident would neither be very reputable to me nor at all useful to you; it would yield rubbish rather than material.

There is a great deal more difficulty attending all narrative of this nature than is imagined by those who have not seriously attempted it; for when varying circumstances, witnessed at the time under great interruption, are sought historically after the lapse of many years, suggestion occurs as remembrance, surmise as fact; the difficulty then, with whatever veracious intention, is to tell the truth, the whole truth and nothing but the truth.

You will find on the opposite page answers to your questions; but should you observe anything at variance with the before named authentic and intelligent statements, you will exercise a very fair caution in receiving my version, since I did not make a memorandum at the time and was on that ground only during the battle.

I have the honour to be, Sir, your faithful and obedient humble servant

HENRY MURRAY
COLONEL 18TH HUSSARS

Memoranda

'What was the particular formation of the 18th Hussars?'

The formation of the 18th Hussars was three squadrons in line. Its left to Genappe road; its right to the 10th Hussars#. Squares to its front according to the position.

The position of the brigade was nearly behind where the plan, attached to Major Gawler's statement 3 places the Brunswickers, its right extending towards Hougoumont, but the left of the 18th was near, rather than 'nearly brushing' the Genappe road.*

Seven o'clock must have been about the time when Lord Anglesey and General Vivian were riding in our front – the action was vehement at the moment.

 # I should so entirely fail in tracing the formations with accuracy, that I should only suggest errors in so doing and therefore return the plan without having marked them whom I have said elsewhere will more usefully supply this deficiency.

** Sir Hussey Vivian says, 'nearly touching', he has seen the ground since I have.*

'What was the formation of that part of the enemy's forces &c.?'

At the precise period about 7 o'clock, the smoke made it impossible to see what was in our front.

None of the enemy came on the crest where the 18th were, nor I believe where the 10th were.

From the time when the 6th Brigade of cavalry replaced the household brigade, until after having moved in column of half squadrons parallel to the position, and wheeled again so as to be moving perpendicularly to their original front. I do not imagine the enemy were at all perceptible; but then the smoke clearing away (though under cannonade on our right flank) the enemy would be seen at all events to the head of the column.

But when the line was formed to the front – (an operation interrupted by cavalry charging the right squadron of the 10th and some casualty from fire amongst the 18th) as also afterwards when the 10th having gone on with General Vivian to charge, the 18th was ordered to remain, there was a continued fire on the 18th from the front, which prevented any accurate observation of the enemy, so that a real knowledge of what they were and how disposed (beyond seeing that they were there and pretty near) was more the result of subsequent sudden contact than previous observation.

It must however be recollected that a short distance will make a great change as to the power of observation.

Hence the view of General Vivian who had been superintending the charge of the 10th must before his return to the 18th, have embraced several points in which the enemy could be seen not attainable to those stationary under fire – and this, although the direction of the charge of the 10th diverged.

'Upon examining the plan you will find that I have marked with a pencil on the different fields in and near which the 18th Hussars were generally posted.'

I have looked over the plan very often and attentively. The general description of the nature of the cultivation is likely to be correct. Yet I can only say it appears to me such. At this distance of time I cannot affirm it.

I perfectly, however remember, that the luxuriance of the first crops we came in upon (on the extreme left, at the commencement of the action) made us sorry to tread it down.

Afterwards, the state of the ground (very wet at first) was so devastated and trodden down that later in the day hardly any opinion could be formed of where its cultivation had been.

With respect to ploughed or fallow land, we may have passed over some, but I should think no more than you have marked in pencil.

We were almost the whole day going (as it is termed / in dirt, and therefore when we touched on the ploughed land it hardly was remarked, for nearly all was deep.

'I shall feel very much obliged by your affording me in addition to the information already solicited, any remarks &c.'

As this answer must embrace various considerations, allow me, Sir, to mention that I was the only Regimental Field Officer with the 18th Hussars during the campaign as my Adjutant was severely wounded at Waterloo; – which occasioned many duties to devolve on me next day, so that I had not leisure to revisit the field of battle before we quitted its vicinity – and I have not been there since.

Seldom using any quarter but the bivouac I did not make memoranda of events then fresh in my recollection; so many years have since gone by that I cannot now pretend to the same accuracy of memory and therefore must be unavoidably more restricted in answering enquiries on the subject.

The 10th and 18th were on the left at the commencement of the battle.

The 18th had bivouacked at Verd–Cocou[A] the night of the 17th, throwing out a picket to Ohain.

Coming down upon luxuriant crops, the brigade took up its position, the 10th being on the right of the 18th in line.

The action soon commenced, and General Vivian[B] rode forward to observe its progress. The brigade stood under cannonade frequently, but not attended with serious casualty.

To us on our regimental posts the prevailing fire seemed towards the centre of the Armies,[C] and to our right, very heavy and continued.

It is impossible at this distance of time that I can trace step by step the progress of the brigade from the left to the right, but I will mention as consecutively as I can the chain of events which constitute my recollection of it.

A Prussian officer came with the intelligence of the advance of that army. After some time, Major the Honourable Henry Percy,[4] one of the Duke of Wellington's aides-de-camp, came to ascertain how soon the Prussians might be expected.

Major Percy told us of the fall of Sir William Ponsonby,[5] and the severe wound (or supposed death) of Colonel Frederick Ponsonby.[6]

After a time we joined General Vandeleur's brigade again to our right.

I may here mention that when we were thus moving to our right the day had improved, and whilst ourselves were less exposed to fire, we had a better view of the action.

When with General Vandeleur's brigade we heard of the wound (then supposed mortal) of Colonel Hay of the 16th Light Dragoons.[7]

Afterwards the 6th Brigade quitted General Vandeleur's and proceeding[D] right in front, and passing a little to the rear, went on again more towards the right. About this time I believe Colonel Quentin, of the 10th, was wounded.

[E]About the time we crossed the Genappe road there was a wonderful column of French pouring down from their position. I mention this because I have been told that it was seven o'clock when we passed Lord Edward Somerset's brigade, but I have no idea that it could be seven till some time afterwards.

The brigade now began to tread the ground of devastation; the pavement of the Genappe road was torn up and scattered.

[F]Lord Edward Somerset's brigade,[8] strengthened by the addition of what had been Ponsonby's, was dwindled to two various squadrons.

General Vivian asked 'Lord Edward, where is your brigade?' 'Here,' said Lord Edward. The ground was strewed with wounded, over whom it was hardly possible sometimes to avoid moving.

Wounded or mutilated horses wandered or turned in circles. The noise was deafening, and the air of ruin and desolation that prevailed wherever the eye could reach gave no inspiration of victory.

Lord Uxbridge, in hussar uniform, mounted on a common troop-horse (his own being exhausted), rode with General Vivian a short time in our front.

Colonel Sir Felton Hervey[9] came to exchange his wounded horse, and in the act of mounting a troop horse of the 18th exclaimed, 'Lord Wellington has won the battle, if we could but get the *damned Belgians*[10] to advance.' Then galloped to the front.

We moved in column of half-squadrons to the right, parallel to the position. Then wheeled the head of the column to the left, so as to proceed perpendicularly to the front.

In the first part of this movement wounded British infantry were lying on the ground, when we changed into the new direction; General Vandeleur's brigade (I believe) on our right cheered.

We were cannonaded upon our right flank, and some casualty I think took place amongst the 10th, who were leading. I have an uncertain recollection, but believe it must have been somewhere about this time I[G] saw Sir Colin Campbell.[11]

As to the fire, by which we were inconvenienced when about to form to our front, proceeded partly from our own artillery's mistaking us when thus advanced, it was understood General Vivian had sent to remedy this mistake.

I cannot determine the time, nor exactly what we were doing, when some Nassau troops with white caps fell back upon us, and were forced forward, in which I remember my adjutant[12] instrumental; nor can I state[H] when it was that I either heard myself, or was told at the moment, the infantry was advancing.

[I]Perhaps it is not irrelevant to mention that when we were proceeding in column of half-squadrons to the front, the earth thrown up by a cannon-shot falling under my horse struck me hard in the face and breast.

[J]In forming line to our front some of the 23rd Light Dragoons and Germans came rapidly across, and the right squadron of the 10th was attacked by cuirassiers. Some casualty from fire happened too amongst the 18th.

General Vivian (who I think had then changed from his own horse to a grey troop-mare of the 10th) had just been giving directions with regard to our formation.

Ordering the 18th to remain where we were, the General went on with the 10th to direct their charge.

The charge of the 10th I believe was in a direction diverging to the right, and bringing their left shoulders forward. [K]The 18th remained under fire, until Sir Hussey Vivian's return to them.

I remember Sergeant-Major Jeffs[13] and others making use of the expression which General Vivian mentions before we moved off to charge; the General being a great favourite with the 18th.

Where we stood in line there were (as I have reason to think) in our front French artillery, cavalry, and infantry near us. General Vivian himself accompanied me to give me the original direction, and in that direction when put into it the regiment proceeded onwards.

That direction diverged to the left (as the 10th charge had to the right), bringing our right shoulders forward.

It may be mentioned that I led from the centre squadron in front of Captain Luard[14] (who very ably commanded it), and whose coverer was Sergeant Colgan.[15]

However slow the description of a charge of cavalry, the grass has no time to grow under their horses' feet.

I understood that Major Harris[16] was wounded in[L] our charge, but when, I am not aware. His animation I well remember when things looked worst.

On proceeding onwards in the direction that had been given us for our charge, we soon crossed a chaussee or road (the horses clattering as they went over at a gallop). When coming from our left and slanting towards our right some French artillery made a push to cross us at a gallop. But it would not do, we were on them (I ordered the guns to be secured, the drivers not hurt); when again we were in with some cavalry (on our right formed up, cuirassiers and other cavalry, and, as I think, some guns), an officer in front of them rode forward and fired at me, but the 18th were among them with their swords. The enemy gave way and were forced over the field.

The charge then ceased to be compact, [M]for the assailants and those who were in retreat were intermingled pell-mell, and that as hard as they could ride.

The cavalry, in trying to escape, rather bore to their right hand, then went quite straight to the rear. So that the original direction of the 18th having been to the left, and that direction (leaning down to intercept the French artillery coming from the left) having been still further increased, was altered by a sudden swerve to the right hand to attack the cavalry formed to our right, and that alteration more or less increased in pursuit. As this was a chase, compactness was out of the question.

But soon we came into ground entirely covered with French infantry retreating, not in a body, but individually, yet with none of that hurry and confusion that might be imagined when thus suddenly ridden in upon, and especially some of the Ancienne Garde might be remarked for their coolness and bold countenance (one nearly bayoneted me as I passed). Numbers of these were cut down, and my orderly (a man named Dwyer[17]) cut down five or six in rapid succession, the pursuit of the cavalry continuing.

On our right were some squares of French infantry, but out of the stream of attack of the 18th as they pressed on the heels of the cavalry.

The first pull upon their horses was where a party of the 18th, with Lieutenant Woodberry[18] I know (perhaps with Lieutenant Waldie[19]), were well formed up. Though few, ready and anxious to act.

The field they had passed was cleared, and a considerable distance had been traversed as hard as the horses could go,[N] and now they stood with some squares of French on the opposite bank halted.

There was a dip or hollow in the ground between the party of the 18th and the squares, perhaps a fence, but quite close.

The squares so posted were inaccessible with any prospect of making impression upon them by even a much larger force of cavalry than the party I have mentioned, especially with troop horses after so hard a gallop.

I moved them a little to the left, where the ground favoured them more, and others joined us.

However, as I was told that the signal had been given for us some time before to retire – as this was too close to the enemy for forming up the regiment after a charge, and nothing was immediately in our power to do – which was evident to all – I put them about in order to fall back upon our reserve.

The charge, as also the previous movements, had been attended with casualty, but retiring with a view to formation proved infinitely more destructive. For as the light was uncertain, they crossed upon some fire, whether the enemy's or Prussian's (perhaps the latter), which mowed them down many at a time more than once.

In returning there was a party of men with me at first; so many fell I do not think another man remained.[O] This happened near a barn or farm building on our right as we came back. I then joined others of the 18th, and the first person of the brigade I met and spoke to was Sir Robert Gardiner.[20]

Lord Robert Manners[21] was forming the 10th when the 18th came to form up with them; Major Grant,[22] I remember, assisting me in doing so.

The attention having been directed to the artillery on our left, it was more as the cavalry formed on the right drew out in their escape that their description was observable to those who had charged them.

It must also be observed that there is not leisure nor opportunity for remarking what is even at an inconsiderable distance whilst engaged in charge or pursuit.

I am not aware of having seen any British infantry whilst we were employed in the pursuit. Where our pursuit ended I do not imagine that any of our infantry could be in our front, that front being occupied by French squares.

But not having been subsequently over the ground on which the battle was fought, I cannot give any guess at the place where the charge which I was concerned in terminated,[P] but that it was far from the place whence we had started for the charge there can be no doubt.

The various little occurrences I can call to mind would occupy some minutes, and the rate of going, taking divergence and check into calculation, must have been at the rate of ten miles an hour at the least, probably more.

The 10th and 18th formed up together, and after a time were moved still further to the right, and, the action having concluded, bivouacked.[Q]

In the attack the 1st Hussars[23] had been in reserve.

In the course of the day the brigade had moved from left to the right.

Sir Hussey Vivian severally addressed the regiments that night in commendation of their conduct.

It may not be quite right for an inferior to give any judgement upon his superior officer, but I have no doubt, that the General's example and the confidence entertained in him by all ranks added to the zeal of the 6th Brigade of cavalry by the knowledge that their exertions would be well directed.

So much has been said of what has been termed the crisis of Waterloo, that the only result, I think, truly established, is that no man can pronounce with certainty what that crisis was, except he who won the battle.

[R]*Not that this uncertainty in the least diminishes the great merit of the 52nd, which in the hands of Colborne did under every danger and difficulty all that might be expected from the discipline and memory of Moore.*

But the 95th had also their remembrance of hard earned distinction and suffered severely.

[S]*In the 71st, their determination was the same for Pack and Cadogan*[24] *were replaced by Reynell.*

[T]*The Guards nobly did their duty, the excellent artillery were not unmindful of theirs and it is only necessary to designate the corps of infantry to establish other as real claims to praise.*

Lord Hill,[U] *Kempt &c. were in the field, and if they did not contribute to success it must have been the first time they failed to do so, but it is known that they did not fail but contributed services of a high order even for these illustrious men to contribute.*

The fall of Picton or[V] *Ponsonby or De Lancey,*[25] *of Gordon*[26] *and Canning,*[27] *the wounds of Elley,*[28] *Fitzroy Somerset*[29] *and others speak no supineness in the Staff; an important thing in a battle.*

The admiration of Bonaparte says something for the[W] *conduct of the Greys, and the rest of the cavalry*[X] *could not be insensible to the pattern of the infantry and Lord Anglesey's illustration of daring.*

What then do all these considerations amount to? Simply, I think, to this: That all the British army that was engaged that day may be satisfied with the recollection of what they did, whether they did much or little depended upon their opportunity sufficient for them, it is that they did not neglect that opportunity.

Too critical an inquiry as to who has the greatest claim to praise engenders a jealousy which never should exist between companions in arms since the noblest results can only be achieved by the union of all hearts and hands in serving their King and Country without rivalry but with virtuous emulation of excellence.

I regret that some alterations requiring me to re-copy my letter and all the answers it contains have again added the delay of some days to its date.

However imperfectly it may now answer your purpose, at all events I hope it will prove that no pains I could employ have been spared to make it worthy of trust so far as the limited information upon which it is founded gave me the power of ensuring its fidelity.

A The rain during the night had been nearly incessant.

B This gave him the opportunity to see much in the early part of the day which was completely unseen by officers with their regiments – Majors Harris and Keane[30] *& Mr Fitzroy*[31] *were I believe with him.*

C Early in the action the fire seemed to gain ground for a time to our right.

D This is recalled to me by its being the last time I spoke to my friend and former brother officer, Major the Honourable Frederick Howard (son of the late Earl of Carlisle), who when gallantly charging with the 10th a square of French infantry, was killed to the great regret of all who knew him. Lord Paget in Spain had noticed his distinguished conduct in action in Sir John Moore's campaign.

E *This I think was told me (relative to Colonel Quentin) by Sir Henry Floyd*[32] *just after we had crossed the Genappe road.*

F *From the time we came up to where Lord Edward Somerset's brigade was, very little was to be seen except (as in a fog) what was immediately near you. This of course was subject to some variation, but I do not think at any time such as to give the commonest range of sight. But no distant object could at any time be seen, and it was one of the annoyances of the moment that you were so completely in the dark as to what was going on, whilst you knew a great deal was going on of great importance.*

G *At the time I only knew Sir Colin Campbell by sight. But from Sir Hussey Vivian's narrative it will be seen that Sir Colin's coming was a material circumstance and was much more likely to be remembered with accuracy by General Vivian.*

H *I think this was when we were midway between the two positions.*

I *The fire came from our right flank and we had altered our course in that direction. Very soon after we had been changed from being horizontal to the position into a direction perpendicular to the front.*

J *Excepting the charge this was the most bustling moment.*

K *I do now wonder whether we had casualties except amongst the horses at that interval. Whilst here Captain Luard's bay horse was shot in the hind fetlock and Captain Duperrier's grey mare was shot in the hip as he was riding with me in front. There was a good deal of fire.*

L *I had thought that Major Harris had been wounded earlier, being led into the mistake by someone having said 'the Brigade Major is wounded' just as we were forming up and the 10th quitted us to charge. The officers who led squadrons were Major Grant (who had been also at the battle of Assaye); Captain Luard; Captain Croker*[33] *broke his sword in the charge (this officer had received a severe sabre wound in the face in a successful charge of the 18th Hussars at Croix d'Orade,*[34] *where they were commanded by Colonel Hughes, in which affair Sir Hussey Vivian who superintended in person was severely wounded in the arm); Lieutenant Hesse*[35] *wounded severely in the arm, this officer about three years ago was unfortunately killed in a duel at Paris by the Comte de Leon, said to be a natural son of Bonaparte; Lieutenant and Adjutant Duperier severely wounded in the head; Lieutenant Machell*[36] *had his brown mare killed; Lieutenant Rowlls*[37] *had his bay horse shot completely through the head (but which with the loss of an eye recovered). This officer pointed out to me at the termination of the charge (before we began to retire) the wound his horse had received, and I advised him to keep on with him.*

M *Supposing the 52nd to have driven the Ancienne Garde from near Hougoumont down the space between the two positions, a surmise that is strengthened by my recollection of my fire working (if I may be allowed the expression) in that direction, and also by the circumstance of the fire when heaviest not having been most galling to us on our position; all which must be conjecture on our part who could not see through the smoke and who could only since learn that the 52nd was the regiment so gallantly and memorably employed in achieving so important a feature of the battle. It yet does not appear to me that anywhere on the line, to the front where we went, the 52nd could be ahead of us. But that they might be very near without mutual recognition is easily to be supposed, where every appearance of troops could only evolve with varying uncertainty from the smoke. I have tried often (so little jealousy I hope can I entertain of assistance we should feel a pride in being indebted to) to ascertain whether the guns coming in on our left might not have been those driven away by the 52nd, of which Major Gawler speaks. But certainly there were, that evening two different descriptions of force were fell in with. The one not beaten, but disposed to be aggressive as proved by the charge of the cuirassiers on the right squadron of the 10th and the resolution shown by the cavalry in other places, and squares of infantry. The other beaten, retiring loosely. These I apprehended were some of the troops beaten by the 52nd. But as the 52nd had driven them the 52nd could not be ahead of them. That even some of these might be left in the rear of the cavalry does not invalidate the argument as it applies to the 52nd. If all these scattered French infantry were not reaped in field it was only because the reapers rode through it too fast. But the 52nd could not have left behind them on that line, the squares of French, they would not have left them unbeaten and unbroken and in that state we saw some squares, after our charge was over, in front of us.*

N *To break into a square, perhaps it would be best to charge in successive squadrons. But with blown horses and up a hill, the square would possess a great advantage; supposing (of which I am dubious) there was not a fence preventing it. But successive squadrons were here out of the question, I had not one.*

O *This happened near a barn or farm building on our right as we came back.*

P *There is a probability that it was beyond Rossomme, since after coming back it was only near there we eventually bivouacked.*

Q *Near Rossomme.*

R *I may here caution that I do not have the slightest shade of doubt upon the accuracy of Major Gawler's narrative of the operations of his regiment, but on those of other regiments he cannot be equally well informed. As relates to the 6th Brigade of cavalry, Sir Hussey Vivian appears to me a very correct statement. No question can advise us to the candour and accuracy of Sir Thomas Reynell's. If all these accounts do not fit into each other in every particular, it is only that some little piece of information is accidentally broken off which should fill up the interstice.*

S *The misinformation of Major Gawler with regard to the exact employment of the 71st shows how very difficult it is to be certain as to the movement of another corps.*

T *A staff officer of great experience and of indisputable merit told me he saw the Guards at one time maintain their ground under a fire almost beyond the power of endurance. If they had broken, here would have been 'a crisis' the wrong way. But they held their ground and therefore contributed much to 'the crisis' in our favour.*

U *Soon after the battle, the way in which it was currently said General Kempt had repelled an overwhelming attack might well be spoken of as a 'crisis'. In fact there may be many such, where not to be at once defeated is a step towards victory.*

V *It was said General Ponsonby met his death in consequence of the tiring of his horse in the deep ground, also that when he had fallen, his Brigade Major Reignolds*[38] *(of The Greys) lost his life in the romantic but devoted endeavour to secure a beautiful miniature of Mary, which the General wore. Major Reignolds had just sustained the loss of his wife and felt the full value of what could at once alleviate and enhance a similar calamity.*

W *Colonel Cheyney*[39] *of the Greys is said to have had a horse killed beneath him at Waterloo.*

X *From the same country, influenced by the same general discipline, and feeling their responsibility as an individual branch of service, though embarked on the same cause and fighting for the same interests as the infantry (whose exertions it was impossible to view without an admiration to which no language will do justice) with a nobleman of high rank and profession and of fame as a cavalry officer at their head, to say the cavalry exerted themselves to do their best; is merely to claim for them the common feeling and specific of anon. It may appear a work of supererogation to say all of this, but of late an endeavour has been made to tarnish the national and military reputation of the British cavalry, an endeavour ungenerous, unjust, and un English, and more likely to be found in narrow prejudice and factious motive than in any real regard or research for historical truth.*

HENRY MURRAY

Letter no. 63

1 Henry Murray joined the regiment as a cornet in 1800, serving in the 16th, 20th and 10th Light Dragoons and the 26th Foot before joining the 18th in 1810. He served in the Peninsula, seeing action at Morales where he was severely wounded in the knee. Afterwards Sir H. Murray KCB, General and Colonel-in-Chief of the 14th Light Dragoons. He died at Wimbledon Lodge on 29 July 1850.

2 Lieutenant Colonel Thomas Reynell of the 71st Regiment was wounded at Waterloo. He had joined the army as an ensign in 1793; he served in Holland in 1794–5, and commanded the Light Company of the 40th Foot in Egypt. He received the RStGO3 and KMT for his services at Waterloo. Afterwards he became General Sir T. Reynell Bart, KCB, and Colonel-in-Chief 87th Foot. His letter was published by Siborne (number 125).

3 This refers to the plan accompanying Gawler's statement in the *United Service Journal,* 1833; this is a copy of W. B. Craan's plan of 1816.

4 Major, The Honourable Henry Percy, 14th Dragoons, Extra Aide de Camp to Lord Wellington. He had been ADC to Sir John Moore at Corunna. He was sent home with the Waterloo despatch and made a brevet lieutenant colonel and CB. He died on 15 April 1825.

5 Major General The Honourable Sir William Ponsonby KCB was killed leading the 2nd (Union) Brigade in the great cavalry charge at Waterloo.

6 Lieutenant Colonel Frederick Cavendish Ponsonby commanded the 12th Light Dragoons at Waterloo. Originally with the 23rd Light Dragoons which he commanded at Talavera. He remained in Spain when his regiment was sent home as an Assistant Adjutant General, serving as such at Busaco and Barrosa. He then took command of the 12th Light Dragoons serving at Salamanca and Monasterio where he was slightly wounded. He was wounded at Waterloo, lying on the field all night. The narrative of his experiences lying wounded on the field near the French lines for is often quoted. Afterwards Major General Sir Frederick Cavendish Ponsonby KCB and KMT, Governor of Malta. He died on 11 January 1837. His letter was published by Siborne (number 57).

7 Lieutenant Colonel James Hay commanding the 16th Light Dragoons was severely wounded. His letter is published in this volume (number 45).

8 The 1st Brigade of Cavalry.

9 Colonel Felton Hervey of the 14th Light Dragoons acted as an Assistant Quartermaster General at Waterloo.

10 This phrase was omitted in the original edition to avoid offence.

11 Colonel Sir Colin Campbell KCB of the 2nd Foot Guards served as Commandant at Headquarters. He had joined the army in 1799 and had followed Wellington closely since India, serving at Assaye and on the Headquarters Staff throughout most of the Peninsular war. He received a cross with bars for Talavera, Busaco, Fuentes d'Onoro, Badajoz, Salamanca, Vittoria, Pyrenees, Nivelle, Nive and Toulouse. He became a General and Colonel-in-Chief of the 72nd Foot. He was Governor of Ceylon 1840–7, but died almost immediately on returning to England on 13 June 1847.

12 Lieutenant Duperier was Adjutant of the regiment; see his letters below (numbers 64–65).

13 This is most likely to be Regimental Sergeant Major Thomas Jeffs, but could refer to Troop Sergeant Major William Jeffs of Captain Ellis's troop.

14 Lieutenant George Luard of the 18th. He joined the 4th Dragoons as a cornet in 1802 and served in the Peninsula, receiving a General Service Medal with seven bars for Talavera, Albuera, Vittoria, Nivelle, Nive, Orthes and Toulouse. He was later placed on half pay as a major in 1826 and died in December 1847.

15 Sergeant Matthew Colgan of Captain Luard's Troop.

16 Almost certainly Captain Thomas Noel Harris, on half pay, Major of Brigade to Sir Hussey Vivian. He originally served in the 1st Dragoons for eight years then sold out. He re-entered

as a cornet in the 13th Light Dragoons in 1811 and was very slightly wounded at Badajoz whilst serving as ADC to Major General Walker. He received a General Service Medal with three bars for Fuentes d'Onoro, Ciudad Rodrigo and Badajoz. He was severely wounded, losing his right arm at Waterloo. He received the PrMOM, KStA and KStV. He retired as a colonel on half pay in 1830 and was made KCH. He was the Chief Magistrate at Gibraltar for many years. He died at Updown, Eastry, on 23 March 1860.

17 The only Dwyer listed in the 18th at Waterloo was Sergeant Jeremiah Dwyer of Captain Ellis's Troop.

18 Lieutenant George Woodberry, he joined the army as an ensign in the 10th Foot in 1812. He was wounded at Vittoria and Mendionde. Eric Hunt has published extracts of his diary in *Charging against Napoleon,* Pen & Sword Books, 2001.

19 Lieutenant James Henry Waldie, he joined the regiment as a cornet in 1812 serving as Adjutant in 1812–13. He went on half pay in 1820, and little else is known of this officer.

20 Lieutenant Colonel Sir Robert Gardiner. He joined the Royal Artillery in 1797, serving in Minorca, northern Germany, Walcheren and the Peninsula. He received a General Service Medal with only three bars for Rolica, Vimiera and Corunna. This is strange as he also served at Barrosa, he was made a brevet major for his services in the trenches at Badajoz, Salamanca and Burgos. After Burgos he was given command of a horse artillery battery and served at Morales, Vittoria, Orthes & Toulouse. Afterwards made KCB, KCH, KStA, and Grand Cross of Charles III of Spain, ADC to George IV, William IV and Victoria. In 1848 he became Governor and Colonel-in-Chief of Gibraltar. He died as General and Colonel Commandant of the Royal Artillery at Claremont on 26 June 1864.

21 Lieutenant Colonel Lord Robert Manners of the 10th Hussars, see his letters above (numbers 50–51).

22 Captain James Grant joined the army in 1797 and served in the Peninsula. He received a General Service Medal for Toulouse. Afterwards placed on half pay in 1819 he became a Major General in the 23rd Foot, CB and Governor of Scarborough Castle. He died at Hillingdon in Middlesex on 5 April 1852.

23 1st Hussars KGL who were brigaded with the 10th and 18th.

24 This reference is obscure, as Sir Denis Pack commanded the 9th Infantry Brigade on the other side of the field to the 71st and Lieutenant Colonel The Honourable Edward Cadogan did not serve at Waterloo.

25 Colonel Sir William Howe De Lancey KCB was knocked from his horse by the wind of a cannonball, which separated his ribs from his spine; he lingered for some days under the care of his wife of two months before passing away. The narrative of his wife, describing his last few days has been published as *A week at Waterloo in 1815*, published in 1906. I defy anyone to read it without shedding a tear.

26 Lieutenant Colonel Sir Alexander Gordon KCB, 3rd Foot Guards, Aide de Camp to Lord Wellington. He was laid in Wellington's bed at the Headquarters in Waterloo village but passed away early on the 19th. When Dr Hume woke Wellington to advise him of Gordon's death he wept openly.

27 Lieutenant Colonel C. F. Canning, 3rd Foot Guards, Aide de Camp to Wellington was killed at Waterloo.

28 Colonel Sir John Elley, KCB, Royal Horse Guards was the Deputy Adjutant General at Waterloo. Elley had risen from a private soldier and had served on the Staff since 1807 as an assistant adjutant general throughout the Peninsula. He was slightly wounded at Salamanca and more seriously at Waterloo. Afterwards made KCH and KMT, Lieutenant General and Colonel-in-Chief of the 7th Hussars. He died on 23 January 1839 at Amesbury.

29 Lieutenant Colonel Lord Fitzroy James Henry Somerset, 1st Foot Guards, acting as Military Secretary to Wellington. He joined the Army in 1804, serving in the 43rd Foot and became

an ADC to Wellington serving throughout the Peninsula. He received a cross with five bars for Fuentes d'Onoro, Badajoz, Salamanca, Vittoria, Pyrenees, Nivelle, Nive, Orthes and Toulouse. He was wounded at Waterloo and lost his right arm. Afterwards Colonel-in-Chief of the 53rd Foot, and Military Secretary to the Commander in Chief. Master General of the Ordnance. Finally he became Field Marshal Lord Raglan commanding the army in the Crimea where he died. Siborne published his letter (number 2).

30 Captain Edward Keane, 7th Hussars, Aide de Camp to Sir Hussey Vivian. He joined the army in 1803 and served in northern Germany, Corunna and the Peninsula from 1813 including Orthes and Toulouse. He was made a brevet major for Waterloo and was lieutenant colonel of the 6th Dragoons 1825–33 when he retired on half pay. Brought out of retirement, he served as a colonel in the Grenadier Guards and retired again in 1838. He died on 2 November 1866.

31 Almost certainly Captain Lord Charles Fitzroy, 1st Foot Guards, Deputy Assistant Adjutants General. See his letter (number 114)

32 Captain Henry Floyd, 10th Hussars. He joined the army as a cornet in 1808. He was made Bart. in 1818. He went on half pay in 1824 and died on 4 March 1868.

33 Captain Richard Croker, 18th Hussars. He joined the regiment as a cornet in 1805 serving in the Peninsula and was wounded at Corunna and Mendionde and severely wounded at Toulouse. He received a General Service Medal with five bars for Sahagun, Nivelle, Nive, Orthes and Toulouse. He was made a brevet major for Waterloo. He went on half pay in the Portuguese Service in 1820 and eventually became a colonel on the retired list. He died at Leamington on 15 January 1854.

34 The action at Croix d'Orade occurred on 8 April 1814 near Toulouse in southern France. Wellington had wished to cross the Ers river, but the French managed to destroy each bridge as they retreated past them until that of Croix d'Orade. Here Sir Hussey Vivian surprised the French 5th and 22nd Chasseurs before the bridge had been broken. By charging immediately with the 18th Hussars, the 22nd was caught unawares and promptly fled over the bridge. The French lost 120 prisoners and the bridge was captured intact. Napier claims the success of this action for the Commander of the 18th, Major Hughes, but Oman sensibly argues that the lion's share of the credit should go to Vivian who ordered the charge. Vivian was wounded by the carbine fire of the 5th Chasseurs as he chased the 22nd Chasseurs. Hughes was not at Waterloo.

35 Lieutenant Charles Hesse, 18th Hussars, was wounded at Waterloo.

36 Lieutenant John Thomas Machell, 18th Hussars, had a horse shot beneath him at Waterloo, and he went on half pay in 1821. He died at Beverley on 13 October 1853.

37 Lieutenant William Henry Rowlls, 18th Hussars, had a horse shot beneath him at Waterloo; he went on half pay in 1817.

38 Major Thomas Reignolds, 2nd Dragoons, acted as Major of Brigade to the 2nd Cavalry Brigade and was killed at Waterloo.

39 Captain Edward Cheney commanded the regiment for the last four hours of the battle and had five horses killed beneath him in twenty minutes! He became a colonel and CB. He died at Gaddesby in Leicestershire on 3 March 1847.

No. 64 Lieutenant Henry Duperier[1]

Roscrea, 10 November 1829[2]

ADD MS 34703, FO 90

To Sir Hussey Vivian

Sir,

I have the honour to acknowledge the receipt of your letter of the 4th inst. and, according to your wishes, I herewith annex a detailed statement of the movements and other *material* circumstances which came under my observation, connected with your brigade on the 16th, 17th and 18th of June 1815, so far as I can charge my memory, up to the moment of my being wounded.

At two o'clock on the morning of the 16th the brigade order was received to assemble at *four* o'clock the same morning on the road to Braine le Compte, or Nivelles (I am not certain which) and, after assembling, the brigade marched towards Quatre Bras, when it halted for a considerable time, in column of route, on the main chaussee,[3] and when ordered to move on made a detour to the left towards the Prussians.[4] After having marched for about *two* hours I received orders to advance, and endeavour to find a place to bivouac the whole brigade; but, on the brigade arriving on that ground, and after having fed the horses, an order came to move on, and, about an hour after I was again sent forward to select a bivouac. I had succeeded, and was waiting for the brigade, when Major, now Colonel, Harris[5] came to me to inform me, that we were not to halt, and we both rejoined the brigade. Shortly after this some Horse Artillery came up at full trot, and the brigade divided the road to let them pass: for some time after this, the brigade trotted, also, and about six o'clock struck off the road to its left across the ploughed ground and between *eight* and *nine* halted for the night, and took up its position amongst the rye on a height, in the environs of Tilly, with orders to send out frequent patrols to the left, to endeavour to ascertain what situation the Prussians were in. Colonel Murray[6] and I went together a considerable distance, but could not obtain any intelligence of them.

On the morning of the 17th the brigade remained in its position until *eleven* o'clock, when perceiving the enemy's lancers advancing in great force, the 18th were ordered to throw out skirmishers into the valley, whilst the brigade deployed into line, but after some skirmishing they were driven in as the enemy advanced with great impetuosity. The brigade then retired by 'threes about' followed by the enemy, whom opened a heavy fire of artillery upon it, after some resistance the brigade retired, first by divisions, and then by files, by cross roads with the enemy close to it, shouting and pursuing. It rained so violently that the road appeared more like a river than what it was, and prevented General Vivian consulting the map. The villages through which the column passed were all deserted by the inhabitants, but in one a man was seen, taken, and forced to come and show the road. He was placed behind Trumpeter Verity[7] of the 18th on his horse. The brigade overtook some horse artillery, and was ordered to halt. The enemy was then close to the left, and their shouts were distinctly heard. A few skirmishers were sent to support the Horse Guards, and after half an hours halt the artillery advanced, and on gaining the heights the noise of the French ceased, and Major Kennedy's[8] squadron was detached in the direction of Wavre.

Towards the close of the evening the brigade took its position in a small copse in the vicinity of a hamlet named Coucou,[9] with orders to patrol as far as the village of Ohain on the left, where, during the night, a patrol of Prussians was met, and at three in the morning a Prussian officer came with a verbal dispatch from Marshal Blücher to the Duke of Wellington: this officer was brought to Sir H. Vivian, who, after communicating with him, caused him to be conducted to the Duke.

Letter no. 64

At *nine* o'clock on the morning of the 18th the trumpets sounded 'To horse', and the brigade marched into position on a height on the left of the British line, where it remained a considerable time much opposed to, and suffering severely from the enemy's cannonade, until Sir H. Vivian caused it to fall back a small distance. Towards *two* o'clock the brigade was moved to the right, in rear of a hedge, and formed in column of half squadrons, where it remained a short time: – it was then moved from there to the right and formed in line in rear of, and close to the Belgian infantry, where the 18th lost a great many men and horses from the musketry of the enemy: It remained in that position until the general charge took place, when it was most gallantly led on by Sir H. Vivian.

Thus, General, I have endeavoured to give you an account of what came under my notice on those *memorable* days, but I must acknowledge that the length of time which has intervened has obliterated many minor incidents from my memory.

Permit me to present my most respectful compliments to Lady Vivian and yourself with my sincere wishes for the long enjoyment of good health and happiness of all the family.

I have the honour to remain, Sir, your most obliged, most respectful and most obedient humble servant

H DUPERIER

---

1 Duperier had been a sergeant major in the 10th Hussars, becoming a cornet in 1808. He was adjutant from 1813 to 1821. He was wounded at Waterloo and went on half pay in November 1821.

2 This clearly is another of the letters previously collected by Sir Hussey Vivian and forwarded to Siborne for his information.

3 The road to Nivelles (the Brussels to Mons road).

4 On to the road leading to Quatre Bras.

5 Captain Thomas Noel Harris, Major of Brigade to Sir H. Vivian. He had served with the Allied armies in Germany in 1813–14 and been at Leipzig. He lost his right arm at Waterloo and received another severe wound. He retired on half pay in 1830 as a colonel. Later he became KCH and Chief Magistrate at Gibraltar. He died at Updown, Eastry, 23 March 1860.

6 Lieutenant Colonel Henry Murray, commanding the 18th, see his letter (number 63).

7 The Waterloo Medal Roll does not list a trumpeter Verity.

8 Major Arthur Kennedy had been wounded on the 16th by his horse standing on his foot as he dismounted. He was not therefore with the regiment at Waterloo and did not receive a Waterloo medal. He had joined the 24th Foot as an ensign in 1803, joining the 18th in 1804. He served throughout the Peninsula campaign, receiving a General Service Medal with six bars for Sahagun & Benevente, Vittoria, Nivelle, Nive, Orthes and Toulouse. He later transferred to the Rifle Brigade rising to Lieutenant Colonel, before retiring on half pay in 1831. He died at Ranaldstown, Ireland in 1855. I must thank Captain Locker retired, OC Home Headquarters, Light Dragoons, for providing some of this information. The Waterloo Roll would indicate that Lieutenant Rowlls commanded Kennedy's troop in his absence.

9 Verde Coucou, which lay just to the east of Mont St Jean farm.

No. 65 From the same
Roscrea, 11 February 1830

ADD MS 34703, FO 122

To Sir Hussey Vivian

Dear General,

I beg to inform you that I have not forgotten the occurrence you allude to in your letter of the 7th instant, which reached me this day, and I take no time in stating what I recollect of the circumstance of the 17th June 1815.

I did not mention it before, considering that an occurrence of so trivial a nature could not be of consequence to any person.

After the French had ceased to harass our rear as we passed thro' a village, I turned down one of the lanes to my right, and called at a house: a woman came out who was all in tears. I asked if she had any Hollands,[1] she replying in the affirmative, I requested some to fill my small flask, which contains about a pint, and that very moment you came out of another lane on my right, and asked me what I was doing: on my informing you, you asked me how I had found that out, and by that time the woman returned and filled my flask (I have kept it ever since, and it hangs in my bedroom over my sword) she was still crying: you then told her not to be uneasy – that she had nothing to do but to put away in safety all the best of her property, under-ground or any where, for that in less than three days we would return and drive the French away for ever.

I have also some recollection of some men coming by at that time, who had, I think, some cattle with them – whom you told them into the forest, out of the way for a time, as we should return the next day and expurgate the enemy, or words to that effect, and I explained this to them partly in Flemish and partly in German, they not understanding your meaning in French, by that time you had drank a glass of the Hollands.

We then galloped off and soon overtook the brigade, shortly after Captain (now Lt. Colonel) Harris, then your aide-de-camp came to me and asked for a little of my Hollands: at first I told him I had none; (for it was then a very scarce article) but he said the General had told him that my flask was full, on that I unbuckled it and he took a hearty sup.

I hope you will pardon me for having gone into this minute detail, but I think it better to be tedious than omit any circumstance which may conduce *[sic]* to your information.

Ensign Kepple is a very *tall* young man and very pleasant.

I am extremely happy to hear that Lady Vivian is well, and beg to present my respectful compliments to her.

I remain, dear General, your most obedient and very humble servant

H DUPERIER

Handwritten note attached:

The circumstances recalled in the letter are as the letter justly discuss, of a trivial nature and of no consequence and no use – but as he had presently in conversation with me after the battle noticed the unfailing accuracy with which I had foreseen the results of our movements[2] – and as he has not at all referred to these circumstances in his report of our proceedings (for which he has given a very sufficient one) – having occasion to write to him I brought it to his recollection, this is the reply, my having done so.

H VIVIAN

16 February 1830

1 Dutch gin.

2 It is clear that Vivian put great efforts into obtaining information from many of his junior officers to ensure his version of events was very persuasive. This, his position as William's commander in Ireland for a period and his hefty loan to help complete the project did undoubtedly give him enormous influence in the finished product. I have not, however, found any evidence of undue bias. I thank John Hussey for bringing this point to my attention.

The 1st Hussars KGL

No. 66 Lieutenant Colonel Augustus von Wissell[1]

Verdun, 18 December 1829

ADD MS 34703, FO 98

[To Sir Hussey Vivian?][2]

Most honoured Sir![3]

Highly I am indebted to you for the very kind and conspicuous answer of the 4th instant you honoured me with, but feel very sorry for the great troubles it gave you. My intention by the addings *[sic]* of the 18th October was only to get in a few words. Your advice, if it was worthwhile to refute the scribblings of those brawlers who wish to blame it right or wrong.[4]

The received honourable testimony you were pleased to give the 1st Hussars late KGL, also the generous approbation of their officer commanding; and the very reason you mention wherefore the thrown accusation 'of neglect or surprise' could not be extended to us on account of the military situation: determined me at once to treat with contempt a long ago made charge and not to enter the lists with the mentioned writers.

On the eve to apprise you of this I was so happy to receive your most friendly lines of the 25th for which I am most thankful and annex a memorandum of all I recollect of the proceedings from the 16th to the 19th of June 1815. I am afraid it will be of no use.

With sincere participation I did read the granting of my wishes for you Sir and honourable family welfare, might you never prove a change of!

Please kindly to accept the assurance of the unbounded esteem and great regards wherewith I have the honour to remain forever,

Sir, your most obedient servant

A WISSELL
SERVING NOW 48 YEARS IN
HS M CAVALRY

Memorandum

Verdun, December 18th 1829

On the 16th of June 1815 about 11 o'clock a.m. the 1st Hussars late KGL stationed at Tournai, received the order to march to Ath and to join near Quatre Bras the brigade of Major General Sir Hussey Vivian. I did so without delay and directed the Captain on outpost to assemble the detachments and follow as soon as possible.

After a very teasing march we had the good luck to come at our destination on the 17th early in the morning. About noon, when our infantry and artillery had been ordered to retire, the cavalry of the enemy moved on in three strong columns one of which took the direction of the brigade posted on the left wing. Orders to fall back having been before received the 1st Hussars got the rear guard, the enemy keeping close on, we had always a squadron at hand to support the skirmishing. Once we reached thus a village crossed, by a rivulet, (the name of it I don't know[5]) where two officers and several men of ours, coming in wrong lane, were cut off, but by their bravery and the swiftness of their horses rescued themselves. The 10th Regiment of Hussars relieved the 1st.

On the 18th the third of the brigade must have been uselessly destroyed by guns had not the conspicuous gallantry of the celebrious *[sic]* General had spared them, for a more deciding purpose, by changing the positions of the regiments. As for himself he ever kept on the heights on lookout and had the commanding officers with him to take his directions for momentary execution.

When about 6 o'clock in the afternoon the Prussian corps of General Bülow appeared, the brigade was successively – on account of walls – moved from the left to the right wing of the battle. The 10th and 18th Hussars having charged the French infantry with great fury, the General ordered the 1st and 3rd squadrons – just formed – to do the same, I told Major Gruben[6] I would go with the first part and he may follow with the remainder. In moving on, it being twilight, an aide de camp came requesting to halt as our own infantry was in front. The regiment went then in pursuit of the enemy, of whom many prisoners were made, till General Vivian – sent order to fall back and in coming up himself he directed to take a bivouac which was done about 11 o'clock at night.

That every one tried to imitate the set forth example of our daring Brigadier is out of question, if any one reached it can only be decided by himself.

A WISSELL, MAJOR GENERAL
LATE LIEUT COLONEL, COMMANDING
THE 1ST REGIMENT OF HUSSARS KGL

---

1 As Count Linsingen was not present at Waterloo, Wissell commanded the 1st Hussars during the campaign. Wissell, listed number 168 in Beamish, joined the KGL in 1803, serving in the Peninsula 1811–14. He rose to be CB, HGO2 and a major general and went on half pay at Verden.

2 This letter predates the request for information by Siborne; one must presume it is another letter collected by Sir Hussey Vivian, then forwarded to Siborne later.

3 The letter is written in English; therefore, although having corrected spellings, I have left the slightly awry English as per the original.

4 The regiment formed the rearguard at the crossing of the Dyle and were forced to rush over the bridges at speed once the rest of the brigade had safely crossed. This appears to have been a coordinated movement, as Vivian had previously dismounted some of the 18th with carbines to cover the crossings and successfully checked the French pursuit. However, it seems that there was some accusation that the 1st Hussars had been driven back precipitately, something that Wissell was keen to refute.

5 This was at the small hamlet of Thy, where two small stone bridges cross the Dyle.

6 Major Philip Moritz von Gruben also of the 1st Hussars, numbered 169 in Beamish. He

joined the KGL in 1804, serving in northern Germany, the Baltic and the Peninsula 1809–14. He was severely wounded at Fuentes d'Onoro. He received a Gold Cross with bars for Salamanca, Orthes and Toulouse. He became a Major General and Colonel Commandant of the 2nd Hussars (Hanover). He died at Diepholz in Hanover on 13 October 1828.

7th Cavalry Brigade

The 3rd Hussars KGL

No. 67 Captain Quintus Von Goeben[1]

Aurich,[2] 13 September 1835

ADD MS 34704, FO 246

Original in German

Your Excellencies

I have the honour and pleasure to answer your honoured letter of 15th of last month, concerning the 3rd Hussar Regiment of the King's German Legion at the battle of Waterloo, and give you all that is in my power to clarify and complete the history of the 3rd Hussars Regiment of the King's German Legion started in 1818. This describes the participation of this regiment in the battle of Waterloo and I am giving this information in writing as it gives approximately each position, movement and surroundings of the regiment as it appeared on that particular day.[3] I have to state regretfully that at the given time period on the model namely 7 o'clock pm at the time of the attack by the French Guards on the right wing of the combined army; the actions of the 3rd Hussar Regiment were not so very remarkable. I believe it must have been around this time when a line of enemy skirmishers approached close to the regiment and I enclose the drawing with the positions of the 3rd Hussar Regiment of the Legion and those of the enemy. Should I not be able to place the regiment accurately, which is quite difficult as the disposition of other troops are not at my disposal, this difficulty could easily be removed, as the position of the other troops given in my statements will also clarify the position of the 3rd Hussar Regiment. Concerning the disposition of the crops in the fields, possibly the statements of the farmers are correct, as the very trodden ground gave no indication of cultivation.

I have the honour to be your obedient servant

Q VON GOEBEN
LIEUT COLONEL

1 Goeben is numbered 253 in Beamish. He joined the Legion in 1805, serving in the Baltic, Peninsula 1808–9, northern Germany 1813–14 and the Waterloo campaign. He was slightly wounded at Waterloo. He received a General Service Medal with two bars for Sahagun and Benevente. HGO3 and HWC, he later became a brevet lieutenant colonel in the Hanoverian Garde de Corps.

2 Aurich is to the north of Emden in north Germany.

3 This report appears as letter no. 68.

No. 68 From the same

ADD MS 34704, FO 248

Original in German
Copy

It was towards 11 o'clock am on 18 June 1815 when the 3rd Hussar Regiment KGL took its place in the position which the combined army under the command of the Duke of Wellington had occupied near the village of Waterloo, and because the regiment only marched in from Brussels in the morning, it was placed at the end of the cavalry column, behind the brigade which stood with squadrons in closed column at the centre of the position on the rise. The regiment was very weak and arranged *in 3 squadrons*, and as it had not been united with the 13th English Light Dragoons Regiment with which it was under the command of Col. F. Arenschildt,[1] the first deployment of the regiment was in companies in half-closed column to the right of the chaussee leading to Genappe; the chaussee leading to Nivelle was just in front of them. When the first cannon shots occurred that started the battle of Waterloo towards 12 o'clock am, the regiment mounted, and it didn't take long before it suffered considerable losses, particularly of horses, as a result of cannon fire. At the beginning of the battle, several brigades were sent from the cavalry column both to the right and left wings, and the regiment made various movements as a result, and passed by the chaussee to Nivelle, partly in order to close up the column, and partly to take cover behind the rise from the increasingly heavy artillery fire. It was in one of these positions toward 2 o'clock pm that the commanding officer of the regiment, Lieut. Col. Meyer,[2] was mortally wounded by a cannon ball. Towards 3 o'clock pm the regiment arrived at the rise behind the infantry which lay *en echequier*[3] in squares, behind the second line consisting of three to four battalions of Grand Duchy of Nassau troops,[4] and hardly had they arrived here, when the heavy Dutch cavalry brigade,[5] which until this point had stood in rear of the regiment, advanced in front of the right wing squadrons of the regiment but came back *en debandade*,[6] so that both these squadrons had a great deal of difficulty holding their positions and avoiding being carried along by it. During this time the left wing squadrons of the regiment, which had remained free of this wild entanglement, attacked enemy cuirassiers of approximately squadron strength, and indeed succeeded in dislodging them. Because both of the other squadrons had now become free they advanced up the rise toward the crown of the position, they immediately received personal orders from Lieut. Gen. Lord Uxbridge, commander of the entire cavalry, to attack enemy cavalry consisting of two or three squadrons of cuirassiers and just as many squadrons of the 1st French Dragoon Regiment,[7] which were sighted in lines at a distance of 400 to 500 feet away. They advanced for the thrust at a brisk trot, and then at a gallop they soon encountered the enemy, which was advancing at a slow trot or pace. They broke through the line at both points of attack, but they were so surrounded by the enemy wings and had them at their back, that only very few of them got away. They rode back separately, pursued by the enemy toward the squares, where the regiment reassembled behind the same, and now recognized the heavy losses they had suffered from these two thrusts, as the entire group had shrunk to only 60 or so men, which was then formed into two squadrons. This assembly of the regiment took place behind the infantry division, which was commanded by Lieut. Gen. Count Charles

Alten, and the Lüneburg field battalion of this division were in front of the regiment.[8]

Shortly thereafter, a closed column of enemy cuirassiers advanced at a pace toward this part of the position in order to break through it, but as a result of cold-blooded and effective fire from the infantry, which allowed the enemy to advance to perfect shooting distance, and by means of this firing and the weakness of the attack, the column was soon stopped with losses and forced to retreat.

Not long thereafter at 4 or 5 o'clock pm, a battalion of the combined army, probably the 5th Line Battalion KGL, attacked the enemy infantry with bayonets at a distance of approximately 600 to 800 feet from the left flank of the regiment, near a hedge, but it was threatened by enemy cuirassiers which advanced quickly and charged the battalion, which had become disordered as a result of the attack, whereupon Captain Kerssenbruch[9] attacked these enemy cuirassiers in their left flank with the remainder of the regiment and without further instructions, so that the same were kept from further pursuit of the infantry. However, as a result of the superiority of the enemy in numbers and weaponry, the regiment soon had to retreat to cover after it took numerous losses during this third attack and had lost Captain B. Kerssenbruch, who had been commander till that point. The enemy then pursued the regiment up to the infantry square, but it was repelled by fire from the aforementioned Hanoverian infantry battalion. However, a few enemy cuirassiers were able to get behind the line of squares, and one of these reckless or drunk cuirassiers was only discovered amid the regiment when it reassembled behind the square and ordered itself into rank and file. When he failed to take his leave he was cut down by the hussars.

The remainder of the regiment, which now consisted of only 40 men, remained at this designated place. Enemy cavalry, whose officers wore large, broad bearskin caps, again appeared at a distance of 400 to 500 feet in a line of two to three squadrons and rode forth singly several times and challenged the regiment to single combat. However, because its strength was so weak it was not able to return the honour, and this enemy cavalry did not carry out anything further, except that several of these big bear-cappers[10] served as targets for Hanoverian field battalion marksmen, and with some success in that an officer was seen to topple from his horse.

At about 6 o'clock pm two squadrons of Scots horse guards came together near the regiment and formed a line with the same, and because the enemy cavalry, which was not combined with the infantry at this time, approached this position at shooting distance, the Scots Greys, who were bigger on horseback, were singled out and suffered considerable losses with great cold-bloodedness, until a number of skirmishers were sent out from the regiment and somewhat held off the cavalry so that their fire was eventually completely silenced and they retreated.*

Toward 7 o'clock pm the Duke of Wellington passed in front of the regiment from the right wing with a small *suite* and returned the same way a short time later, whereupon an order was issued to us by one of his aides-de-camp to go back to the chaussee leading to Nivelle, and to follow the army. At this point we heard artillery fire from the approaching Prussians. Hardly had the regiment gone a few paces than a brigade of English light dragoons in column of divisions came marching by from the left wing of the position, swung about on the spot where the regiment had been until then and where the infantry now also took its place. They then all advanced and the regiment followed. The increasingly distant sound of enemy fire signalled the retreat of the same until dark, when it became completely silent, etc.

Correct copy

Q VON GOEBEN COLONEL

*Presumed time to be depicted in the model, whereby it is further to be noted of the designated surroundings of the regiment in the present description of the battle of Waterloo that Hougoumont lay about a ¼ mile to the right and La Haye Sainte about 600 to 800 feet to the left and forward of the position of the regiment.

---

1 The 13th Light Dragoons were originally meant to form part of Colonel Arenschildt's 7th Cavalry Brigade. Because of the absence of the 2nd Hussars KGL on the frontier and possibly because of the late arrival of the 3rd Hussars, the 13th were transferred to Major General Grant's 5th Brigade.

2 Lieutenant Colonel Frederick Lewis Meyer, numbered 816 in Beamish. He joined the Legion in 1803, serving in the Baltic 1806–7 and the Peninsula in 1808–14. He was slightly wounded at Fuentes d'Onoro in 1811 and mortally wounded at Waterloo. He died at Brussels on 6 July 1815.

3 In checkerboard formation of squares.

4 The Nassau Brigade commanded by Major General von Kruse.

5 The Dutch cavalry division of Lieutenant General Baron de Collaert.

6 French for 'helter skelter'.

7 The 1st Dragoons were not present at Waterloo, perhaps he means the 1st Dragoon Brigade of General of Division Baron L'Heritier's 11th Cavalry Division, consisting of the 2nd and 7th Dragoons.

8 The 3rd Division of Lieutenant General Count Alten included the 1st Hanoverian Brigade, which included the Lüneburg Field Battalion.

9 Captain Agatz von Kerssenbruch, numbered 801 in Beamish. He joined the Legion in 1805, serving in Hanover 1805, the Baltic 1806–7, the Peninsula 1808–9 and northern Germany 1813–14. He was killed at the battle of Waterloo.

10 The French Horse Grenadiers.

THE ARTILLERY

The Royal Artillery Staff

No. 69 Captain Henry Baynes[1]
Guernsey, 21 December 1834

ADD MS 34704, FO 71

Sir,
I have the honour to acknowledge the receipt of your note and circular, which has not reached me till after considerable delay, in consequence of its having been addressed to Bedford Square, Brighton.

I should have much pleasure in giving you information on any of the points connected with the object you have in view, but am precluded from doing so, by the circumstance of my having been wounded and removed from the field previous to the period of the battle adopted for presentation in the model.

A reference to the M. General[2] of Artillery at Woolwich, or to Colonel Sir John May (who was at the head of the artillery staff at Waterloo[3]) appears to me to be the most likely means to obtain correct information as to the respective positions of the numerous troops and brigades of artillery,[4] which of course from the nature of the service were in all the different parts of the field; and indeed it would be difficult for any one to state the position of each without reference to the officers who were with them, this however might be done, at least to a considerable extent, by a person at Woolwich.

I remain, Sir, your obedient servant

HENRY BAYNES

---

1 Baynes joined the Artillery in 1801, serving in Naples in 1805 and the Peninsula from 1809 to 1813. He received a General Service Medal for Talavera where he was slightly wounded in the head. He was slightly wounded in the face and body at Waterloo. Afterwards brevet major and KH; he went on half pay in 1826. He died on Guernsey on 15 July 1844.

2 The Master General was head of the Ordnance.

3 He had served in the Royal Artillery since 1795, first serving afloat on a bomb vessel from 1797–1801. He served at Copenhagen in 1807 and in the Peninsula. He received a Gold Cross with three bars for Badajoz, Salamanca (wounded in the thigh by two musket balls on the following day), Vittoria (he received a violent contusion), San Sebastian, Nivelle, Nive and Toulouse. He was made KStA, KTS, KCH. He became a colonel and died on 8 May 1847. The head of the Artillery at Waterloo was Colonel Sir George Adam Wood.

4 Horse artillery batteries were designated Troops, and foot artillery batteries as Brigades.

The Royal Horse Artillery

Lieutenant Colonel Webber Smith's Troop

No. 70 Captain James Webber Smith[1]
Castle, 21 May[2]

ADD MS 34707, FO 46

My dear Siborne
Any assistance you may require will be given by our artificers on your sending to Colonel Cobbe or the Adjutant (duty officer) at Island Bridge.[3]

The German and Hanoverian Horse Artillery at Waterloo had shabraques like the Rockets[4] and black pouch belts over the left shoulder.

Very truly yours

J WEBBER SMITH

---

1 Webber Smith was ranked as a captain in the Royal Artillery regiment but a lieutenant colonel in the army. He had joined the Artillery in 1795 and served at Minorca in 1798, Malta in 1800, Porto Ferrajo in 1802, Walcheren in 1809 and in the Peninsula 1813–14. He received a Gold Medal with one bar for Vittoria and San Sebastian and a General Service Medal with bars for the Nivelle and Nive. He received the CB for Waterloo. Afterwards Major General and Director General of Artillery 1844–8, then Colonel Commandant in 1848. He died at Brighton on 21 March 1853. Siborne published a previous letter of his (number 79).

2 Dublin Castle, Headquarters of the British army in Ireland. Probably written around 1840.

3 This must refer to any assistance that Siborne required to transport the model to London; he could apply to Lieutenant Colonel George Cobbe, RA.

4 The shabraque was a decorative cloth that rested on the horses back beneath the saddlery. Here he likens that of the German Horse Artillery to those of the British Rocket Artillery.

Lieutenant Colonel Sir Robert Gardiner's Troop

No. 71 First Lieutenant Robert Harding[1]
Cookerham,[2] 10 December 1834

ADD MS 34704, FO 32

Sir,
I have been favoured with your communication of the 11th of November (which only reached me a few days since) in which you request answers to certain queries relative to the position and other circumstances connected with Sir Robert Gardiner's troop of Horse Artillery, on the field of Waterloo. I regret the vagueness of any information I can at this distance of time furnish you with, unaided by having had any subsequent opportunity of going over that memorable ground. I should the more particularly regret this, were it not that from the circumstance of Sir Robert Gardiner's troop having been

attached on this occasion to Sir Hussey Vivian's hussar brigade, I am well aware you must have at your command the very best information connected with the instructions and such of that brigade, that could by all possibility be given.

At the moment you particularly allude to in your first question – the troop having moved with the brigade from the left of the position, was halted with it in a slight hollow in the rear of I believe the right centre of our line and was not at that time engaged. The brigade almost immediately after advanced to charge – when if I recollect right, we passed the high road and came into action a few hundred paces to the right of La Haye Sainte – our fire being directed principally against some batteries of the enemy's on the opposite side of the hollow which were annoying the advance of our troops.

As regards the crops on the ground over which we moved, I have no distinct recollection beyond that of the great part of it being in cultivation.

I cannot conclude without offering you my sincerest wishes for the success of the undertaking so meritorious, and of such general public interest and importance.

I have the honour to be, Sir, your humble servant

ROBERT HARDING

---

1 Harding served in the Peninsula and received a General Service Medal with five bars, for Salamanca, Vittoria, San Sebastian, Orthes and Toulouse. He retired on half pay as a second captain in 1825 and died on 12 November 1849.

2 I can only trace one Cookerham in the UK. This village is situated approximately 5 miles south of Lancaster in Lancashire.

Captain Edward C. Whinyates's Troop

No. 72 Captain Edward C. Whinyates[1]
Carlisle, 17 August 1840[2]

ADD MS 34707, FO 187[3]

To Sir Hew Dalrymple Ross[4]

My dear Sir Hew

I return the plan,[5] and send you what recollections I have of the position of my troop of Horse Artillery at the battle of Waterloo.

On the bugle sounding for the line to turn out, it assembled, with 3 or 4 or 5 troops of Horse Artillery behind the position in the hollow ground, and on the left of the Brussels road.

The troops soon received orders to proceed to different points. A line of foreign troops in our front were overpowered,[6] and some British infantry marched up to replace them, and Lord Anglesey having formed some regiments of cavalry, immediately on the left of my guns they moved forward, and passed the hedges and hollow road in our front. I received orders at the same time to advance, which, I did on the right flank of the cavalry, and on arriving at the hedge and hollow road, Colonel Macdonald[7] of the Horse Artillery ordered me to leave the guns on the position, and advance with the mounted rocket sections. We accordingly did so, and advanced some hundred yards down the sloping ground in front of the position, and fired some discharges of rockets. We then returned to the guns left on the position, which were then on the Brussels side of the hollow road which runs along the front of the position. We then crossed, the two banks and hedges, and occupied the ground on the French side of the road, when the infantry losing (unnecessarily) many men by rifle shots sent me word, they should occupy the other bank of the road and we returned there with haste.

The position was somewhere about the spot in the parallelogram in the plan where the 79th are represented to be.

Major Dansey[8] with 2 guns was detached early in the battle to the abatis[9] on the Brussels road, where he was almost immediately wounded. The Troop remained in this position during the day, and was engaged there, when the French finally gave way.

I am, my dear Sir Hew, very truly yours

E C WHINYATES

---

1 Whinyates joined the Artillery in 1798 and served in Holland in 1799, Madeira in 1801, Copenhagen in 1807, and the Peninsula in 1810–13, receiving a General Service Medal with two bars for Busaco and Albuera. At Waterloo, he had three horses shot beneath him and was then struck by a roundshot on the leg and severely wounded in the left arm towards the close of the day. He was made a brevet major for Waterloo and received a pension for his wounds. Afterwards General Sir E.C. Whinyates, KCB and KH, he was Colonel Commandant of the Royal Horse Artillery in 1864. He died at Cheltenham on 25 December 1865.

2 This letter predates his letters published in Siborne's *The Waterloo Letters* (numbers 83 to 85).

3 The British Library catalogue incorrectly records that this letter is by Mrs S. Whinfield. A further letter Add MS 34707, fo 251, is also by Whinyates not Mrs. Whinfield as recorded. This letter is actually published in Siborne's *The Waterloo Letters* (number 83).

4 Captain Sir Hew Dalrymple Ross KCB commanded 'C' Troop of the Royal Horse Artillery at Waterloo. He had joined the Artillery in 1795 and served in the Peninsula from 1809 to 1814, receiving a Gold Cross with six bars for Busaco, Fuentes d'Onoro, Ciudad Rodrigo, Badajoz, Salamanca, Vittoria, Pyrenees, Nivelle and Nive. He was wounded in the shoulder at Redinha, wounded in the leg at Foz d'Aronce and dangerously wounded in the head at the siege of Badajoz. He became KStA for Waterloo. He was the first artilleryman ever to become a Field Marshal. He died as Lieutenant Governor of Chelsea Hospital in December 1868. His letters were published by Siborne (numbers 91–92).

5 Unfortunately, this plan appears to no longer exist.

6 This refers to the retreat of Bijlandt's brigade during the advance of D'Erlon's corps and the movement of Kempt and Pack's brigades to counter this.

7 Lieutenant Colonel Alexander Macdonald commanded the six Horse Artillery troops attached to the cavalry at Waterloo. He joined the Artillery in 1794, but only seems to have seen action at Waterloo, for which he received the CB. He became a major general in 1837 and died at Leamington on 21 May 1840.

8 Second Captain Charles Cornwallis Dansey was severely wounded while leading a rocket detachment to the abatis. Dansey joined the Artillery in 1803 and served at the sieges of Ischia and Santa Maura in the Ionian Islands and in the Peninsula. He received a General Service Medal with six bars for Badajoz, Salamanca, Vittoria, San Sebastian, Nivelle and Nive. Afterwards CB and colonel. He died on 21 July 1853. His letters were published by Siborne (numbers 87 & 88).

9 An abatis is an obstruction made of trees and branches to prevent use of a feature, such as a road to the enemy. Two abatis were built across the Brussels road, one near the southern

edge of La Haye Sainte, the second at the northern tip of the sand pit. It is almost certain that Dansey's party fired their rockets from the abatis near the sand pit.

No. 73 From the same
Carlisle, 20 November 1842

ADD MS 34707, FO 466 10

This letter was previously published in Siborne's Waterloo letters (number 84); however a large part of the text was omitted. I have therefore chosen to reprint it in full; Siborne omitted the text in italics.

Dear Sir

I beg to acknowledge your letter of the 16th requesting information on some points relative to my troop at the battle of Waterloo, and hasten according to your desire, to reply to the references as well as my memory will permit.

In answer to the question 'Had you a certain number of men employed *exclusively* in managing the rockets, in addition to the ordinary numbers attached to other troops? And if so what was the probable amount of that additional strength?'

I have to state that the mounted rocket sections were also gun detachments and were *not exclusively* employed in managing rockets.

When Colonel Macdonald ordered the advance with rockets, all the gun detachments (except the two dismounted men at each gun who are called limber gunners, and which two are carried on the limbers, and have no horses) left their guns behind them and moved quickly being on horseback down the slope in front of the guns.

When halted and brought into action, they dismounted from their horses to fire *ground* rockets, that is rockets not laid at angles of elevation but rockets that ricochéd along the ground. There were crops of rich standing grain in front of the rocket sections when the men dismounted, which screened all objects in front, and the rockets were fired through them in the direction of the enemy's troops in position.

The foregoing statement replies to the supposition in the following paragraph of your letter 'that if at any time it was necessary to leave the guns in position while the rocket section proceeded to some other point, enough men were left to work those guns.' This was not the case, the two limber gunners attached to each gun only were left when the mounted men moved down the slope in advance.

With respect to the costume and equipment of the rocket troop at the battle of Waterloo, the men were dressed like the Horse Artillery viz. with a laced jacket (having three rows of buttons in front) and helmet. Their appointments (both of horse and man) however differed from those of the Horse Artillery. They had a pouch belt which the Horse Artillery had not. Each mounted man carried fasces of 3 or 4 rocket sticks in a bucket in a manner similar to the mode of lances and dragoon carbines are carried. These sticks were carried on the right side of the horse. Besides these the centre of threes carried a small trough on his saddlebag on which the rocket was laid when fired, and every man in the rocket sections carried rockets in his holsters. Should you entertain any intention of representing the costume of the troops, the small flag attached to the rocket stick should not be introduced. It was added by the Captain as an ornament, and was discontinued and not part of the real equipment. The horse appointments were those of the light cavalry and the N.C. officers and gunners had blue shabraques laced with yellow.

I am sorry I cannot add anything to what I have before sent on the movement of the Troop at the time of the advance of the cavalry.

With respect however to the supposition at the conclusion of your letter, 'that the rocket sections advanced to the knoll on the left of the sandpit (opposite La Haye Sainte) and as that moment Kempt's brigade was driving before it a French column in the direction of the knoll, this, also other hindrances could delay the advance of the rockets, and perhaps by the time they got fairly established on the knoll, our cavalry were in full retreat, and the rockets perhaps playing over their heads against the enemy's reserves.'

I have to remark that the rocket sections never were on the knoll, and did not fire over the heads of the cavalry, but descended the slope in front of their guns, and fired ground rockets which ranged up the ascent to the enemy's position.

I myself saw no dragoons in front of the rocket sections, and I am not sufficiently acquainted with the cavalry movements at that moment to say if they ever did engage the enemy on his position directly in my front. If they did so they must have extended to the right of their original direction of advance.

However I was informed (but how correctly I cannot say) that a wounded officer of dragoons left disabled close to the enemy's line had said that rockets passed over him, and he heard the exclaiming about them and saying we wished to burn them alive. But the rockets which passed over this officer may have been wide straggling ones out of the general direction of fire.

I regret I cannot afford you so much information as will make plain the circumstances of a scene of such diversity and constant change. I was necessarily an actor and my mind and time were engrossed by my particular duties, to the prevention of observation of general events.

My former statements will have explained that the troop having received orders moved on the flank of the cavalry up to the position, that at arriving at the double hedge, and hollow road, and consequently on the position it received Col. Macdonald's orders to advance with the rocket sections which was immediately done. That moving down the slope in front of the guns which were left in position we came to action and fired ground rockets and shortly after received Colonel Macdonald's orders to rejoin the guns which we did accordingly.

I am, dear Sir, truly yours

E C WHINYATES

---

1 This letter is incorrectly recorded as written by Mrs S. Whinfield in the British Library catalogue.

No. 74 First Lieutenant Thomas Fox Strangways[1]

Woolwich, 22 March[2]

ADD MS 34708, FO 336

Dear Siborne

I would have had great pleasure in giving you any information as to where our guns, that is Colonel Whinyates' troop, were in position at 7 o'clock on the 18th June 1815, but I was wounded and retired previous to that hour of the day.

I should say that between five and six o'clock, our guns were farther from the high road than you have placed them and I don't think they ever were moved nearer to it. I have put a black dot where I should say our right gun was. We were most of the day in front of the Wavres road, but at the time you mention and previous to that, in the rear of it, about ten or fifteen yards I should say.

The ground was so soft from heavy rain that our guns were moved behind the Wavres road and after that, hardly moved at all.

When our guns were in advance of the Wavres road, they were only just in front of it and that must have been about two o'clock. Also about that time, we advanced with rockets perhaps 100 yards, and fired some volleys, leaving our guns for that very short period in our rear.

We were the only troop that had rockets as well as guns (6 pounder).

We had two guns detached under Major Dansey,[3] which were I believe placed on the chaussee from Brussels.[4] No English troops in our front would have suffered from our guns, as we should not have kept up the fire we did.

Colonel Whinyates is at Woolwich, Major Dansey abroad, either at Rome or Naples.

I wish I could have given you more information, which I would do with great pleasure when able. We expect to be in Dublin next year and as our promotion is so slow probably Walcot[5] and myself will again accompany the troop.

---

1 Strangways had joined the Artillery in 1806 and served as a subaltern with the rocket troop sent to Germany in 1813. He was present at the battles of Gohrde and Leipzig, receiving the SwOS and KStA for commanding the troop when Major Bogue was killed in action. He was dangerously wounded at Waterloo but made a miraculous recovery. Afterwards, as a Brigadier General serving in the Crimea he was killed by a shell at Inkermann.

2 Probably written around 1837, as it appears to precede the following letters, which can be identified to that year.

3 Second Captain Charles Cornwallis Dansey.

4 This note appears to indicate that the two guns were placed on the high road near the cross roads, but this is the same position where Sir Hew Ross describes having two of his guns. It is unlikely four guns would be positioned here and it seems difficult to make both statements tally.

5 Edmund Yeamans Walcot had served at Waterloo as a second captain in Lieutenant Colonel Webber Smith's horse artillery troop. He joined the Artillery in 1802 and served in the Corunna campaign. He retired on full pay in 1845 as a lieutenant colonel. He died at Winkton, Hampshire, on 28 February 1847.

No. 75 From the same

No date[1]

ADD MS 34708, FO 341

Major Whinyates' troop [of the] Royal Horse Artillery about 7 pm was posted in line, a little in the rear of the cross road leading from Wavres and the Brussels road, and to the left of the high road from Brussels to Genappe.

It is the last of my recollection for I was wounded about that time, there were considerable sorties of cavalry and infantry in front of the troop, but as to their particular formation I cannot say.

I believe that all the ground immediately near the troop was in crops of some kind but I cannot specify the particular kind.

Major Whinyates' troop discharged several rockets during the day, principally at two hundred yards in advance of the cross road, leaving the guns in the position before named.

The six guns[2] (6 pounders) were during the greater part of the day sometimes in front and sometimes in the rear of the cross roads leading from Wavres.

THOMAS FOX STRANGWAYS
CAPTAIN, ROYAL HORSE ARTILLERY

1 Probably written in 1837.

2 This statement does not agree with those of Sergeant Dunnett or his own previous letter, which state that two guns had been detached and did not rejoin until the following day.

No. 76 From the same
Woolwich, 30 April[1]

ADD MS 34708, FO 342

Dear Siborne

I feel quite positive as to there not being any guns on the mound in front of the sand pit and marked *a* in your plan, during any time of the day of the 18th. Whinyates' troop about the time Picton was killed advanced with their rockets, I should say a little to the left of the point *a* and fired several, when we fell back on our guns, which we had left immediately in front of the cross road, and there we remained in position some time before we occupied the position as marked in your plan behind the cross road.[2] The two guns were withdrawn from the high road, but at what time of the day I do not know.

In the retreat from Genappe, Whinyates' troop fired several rockets along the chaussee but to the best of my recollection our guns, all light 6-pounders, were not fired at all.

I understand Rudyerd[3] is abroad and that the agents Messrs. Fox and L. have instructions to forward his letters to him.

I hope you are successful in obtaining a good situation for your model when it comes to London and as the coronation will make my place so thronged I expect you will be overwhelmed with visitors. I have consulted Whinyates and he has nothing more to say than I have written.

Believe me, very truly yours

THOMAS FOX STRANGWAYS

I wish I could be of more use to you.

1 No year is given, but as the letter refers to the coronation, it is reasonable to presume that it was written in 1838, as Queen Victoria's coronation took place on 27 June 1838.

2 The plan appears to be no longer extant.

3 Samuel Rudyerd served at Waterloo as a second captain in Major Lloyd's battery of foot artillery. He had joined the Artillery in 1803 serving in the East Indies before the Waterloo campaign. He rose to colonel in 1846 and died at Whitby on 29 July 1847. The reason for mentioning him is not clear. His letters were published by Siborne (numbers 98 & 99).

Letter no. 77

No. 77 Sergeant Daniel Dunnett[1]

Walton House, near Aylesbury, 1 May 1843

ADD MS 34708, FO 96

To Sergeant Dickson, Royal Horse Artillery

Dear Dickson

In compliance with your request in respect to the circumstance attending the rocket party mentioned in Captain Siborne's letter. I feel very anxious to give all the information in my power.

With respect to the first question, the French *column* did certainly appear to be advancing for the purpose of attacking the farmhouse.[2]

As to the 2nd question I can say that the firing of the rockets did give a severe check to the advance of that column which did not appear to resume its advance during the time we were firing, but our rockets being expended, we joined our guns a little to the rear. Whether the same column did afterwards advance and take the farmhouse, I am unable to say, the column mentioned appeared to be a very strong one and if there were two columns, they must be very close together. I recollect when our rockets being expended we fell back on our guns, they were then in command of Lt Wright[3] and being then late in the evening, the right division[4] did not join the other part of the troop till the morning of the 19th.[5] I retired with my party in consequence of having discharged all our rockets, to the guns as mentioned above (you will remember the morning of the 19th) when a cart came along with a *cask of rum* and no one with it but a country person and I ordered one of the men to fetch me a falling ladle off one of the drivers, with which I paid on the head of the cask till I arrived at the rum, and I am happy to say that though I directed the men to fill their *canteens* they *every man* kept perfectly sober although they had been nearly 2 days without provisions.

Make our kind respects to Mrs Dickson and family, and believe me to remain your well wisher,

D DUNNETT

---

1 Sergeant Daniel Dunnett took command of the rocket detachment at the abatis when Captain Dansey was severely wounded. He ordered the detachment to continue firing, only returning to his divisional guns when all their rockets had been discharged. (See Dalton *Waterloo Heroes*, p. 273).

2 La Haye Saint farmhouse.

3 First Lieutenant Amherst Wright joined the Artillery in 1806 and served in Copenhagen in 1807. He was attached to the Swedish Army in 1813–14 being present at the siege of Wittemberg and capture of Hanover and Lubeck. He received a Gold Medal and was made SWOS by the Prince Royal of Sweden for the siege of Gluckstadt. Dalton records him as being wounded at Waterloo, but this is not confirmed by any other source. He afterwards retired on full pay as a major in June 1840 and died soon after at Malta on 27 September 1840.

4 The six-gun troop was divided into three divisions of two guns each commanded by a Lieutenant. The division of Lieutenant Wright was obviously detached from the other two divisions and placed near the crossroads. The most obvious location would be on the road in the rear of the abatis, but most accounts agree that the two guns placed here were a division of Sir Hew Ross's troop. There is some evidence in other letters that the guns were run down the slope to the vicinity of the sand pit, but this is far from certain.

5 The remaining two divisions commanded by Whinyates throughout was then positioned on the ridge where Roger's battery had originally been sited, but had been moved to the right at about 2.30 pm.

No. 78 Sergeant John Dickson[1]
Woolwich, 24 April 1843

ADD MS 34708, FO 90

Sir

I beg to acquaint you that the non commissioned officers party with rockets, detached from the troop at Waterloo, came into action on the high road, considerably in advance of our line, and after firing a few rockets we fell back to where our horses were standing (about the centre of our line).

Captain Dansey was wounded leading the party into action on the high road, and was taken to the rear. Consequently the party was left under the command of Sergeant Dunnett (see accompanying letter)[2] when the circumstance mentioned in your letter occurred. The party was standing on the left of the high road, and the French column was rather to our left front. The enemy was not then in possession of the farm of La Haye Sainte, but they were so not very long afterwards. I cannot say at what o'clock it was, for I had no opportunity of enquiring.

Yours,

JOHN DICKSON SERGT RHA

1 I cannot positively identify this person who obviously served with the troop at Waterloo. The only possibility listed in the Waterloo Medal Roll is Driver John Dixon, but there is no evidence to confirm that it is he.

2 This refers to letter 77.

No. 79 From the same
Woolwich, 2 May 1843

ADD MS 34708, FO 94

Having communicated the contents of your letter of 27th April '43 to Mr Daniel Dunnett and requested him to send me an account in writing (as far as he could recollect) of what transpired during the evening, after firing the rockets mentioned in my last, and I herewith send you a portion of his letter (having drawn the pen through such part of it as related to family matters) and about a favourite horse of the Sergeant's having been shot.

With respect to your 1st question, whether the column was altogether prevented from making that attack in consequence of the discharge of rockets; as well as I can recollect, the column did not appear to advance during the short period we remained in that part of the field; but as our rockets were all expended we were moved a little to our rear and then to our left and rejoined our guns under the command of Lieutenant Wright.

Some short time afterwards on looking towards the farmhouse, I saw it in possession of the French and a number of our soldiers appeared to be retreating from the farm, but whether [by] the same column we fired the rockets into I cannot say. When the

Sergeant fired the rockets, the column appeared advancing in a direct line for the farm, and our attention was wholly directed to one column, I did not observe two.

After the rockets were all expended, the Sergeant retired, and rejoined the two guns that were detached from the Troop under Lt A. Wright .[1]

Yours,

J DICKSON SERGT. RHA

---

1 First Lieutenant Amherst Wright was in command of the detached division following the wounding of Captain Dansey. He seems to have stayed with the guns when the rocket squad moved forward to the abatis. This statement confirms that of Daniel Dunnett regarding the positioning of the two guns forward of the main position.

No. 80 Sergeant Michael Taylor[1]

No date

ADD MS 34708, FO 367

Sir,

Major Whinyates' brigade was situated in advance on the summit opposite to the farm La Haye Sainte, the 2 right guns upon the main road to Genappe, commanded by Captain Dansey.[2] I saw no such troops as you mention belonging to the German Legion,[3] I saw the Horse Guards charge the cuirassiers.

I saw the panorama of Waterloo[4] and consider that Major Whinyates' troop was there neglected.

During the action and early, Colonel Alexander Macdonald R.H.A.[5] came to Whinyates and says 'Now Whinyates, for your honour, take your mounted rocket tuns in advance'. He did so in rear of La Haye Sainte and divided his fire in two directions, the left on a brigade of French cavalry and the right on a column of infantry. We put the former in great confusion then retreated to our guns. No notice is taken of this in the panorama. I noticed this same thing to you before.

Sir, I am your most obedient servant,

M TAYLOR

---

1 He served with Whinyates' troop at Waterloo.

2 Again, the letter confirms that Dansey's division of guns were on the road, they must have been close to the two guns of Ross's troop situated at the crossroads yet they never comment on the others presence.

3 This refers to statements made by some officers of the 2nd KGL Brigade, that some of their troops crossed the chaussee to aid in the defeat of D'Erlon's corps.

4 This does not refer to the panorama painted by Louis Dumoulin, which can still be seen at Waterloo, as this was not produced until 1910. It refers to a panorama of the battle exhibited at London in the 1830s.

5 Lieutenant Colonel Alexander Macdonald commanded the six Horse Artillery troops at Waterloo.

Lieutenant Colonel Sir Hew Ross's Troop

No. 81 Second Captain John Boteler Parker[1]
Military Academy, Woolwich, 14 May 1835

ADD MS 34705, FO 265

Sir

It is necessary I should apologise for having so long delayed answering your queries, which would not have been the case, if I had felt in possession of any information worth your acceptance. I now return your plan with such observations as occur to me to be useful.

Question	**Answer**
1 What was the particular formation of the Troop about 7 o'clock etc.	Cannot say having been carried off the field wounded before that hour.[2]
2 What was the formation of that partof the enemy's forces etc.	Answered above
3 Would you have the goodness when examining the plan you will find I have marked with a pencil etc.	I have examined the plan and cannot see any pencil marks denoting the position of Sir Hew Ross's troop, but if the writing in pencil specifying to several corps is intended to mark it, I think it mistaken, as I have no recollection of the troop having gone off the plateau near La Haye Sainte and in front of the sunken road which traversed across our rear. One or two guns, I am unsure which were detached into the high road. I think the nature of the several corps adjoining our position are properly presented on the plan.
4 I shall feel very much obliged by your offering any etc.	At so great a distance of time I do not feel qualified to attempt to offer any information that you are not in possession of, but rather than not, I prefer answering in the risk of repetition. The enemy took early possession of La Haye Sainte (clearing the Germans out) and kept possession of it to our cost the whole day. Nor was any attempt made that I am aware of to dislodge them. This facilitated the advance of their cavalry both cuirassiers and lancers who charged the guns and obliged us partially to abandon them for a short time.

I have marked in red ink the ground the troop occupied so long as a semicircle in the field.[3]

I am, Sir, your obedient servant,

J B PARKER

1 He was the second son of Admiral Sir Hyde Parker. He joined the Artillery in 1802, serving at Walcheren and the Peninsula in 1812–14. He received a General Service Medal with three bars for San Sebastian, Orthes and Toulouse and a Gold Medal for Vittoria. He became a brevet lieutenant colonel on 18 June 1815. Afterwards he rose to Major General and CB. He was Lieutenant Governor of the Royal Military Academy at Woolwich from 1 April 1848 until his death in March 1851.

2 Parker lost his left leg at Waterloo.

3 The map shows nothing of consequence and therefore is not produced here.

Major Beane's Troop

No. 82 First Lieutenant James Robertson Bruce[1]

Downhill,[2] 10 December 1834

ADD MS 34704, FO 28

Sir

I regret very much that at this distance of time I cannot give you any satisfactory answer to your several queries, in relation to the formation of Major Beane's troop and that of the enemy's forces immediately in front of it at the time you specify (about 7pm). To the best of my recollection the troop was in action at this moment, the six guns in line under command of Lieutenant Maunsell,[3] Major Beane[4] having been killed and Captain Webber[5] wounded (slightly) early in action.

I have no reason to doubt the correctness of your information as to the crops on the field of Waterloo on the day of the battle, but many of them were so trodden down before Major Beane's troop came on the ground that it was impossible to distinguish what they were.

I must again express my regret at not being able to give you the information you require for so interesting a work.

I have the honour to be, Sir, your obedient humble servant,

J R BRUCE

1 Afterwards Sir James Robertson Bruce, Bart. He retired on half pay as a first lieutenant on 16 June 1820 and died in 1836.

2 Downhill can be found west of Coleraine in Londonderry, Northern Ireland.

3 First Lieutenant John E. Maunsell retired on half pay as a second captain in 1826; he died on 20 November 1869. His letter was published by Siborne (number 93).

4 Major George Beane had commanded the troop since 1813; he had previously served at Corunna, Vittoria, San Sebastian, Orthes and Toulouse. He died at about the time of the attack of the Imperial Guard. After the battle, Captain Alexander Mercer, famous for his *Journal of the Waterloo Campaign*, published in 1870, succeeded him.

5 Second Captain William Webber joined the Artillery in 1803 and was present at the capture of Surinam in 1804 (where he was wounded), the Peninsula (including Vittoria), the Pyrenees, Orthes, Toulouse and then Canada in 1814. He was severely wounded at Waterloo by a heavy fall from his horse, which was killed by a shell when at the gallop. He went on half pay as a major in 1826 and became a lieutenant colonel in 1837. He died at Hexworth House, Cornwall, on 1 March 1847. R. H. Wollocombe published his Peninsula journal entitled *With the Guns in the Peninsula* (London, Greenhill, 1991).

The Royal Artillery

Captain Bolton's Battery

No. 83 First Lieutenant William Anderson[1]

Tower, London, 10 June 1838

ADD MS 34706, FO 480

Sir

In reply to your letter of the 10th, I beg to inform you, that at the time I was ordered to withdraw the abandoned pieces on the 18th June, I was led to believe that they belonged to the Belgians, I am still under the same impression, but not having seen any of the gunners by whom they had previously been worked, it is of course possible that I am under a mistake, and that they belonged to the Brunswickers and were the guns to which you refer.

The limbers by which the guns were withdrawn belonged to the batteries under the command of Colonel Rogers,[2] and Major Sinclair,[3] and consequently were British. They were limbered up by the gunners belonging to Captain *Bolton's Brigade*,[4] and withdrawn to the rear without gunners.

I was ordered to take them across the Nivelle road, upon moving to the rear I led nearly perpendicularly for a *short* distance, then *continued to Mont St Jean*, when finding that I was thereby exposing them to a very heavy cannonade, I threw our shoulders forward, and crossed the Nivelles road to the right of the position from where they had been withdrawn,[5] and there they were left, the limbers rejoined their respective batteries.

I remain, Sir, your obedient humble servant,

W C ANDERSON
CAPTAIN REGIMENT OF ARTILLERY

---

1 Afterwards he was a major general; he died in Edinburgh on 30 August 1865.

2 Major Thomas Rogers commanded a foot artillery battery, which had already been hotly engaged at Quatre Bras. He gained a CB for Waterloo. He died as a colonel at Woolwich on 9 August 1839. His letters were published by Siborne (numbers 101 & 102).

3 Second Captain James Sinclair commanded a foot artillery battery at Waterloo. He had served in the Peninsula and had received a General Service Medal with seven bars for Corunna, Badajoz, Salamanca, Vittoria, the Pyrenees, Nivelle and Nive. He retired on full pay as a lieutenant colonel in 1841 and died on Jersey on 15 May 1851.

4 Captain Samuel Bolton commanded a foot artillery battery and was killed during the attack of the Imperial Guard.

5 In a footnote on p. 330 of his *History of the Waterloo Campaign* (Greenhill reprint, 1990), Siborne refers to Anderson's letter and concludes that the guns were from a Brunswick battery. However, Siborne further quotes Anderson as stating that the guns were in the first line and that one cannon could not be removed as too near the French. This additional information is presumably from a previous letter, which is no longer in the files. The Brunswick batteries are generally believed to have been in reserve most of the day, only coming into action in support of the Brunswick infantry squares that stood in second line and receiving few casualties, therefore the guns are unlikely to belong to them. The Dutch/Belgian batteries known to have been in this part of the field are the Belgian Horse

Battery of Captain Krahmer de Bichen which was involved in the defeat of the Imperial Guard and is described by Ensign Macready as having fought bravely; and the two halves of the Dutch horse battery which fought separately, commanded by Captains Petter and van Pittius respectively. The identity of these guns is therefore not clearly established, but the likelihood is that Anderson was correct that they were Dutch/Belgian and belonged to one of the half batteries of Petter or van Pittius.

No. 84 Gunner Robert Mackay[1]
31 July 1836

ADD MS 34706, FO 124

Captain Bolton's Battery

I cannot describe the position of the battery when near A in black[2] better than that it was a rise of ground some distance in the rear of the road and rather to the left of Hougoumont.[3] The battery was first with its left towards the enemy, the farriers passing along a narrow road with the cars in rear of their respective guns, and a troop of Horse Artillery was at the same time on the top of that rise, facing the enemy at regular distance. Whose troop it was I cannot say but I went and shook hands with a man by the name of Ormerod[4] who formerly belonged to the Royal Artillery. Whilst in that position, gun no. 1 with its people was ordered to go and dismount a French gun who nearly could enfilade our position. On the guns return I was informed by the men that they dismounted the gun with the loss of Gunner Charles [Quinn?].[5] Some time afterwards I saw an aide de camp go to Captain Bolton; when the battery was then ordered in position of action to our proper front and rather to the left.[6] A brigade of light cavalry was then to our left front (one of the regiments was the 12th Light Dragoons) who went over the front position at a canter and soon returned with a brigade of French lancers after them (as I thought dressed in red) who received the fire from the faces of several squares and of our battery with round shot through the intervals of squares which made them retire. Our cavalry drew them three times in to that snare, the third time the French followed ours in rear of the squares and both charged; the French having the hill, they passed through each other, formed and charged again, when the French retreated. I believe the 12th had a captain killed on that occasion.[7]

We were then ordered to position C. Captain Bolton would not move for the first order – because it did not come from General Clinton.[8] Upon receiving the proper order we moved to *P.C.R.*; near the position we passed in rear and to the left of a square of the foot guards (1st Regiment), where there was a battery with only a bombardier and 2 gunners belonging to the 10th Battalion of Artillery[9] to man it. Therefore Major Napier[10] could have made use of 10 guns and one howitzer instead of five guns had he the men to work them.

ROBERT MACKAY SERGEANT MAJOR
1ST BATTALION GRENADIER GUARDS –
THEN GUNNER IN CAPTAIN BOLTON'S BRIGADE OF ARTILLERY

1 He is recorded as Gunner Robert McKey in the Waterloo Medal Roll. He is shown as having been discharged and subsequently joined the Grenadier Guards.

2 The plan referred to appears to be no longer extant.
3 The battery stood on a ridge just north of the Nivelles road, facing towards Nivelles.
4 Probably Gunner John Ormrod of Major Norman Ramsay's troop of horse artillery, stationed on the crest just above Hougoumont. There are no officers of this name listed as present at Waterloo.
5 There is no person listed by the name of Charles Quinn listed for the battery in the Waterloo Medal Roll, but there is a Gunner Hugh Quinn, though he is not listed as killed.
6 The battery was moved at approximately 3 o'clock to the left and on to the front ridge between Beane's and Kuhlmann's guns.
7 Mackay presumably refers to Captain Edwin Sandys of the 12th Light Dragoons, as the Waterloo Medal Roll states that Captain Sandys died of his wounds soon after the battle.
8 Lieutenant Colonel Sir Henry Clinton commanded the 2nd Division, which included Bolton's battery.
9 The Royal Artillery regiment consisted of 10 battalions of ten companies, each manning a battery. The reference to the artilleryman's battalion is unusual as it only functioned as an administrative organization; it was more normal to refer to their battery by the relevant commander's name. It is unclear as to whose guns these could be, but may well be the same guns referred to by First Lieutenant Anderson, before they were removed.
10 This refers to Second Captain Charles Napier, who succeeded to the command of the battery on Captain Bolton's death towards the close of the battle.

Captain Sinclair's Battery

No. 85 First Lieutenant William Poole[1]

Terrick, near Whitchurch, Salop, 27 November 1834

ADD MS 34703, FO 285

Sir,

In replying to your circular of the 19th inst., I have to regret extremely that I am unable to supply you with any information that can be of any service to you in the very interesting undertaking you have in hand. Captain Sinclair's battery to which I belonged, was in reserve, and was not called up until a considerable time after the commencement of the battle, very shortly after which I was struck on my thigh with a splinter of a shell and left the field.

I have the honour to be Sir, your most obedient humble servant

W H POOLE, CAPTAIN
1/2 PAY OFFICER, ROYAL ARTILLERY

---

1 Poole retired on half pay as a second captain on 22 January 1834 and died at Terrick Hall, Whitchurch, on 20 January 1859.

Major Roger's Battery

No. 86 Second Lieutenant Henry Dunnicliffe[1]

Newport, 21 November 1834

ADD MS 34703, FO 297

Sir
I regret that it is not of my power to state the *precise* situation of Major Roger's battery at 7 pm at Waterloo. I never had otherwise than a very imperfect idea of the field, which I have never subsequently visited.

As far as my recollection goes, about 7 pm our battery was ordered to take up a position to the right of La Haye Sainte. We proceeded, accordingly, some distance – I can't really state what – up the Nivelle road and turning to the left ascended the heights, when we commenced a cannonade directed towards La Belle Alliance. There were some other batteries on the ground – mostly to our left. It would be useless for me to attempt to designate our position on the plan, I might only fix on some spot already *positively* appropriated; and thus mischievously create much doubt and perplexity in your mind.

Neither can I speak more decidedly as to the exact description of troops immediately vis-a-vis. I perfectly remember, however, the 24th Light Dragoons[2] charging down the hill immediately on our right of the two guns I commanded.

I should conceive that your best and surest sources of information would be officers commanding corps, divisions, regiments and batteries, and the staff.

With every wish for your complete success in the arduous but highly creditable undertaking you have embarked upon.

I have the honour to be, Sir, your most obedient servant,

HENRY DUNNICLIFFE

1 Henry Dunnicliffe is listed at p. 227 of Dalton's *Waterloo Roll Call* as having received a Waterloo medal as an unattached officer; this letter clarifies that he served with Roger's battery. He retired on half pay on 1 April 1819 and died at Richmond on 8 April 1866.

2 This is obviously a mistake, as the 24th Light Dragoons were not present at Waterloo. It is now impossible to identify the dragoons with any certainty.

KGL Artillery

Major A. Sympher's Horse Artillery Troop

No. 87 Second Captain Frederick Erythropel[1]

Basbeck,[2] 15 February 1835

ADD MS 34704, FO 253

Original in German

Your Excellency,
I have the honour to respond to your letter as follows.

The 1st Horse Artillery battery of the King's German Legion, with five nine-pounders and one howitzer under the command of Major Sympher[3] were at the various positions *a, b* and *c* as shown on the plan,[4] on the day of the battle at Waterloo on 18 June 1815. The battery was held in reserve at *a* and remained there until the enemy cavalry undertook a general attack, whereupon it was ordered to move to *b*, where it fired at the enemy which was established at *c*. This made him withdraw and we occupied the heights at *c* without suffering much loss from the enemy infantry fire which was still taking place behind the heights, but they were forced to withdraw as soon as we fired and our battery remained at c till the defeat of the enemy guards when they were pursued by the army where you took part.[5] During the time our battery was at *c*, it was attacked fiercely by an enemy battery, which was placed to their right, approximately in the direction of *d*.

As the enemy guards formed a march formation in order to attack our lines I was wounded and had to leave the battlefield and cannot tell you anything further about the result of this encounter.

The marked points *a*, *b*, and *c* can be taken as quite accurate while the position *d* marked in the surrounding area where the battery stood is more vague; this is particularly so at *c*.

I have the honour, your Excellency, to be your obedient servant,

ERYTHROPEL

---

1 Erythropel is numbered 43 in Beamish. He joined the Legion in 1805, serving in Hanover in 1805, the Baltic in 1807 and northern Germany in 1813–14. He was severely wounded at Waterloo. He later became a brevet major on half pay.

2 Basbeck is near Bremervörde, some 40 km west of Hamburg.

3 First Captain Augustus Sympher, numbered 29 in Beamish. He joined the Legion in 1804, serving in Hanover in 1805, the Baltic in 1807 and northern Germany 1813–14. He was slightly wounded at Waterloo. He was made CB, HGO3 and became a brevet lieutenant colonel in the Hanoverian Artillery and died at Hanover on 11 December 1830.

4 This plan does not appear to be extant.

5 It is not clear to whom this letter is written.

Major Kuhlmann's Horse Artillery Troop[1]

No. 88 Second Lieutenant Lewis Von Wissell[2]
24 February 1835[3]

ADD MS 34704, FO 262

Original in German

My memory of the battle of Waterloo after such a long time is as follows:

1 The 2nd horse battery of the Legion was near Capt. Sandham's[4] brigade of the British artillery, which was joined to the guard's division, which was if I am not mistaken under the command of Gen. Cooke.[5]

2 The battery occupied the approximate position which I marked on the map,[6] where they remained from early morning till about 6 in the afternoon; but due to a shortage of ammunition, as they were involved in the fighting on the 16th and 17th, they had to withdraw and reoccupy their original position. The French guards were already pushed back and the English army advanced, whereupon there was a total rout of the French army. Unfortunately, I cannot give answers to the further points raised in the questions.

3 The battery was forced to fire immediately at the beginning of the battle on a French infantry column, which was advancing around Hougoumont in a north-westerly direction, but due to the powerful artillery fire it had to turn around, whereupon the French redirected their attack against the protected north-easterly side. Our battery did not respond to the fire of the French artillery but we did fire if stragglers from the enemy infantry appeared towards Hougoumont.

4 Around 4 o'clock the French cavalry appeared to be beaten in the centre as it arrived with only a few squadrons with their front line at right angles to ours and close to the battery. We could not see from our position what was happening in the centre and at La Haye Sainte.

5 Soon afterwards repeated attacks by the enemy cuirassiers occurred; they penetrated the battery every time but were pushed back by both dragoon regiments[7] to their lines. The artillery troops went back to safety near the standing squares and then rushed forward again to the liberated positions.[8]

L v WISSEL
FORMERLY 2nd LIEUT OF THE 2ND HORSE BATTERY
KING'S GERMAN LEGION

1 First Captain Henry Jacob Kuhlmann numbered 28 in Beamish. He joined the Legion in 1804, serving in Hanover, and northern Germany in 1813–14. He received the CBO and HGO3 and became a brevet lieutenant colonel in the Hanoverian artillery and died at Stade near Hamburg on 19 March 1830.
2 Wissell is numbered 66 in Beamish. He joined the Legion in 1813, serving in the Netherlands. He was made HGO3 and HWC, and later became a captain on the staff of the Hanoverian artillery.
3 The location is unreadable.
4 Captain Charles Sandham commanded a foot battery in the Royal Artillery. He retired on half pay as a brevet major in 1822 and died at Rowdell in Sussex in 1869.
5 Major General George Cooke commanded the 1st or Guards Division.
6 The map does not appear to be extant.
7 The two KGL dragoon regiments which formed part of Major Dörnberg's 3rd cavalry brigade.
8 The artillerymen retreated to the protection of the infantry squares during the cavalry charges and returned to the guns as soon as the French cavalry retired.

Captain A. Cleeve's Foot Battery[1]

No. 89 First Lieutenant William Von Goeben[2]
Celle, 7 February 1835[3]

ADD MS 34704, FO 226

Lieut. Sir,
I am very sorry not to be able to give the desired explanations about the battle of

Waterloo, as I was already severely wounded two days before at the action of Quatre Bras.

The battery I was attached to at that time, was commanded by the late Lieutenant Colonel Cleeves.[4] Another officer of the battery – Lieutenant Hartmann[5] – was likewise wounded at Quatre Bras and absent from the brigade, and an officer of the British Artillery, who had assumed my place, was killed at Waterloo.[6] I must therefore doubt, that you will get an explanation on the questions sent to me by an officer of the battery, if Lieutenant Ludowig[7] is not perhaps able to furnish you with details. I know Lieutenant Ludowig was attached to our brigade, but I am not certain, if he was with the battery at Waterloo, as I believe to remember, that he was likewise wounded at Quatre Bras.

I have the honour to be, Sir, your most obedient, humble servant,

W DE GOEBEN

LATE K G ARTILLERY

---

1 Captain Cleeve's battery was brigaded with Major Lloyd's Royal Artillery battery and formed the artillery of the 3rd Division of Lieutenant General Baron Alten. The artillery brigade was commanded by Lieutenant Colonel Williamson.

2 He received a Waterloo medal and went on the retired list at Celle as a brevet major.

3 Celle is north-east of Hanover.

4 Captain Andrew Cleeves, number 34 in Beamish, was severely wounded at Waterloo. He joined the Legion in 1803 and served in Hanover, the Baltic and the Peninsula between 1808–14. He received a Gold Cross for Albuera. He became a brevet lieutenant colonel in the Hanoverian service and died at Selby in Yorkshire on 8 June 1830.

5 First Lieutenant Henry Hartmann, number 56 in Beamish, joined the Legion in 1811, serving in the Peninsula in 1812–14, receiving a General Service Medal with eight clasps for Salamanca, Vittoria, Pyrenees, San Sebastian, Nivelle, Nive, Orthes and Toulouse. He is shown as having been severely wounded at Quatre Bras and received a Waterloo Medal, and was made HWC and HGO3. Placed on British half pay in 1816, he became a captain in the Hanoverian artillery.

6 Siborne and Dalton identify this officer as First Lieutenant Robert Manners detached from Major Roger's battery of foot artillery. Dalton mistakenly states that he was at Ligny rather than Quatre Bras on 16 June. He is recorded as being wounded at Waterloo, but died of his wounds on the 18th.

6 This can only be Second Lieutenant Charles Hermann Ludowieg, number 67 in Beamish, who joined the Legion in 1814. He is not recorded as being wounded but received the Waterloo medal, indicating that Goeben was correct and that he did serve with the battery at Quatre Bras but also served at Waterloo. He was put on British half pay in 1816 as a brevet captain living in Stade.

Letter no. 90

The Hanoverian Artillery

Captain von Rettberg's Hanoverian Foot Artillery Battery

No. 90 Captain Charles von Rettberg[1]
Stade,[2] 10 February 1835

ADD MS 34704, FO 229

Original in German

Sir,

I hurry to answer your honoured letter dated Dublin, 27 January 1835, to tell you that at the end of February 1815 I remained on the Continent with the artillery of the King's German Legion in Ostend… and was ordered personally to go to Brussels in order to take over the command of the newly organized Hanoverian 2nd foot Battery which was added to the Hanoverian reserve corps. About 16 June my battery was ordered by the Duke of Wellington to join the 4th Division which was then under the command of Sir C. Colville, which was then stationed at Oudenarde. The march route was not advised to me, and on 16 June I then received the order to join the 5th Division of Sir T. Picton, and I marched with the same to Quatre Bras.[3] We took part in the fighting where I lost more men than at Waterloo – went back on the 17th with the 5th Division into position at Mont St Jean and was positioned on the left of the chaussee.

I beg to be excused this digression because I believe it is important to give an explanation as to how I came with my battery to be with the 5th division as you will see from the General Orders that I was to join the 4th division which was known to be in reserve and took no action in the battle.

In the *Notice Historique sur la bataille de Waterloo* by W B Craan[4] published in Brussels in September 1816, where the publisher appears to deal with the disposition of the army I have noticed that my battery was mixed up with another battery under the command of Captain Braun.[5]

On 18 June my battery was placed at A,[6] my ammunition coaches were placed at B. On the right and under the circumstances, correctly so called the Scottish brigade which brigade consisted of the 1st Royals, 42nd and 92nd Regiments was placed behind me in a valley and the cavalry brigade of Sir F. Ponsonby was approximately at C. Opposite us stood a numerous French artillery at C–C. Behind them in the valley covered by D was the French reserve. On the right of the Scottish brigade was an English rocket battery[7] at G I believe and the other Hanoverian battery under Captain Braun who was earlier injured around position H.

I remained in the position with my battery the whole day till the end of the battle. To the left of me was a Dutch battery.[8] Around 1 or 2 o'clock we were attacked by a strong French column at point D that however walked up the height leading towards us in apparent disorder. They did not come in close formation and pushed on to my right wing where I had my howitzers and became involved in hand to hand fighting with the Scottish brigade who defended their glory. Sir F. Ponsonby attacked immediately with his brigade that stood at F, whereupon the enemy took flight in the greatest possible disorder. The British cavalry went too far and was forced to retreat by a superior number of enemy cavalry. The enemy left behind a substantial number of prisoners.

After this failed attack by the enemy nothing special happened to the front of my battery, the French increased their artillery fire against us and a continuous cannonade took place between us that lasted till the evening. The enemy concentrated his fire on the pass at La Haye Sainte and at our right wing.

Around 4 o'clock I saw that our right wing was very much under pressure and at the same time I noticed that the Prussians were approaching on the left of Plançenoit and that a substantial corps of the French advanced against them.

I thought that the enemy would be somewhat weakened in their efforts against our right wing but the opposite was the fact. Their effort against our right wing and their march past La Haye Sainte was doubled.

I had with my battery the most beautiful position that one could wish for artillery. Just in front of me was the road from La Haye Sainte to Wavre with a hedge on our side. I stood about 8–10 feet higher then the road. Immediately on the other side of the road the terrain ran gently down towards the enemy. I had arranged to cut down the hedge in the morning to have a free view.

I rode over the battle ground many times in the years 1816–18 from Conde and found the ground in a reasonable condition, which the French in their stories describe for them as the unfortunate facts of the battle, that we had the fortune because of the cut down hedge in my front and the yellow clay which the enemy could easily see.[9]

The loss of my battery was in relation to the others therefore very minimal. The rocket battery and the 1st Hanoverian foot battery on my right suffered because they were disadvantaged somewhat in comparison with me as their positioning was less suitable.

In the evening of this for me unforgettable day, I was at about 7 pm busy at my ammunition wagons at B and I was startled by an unknown bugle call and saw a great number of Prussian cavalry very close to the wood at B coming on. Leading them was General Lieutenant von Ziethen[10] himself. He asked for the shortest way to the main road that runs along by La Haye Sainte. I rode after him and I showed him my joy that the Prussians came to our aid to which he replied that on his march on the flank of the French army he saw there was already some disquiet and he believed that they would be soon retiring. Soon after the catastrophe took place.

The fire from our left wing was much reduced, I could become a viewer of what was happening on our right wing, how our brave troops with a hurrah! advanced and the enemy fled in unbelievable chaos. After half an hour the enemy was not to be seen and some men in the battery let their happy song sound. I did not follow the fleeing enemy because I had no ammunition and also no order to pursue.

Sir T. Picton was already dead in the morning and I reported therefore next morning, the 19th to Lieutenant General Sir J. Kempt who was in the rear house of La Belle Alliance, that we were ready for whatever service he required. He gave me the order to count the guns that were abandoned by the French, I found 26 pieces, but many of these were not recoverable as they were placed at J. where the exits to the lane were too steep.

They wished that I should reply in German, excuse me therefore for my meandering which is part of our language and also a 44-year-old serving soldier who gets great pleasure in talking about taking part in battles.

I have great honour to greet you respectfully,

C RETTBERG
LIEUT COLONEL
COMMANDER 2ND BATTALION HANOVERIAN ARTILLERY

PS I marched with the 5th division in the afternoon of the 19th June from the battlefield to Paris, on the 28th I went from Roye to the 4th division at Montidier. I parted from the 5th Division very unhappily and from their then commander Sir James Kempt who showed remarkable bravery, the greatest concern and maximum care for his troops during the march.

---

1 Rettberg is numbered 33 in Beamish. He joined the KGL artillery in 1804 and became a captain in 1806. He served in Hanover, the Baltic, in the Peninsula from 1808–14 and then in the Waterloo campaign. He received the Gold Cross with bars for Talavera, Busaco and Badajoz. He was made HGO2 and HWC. Afterwards he went on British half pay in 1816 and became a colonel in the Hanoverian artillery.
2 Stade is just to the west of Hamburg.
3 This information is of interest as it is usually stated that Rettberg's battery did not serve at Quatre Bras.
4 This refers to the map of the field of Waterloo, produced by the Belgian engineer de Craan by the orders of King William. It showed the positions of all the allied units.
5 Captain William Braun's 1st Hanoverian foot battery was originally posted at Mont St Jean farm, but moved into the line to the right of Rettberg at approximately 2 pm.
6 This obviously refers to a map, which appears to be a copy of that of Heise, namely map two accompanying letter number 93.
7 Captain Whinyates' battery; see the letters from his troop on pp 72-80.
8 This must refer to Captain Bijeveld's Dutch horse battery stationed above Papelotte.
9 He indicates that the hedge gave him a clear arc of fire and that the yellow clay would cause the attackers to slip and slide as they attempted to close with the battery making it nearly unassailable.
10 Ziethen commanded the Prussian 1st Corps.

No. 91 From the same
Stade, 25 July 1836

ADD MS 34706, FO 377

Original in German
Written to Lt Benne
Marked as received at Hanover 18 September 1837

Dear Sir,

I have made no copy of my letter of 10 February 1835 and so please forgive me if I should repeat something. I was moved with the 2nd Hanoverian battery from Namur to Brussels a few days before 16 June according to General orders and transferred to the English division which was commanded by Lieutenant General Sir Charles Colville. The march route to Oudenarde had however not been received when I received orders to join the Duke of Wellington's 5th Division, which at that point as Sir T. Picton had not joined was therefore commanded by Sir J. Kempt.

About 3 o'clock in the afternoon I arrived at Quatre Bras, an adjutant advised my position and I had at the same time the opportunity to see the enemy cavalry, which soon attacked but was beaten back, being effectively fired upon. Somewhat later, I believe about 5 or 6, I was ordered to B,[1] to the right of General Alten's division, as he was short of artillery. I realised the danger of this position for my battery, because the French artillery which was numerically superior to us, at D was also placed most advantageously, as I could see the barrels of their guns only and placed my pieces therefore as far apart as possible, leaving only as many cannons in place as were necessary and sent the ammunition caissons into a protected position at JL. Irrespective of these precautions, I lost a lot of people and horses as the fire lasted till late at night, I think 9 pm. A Second Captain from Captain Lloyd's battery, whose name I forget,[2] came with a howitzer and placed himself voluntarily under my command, while the other guns of Captain Lloyd's battery were under fire by the enemy.

I sent an officer around 11 o'clock with a report of the losses suffered and ammunition expenditure to the headquarters of the artillery at Quatre Bras and received a reply that the ammunition would be replaced next morning. However this did not happen and possibly could not happen as the army started to withdraw. The horses were not fed for many hours and not watered at all, it was very warm. The column made a short stop not far from a brook. I rode to Sir T. Picton who had arrived the previous afternoon, I saw him sitting against a shed and heard later that he was already wounded at Quatre Bras – to ask his permission to move to allow the horses to drink. He refused this however with the addition that we should be soon in our new position and would have plenty of time to do so then.

We arrived soon under a very heavy rain, between 7 and 8 in the evening in our position near St Jean (Waterloo), where I established my position at F. I stood here all

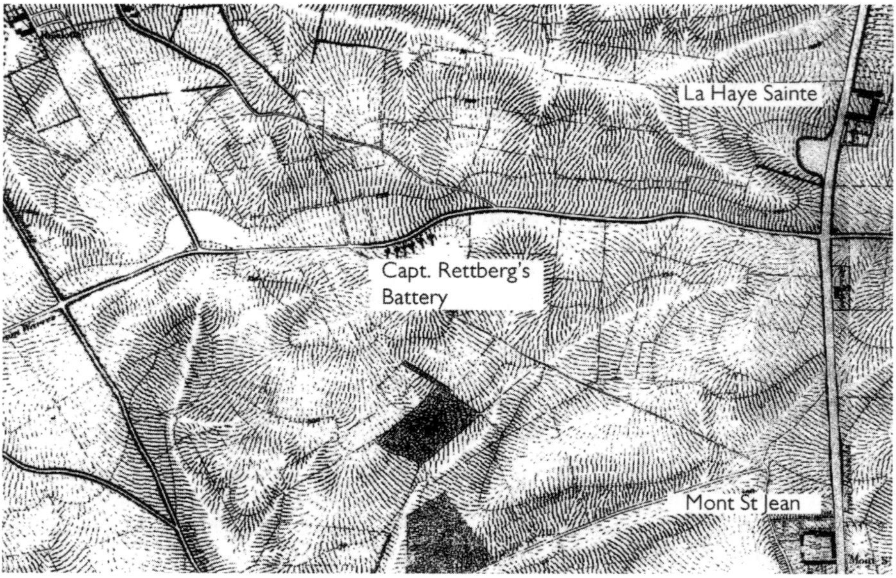

day as I had not received any ammunition replacement so I finished around 7 in the evening. The Prussians arrived and one battery relieved me as I had used up all but a few rounds of my ammunition. I led the battery to K about 200 paces back, where General Von Ziethen with the Prussian cavalry were posted. This allowed me to go to the centre of our army along the main road from Brussels to Charleroi. The other minor happenings I do not recall. I rode again to my battery that had stood all day on the heights and waited with great longing for the replacement ammunition which however, to my great regret did not arrive, as the despatched officer could not get through with the carriages, as I found out later. But I saw the happy and for us so glorious outcome of the battle. What I saw agrees totally with the statement of Lieutenant Lewis Heise.

The remaining details of the battle are extracted from the reports, I could still write a number of sheets about it, which may not suit you as it may not serve your purpose. I enjoy talking with my contemporaries whom have mainly survived after 45 years in the service, about the memorable battle as well as the marches in the Peninsula where I was from 1808 till the spring of 1815.

An important trip through peaceful Germany, which I undertook last summer, was the reason why this letter sat so long, and I must admit that after my return from this expedition I forgot about it completely. It is now my heartfelt intention that you, my dear Sir, may find within material that will suit your purpose, and hope that it does not reach you too late for that purpose.

C RETTBERG

---

1 This refers to a copy of the map that appears with Lieutenant Heise's letter, map 1 letter number 93 below.

2 The only second captain in Lloyd's foot artillery battery was Samuel Rudyerd. He eventually attained the rank of colonel in 1846 and died at Whitby on 29 July 1847.

No. 92 Lieutenant Lewis Heise[1]
Hanover, 23 April 1835

ADD MS 34705, FO 190

Original in German

The 2nd Hanoverian 9-pounder foot artillery battery under the command of Captain von Rettberg[2] was attached to the 4th Division[3] of the English army and at the outbreak of hostilities was located in the city of Brussels. On 16 June 1815, the battery received orders to attach itself to the 5th Division under the command of General Picton, and the battery reached the battlefield of Quatre Bras that afternoon at 3 o'clock.

They remained there until the morning of 17 June, when they received an order to retreat to the position of Waterloo. The battery reached its position toward evening, and was placed at the left wing of the first line in the position noted on the plan. To the left, next to the battery, stood a Hanoverian infantry brigade,[4] and some distance from it were English cavalry (heavy dragoons).[5]

At 11 o'clock in the morning of 18 June, the battle was commenced from the French side with heavy cannon fire. After the battery had fired on the enemy artillery for some time, there was movement in front of the battery by a strong column of enemy cuirassiers. This column advanced to within 200 paces of the battery, but was then forced to retreat in the face of heavy fire. After the battery again fired on enemy artillery for about another hour, it was then attacked by enemy infantry. This attack, too, was repulsed with the help of the Hanoverian infantry brigade. Towards 4 o'clock in the afternoon, enemy cavalry made its final and most furious attempt to throw its troops at our left wing, and the attack was mainly directed against the battery. Strong columns of cuirassiers stormed forward in spite of heavy fire until they were very close to the battery; however, they were beaten back by the English heavy dragoons.

After this last attack, the battery was only able to return weak fire against enemy artillery because it had not been resupplied with munitions, which had largely been used up during the fierce enemy attack. This weak fire was continued by the battery until the arrival of Prussian troops, which occurred toward evening at about 6 o'clock. Because this battery had not a shot left upon the arrival of the Prussian troops, it was replaced by a Prussian battery, which immediately set itself up there and commenced with a brisk fire. The battery retreated several hundred paces to the rear and remained there throughout the following night.

LEWIS HEISE
LIEUTENANT K G ARTILLERY
COMMANDER TO THE HANOVERIAN ARTILLERY IN THE YEAR 1815

1 Heise is recorded in Beamish as number 64. He joined the KGL Artillery in 1812 and served in the northern German campaign of 1813–14. He is recorded as having been slightly wounded at Waterloo. He retired as a captain on half pay in Hanover in 1816.
2 First Captain Charles von Rettberg.
3 The 4th Division of Lieutenant General Sir Charles Colville was stationed at Hal throughout the battle of Waterloo and saw no action. Rettberg's battery together with the 4th Brigade, was detached to Picton's division and served with it at Quatre Bras and Waterloo.
4 The 4th Hanoverian Brigade of Colonel Best was immediately to their left and the 5th Hanoverian Brigade of Colonel von Vincke further to the left.
5 The cavalry to the left were those of 4th Cavalry Brigade of Major General Vandeleur and the 6th Cavalry Brigade of Major General Sir Hussey Vivian. Heise is mistaken in one detail; all of these cavalry were light dragoons and hussars not heavy cavalry.

No. 93 From the same
Hanover, 20 February 1837

ADD MS 34706, FO 375

Original in German

The 2nd Hanoverian 9-pounder foot battery under the command of Captain von Rettberg was in Brussels in June 1815 at the outbreak of hostilities. The battery had been attached to the 4th Division; however, during the night of the 15th to the 16th, it received orders to join up with the 5th Division under the command of General Picton. On the morning of 16 June, the battery marched from Brussels with this division and the Brunswick troops and reached the Quatre Bras battlefield at about 3 o'clock in the afternoon. Immediately upon arrival, the battery was positioned on the left flank of the

English Corps, and participated vigorously in the battle until about 9 o'clock. During that night, the battery occupied the ground that it had taken during the battle. The foot battery under Captain Cleeves[1] of the K. G. Legion positioned itself at the same time that day several hundred paces to the right of this battery. This battery also fought immediately after arrival in the battle and remained on the ground it occupied until next morning. On the morning of 17 June at about 9 o'clock, the battery received the order to retreat, and somewhat later, two of the battery's guns were ordered to the rear guard. Towards evening, when these cannon were reunited with their battery, they reached their position at Waterloo and were positioned as depicted on the plan.

I have reported previously on the role played by this battery at the battle of Waterloo, and I am not capable of saying anything more about it.

LEWIS HEISE
IN THE YEAR 1815 LIEUTENANT, K G ARTILLERY
ORDERED TO THE 2nd HANOVERIAN FOOT BATTERY

---

1 Captain Cleeve's Battery of the 3rd Division was stationed near the crossroads.

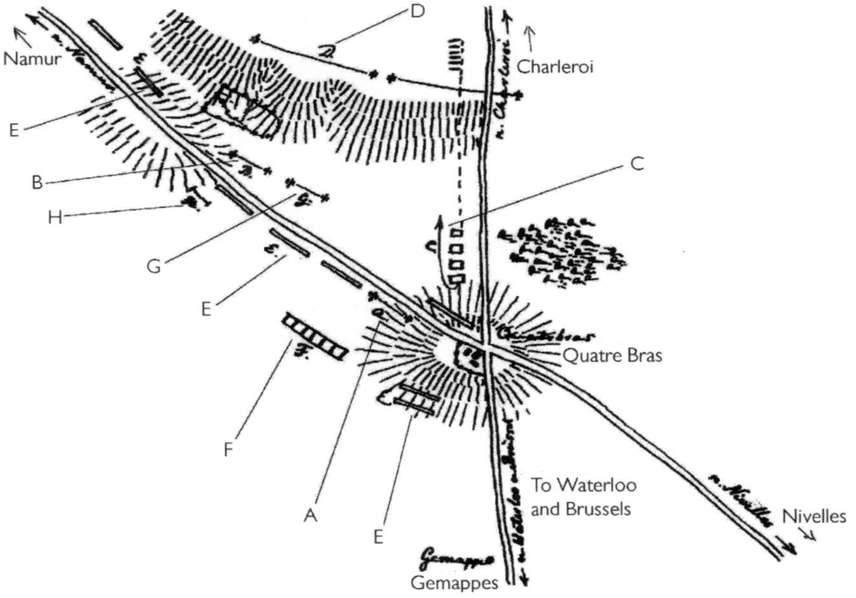

Sketch 1

Position of the 2nd Hanoverian battery under the command of Captain von Rettberg in the battle of Quatre Bras on 16 June 1815.

Key

A	Initial position of the 2nd Hanoverian battery	E	Allied Army infantry on the left wing
B	Second position of the same	F	Brunswick cavalry
C	Attack by the French using cavalry	G	Battery of Captain Cleeves
D	French artillery during the battle	H	Position of the ammunition wagon

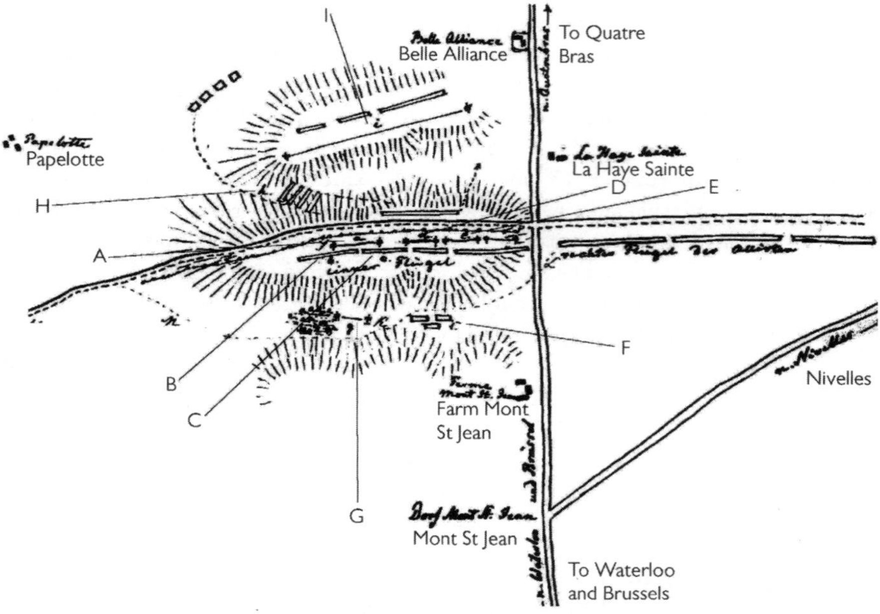

Sketch 2

Position of the 2nd Hanoverian battery under the command of Captain von Rettberg in the battle of Waterloo.

Key

A The 2nd Hanoverian battery
B Hanoverian brigades of von Vincke and Best Belgian brigade
D English rocket battery
E The 1st Hanoverian battery
F English cavalry
G Ammunition wagons of the 2nd C Hanoverian battery
H French attack
I French artillery

FIRST DIVISION

1st Infantry Brigade

No. 94 Ensign Augustus Cuyler, 2nd Battalion Coldstream Guards[1] Extra Aide de Camp to Major General Cooke

Royal March, Dublin, 13 November 1833

ADD MS 34703, FO142

Sir,
In reply to your letter of the 26th instant which I have only just received; I beg to state that your model of the battle of Waterloo is a most accurate delineation of that action.[2] Having been employed on the Staff of the army at that time I can speak with great truth and confidence to this point – and it is very much superior to any other models of actions which were to be seen in Paris in 1815 and by which the French set so much store as a matter of instruction to young officers. It is in my humble opinion most valuable, exhibiting to them the exact position of troops where engaged, and showing them the application of movements and drill in the moment of difficulty.

I have the honour to be, Sir, your most obedient servant,

AUGUSTUS CUYLER
LT COLONEL

1 Second son of General Sir Cornelius Cuyler (1741–1819), Colonel of the 69th Regiment. He joined the 2nd Foot Guards as an ensign in 1812 having previously held the same rank in his father's regiment. He eventually became a lieutenant colonel on half pay unattached in 1826.
2 The letter mentions the model in 1833, whereas it was not exhibited until 1838. He must be referring to a plan of the proposed model.

No. 95 Lieutenant Colonel Henry Rooke, 3rd Foot Guards, Assistant Adjutants-General[1]

Martinsherne, Berkshire, 1 December 1835

ADD MS 34705, FO 358

My dear Cuyler[2]
I am almost ashamed of having allowed so long a time to elapse without having answered your letter of the 12th of October, but I assure you it has not been altogether from neglect or forgetfulness, but having written to my father a long and particular account of all that came under my observation immediately after the 18th of June, I thought that I might have found some information in that letter which might be of use

to Mr Siborne, and would be more correct than any that I could offer at this distance of time, particularly as I have never been over the ground since, nor have I read any of the numerous statements which have been published on the different disputed points. My sister, in whose possession I believed the letter to be, was absent, and I have waited for her return, but I found she has not got it. I will beg of you to make my excuses to Mr. Siborne for any seeming inattention to his request and assure him that I should be most happy if I could give him any information that could be of service to him. I am sorry to say that I was not with the First Brigade at the moment he particularly refers to, and therefore I cannot positively answer the question he seems most anxious about. I had left them about two minutes previous to that. The Division was in want of ammunition. Two or three officers had been sent to order it up but could not find it and Sir John Byng[3] wished me to go as I knew where it was placed. Before I got back the attack had been made and the Brigade had since advanced. I will however endeavour to answer the questions Mr. Siborne has put to *you* as well as I can.

Question 1 When the French column of the Guard advanced immediately opposite the right companies of the 1st Brigade of Guards actually reached the crest of the position where was the Brigade posted while throwing its fire into the column? In front or in rear of the cross road which runs along the ridge?

I cannot say how the Brigade was posted at that precise moment not being with them, but a very short time previous to the advance of the French they were lying down immediately under the crest of the ridge.

Question 2 How long had the Brigade continued in that position previous to that particular moment?

The Brigade had remained in that position the greater part of the day, excepting when they were formed into squares.

Question 3rd Had the Brigade in an earlier period, been posted much in advance of the cross road?

And **Question 4th** If so what led to the retrograde movement?

I do not speak with reference to the cross road, for I cannot recollect the exact position of it being early in the day, the Brigade was a little more advanced, but was ordered by the Duke of Wellington to move behind the hedge so as to be partly sheltered, when lying down, from the enemy's guns.

After forming squares, the second time I think, the line was formed again by wheeling at the wings, so they stood, four deep and they remained so for the rest of the day.

In the printed letter, I see a question as to the crops on the field. Immediately in front of the 1st Brigade was a field of rye, so high that the horses of the cavalry were nearly head high.

I do not think the few remarks I have made are worth troubling Mr Siborne with a letter, perhaps you will be good enough to communicate them to him.

Believe me my dear Cuyler yours very truly

H W ROOKE

1 Rooke joined the army as an ensign in 1798 serving in Holland in 1799. He did not see active service again until Holland in 1814. Afterwards Major General Sir Henry Willoughby Rooke CB and KCH, he died on 2 May 1869.
2 Ensign Augustus Cuyler of the 2nd Foot Guards. See letter 94.
3 Major General Sir J. Byng commanded the 2nd Brigade of Guards in the 1st Division

The 1st Foot Guards, 2nd & 3rd Battalions

No. 96 Captain and Lieutenant Colonel Alexander Fraser, Lord Saltoun[1]
Dunne, 14 November 1834

ADD MS 34703, FO227

Sir,

Your promised letter of the 7th November reached me yesterday at this place. In reply to your questions regarding the battle of Waterloo I have just to remark that the 1st Battalion of the 1st Regiment of Foot Guards did not serve at Waterloo but at that period was doing duty in London. It was the 2nd Battalion and the 3rd Battalion of the 1st Regiment of the 1st Guards that formed the 1st Brigade of Guards of that army.

Near the time of the battle to which you refer the formation of the 1st Brigade of Guards was in line of four deep by the Duke of Wellington's express orders. Consequently it follows that the extent of front occupied by this brigade would only be equal to that of one battalion in line of two deep.

The formation of that part of the enemy forces immediately in front of the 1st Brigade of Guards was in column.

I have received the plan you have sent me but I cannot find any remarks in pencil relative to the nature of the crop nor can I at this distance of time give you any information on that subject. I regained my battalion about three o'clock on that day having up to that period served in the orchard of Hougoumont and at that time the crop had been so trodden down that I can make no remarks upon it.

You are quite correct with respect to the hedge introduced on the plan by the ground at Hougoumont, no such hedge existed at that time nor was there any wood in that direction but mainly a earth bank as you describe it to be in your letter. The hedge which bound the orchard on that side was of hawthorn or stunted beech and very strong.

I have marked[2] as nearly as I can remember the ground occupied by the 1st Brigade of Guards at the period of the action you mention. It was on the crest of the hill having La Haye Sainte, which at that time had been taken by the enemy at some distance to our left the enemies columns about 5,000 strong advanced as nearly as possible on the centre of our line.

In referring to the plan to mark the position of the brigade I found your remarks in pencil but from the reason above stated I can give no information on that head.

Your servant

SALTOUN

1 Son of Alexander Fraser, 15th Lord Saltoun. He joined the army as an ensign in 1802 and served in the Peninsula, receiving a General Service Medal with three bars for Corunna, Nivelle and Nive. He had four horses shot beneath him while leading the defence of Hougoumont orchard. He returned to the battalion with only a third of his men. He was made KT, KCB, GCH, KMT, KStG and later Colonel-in-Chief of 2nd Foot. He commanded a brigade in the war with China in 1842. He died on 18 August 1853 at Rothes. Siborne published a later letter (number 106).

2 The plan does not appear to be extant.

No. 97 Captain John Reeve[1]
Leadenham,[2] 26 March 1835

ADD MS 34705, FO 114

Sir,

In reply to your letter of March 9th touching the position of the 1st Brigade of Guards in the battle of Waterloo and other queries relating thereto, I beg after due consideration and reflection to communicate to you what information I am able to give.

When the French Imperial Guard made their attack about 7 o'clock pm the 1st Brigade of Guards were lying down in a line of four deep resting upon their arms and as far as my recollection carries me, occupied the position which I have marked upon the plan,[3] being covered by some broken and gently rising ground in their front. They had been thus situated for about the space of 20 minutes previously to the enemy's last attack, all firing in their immediate front having ceased. The enemy, advanced in two parallel close columns of infantry of the Imperial Guard in a front of Grand Divisions preceded by a very strong line of sharpshooters who came on in a most gallant and determined manner, shouting and keeping up a most destructive fire. On the enemy's columns arriving within about 30 paces of our line they halted, but from the warm reception they met with, instead of deploying they commenced firing several file deep evidently in confusion; at that moment we charged them – they began to waver; went to the right about and fled in all directions. The mass of their columns apparently first beginning to show disorder and ran: we passed them to the low ground in the direction of La Belle Alliance and to the best of my recollection to the spot marked on the plan when Sir Felton Hervey ADC.[4] came to us with an order to halt and form Column of companies at half distance which we did.

The ground upon which we were formed at the moment of attack was clover as marked in the plan, that on which we halted had been a green crop but was then trodden upon. The enemy as they ran off occasionally turned round and fired a few random shots at us.

I am, Sir, your obedient servant,

JOHN REEVE
COLONEL HALF PAY UNATTACHED

1 From the Reeve family of Leadenham Hall, Grantham. He joined the army as an ensign in 1800 and served in the Peninsula, receiving a General Service Medal with three bars for Corunna, Nivelle and Nive. He attained the rank of Lieutenant General and Colonel-in-Chief of the 61st Regiment. He died on 3 October 1864.

2 Approximately 12 miles north of Grantham.

3 The plan is no longer extant.
4 Colonel Felton Hervey of the 14th Light Dragoons acted as an Assistant Quartermaster General at Waterloo.

No. 98 Lieutenant Charles Parker Ellis[1]
The Hill, Brampton,[2] Cumberland, 25 March 1835

ADD MS 34705, FO 101

Sir,
I have the honour to acknowledge the receipt of your letter of the 9th instant, and am sorry that it is not in my power to give you the information you require as to the formation of the 2nd and 3rd Battalions of the 1st Foot Guards on the evening of the 18th of June, as I was with the light company of the 3rd Battalion employed in the defence of Hougoumont, and left the field wounded at three o'clock.

I understand from Lord Saltoun[3] that he has answered your letter fully, and you cannot have better authority than his. The map which you sent me appears to be, from my recollection of the field, a particularly correct one, and I should feel much obliged by your allowing me to retain it in my possession, if however you wish to have it returned, I will send it back by return of post.

The wood at Hougoumont, was an open grove, and not so thick a wood as appears in your plan.

I have the honour to be, Sir, your obedient humble servant,

CHARLES ELLIS
LIEUTENANT COLONEL

1 He joined the army as an ensign in 1811 and served in the Peninsula, receiving a General Service Medal with two bars for Nivelle and Nive. He was dangerously wounded at Waterloo. Afterwards he went on half pay late of de Roll's regiment in 1831 and became colonel. He died at Cleevedon on 6 August 1850.
2 There are two Bramptons in Cumberland, it is not clear which one this is.
3 See his letter number 96.

No. 99 From the same
The Hill, Brampton, Cumberland, 6 April 1835

ADD MS 34705, FO 140

Sir,
I received your letter of the first of the month this morning, and I can only repeat my regrets that it should not be in my power, from reasons which I stated to you in my first letter, to give you any correct information, from my own personal observations, as to what occurred at the time of the attack of the Imperial Guards; but I think it as well at the same time to state what I have heard from officers of the First Brigade who were present, and upon whose information I think I can rely, and which I hope may be of use to you.

The first attack of the Imperial Guards[1] was (I believe) composed of the old guard; and this first attack was repulsed, and I may add, the attacking column almost destroyed, by the *First Brigade*; no other corps having anything whatever to do with that attack.

The second attack was composed of the young guard, and that was defeated *jointly* by the First Brigade and Adam's brigade – while the First Brigade were engaged with the front of the column, Adam's brigade charged on the flank,[2] and which attack I believe they sustained but a very few minutes.

It is very strange, and I regret it much, that no officers who were present at the time should have answered your letter; for I feel, myself, that love for my old corps, in which I served nearly twenty years, that I cannot bear to think that their services on that day should not be duly recorded. And more particularly so as by referring to the returns, you will see that that regiment suffered more severely than any in the army.[3] I will send your letter to Lord Saltoun and I have no doubt but that he will write to you fully on the subject, and he can give you the very best information. I cannot close my letter without thanking you very much for the plan of Waterloo, which you have kindly given me.

Believe, me dear Sir, yours truly,

C ELLIS

---

1 The two attacks to which Ellis refers were actually one attack, but the two columns of the Imperial Guard reached the crest in succession; hence the first was defeated before the second attacked.

2 This refers to the flank attack of the 52nd Regiment led by Sir John Colborne.

3 Records show that the loss in killed and wounded of the two battalions of the 1st Guards at Waterloo as 487 rank and file out of an effective strength of 1,628, a loss of 28%. This was a severe loss, but other regiments have a greater claim to the dubious honour of sustaining the highest losses that day.

No. 100 From the same

The Hill, Brampton, Cumberland, 19 April 1835

ADD MS 34705, FO 155

Dear Sir,

I received your letter of the 10th instant this morning, and I have sent the copy of your letter to Sir John Byng,[1] by this post and Lord Saltoun who I have no doubt will write to you very shortly. Indeed I had written to urge him to do so before I received your last letter; whenever he does write I feel confident, from my knowledge of him, that he will enter fully into the subject, and give you every information in his power.

Sir Peregrine Maitland[2] is now in England, and if you have not already applied to him, perhaps it would be advisable to do so, as he commanded the First Brigade, and was not wounded. I have read your letter to Sir John Byng with great attention, I will tell you fairly in what your view of the case differs from mine, with respect to the information which I have been able to collect. I believe the first attack of the Imperial Guards to have been composed, of a *very much* larger force than four battalions, moreover the attack was *decidedly* in column and *not in line*, upon this point I have no doubt, for I have never heard it stated otherwise by any officer, besides which the French rarely, if ever, attacked in any other formation. The column presented a front of about 200 men which might have led to the mistake, and after receiving about ten rounds of a close and well directed fire, they began firing from the rear of this column and killing themselves, and at this moment (as described to me) the column seemed to burst, if I may use such an expression. The French officers were observed to be very active in trying to form a line, and it was then the brigade charged them, and with complete success. I have mentioned these minor circumstances as proof of the attack having been made in column.

I observe that you are aware of the brigade having been formed four deep, but perhaps you are not aware that they were completely clubbed, having been wheeled outwards into line from square, which square had been previously formed from a column of quarter distance, consequently the grenadiers were in the centre of their respective battalions, and number nine company (the light companies being detached to Hougoumont) had a subdivision on each flank. I do not mention this as being such as to be of any use to you, but merely to show the extraordinary steadiness of British infantry. My idea has always been the same as yours, that the First Brigade did not advance immediately after the repulse of the second attack of the Imperial Guards. Wishing you every success in your arduous undertaking.

Believe me, dear Sir, yours very sincerely,

CHARLES ELLIS

Note in same hand

I have sent the map of Waterloo to Lord Saltoun thinking that it may be of service to them while reading your account of the movements of the different brigades.

---

1 Sir John Byng commanded the 2nd Brigade of Guards at Waterloo. He joined the army as an ensign in 1793 and served in Holland, Hanover, Copenhagen, Walcheren and the Peninsula. He received a Gold Cross with one bar for Vittoria, the Pyrenees, Nivelle, Nive and Orthes and a General Service Medal for Toulouse. He was made GCB, GCH, KMT and KStG, and became a field marshal in 1855 and Colonel-in-Chief of the 29th Regiment. Created Baron Strafford in 1835 and Earl Strafford in 1847. He died on 3 June 1860.His letters were published by Siborne (numbers 112 & 113).

2 Sir Peregrine Maitland commanded the 1st Brigade of Guards at Waterloo. He had joined the Guards as an ensign in 1792 serving in Holland, the Corunna campaign and the Peninsula, receiving a General Service Medal for Corunna and a Gold Medal for the Nive where he commanded the 1st Brigade of Guards. He received the KCB, KStV and KW. He was Colonel-in-Chief at Madras in 1836, Governor and Colonel-in-Chief at the Cape of Good Hope in 1843 and Colonel-in-Chief of the 17th Regiment. He died on 30 May 1854. His letter was published by Siborne (number 105).

No. 101 Lieutenant Charles F. Rowley Lascelles[1]

Harewood House, Leeds, 19 March 1835

ADD MS 34705, FO 79

Sir,

I had the honour to receive your letter last night, enclosing a plan of the battle of Waterloo, requesting me to answer the following questions.

What was the particular formation of the 1st Foot Guards at the moment, (about 7 o'clock pm) when the French imperial Guards advancing to attack the right of the British forces reached the crest of our position?

We were formed in line four deep.

What was the formation of that part of the enemy's forces immediately in front of the regiment? The Imperial Guard came up in close column, and began to open out into line, but did not complete the manoeuvre.

I do not recollect anything about the crops as it is so long since the battle of Waterloo. I have marked your map[2] as well as I can remember at this length of time where the battalion was formed at this time of the attack of the Imperial Guards, as also their position (the Imperial Guards) at the bottom of the hill at the moment of that attack.

The Light Infantry Companies of the 2nd and 3rd Battalions, were detached under the command of Lord Saltoun at Hougoumont. If I remember right the 95th Rifles (part of General Adam's brigade) were on the right of the 2nd Battalion, between it and Hougoumont. I beg leave to state that I was in the 2nd Battalion 1st Foot Guards during the campaign of 1815.

I have the honour to be, Sir, your obedient servant,

C F R LASCELLES
CAPTAIN 1st BATTALION
GRENADIER GUARDS

---

1 Lascelles joined the Guards as an ensign in 1812 serving in the Peninsula in 1814 and received a General Service Medal with two bars for Nivelle and Nive. Dalton indicates that he was wounded at Waterloo but he was not listed as wounded on the *London Gazette*. He seems to have seen the battle through and it is quite possible that Dalton is in error as Henry Lascelles of the regiment was wounded. He became Lieutenant Colonel commanding the 1st Foot Guards on 10 April 1849 and retired on full pay before 1855. He died on 8 November 1860.

2 This plan does not appear to be extant.

No. 102 Ensign Robert Batty[1]

Coaxdon Hall, near Axminster, 2 May 1835

ADD MS 34705, FO 227

I had the honour to receive your letter dated 9th March and subsequently dated 25th April on Tuesday last, the 28th of April.[2]

I take the earliest opportunity of forwarding to you some remarks on the points referred to in your communication. They are deduced from a variety of materials which I have collected with a view to an improved and corrected edition of *An Historical Sketch of the Campaign of 1815 with plans* which I published in 1820 and I hope they may prove of use to you in your very interesting undertaking.

I must however observe to you that I was only an ensign in command of a company on the 18th of June; and that I was wounded prior to the attack made by the French Imperial Guards so that, unfortunately I was unable to witness it.

I have the honour to be, Sir, your most obedient servant

ROBERT BATTY
LT COL HALF PAY UNATTACHED

1 Batty served in the Peninsula and received a General Service Medal with two bars for Nivelle and Nive. Later he became a lieutenant colonel on the half pay list and died on 20 November 1848.

2 In the corner of the letter is a note in Siborne's hand, explaining the premise of his letter to Batty. It reads 'Wrote to Lt. Colonel Batty 13th October to enquire whether his account of the formation for attack by the Imperial Guard was divined from the testimony of French officers'.

No. 103 From the same
Coaxdon Hall, near Axminster, 17 October 1835

ADD MS 34705, FO 339

Sir

Your letter dated the 13th instant reached me yesterday; and in answer to your queries respecting the formation of the French Imperial Guard – I beg to acquaint you that I had every reason to believe that the account given to me of the formation of the French columns of the Imperial Guard for the attack of the British right was strictly accurate; as also the strength of the battalions engaged. The authority on which I chiefly relied was an officer of the grenadiers of the Imperial Guard, *who was himself wounded in the attack,* and a gentleman of more than ordinary intelligence. Finding, too, that the accounts of our officers in the 1st Brigade of Guards, who were eyewitnesses, perfectly accorded with the account I had obtained of the enemy's formation. I may add that, in collecting my information respecting the battle of Waterloo, I generally placed a plan of the ground before my informants, in order that there might be less chance of misapprehension.

I am not sure whether I stated in my former letter that the 1st Regiment of the Grenadiers of the Old Imperial Guards (1,300 men) formed into two battalions was placed in reserve on the heights near Belle Alliance at the time when the other Regiments of the Grenadiers and Chasseurs of the Imperial Guard advanced to attack the British in the manner described in my former letter. It was this position of the Old Guard which formed squares and endeavoured to cover the retreat of the broken columns at the close of the day.

I remain, Sir, your most obedient servant

ROB BATTY

No. 104 From the same
Coaxdon Hall, near Axminster, 5 February 1837

ADD MS 34706, FO 211

Sir

In reply to the queries you propose, I beg to acquaint you that I received the information respecting my friend Staveley's[1] communication with the Prussians from *himself*; and I have no doubt whatever that he is accurate as to the *time* when Bülow's[2] corps was in the act of crossing the ravine between St Lambert and Lasne; and advancing in the direction of the wood of Frischermont.

At what precise moment the Prussian skirmishers became first engaged with the French scouts it is difficult to decide, but it must have been a very considerable time before any force of consequence could even *arrive on the actual field of battle* and be effectively engaged.

When in Paris, in 1815, I was informed by Prussian officers, that the leading columns of Bülow's corps had to wait a long time before sufficient numbers could be brought up to enable them to take any important share in the contest, the soldiers meanwhile laying on the ground and resting after an excessively fagging march through muddy and intricate cross roads.[3]

It has always appeared to me that the general opinion of the Prussians having been engaged at Waterloo early in the afternoon is wholly erroneous. Both the French and Prussians are, naturally, anxious to fix as early an hour for this event as they can. The former to make out a case of having to contend with superior numbers: the latter to claim as great a share in the honours of the day as possible.

Napoleon having early intimation of the intended stroke against his right flank, took the precaution of placing Domon[4] and Subervie's[5] cavalry to keep them in check and when the Prussians made a nearer approach the French drove them back and kept them at bay for some time.

I am happy to hear that you are making progress with the model.

And remain Sir your very obedient servant

ROBERT BATTY

---

1 The only Staveley recorded by Dalton at Waterloo is Major William Staveley of the Royal Staff Corps. He joined the army aged 14 years, serving in the Caithness Legion where he rose to captain. He then joined the Royal Staff Corps as an ensign in 1804 becoming a deputy assistant quartermaster general in 1813. He served in the Peninsula and received a General Service Medal with eight bars for Talavera, Fuentes d'Onoro, Ciudad Rodrigo, Badajoz, Vittoria, Nivelle, Nive and Orthes. He received the CB and became a brevet lieutenant colonel for Waterloo. He went on half pay in 1825 but later became Commander-in-Chief at Madras and Colonel-in-Chief of the 24th Foot. He died in Ireland in March 1854. His identity is confirmed by Batty in his *Historical Sketch of the Campaign of 1815,* reprint, London, Trotman, 1981, p. 105.

2 General Friedrich von Bülow, commanded the Prussian IV Corps.

3 Wellington had expected the Prussians earlier in the day, especially after they had been sighted in the forenoon. However, they were much delayed in forming up for the attack, owing to the straggling nature of the Prussian advance through the defiles. It is seen here that the leading elements lay down to await the following troops to close up before advancing to attack the French wing.

4 Général de Division Baron Jean Simon Domon commanded the French 3rd Cavalry Division.

5 Général de Division Baron Jacques Gervais Subervie commanded the French 5th Cavalry Division.

No. 105 Ensign Thomas Robert Swinburne[1]

9 Carlton Place, Edinburgh, 1 March 1847

ADD MS 34708, FO 346

Letter no. 105

Sir
In reply to your favour, I fear I shall not be able to afford you much information relative to the battle of the 18th of June, my pocket map and what little memoranda I may have made at the time are in England and I have not access to them.

I was a subaltern in the 3rd Battalion 1st Foot Guards and the battalion formed in column of grand divisions,[2] afterwards in square to receive the repeated charges of the French cavalry, mostly cuirassiers. About the period you allude to, we retired up a rising ground and the men were ordered to [go] back and lie down behind a grassy bank, which I believe was a division of the fields. We had retired in line and the French Guards had deployed and followed us up closely. On their gaining the crown of the hill (if I may so call it), there was a call for skirmishers to check the French advance. I went forward with a few men pretty close to the French, who continued advancing to the spot where our battalion was lying. I got back to the company I had the command of, shortly before we were ordered to rise and fire a volley and charge. This the French received and I think they were not more than 15 yards from us; they were so close that some of our men fired from the charging position (I mean without bringing the musket to the shoulder). The fire was very destructive, as there was a hedge of bodies lying and over which we passed in the charge after them down the slope. In this charge (that is on the way between our position and La Belle Alliance where we bivouacked) there was some ploughed ground but from the rain that had fallen during the night the constant crossing it by the cavalry and the many loose horses that galloped after the advancing and retiring squadrons, the whole was very *puddley*, and the crops destroyed.

During the day we were mostly opposed by the heavy cavalry who rode very boldly up to our square and past us on each side, receiving our fire from either flank of the square both on their advance and retreating they went well to the rear and completely surrounded our battalion.

In the early part of the day, as I mentioned before, we were in grand divisions, then in squares as the French cavalry advanced against us and deploying as they retreated.

It will perhaps be unnecessary for me to say, I went on with my battalion to Paris and have never had an opportunity of seeing the field since, but I think my recollection of what I saw, which from the situation I was in, was not a great deal, is pretty correct.

If it is in my power to answer you any further question [or] give any information I shall be most happy to do so and remain your obedient servant

T R SWINBURNE
MAJOR HALF PAY UNATTACHED

Note in same hand:
I may not be accurate as to the exact spot where we were stationed and front whence we charged, but it was a grassy bank on the top of a slope.

---

1 Swinburne joined the army as an ensign in 1813. After Waterloo, he was present at the taking of Peronne, a fortress that had never been stormed before. He transferred to the 3rd Dragoon Guards as a captain in 1823 but went on half pay in 1825, eventually attaining the rank of major general. He died on 28 February 1864.

2 The eight centre companies of a battalion were split into four grand divisions of two companies each.

No. 106 Ensign Daniel Tighe[1]

Rapann,[2] 21 March 1835

ADD MS 34705, FO 83

Sir,

The concluding paragraph of your letter of the 16th instant in some measure will justify me in attempting to give you the information sought for as regards the position of the 1st Foot Guards on the evening of the most memorable day of the 18th June 1815. It being now nearly 20 years since the battle of Waterloo, and as I have no memorandum by me, and have never had an opportunity of going over the ground since; I cannot hope that what I write will in any way assist you, though perhaps it may imitate information received from other quarters. I have marked with pencil on the map – the movements of my Brigade consisting of the 2nd and 3rd Battalions of the same regiment, the 1st Foot Guards from the night of the 17th having bivouacked that night on the left of the road leading from Brussels to Nivelles. (A) About 11 o'clock am on the 18th we were formed into hollow squares, (B) protected by a rising ground in front, in the rear of which the artillery attached to the 1st Division was posted. We were at that time completely guarded by the bank in front from discharges of musketry, but suffered much from the shells thrown into our squares with great effect, we afterwards moved, being still in squares, a little to the left, where we had to withstand repeated charges of the French cuirassiers, who had gained temporary possession of the artillery in front, towards the evening, the attacks of the French cavalry having cleared, we advanced in line (to C) where we lay down under cover of a small dyke, (which may have been the side of the bye-road to Wavre on your map, but of which I have no recollection, if so I have marked our position as too much in advance-) volleys of musketry passing over us but without much effect, we remained a considerable time in this position, till on the advance of the Imperial Guard we got the word to advance in line (to D) and poured in a rapid fire into the advancing columns of the Imperial Guard which they stood but a short time and retreated in full disorder. I conceive this advance of the Imperial Gds. to

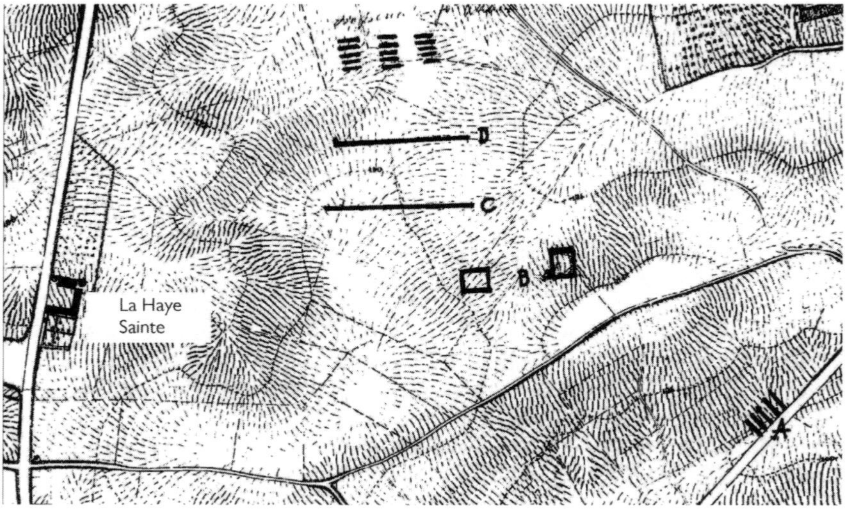

be almost the time alluded to in your letter. We afterwards proceeded to La Belle Alliance and bivouacked there, large bodies of Prussian cavalry advancing along the chaussee in pursuit of the French. With respect to the nature of the crops in different parts of the field I can afford no information, nor as to the several movements and position of the rest of the army – the rising ground in our front preventing us from seeing much. On our advance towards La Belle Alliance several battalions of Belgians accompanied us on the left in regular order, having taken no part in the battle.

I have the honour to be, Sir, your most obedient servant

D TIGHE

---

1 He went on the half-pay list in 1821and died on 20 December 1881. Little else is known regarding this officer.

2 I cannot identify this place.

2nd Infantry Brigade

The Coldstream Guards, 2nd Battalion

No. 107 Lieutenant George Bowles[1]

London, 2 May 1835

ADD MS 34705, FO 235

Lt. Colonel Bowles presents his compliments to Lieutenant Siborne and regrets very sincerely that owing to his absence from London his letter of November relative to the battle of Waterloo should have remained so long unanswered. From the length of time which has now elapsed since the period alluded to Lt Col. Bowles cannot undertake to speak with any degree of correctness as to the crops on the ground on the day of the battle.

The Coldstream Guard were employed in the defence of Hougoumont and were nearly all in or near that post during the whole of the afternoon of the 18th. But as they were dispersed by detachments also in the orchard, garden, etc., mixed up with the Light Companies of the 1st Brigade of Guards as well as with the battalion of the third (Scots Fusiliers) Guard, it is scarcely possible to mark with any degree of accuracy the position of the battalion at the termination of the action.

Lt Col. Bowles regrets sincerely that he can send nothing more satisfactory in answer to Lt Siborne's queries and trusts he will excuse the delay which has taken place in making this communication.

---

1 Bowles joined the army as an ensign in 1804 and served in Germany in 1805, Copenhagen in 1807 and the Peninsula in 1809–14. He received a General Service Medal with six bars for Talavera, Ciudad Rodrigo, Salamanca, Vittoria, Nivelle and Nive. He became a brevet major for Waterloo. Afterwards General Sir George Bowles KCB, Colonel-in-Chief of 1st West India Regiment and Lieutenant of the Tower of London. Master of the Household to Queen Victoria 1845–51, he died in London on 21 May 1876. His letters and memoranda are printed in the *Letters of the 1st Earl of Malmesbury, his family and friends*, vol. 2, 1870.

No. 108 Lieutenant William Lovelace Walton[1]

49 Upper Leysmill,[2] 10 December 1834

ADD MS 34704, FO 36

Sir,

In answer to your letter requesting me state 'what was, the particular position of the 2nd Battalion Coldstream Guards, at about 7 o'clock pm on the 18th June 1834'? I have the honour to remark that to the best of my recollection (aided by what I can ascertain from the few men we have now in the Battalion who were there, 31 only, and many of those wounded early in the day) there were two companies near the spot marked by an A[3] in the plan. 6 Companies were on the other side of the farm, near the spot marked B. The reserve of two companies with the colours was some distance in the rear, near the first position taken up by the Battalion, before they were led by detachments of two companies at a time down to Hougoumont. With regard to the position of the enemy in the immediate front of the Battalion, I believe they occupied the wood, and lined the skirts of it, parallel to the fence which bounded the orchard of Hougoumont.

As to the crops on the ground, but all I can recollect is, that the field in which the Coldstream's bivouacked in the night of the 17th was, I think, fallow, and the field between the position the battalion front took, and the farm of Hougoumont, must I think have been grown with rye, and it was at that time a considerable height.

I have the honour to be, Sir, your most obedient servant,

W L WALTON LIEUTENANT COLONEL
CAPTAIN COLDSTREAM GUARDS

---

1 Walton joined as an ensign in 1806 and served at Copenhagen and in the Peninsula, receiving a General Service Medal with two bars for Talavera and Busaco. He was appointed Brigade Major to the 2nd Brigade of Guards on the march to Paris following the death of Captain Stothert. Afterwards a general and Colonel-in-Chief, Fusiliers, he died on 11 January 1865.

2 The address is extremely difficult to read, however this tiny village near Arbroath was the only one that seems to fit what can be deciphered.

3 Unfortunately as with most of the files, the plan appears to be no longer extant.

No. 109 Ensign Henry Gooch[1]

Bureton, 10 March[2]

ADD MS 34708, FO 299

Sir

Having been absent from London, I only received your letter two days ago. I wish it was in my power to give you any useful information in answer to your questions but I fear it is not so. With the exception of two companies, the 7th and 8th, the whole of the 2nd Battalion of the Coldstream, were in the garden and courtyard of the Chateau of Hougoumont at the moment of the last attack by the French Guards. I have marked what I have heard was the position of those two companies with the colours. Having myself been in the light company and posted at Hougoumont from the night of the 17th till after the battle, I saw very little of what took place except immediately about me. I have marked where the light companies of the Coldstream and 3rd Guards were

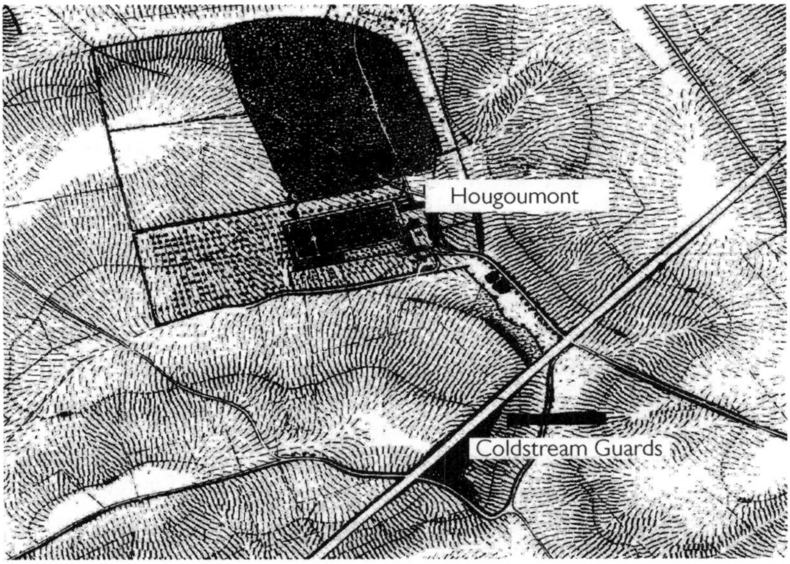

stationed to receive the 1st attack on Hougoumont and from whence we were driven into the Chateau by the gate facing our position. On another attack we charged and drove the French along the road leading to the wood. At the time of the attack of the French Guards, our attention was fully occupied by the enemy who were attacking us on all sides.

I have the honour to be your humble servant,

H E GOOCH

---

1 Gooch joined the army in 1812 and served in Holland in 1814 and the Waterloo campaign. He was promoted to lieutenant and became captain in 1819. He quit the service as a lieutenant colonel in 1841.

2 No year can be ascertained but it was probably written around 1843.

The 2nd Battalion, 3rd Foot Guards

No. 110 Captain Douglas Mercer[1]

Stoke by Nayland, Colchester, 9 November 1834[2]

ADD MS 34703, FO 203

I have the honour to acknowledge the receipt of your communication dated Dublin November 3rd and in reply beg leave to state in regard to your first query that the 2nd Battalion 3rd Foot Guards (now the Scots Fusilier Guard) about 7 pm on the 18th June occupied the hedge in front of the orchard of Hougoumont, or rather the hedge which bounded the orchard on the side of Rossomme. The light infantry company was detached on the inside of the building. The battalion in the orchard was in extended order for the purpose of occupying and defending the whole length of the hedge, which owing to our great loss, was much more than we could occupy in close order.

Here it was that our chief loss in officers and men occurred. The hedge afforded but small protection, the earth bank being but little raised above the general level of the ground, while our flanks at *B & C* were opposed at the latter to the fire of light troops, who occasionally advanced through the wood at *C*, while on our left, at *B*, there were dense bodies of the enemy lying in the high grain which was only trodden completely down on the Grand Advance,[3] which took place at the moment represented in your plan. These masses on our left were likewise covered by light infantry.

With regard to your second query, I have to observe that I believe that that part of the French force immediately in front of us, at the time more particularly referred to in your letter, was composed of light troops.

I relieved Lord Saltoun[4] in command of the orchard, I should think between 2 & 3 o'clock. I took down with me the last detachment of my battalion consisting of 3 companies, the other companies in succession, having previously been sent to the orchard to reinforce the troops already there. These last were composed of detachments from the brigade *generally* and when I arrived at the extreme of the orchard with my party, I met Lord Saltoun, who told me he was about to return to his battalion on the heights we had just quitted, in consequence of his having lost almost all his men.

In effect, on looking over the party in the orchard, I found scarcely any other than those belonging to the Scots Fusilier Guards. The dead lay very thick on the whole length of the ground we occupied.

After a time the enemy drove us back as far as the hedge in our rear, which I have marked *D-E*. Here we remained for a short time when we made a rush and driving the enemy back we reoccupied the hedge in front from which we had been driven.

This position we maintained until the arrival of a staff officer who informed us that the French were in retreat, when we forced our way through the hedge and pursued the enemy as long as it was considered of use. Strong columns of the enemy were lying on the ground on our left and I think for a considerable time they were advanced as far as what I should consider a prolongation of the line *E-D*. I have made a pencil X at the spot where I conceive they must have been in chief force.

Before moving down to the orchard, I strongly think the Battalion occupied the height I have marked with a *line & A* in pencil. With the exception of the orchard, the ground we occupied or passed over during the day as marked and generally with crops of high grain.

At the corner of the orchard which I have marked *C* there was a gate and at the opposite corner *B*, there was a considerable opening at the junction of the two hedges. These apparently trivial circumstances we found of great importance and very detrimental to our position. We could not remedy these defects on account of the proximity of the enemy. I should think that the pencil marks which you have made respecting the grain and such are correct, but I only recollect the fact of the ground being mostly covered with crops without being positive to which species of grain they might have been.

The field immediately in our front and which I have marked with two XX, I have already stated as probably occupied by light troops; I likewise *thought* that the French

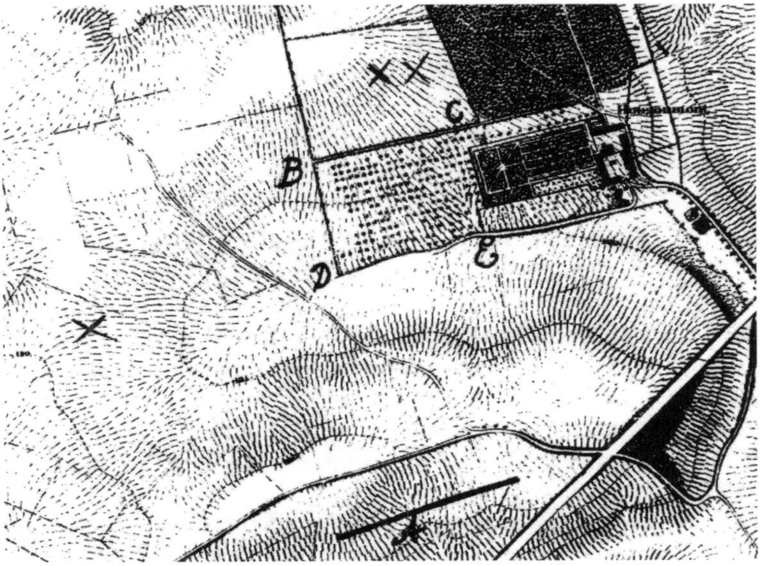

were in great force upon our right and beyond the building of Hougoumont and this I concluded from the fact of the fire which crossed us in almost all directions.

My letter has been extended beyond the limits to which I had at first wished to confine it, and I think that an apology is due to you for my having considered that the little information I could give upon this interesting subject was of value sufficient to entitle me to take up your time by its perusal, but the last paragraph in your letter must be my excuse.

I trust it will not be long, before I have an opportunity of viewing, with the rest of the public, the model, which I have understood to be so worthy of the event it represents.

I regretted much that circumstances deprived me, while in Dublin last summer, of that advantage.

I have the honour to be, Sir, your most obedient humble servant,

DOUGLAS MERCER

---

1 He joined the army as an ensign in 1803 and served in Hanover, Walcheren and the Peninsula as ADC to Major General Dilkes who commanded at Cadiz. He joined Wellington's army for a short while, acting as ADC to Sir B. Spencer and was slightly wounded in a skirmish near Sobral in 1810 and promptly returned to Cadiz. He was also slightly wounded at Barrosa in 1811and soon after returned to England with the battalion. However, he transferred to the 1st Battalion and returned to the Peninsula where he served until 1814, being present at El Bodon, Ciudad Rodrigo, Salamanca, Burgos, the passage of the Bidassoa and the Nive. Mercer received a General Service Medal with five bars for Barrosa, Ciudad Rodrigo, Salamanca, Nivelle and Nive. There is an indication that Second Major Hepburn was involved in the defence of the buildings at Hougoumont and that Mercer therefore commanded the battalion during the battle. He received the CB for Waterloo. Many years afterwards he assumed the additional surname of Henderson and

attained the rank of Lieutenant General and Colonel-in-Chief, 68th Foot. He died at Naples on 21 March 1854.

2 Stoke by Nayland is approximately six miles north of Colchester.

3 The final advance of the Allied armies.

4 Captain and Lieutenant Colonel Alexander, Lord Saltoun of the 1st Regiment Foot Guards; see his letter (number 96 above).

No. 111 Lieutenant Edward B. Fairfield[1]

Mount Eagle, Castle Island, 6 August 1836[2]

ADD MS 34706, FO 129

Dear Sir,

Colonel Berkeley Drummond[3] has been staying with me for some time – and told me that you were anxious to obtain some information as to the sort of 'Defence' which was executed inside the wall at Hougoumont.

I was for many years in the 3rd Regiment (since June 1815) and have heard many officers describe the action of the 18th of June.

In the year 1816 I made some drawings of the different objects of interest and now enclose you the only one I can at this moment put my hand on. I cannot vouch for the accuracy of the drawing at this distance of time.

There is a fault in the perspective at the angle of the wall – this I think I made purposely in order to show that the wall stood someway in advance of the farm wing.

I should say that I remember seeing a sort of rough platform inside the wall, made of stone. Taken I think from a cross wall which separated the homestead from the kitchen garden.

I will endeavour to show my recollection of the appearance of the platform by a rough drawing from the main house and grounds.

I think that there was a way in to this 'space' from a window which had been broken away to make a passage.

The wall was higher perhaps than my sketch would represent.

Whether the platform was at the angle A or commenced at B[4] I cannot positively say – but as it must have been a great object to defend the curtain, I have little doubt but that it was at A. Captain Evelyn[5] and the Light Company of the 3rd Regiment made the 'Defence'. Evelyn was a very ingenious man, and acquired great credit in the regiment for the manner in which he affected the duty allocated to him. Captain Elrington[6] (Who has now left the regiment and is living in Wales) has I am quite sure a most accurate recollection of every particular of the French attack in this quarter – he was stationed I know at the gate[7]– and used to describe the affair with the greatest accuracy of detail.

Drummond left me without taking the drawing, and I now send it to you – and if it is of the slightest use – I shall be most happy to think that I have been able to afford you any information however trivial.

The work on which you are now employed as so apparently national that every person must feel an interest in hoping, that your labours will soon be answered with success.

Believe me, faithfully yours

CHARLES FAIRFIELD

1 I have discovered nothing regarding this officer's later life.
2 The only Castle Island I can discover is a tiny island in Roaring Water Bay just south of Bantry Bay on the south-west edge of Ireland.
3 Lieutenant William Drummond, who had joined the army as an ensign in 1806 and served in the Peninsula from 1809–12 and in Holland in 1814. He received a General Service Medal with three bars for Talavera, Badajoz and Fuentes d'Onoro. He became a brevet major for Waterloo and eventually became a colonel in 1837.
4 There is no point B shown on the drawing.
5 Lieutenant (Captain in the army) George Evelyn was wounded at Waterloo and quit the service in 1824. He died on 15 February 1829.
6 Lieutenant (Captain in the army) John Elrington, he died in November 1843.
7 He is probably referring to the North Gate, famous for the incident of the 'closing of the gate'.

No. 112 Ensign Thomas Wedgwood[1]
Mar Hall, 12 March 1835

ADD MS 34705, FO 46

Sir,
In answer to your circular, which in consequence of my being absent from my regiment, I have only just received, I am sorry to state that I am unable to give you any information, that could be in the least useful to you. On the evening of the 18th of June, I was myself stationed almost entirely within the walls of the chateau[2] and garden or else in the orchard and wood immediately outside and am quite ignorant of the nature of the crops growing in its vicinity, with the exception that they were chiefly standing corn.

To the best of my recollection, the 2nd Battalion 3rd Guards was, about 7 pm stationed within the walls of the Chateau, but were at that time not much pressed by the enemy. I remember, that I was myself completely ignorant of what was going on, or what the result of the action was likely to be until we saw parties of the French passing us in full retreat, with the Brunswickers in pursuit on both sides of the house.

I believe there was a large gateway, to which the road through the wood, led, which is not marked in the plan sent.

I have the honour to be, Sir, your obedient humble servant,

T WEDGWOOD
CAPTAIN AND LIEUTENANT COLONEL
1st FOOT GUARDS

---

1 Afterwards a lieutenant colonel, he died at Tenby, South Wales, on 7 November 1860.

2 The château of Hougoumont.

No. 113 Ensign Henry Montagu[1]

Portland Square, 16 March[2]

ADD MS 34708, FO 311

Sir

The information I can give you regarding the battle of Waterloo, I fear will be of little service to you.

I was attached to the 8th Company of the battalion and remained on the position above Hougoumont till about 2 o'clock, when the 6th, 7th and 8th companies marched down together, to the orchard on our left of the garden. On reaching the left corner of the lower fence, the 6th and 7th companies filed inside the hedge, while the 8th marched in file, up to the gate leading into the grass field beyond the orchard, where there was a road which led through the field, and along the outside of the garden wall. There we began to form companies, when the French troops, standing in line in a rye field, immediately in our front, commenced firing by sections on us. As we got the company in line, we replied as well as we could by file firing, but being much [outnumbered?] lost many men, and were obliged to retire slowly, firing, to the lower corner, when there was a deep lane. Here we remained, being shortly afterwards [reinforced] by 2 companies of a Hanoverian regiment.[3] I remained here a considerable time with Colonel Mercer,[4] who was occupied, reforming stragglers and men who returned from carrying wounded officers to the rear.

The bodies of French cavalry passed over the hill in rear of us and were supported by a brigade or division of infantry which halted within short musket range but did not fire on us. After a considerable interval the French cavalry was driven back and almost immediately after I was ordered to take command of the grenadier company which had lost all its officers. I found it very well formed, occupying the strong fence above the hollow lane, at the bottom of the orchard. I remained with it keeping up a desultory fire, till suddenly, a shout arose on all sides, when, we passed out of the ditch and charged across the orchard driving the French before us, and passed another road by the gap at the left corner of the garden wall. The ditch had been cut deep, and had been full of water, but when I reached it, was completely filled with killed and wounded so as to form a complete bridge.

We skirmished for a time in the wood when we were recalled into the courtyard, to be reformed and were relieved by some Brunswick or Hanoverian Jägers.[5]

The battle was then over although the fire was kept up in the wood for some time. As far as I recollect, the notes of the cultivation of the fields, in the plan, are correct, except that I think we were formed in the morning in a clover patch.

I have the honour to be, Sir, your obedient servant

HENRY MONTAGU

PS I believe that I have omitted to state that the whole battalion was occupied all day in lining the hedges of the orchard and the inside of the garden wall and were posted in this manner at 7 o'clock.

---

1 Montagu joined the army as an ensign in 1814. Afterwards he attained the rank of general, commanding the 1st Division in the Crimea. He became Colonel-in-Chief of the Scots Guards in 1875 and died on 25 May 1883.

2 No year is recorded but it was probably written in 1843.

3 Probably two companies of 1/2 Nassau commanded by Captain Bügsen, whose 800 troops made up a sizeable portion of the defenders of Hougoumont, but they are rarely mentioned by British historians.

4 Captain and Lieutenant Colonel Douglas Mercer (see his letter number 110).

5 It is difficult to be sure which unit this was. The only Jäger at Hougoumont were the 100 men of the 1st Company of the Field Jäger Corps, but they returned to the main position after the first attack had been repulsed and are not recorded as having returned. The forces that supported the clearance of the wood were the 2nd Line Battalion KGL and the Saltzgitter Landwehr Battalion.

SECOND DIVISION

3rd Infantry Brigade

No. 114 Captain Lord Charles Fitzroy, 1st Foot Guards, Deputy Assistant Adjutant-general[1]

Wakefield Lodge, 19 January 1835

ADD MS 34704, FO 185

Dear Siborne,

If it lay in my power I should be delighted to assist you in your ingenious and arduous work. The moment of advance I think I never can forget. The brigade under General Sir F. Adam[2] was first ordered to advance and bring its right shoulders forward. The Guards advancing and bringing their right shoulders forward brought them on the left of Adam's Brigade with a wide interval. The whole advancing brought the Guards in immediate contact with the Imperial Guards; an honour which others (Adams brigade) claimed, but had no more right than a ship in sight when another ship engages and captures an enemy.[3] While this conflict was going on Sir H. Vivian's brigade came on to the field rather in rear of the left of Adams brigade; upon the *'sauve qui peut'* of the French,[4] this (Vivian's) brigade moved by the right of Adams brigade and charged to the front.

I recollect one circumstance before the advance, which was, many of the French Light Cavalry after charging our squares in rear, attempted to return by the road to Nivelles leaving Hougoumont on the left, but were stopped by an abatis, and were all killed or wounded by the 51st Lt Infantry stationed on our right of the road.

Give me any occasion to assist your undertaking and I will willingly perform it.

Your very faithful

CHARLES FITZROY

---

1 Fitzroy was the second son of the 4th Duke of Grafton. He had previously served in the Peninsula, receiving a General Service Medal with eight bars for Ciudad Rodrigo, Badajoz, Salamanca, Vittoria, Pyrenees, Nivelle, Nive, Orthes and Toulouse. He became a brevet lieutenant colonel, 27th Foot, in 1821 and MP for Bury St Edmunds. He died at Hampton on 17 June 1865.

2 Major General Frederick Adam commanded the 3rd Brigade at Waterloo. His brigade, which included the 52nd, was embroiled in a heated argument with the Guards for the honour of defeating the Imperial Guard. Charles Fitzroy as a Guards officer perhaps unsurprisingly argues for the honour of his old corps.

3 This refers to the time-honoured arrangement for sharing prize money in the Royal Navy, which had been called into disrepute during the late wars. The rules allowed that when a

Royal Naval ship captured a prize, any other naval vessel in sight could claim a full share of the prize money despite often having done nothing to help secure the capture. This had led to many acrimonious court cases.

4 The reputed cry of the French troops as they fled the field at the culmination of Waterloo.

No. 115 Captain William George Moore, 1st Foot Guards, Deputy Assistant Quartermaster General[1]

31 New Bond Street, London, 13 July 1835

ADD MS 34705, FO 309

Sir,

Your letter of the 14th December last has only just reached me. The delay has arisen in consequence of my removal from the staff in the Mediterranean, and my present change of residence.

I regret extremely that it is not in my power to give you any information, worthy of communication, respecting the position of the 2nd Division at the moment you have selected, as I was at that time in the wood (or orchard) of Hougoumont. You will of course have learnt from various publications that the 52nd Regiment, commanded by Sir John Colborne,[2] brought up its right shoulders and fired into the flank of the Columns of the Imperial Guard, which was advancing to the attack of our centre. It is certain that the movement took place, although I did not see it myself from the cause I have above mentioned.

I have the honour to be, Sir, your most obedient humble servant,

W G MOORE[3]

---

1 Moore joined the army as an ensign in 1811. Afterwards he became Lieutenant General Sir William George Moore, KCB, Colonel-in-Chief of the 60th Rifles. He died at Petersham on 23 October 1862.

2 Lieutenant Colonel Colborne, afterwards Field Marshal Lord Seaton, GCB, GCH and Colonel-in-Chief of the 2nd Life Guards. He joined the army as an ensign in 1794 and served in Egypt and at Maida before becoming Military Secretary to Sir John Moore and then serving under Wellington throughout the Peninsula campaign. He received a General Service Medal with five bars for Egypt, Maida, Sahagun & Benevente, Busaco and the Pyrenees and a cross with three bars for Corunna, Albuera, Ciudad Rodrigo (where he was severely wounded), Nivelle, Nive, Orthes and Toulouse. He was Governor of Canada at the time of the rebellion. He died on 17 April 1863. His letter was published by Siborne (number 123).

3 The signature definitely reads W. G. Moore, causing me to assign the letter as I have. However, as the letter mentions the 52nd Regiment, it is just conceivable that Lieutenant G. Moore of the 52nd Regiment wrote it. I base my decision to place it with the above officer because Lieutenant Moore never progressed to the Staff as mentioned by the writer and no officers of the 52nd served in the orchard of Hougoumont as far as I know.

The 52nd Regiment, 1st Battalion

No. 116 Captain Patrick Campbell[1]
United Services Club London, 22 November 1834

ADD MS 34703, FO 307

Sir
In acknowledging the receipt of your letter of the 17th instant with its enclosures I beg leave to state, that having been on leave of absence, I was unable to join my regiment until about four o'clock[2] on the memorable 18th of June. I found it drawn up in line with the [95th] Rifles on its left, I think about an hour after I joined we were very sharply engaged with an immense column of the enemy who appeared to me to be retreating and in confusion,[3] about this time the Duke came up to the left of the regiment, and was very much exposed to a sharp fire of musketry.

Major General Sir J. Colborne commanded the regiment and he can give you every information respecting its position from its commencement.

I regret much it is not in my power at this late period to assist you with any information worthy of your notice further than what I have stated.

I have the honour to be, Sir, your most obedient servant,

P CAMPBELL
LATE 52nd REGIMENT

---

1 Campbell originally joined the 53rd Foot as an ensign in 1797; he joined the 52nd as a lieutenant in 1800. He had served in the Peninsula, receiving a General Service Medal with five bars for Busaco, Vittoria, Pyrenees, Orthes and Toulouse. He had actually commanded the 52nd at Nivelle and the Nive, receiving a Gold Medal. Wounded at the crossing of the Bidassoa and at Orthes, he was placed on half pay on 4 May 1818 at his own request, on account of his wounds, and granted a pension of £100 per annum for them, including the loss of his right eye. He became a lieutenant colonel on half pay in 1830 and CB.

2 In the afternoon.

3 This adds another line to the old argument between the 52nd and the Guards as to who actually defeated the French Imperial Guards. Campbell certainly indicates that the French Guards were already in retreat before the 52nd attacked and had therefore been repulsed by the Guards before their flank attack.

No. 117 Captain William Chalmers[1]
No date

ADD MS 34705, FO 165

Memorandum relative to the battle of Waterloo

The strength of the 52nd Lt. Infantry was 1,148 including all ranks on going into action, and when the army formed squares the 52nd Regiment composed two squares. The right one commanded by Sir John Colborne, the left by brevet Lieutenant Colonel Chalmers,[2] immediately on the left of the latter were posted four companies of the 95th Rifles under the command of Lieutenant Colonel Fullarton[3] (also in square) and were suffering rather severely from a corps of French sharpshooters posted behind a kind of natural banquette on their left, Colonel Fullarton's square was too weak to admit of his detaching any men to drive off the French sharpshooters and in consequence Col. Chalmers took a detachment of the 52nd Regiment, passed the 95th square and drove off the tirailleurs. Colonel Chalmers has no recollection of any other skirmishers being thrown out during the day, but when the 52nd Regiment was standing in double line he distinctly remembers that a staff officer rode past the regiment saying '52nd there is nothing in your front but the enemy and therefore look out'. Shortly after this caution a melee of French and English dragoons rode right in upon the line and received its fire.

Note in the same hand

The above statement was taken from Col. Chalmers own lips by me on the 7th February and shown to him on the following day.[4]

SIGNED J C
LIEUTENANT COLONEL[5]

---

1 Chalmers joined the 52nd as an ensign in 1803 and served in the Peninsula, receiving a General Service Medal with eight bars for Barossa, Ciudad Rodrigo, Badajoz, Salamanca, Vittoria, Pyrenees, San Sebastian and Nivelle. He served as brigade major at Waterloo and had three horses shot beneath him. He was made a brevet lieutenant colonel on 18 June 1815. He retired on half pay in 1817 from ill health and he became the Clerk of the Peace and Registrar for the county of Forfar in Scotland. Afterwards General Sir W. Chalmers, he received the CB and KCH, and became Colonel-in-Chief of the 78th Highlanders.

2 Dalton confirms that Chalmers commanded a wing of the regiment on the day, despite being fourth in seniority. This can be explained; Major Charles Rowan was wounded and senior Captain Campbell informs us that he was away from the regiment until 4 pm thus making Chalmers second in command.

3 Captain James Fullarton would have commanded the two companies of the 3rd Battalion of the 95th present at Waterloo, after the wounding of Major John Ross. Fullarton is shown as receiving a wound himself at Waterloo. Chalmers mentions that the square comprised four companies; it is therefore highly likely that two companies of the 2nd Battalion 95th were attached to them. Dalton, the Army List and the Waterloo Medal Roll all spell his name Fullerton, but states that he was the son of Lewis Fullarton in the notes. Chalmers uses Fullarton throughout, which I believe to be correct.

4 This memorandum is in the handwriting of Captain John Cross.

5 There is a small note added written in Siborne's hand 'through Col. W. Rowan'.

No. 118 Captain William Rowan[1]

Belfast, 14 September 1843

ADD MS 34708, FO 31

My dear Sir,

When your letter of the 9th instant reached me, knowing that Lord Seaton[2] was then on the Continent and might not receive the private communication you had addressed to him (I believe, however, he is now in England) and not wishing to trust entirely to my own treacherous memory, I wrote to my brother Charles,[3] who was major of the battalion at Waterloo and to Lt Colonel Cross[4] of the 68th, then a captain, to ascertain particularly whether the regiment fired into the 'attacking column of the Imperial

Guards immediately before it charged it's left flank.' It appears that my brother was knocked off his horse about the time we wheeled to the left, by the fire from the flank men of the French column and previously to our returning the fire.[5]

I enclose herewith a memo from Cross[6] which is quite conclusive as to two or three companies at least having fired into the French column.

Cross happened to meet Colonel Chalmers who was a brevet major at the time and like myself officiating as a regimental field officer, in consequence of the very reduced strength of the corps both in officers and men. I send also a memo from Chalmers,[7] but I think he must mean that we had 1,148 of all ranks in the country, having shortly before received all the effective men of our 2nd Battalion;[8] from that number must be deducted the sick, batmen etc. etc. which left about 1,000 bayonets when in squares, that is for some time previously to forming line formation, he was the senior officer to the one square and my brother with the other, Sir John Colborne commanding the whole. We all had our horses taken to the rear at either two or three which rendered us less efficient and less able to see what was passing around us.

Are you aware that when the Duke made his formal entry into Paris on the 8th of July our Brigade only accompanied him. At the Barriere de L'Etoile he and all his Staff placed themselves in front of the 52nd, and with band playing, Colours flying and such, we marched down the Champs Elysees, the 52nd taking up its bivouac close to the Duke's residence, where it remained as his body guard until the end of October.

Do not take the trouble to acknowledge this unless I can be of any further use.

Believe me, very truly yours,

W M ROWAN

---

1 William Rowan joined the army as an ensign in 1803 and served in the Corunna campaign, Walcheren and the Peninsula. He received a General Service Medal with six bars for Vittoria, Pyrenees, Nivelle, Nive, Orthes and Toulouse. Dalton states that he was wounded at Waterloo, but William makes no mention of it. Afterwards Field Marshal Sir William Rowan, GCB and Colonel-in-Chief of the 52nd Regiment. He died at Bath on 26 September 1879.

2 Lieutenant Colonel Colborne, afterwards Field Marshal Lord Seaton.

3 Major Charles Rowan joined the army as an ensign in 1797 and served in the Peninsula as Assistant Adjutant General to the Light Division. He received a General Service Medal with three bars for Ciudad Rodrigo, Busaco and Fuentes d'Onoro. He was wounded at Waterloo and received the CB. Afterwards he retired as a brevet lieutenant colonel and became Sir Charles Rowan KCB, Chief Commissioner of the Metropolitan Police. He died on 8 May 1852.

4 Captain John Cross, his letters are printed in this volume (numbers 120–2).

5 This must be the moment at which Charles was wounded.

6 This is printed within the letters of Cross.

7 This memo is printed within Chalmers' letter (number 117).

8 It was a long-established practice to empty the 2nd Battalion of its best men to strengthen the 1st Battalions when sent on active service. In recent years the practise had waned as the demands for troops had led to many 2nd and even some 3rd Battalions actually being sent abroad on active service. The 2nd Battalion of the 52nd had spent many years in England and was still able to furnish large numbers of recruits; indeed the 52nd was one of the strongest regiments at Waterloo.

No. 119 Captain Charles Diggle[1]
Royal Military College, 17 November 1834

ADD MS 34703, FO 242

Sir
I have, to the best of my recollection, marked the position of the 52nd Regiment in line,[2] at about seven o'clock when the attack was made on the right of the position, by columns of the Imperial Guard. The skirmishers of the regiment had just fallen back on the battalion, which was advancing to resist the attack when I was severely wounded and left the field.

The ground was so completely trodden and cut up that I cannot speak as to the nature of the crops but the greater part appeared to have been grain, much longer in the advanced part of the field, marked in your plan as occupied by the 52nd Regiment. It sustained in the course of the afternoon when in squares of wings,[3] repeated attacks from the cuirassiers of the Imperial Guard.

I have given you the location of the regiment to the best of my belief, and can only regret that I cannot grant you more aid in the prosecution of so valuable a work as doubtless your model will prove.

I have the honour to be, Sir, your obedient servant,

C DIGGLE

---

1 He joined the army as an ensign in 1804, serving in the Peninsula and he received a General Service Medal with two bars for Corunna and Busaco. Afterwards he became a major general and KH; he then went on half pay in 1843. He died at Cheltenham 18 September 1862.
2 This plan appears to be no longer extant.
3 The regiment formed in two squares each consisting of one half (or wing) of the battalion. This unusual occurrence probably occurred because of the unusual number of men in the battalion, having entered the field with 1,148 men.

No. 120 Captain John Cross[1]
Gibraltar, 17 April 1835

ADD MS 34705, FO 163[2]

Sir
I have the honour to acknowledge the receipt of your letter of the 21st February last, accompanied by a plan of the field of Waterloo, and in reply to the queries contained in your communication, I have to state that the formation of 52nd Regiment at the period alluded to was in line, formed four deep, and rather behind the crest of the height upon which the regiment was drawn up.

The enemy's attacking force at this point was formed in column either at close or quarter distance, but did not come up directly in front of the 52nd but at some distance from its left flank (a few minutes previous to this attack, a French officer who had just deserted intimated that the attack was going to commence) and as soon as the French column approached sufficiently near, the 52nd changed front to the left (so as to take the column in flank) fired, and immediately charged, continuing on as far as a small coppice to the right of La Haye Sainte[3] where the 52nd and Rifle Corps made a momentary halt and opened a fire upon the fugitives, (this halt did not exceed one minute and a half.) The 52nd then pursued on along the high ground to the right of the Genappe road leaving a large body of the enemy behind them in this hollow road, which seemed to make it doubtful whether the 52nd had not pushed on too far from the general line without support. The word, Halt, was given and at that instant the enemy rushed up out of the hollow road to form on the ground which the 52nd then occupied, but the attempt was very feeble. The 52nd crossed the Genappe road obliquely at this point and continued the pursuit up the hill until they reached two well-formed squares of infantry posted on an eminence. The 52nd without the slightest hesitation charged them in line, the squares fired and then broke.

I have a very distinct recollection of these circumstances and in the summer of 1818, I went over the ground and traced out the route of the 52nd as above detailed with the exception of the small coppice which I could not then discover, it might probably have been ploughed up.

I have the honour to be, Sir, your most obedient humble servant,

JOHN CROSS
LT COL, 68th REGIMENT

---

1 Born in County Armagh in 1787, he joined the regiment as an ensign in 1805 and served in Sweden and the Peninsula receiving a General Service Medal with ten bars, for Corunna, Badajoz, Fuentes d'Onoro, Ciudad Rodrigo, Vittoria, Pyrenees, Nivelle, Nive, Orthes and Toulouse. Cross served with the 1st Battalion from 1812–16 as a volunteer, being effective in the 2nd Battalion. He received a severe contusion at Waterloo but did not leave the field. Subsequently he commanded the 68th Regiment and retired as a colonel in 1843. He was made KH and Lieutenant Governor commanding the forces in Jamaica. He died on 27 September 1850.

2 The British Library lists fo 163 as by Crown, this is a mistake, no officer of this name served at Waterloo. It is certainly by Cross.

3 This may have been the orchard of La Haye Sainte.

No. 121 From the same
No date

ADD MS 34705, FO 166

Memorandum relative to the battle of Waterloo

Captain Cross commanded the left company of the 52nd Regiment when formed in double line at the battle of Waterloo, and at the period which is now generally termed the crisis of this battle, Captain Cross by *order of Sir John Colborne*, wheeled his company about the eighth of a circle, to the left in order to effect a change of position, so as to throw the front of the 52nd line on the left flank of the French attacking column, and as soon as either *two or three* of the companies on the left of this line had fired, Sir John Colborne ordered the line to charge, which broke the French column, and the pursuit was continued by the 52nd and a part of the 95th Rifles into a little copse wood close to La Haye Sainte where those regiments stopped about three or four minutes firing on the fugitives, then resumed the pursuit down into the bottom of the valley, but keeping on the bank to the right hand side of the hollow road, by which means the 52nd got ahead of a great body of the French and again made a momentary halt, and at this instant the fugitives rushed out of the hollow road apparently with the intention of forming on the very ground that the 52nd occupied, and at this instant, Captain Cross called out that they were going to surrender and not to fire upon them, but this proved quite a mistake for the foremost of the enemy commenced firing as they got up the bank, but were unable to make the slightest stand there. The pursuit was resumed by the 52nd across the hollow road, and the regiment subsequently brought up their left shoulders and *recrossed* the road and were proceeding at the double march in line to the attack of the three French columns (or squares) posted on an eminence to the right of the Belle Alliance road, and when at the distance of about 150 yards those columns fired and broke, after which the whole French army was in full flight.

SIGNED JOHN CROSS
LT COLONEL

Note in Siborne's handwriting
This differs from all other evidence. I have always understood that no part of the Brigade crossed the road until after the defeat of the 3 squares on the height.

W SIBORNE

No. 122 Lieutenant Colonel John Colborne[1]
No date

ADD MS 34708, FO 319

You must in your account of the great battle, never lose sight of the title of your sketch, *'The Crisis'* the decisive moment at which the contest changed for the better. To establish the precise time when the battle was no longer doubtful, and the movements which were the immediate cause of hastening the crisis, is the object of the writer, and as he is persuaded that the movement of Sir Henry Clinton's division, and of General Adam's brigade, and of the 52nd Regiment in particular, tended greatly to hasten the crisis, it is necessary to describe the several positions of the division from ½ past 3 o'clock to ½ past 7. Fixing from 7 to ½ past 7, the critical half hour, but time passes so quickly in an action and every one is so occupied in performing his own duty that it will be difficult to find persons agree as to time.

However it may be clearly demonstrated that while the columns of Napoleon which made the unsuccessful attack, on the point which is usually called our right centre, and which advanced in full march towards the troops occupying our centre, the Brunswickers retiring, and the British Guards closing in; no one who was looking steadfastly at the movement of the Imperial Guards at that time, could say that the battle did not look critical, or, but that the Imperial Guards had the appearance of success, and also that our centre was on the point of being penetrated. This then we must fix as the time when no change for the better, on our side, had taken place, that we were in the greatest danger, but the moment the Imperial Guards halted and formed squares in consequence of a menaced attack on their left flank, our prospects were immediately changed for the better, it was 'the crisis', and half an hour after, when they were thrown into confusion and they retreated towards La Belle Alliance, the battle was won.

They had no reserve formed worth the name of a reserve, all attacks of cavalry or infantry after that moment, were the necessary consequences of their flight, and an endeavour to save such part of the crew of the wreck, as could be brought off without incurring further risk.

Therefore, however splendid the conduct of any corps might have been after the first flight of the French in reaping the fruits of the victory and in completing the route of the retiring columns; they took no part in the critical affair on the plateau of La Haye Sainte, or plain below it which the left flank of Napoleon's column overlooked.[2] Assuming that the three regiments, the 52nd, 71st and 95th,[3] passed the cross road which runs a few hundred yards in the rear of La Haye Sainte, and forms an acute angle with the Nivelles road,[4] at ½ past 3 or 4 o'clock; the 52nd halted in the low ground three or four hundred yards in front of that road, and about 700 yards from the nearest angle of Hougoumont, remaining there an hour. The 52nd being a strong Regiment formed two squares, the 71st formed square two hundred yards to the right of the 52nd, and on the approach of the French cavalry towards the 71st, the 95th apparently not more than two companies,[5] formed close to the rear of the 52nd.

Colonel Nicolay of the Staff Corps[6] and several officers ran into the squares of the 52nd. Two guns were on the high bank or ridge in front of the 52nd, apparently about 200 yards from the squares,[7] but were only to be seen by the mounted officers. A mounted officer who had ascertained the exact position of these guns, called out from the commencement of the ascent to a captain of the 52nd, to say whether he could see the guns from his part of the square. These guns and a howitzer fired constantly over the squares, the right and front faces of the right square of the 52nd opened a fire obliquely on the French cuirassiers who made a movement to the rear of Hougoumont toward the 71st. The remainder of Clinton's division[8] were formed to the rear of the right of the 71st Regiment.

The Duke of Wellington sent a message to the 52nd by Colonel Hervey,[9] to retire up the hill about ½ past 5 o'clock, but Colonel Hervey was requested to inform the Duke that the regiment was not in danger from the guns in front, if the order was given from the apparent vicinity of the guns.

However on the Nassau Regiment or some of the allied troops[10] running rapidly out of the wood of Hougoumont towards our line, the 52nd prepared to retire and formed two lines, the right subdivisions forming one line and the left subdivisions the other, and retired leisurely up the hill towards the cross road which they had passed an hour before.

While they were retiring a field officer of cuirassiers galloped out of the enemy's column and came in full speed down the hill towards the 52nd, hallooing lustily 'Vive le Roi' as he approached. This officer mentioned the point where Napoleon was and that the Imperial Guards were on the march to make a grand attack. The 52nd halted in two lines ten yards behind the cross road where the ground sloped towards our position. The officer of the Cuirassiers pointed to the exact spot where the Imperial Guards and Napoleon were.

The guns under Colonel Gold[11] on the crossroad were all silent, scarcely any firing except in the rear of La Haye Sainte and in that part of our centre.

The dense columns of the French were in full march on the plateau of La Haye Sainte near the farm, and the front of the columns at this time appeared to form a right angle with the 52nd, supposing the left of the line of the 52nd to be produced.

A few minutes before this an officer had occasion to look at his watch, and said 'the wounded had better be left where they are, the action must be over in half an hour'[12] it was then nearly 7 o'clock. Therefore, at 7 we will say the 52nd wheeled, the left company nearly a quarter circle to the left, and formed the remainder on the new line, with the intention of moving on the left flank of the Imperial column, and firing into the column, to retard the movement.

The 52nd thus at 7 o'clock were formed into two lines, not four deep, but each left subdivision in rear of its right, the whole forming two complete lines, the rear line keeping the wheeling distance of a subdivision from the front line.

At this time the 95th, apparently a small number, formed on the left of the 52nd. A strong company of the 52nd was sent to skirmish in front, and to fire into the Imperial column. At this moment General Adam came to the 52nd from the 71st, and desired the 52nd to move on. The Duke it appears at the same time, had sent Colonel Percy[13] to the 52nd to move on, the 52nd however were already in motion, its right flank totally unprotected, and marched off in two lines well formed and covered by the skirmishers commanded by Lieutenants Anderson[14] and Campbell,[15] who had directions to push on, and to look to the whole battalion as their support.

Whether the 95th moved off with the 52nd is not certain,[16] they certainly did not continue on the left flank the whole time of the march towards the front. The 52nd moved steadily on, the instant that the French columns felt the fire of Anderson's skirmishers they halted, appeared to be in some confusion and opened a heavy fire on the 52nd; the two officers of the skirmishers were wounded and the greater part of the men, the right of the battalion also suffered considerably. The 52nd still moved on passing the entire front of Byng's brigade of British Guards, who were stationary and not firing,[17] about three hundred yards or so to their front, and forming possibly a right angle or perhaps an obtuse angle with the line of the Guards. At the moment the 52nd commenced the movement, Lord Hill was near the British Guards commanded by Maitland, and no movement on their part had then taken place. Therefore it is imagined, that when the 52nd commenced the movement, they were shortly followed by the 71st and the whole of General Clinton's division, the Imperial troops saw that their flank and rear were menaced by a mass of troops marching on their flank, they halted, but the moment this halt took place, our centre made a forward movement which was resisted by the attacking corps of the French.

The 52nd in the mean time had proceeded within a short distance of the rising ground on which the French were formed, when a body of British cavalry were perceived in full speed approaching the front of the left company of the 52nd. The officers of the company gave the order to fire, supposing they had come from the enemy's column. The three adjoining companies wheeled back to form square. The Battalion at this time was under a heavy fire from the Imperial Guards and the Regiment was halted for a few minutes to enable the three companies to rectify their line. At this moment, while the three companies were forming up, the Duke was close in the rear, and said 'Well never mind, go on, go on.' This halt brought the 71st close on the right of the 52nd, which corps had not been so much exposed to the fire as the 52nd. The 52nd then advanced at full speed, the greater part of the French gave way in confusion, but some remained formed close to the deep road running direct from La Haye Sainte to La Belle Alliance. Captain Cross called out 'they are coming over, don't fire',[18] the French however opened a straggling fire, some running across the road and a few remaining till the 52nd were within six or seven yards of them. The whole of the 52nd charged briskly till they were impeded by the deep road, halted for a minute or two till they received the word to pass. They had some difficulty in getting over; when they had passed they formed line and wheeled to the right.

They found a gun on the plateau fully horsed and moved on in line keeping their right on the road, passed La Belle Alliance, and were joined by the skirmishers at the head of Bülow's corps,[19] that shortly after that came obliquely from the left.

In the mean time the 71st had proceeded towards Rossomme[20] and did not pass the road when the 52nd did. The whole of the Division of Sir H. Clinton, the moment the French were observed in retreat and in confusion, had struck to their right towards Rossomme. The 52nd passed about 80 pieces of cannon or tumbrils,[21] within a quarter of an hour after they had passed the Charleroi road from Waterloo.

The skirmishing or attack that took place in the retreat from Rossomme or Plançenoit, the 52nd took no part in; they halted when the evening closed. Bülow's corps in column passed the 52nd after the regiment had halted.

The writer has never been on the ground since, but he is positive, as far as his memory can be relied on, that these facts are correctly stated, and it is thus certain that no corps whatever passed between the 52nd and the French, from the time the 52nd moved on the flank of the French, for the 52nd were under a heavy fire the whole time and were opposed to the moment they touched the Charleroi road. When they were formed to the left of the Charleroi road, no corps was near them. The only corps of cavalry near the 52nd or the French column during this attack was the regiment of cavalry that moved in the direction of the left company of the 52nd.

Thus, it appears that the movements to which Sir H. Vivian alludes must have been the attack made in retreat, and that all the troops that came in contact with the French must have moved across the track of the 52nd in their movement from the cross road to the Charleroi road, and while the 52nd were charging up to the plateau of La Haye Sainte.

NO SIGNATURE

---

1 The statement is not signed or dated. The British Library records it as written by William Rowan, but it is certainly not in the same hand as his other letters. It is almost certainly written to Major Gawler as it mentions his article. The handwriting is the same as Letter 121, but cannot be by Cross, as in this letter he states that he had not been to the site of the battle since, which Cross clearly had done in 1818. Perhaps Letters 121 and 122 are copies made by some clerk from the originals. Moore Smith published letter 122 in his biography of Colborne, presumably from the original, although he does not supply a date and I have no reason to doubt this. I must thank John Hussey for bringing this to my attention.

2 This refers to the claims of Sir Hussey Vivian and his cavalry brigade regarding the overthrow of the French Army.

3 The 3rd Brigade of Major General F. Adam consisted of the 1st Battalions of the 52nd and 71st with the 2nd Battalion 95th and two companies of the 3rd Battalion 95th.

4 This refers to the junction of the road from Mont St Jean to Nivelles and the road running from the centre of the British line to Braine L'Alleud.

5 This refers to the two companies of the 3rd Battalion 95th commanded by Major John Ross.

6 Lieutenant Colonel William Nicolay of the Royal Staff Corps. He joined the army as an

Ensign in 1790 and served in India (Seringapatam and Pondicherry), St Lucia and the Peninsula. He received a CB for Waterloo and became a major general in 1819. Later he was the Governor of Mauritius in 1832, KCH and Colonel-in-Chief of the 1st West Indian Regiment. He died in 1844. The Royal Staff Corps was attached to the Quartermaster General's department. It had been raised by the Duke of York as a corps of Engineers under Army control, rather than the Board of Ordnance, for producing fieldworks, etc.

7 This suggests that cannon fired at the French cavalry over the squares, which seems to have caused some nervousness!

8 The 2nd Division of Lieutenant General Sir H. Clinton consisted of Adam's 3rd Brigade, the 1st Brigade KGL and the 3rd Hanoverian Brigade. These brigades were posted just to the north of Hougoumont near Merbe Braine.

9 Colonel Felton Hervey of the 14th Light Dragoons acting as an assistant quartermaster general on the Staff.

10 This can only refer to remnants of the Hanoverian units 1st Company Field Jäger and detachments of the Luneburg and Grubenhagen Battalions when the detachments of these corps were pushed out of the wood and formal gardens of Hougoumont. They were possibly accompanied by a few men of the 1/2 Nassau Battalion who didn't manage to retreat into the chateau. The 1/2 Nassau commanded by Captain Bügsen continued to aid in the defence of the Chateau for the remainder of the day.

11 Lieutenant Colonel C. Gold commanded the two batteries of foot artillery attached to Clinton's 2nd Division, namely Captain Bolton's horse artillery troop and Major Sympher's horse artillery troop KGL. They had spent most of the day covering the road to Nivelles. Around 4 pm they had moved into the front line on the ridge.

12 That is, to leave the wounded, so that they did not encumber the advance or retreat that looked increasingly likely.

13 Major, the Honourable Henry Percy of the 14th Light Dragoons who acted as an extra aide de camp at Waterloo.

14 Lieutenant Mathew Anderson of the 52nd was wounded at Waterloo and retired from the service in 1821.

15 Lieutenant George Campbell of the 52nd was wounded at Waterloo and retired from the 49th Foot on half pay in 1823.

16 The 2nd Battalion 95th formed in line to the left of the 52nd and joined their movement across the front of the British position. The two companies of the 3rd Battalion 95th apparently formed as a reserve in the rear of the 71st, possibly to help protect the brigade's exposed right flank from any possible counter attack.

17 Major General Byng's 2nd Brigade of the Guards. This statement seeks to prove that the Guards had little to do with the defeat of the attack of the Imperial Guard. This has been a source of contention between the various regiments ever since, as each has claimed the sole honour of defeating the Guard. In reality, they all seem to deserve the honour of jointly defeating the Guard.

18 That is, defecting from Napoleon's army and coming over to the cause of Louis XVIII. It was imagined by the Allied officers that the French would leave the ranks of Napoleon's army in droves when given the opportunity. However, apart from the few infamous officers that defected to the Allies, the French rank and file remained loyal to the bitter end.

19 General Count Friedrich von Bülow commanded the Prussian IV Corps, which met up with the Allied advance near La Belle Alliance.

20 A village on the high road to Charleroi, just beyond the rear of the French Army.

21 Ammunition caissons.

No. 123 Ensign William Leeke[1]
Holbrook Hall, near Belper, Derbyshire[2]

ADD MS 34708, FO 136

Dear Sir
Understanding from my friend Colonel Gawler[3] that you are about to publish your history of the battle of Waterloo by subscription. I beg leave to trouble you with my name to be added to your list of subscribers. I was an ensign in the 52nd at Waterloo and I mention my present occupation, as I suppose the subscribers will be properly designated in your list. In acknowledging the receipt of this, will you kindly say when the work is likely to be published.

I am, my dear Sir, faithfully yours,

WM LEEKE

Are you aware that Lord Uxbridge[4] was wounded in the rear of the centre of the 52nd when they were just attacking the French reserves; at the moment he was begging the Duke of Wellington not to expose himself, as he was then doing.

This was told me by Sir Colin Campbell*[5] who laid hold of Lord Uxbridge till his Aide de Camp came to his assistance. I presume anything of this sort would now be too late to be embodied in your history.

*He gave me the words of the Duke's reply, which I will send you, if you should wish it.

1 Leeke quit the service in 1824 and was ordained in 1829 to the curacy of West Ham, Pevensey. He became the incumbent of Holbrook in 1840 and died there on 6 June 1879. He published a volume entitled *Lord Seaton's Regiment at Waterloo* in 1866.
2 Approximately 15 miles north-west of Nottingham.
3 Lieutenant George Gawler of the 52nd at the time of Waterloo.
4 Lieutenant General The Earl of Uxbridge commanded the cavalry at Waterloo.
5 Colonel Sir Colin Campbell, KCB, of the 2nd Foot Guards, acted as Commandant at Headquarters at Waterloo.

The 95th Rifles, 2nd Battalion

No. 124 Major Amos Godshill Norcott[1]
Jamaica, 30 March 1835

ADD MS 34705, FO 121

Sir,
I have been unable to answer your letter of the 9th December last until now, and I fear that I but do so ineffectually, so many years having rolled away since the great Waterloo day and of course, much of the information you desire has passed from memory with them, but I have done my best to assist your wishes.

I have the honour to be Sir your most obedient servant

NORCOTT

Answer to no.1 query	In square, from which it rapidly formed into line four deep and advanced, in conjunction with the other corps on its right and left to attack.
Answer to no.2 query	Dense masses of cavalry, infantry and artillery, some in square halted, others in column attacking and advancing.

Note – The 2nd Battalion Rifle Brigade received and repulsed when in square, five charges of cavalry. It lost about half its number of officers and men. The three senior officers all dangerously wounded,[2] the others severely.

1 Born in London in 1777, Norcott joined the 33rd Foot as an ensign in 1793 and served in Holland, Cape of Good Hope in 1796 and Manilla in 1797. He transferred to the 95th as a Captain in 1802, serving at Buenos Aries in 1807, the Corunna campaign, Walcheren and the Peninsula (Cadiz, Barossa, Nive, Orthes and Toulouse). He was severely wounded at Tarbes and was severely wounded in the shoulder at Waterloo, having his left arm broken. He received a Gold Medal for Barossa and a bar for the Nive. He received CB, KCH, KStA and KMB for Waterloo. He became Colonel of the Rifle Brigade in 1819 and a major general unattached in 1831. He died at Cork in 1838.

2 Majors Norcott & Wilkins and Senior Captain Miller were all wounded at Waterloo.

No. 125 Major George Wilkins[1]

Walton on Thames, 27 September 1838

ADD MS 34706, FO 486

Should the officers commanding corps on the field of Waterloo at the time represented in the model, be named, the following remark will afford information.

Lieutenant Colonel Norcott, 2nd Battalion 95th Regiment, now Rifle Brigade, was wounded and left the field early on the 18th June, that is to say immediately on forming line after advancing in front of our guns.[2]

The command then devolved on Lt Colonel Wilkins who held it until both himself and horse were felled to the ground by the enemies *[sic]* artillery at the time he was receiving the personal orders of the Duke of Wellington preparatory to the last charge of the enemies Imperial Guard.

G WILKINS LIEUTENANT COLONEL

Postscript in the same hand:

Should any doubt exist as to the correctness of what is stated on the other side, the Adjutant Lt Smith,[3] who reported to Lt Colonel Wilkins the fate of Lt Colonel Norcott, is now a Barrack Master in Ireland and who is much acquainted with every circumstance. G.W.

1 He joined the army as an ensign in 1794 and served in the Peninsula, for which he received a Gold Medal for Salamanca and a General Service Medal with two bars for Vittoria and the Pyrenees. He received the CB for Waterloo. He retired as a brevet Lieutenant Colonel in 1817 and later received the KH. He died at Shirley in Southampton on 8 November 1862.

2 Norcott's letter would seem to indicate that he was with the regiment when the great cavalry attacks were in progress, whilst Wilkin's statement indicates that Norcott was severely

wounded much earlier and removed to the rear.
3 First Lieutenant Thomas Smith, see his letter below (number 130).

No. 126 From the same
Walton on Thames, 18 July 1839

ADD MS 34707, FO 97

Lieutenant Colonel Wilkins late of the Rifle Brigade, had the honour to address Captain Siborne some time ago on the subject of his contemplated publication in which as Colonel W. understood that the officers who commanded battalions on the field of Waterloo would be named.

Lt Colonel Wilkins again begs to remind Captain Siborne that he had the honour with the rank of Lieutenant Colonel to command the 2nd Battalion 95th Regiment (now Rifle Brigade) from the time Lt Colonel Norcott left the field wounded, which was on forming the front line after the advance of the battalion in front of our artillery,[1] where Lt Colonel Wilkins was severely wounded by a grape shot when in square, preparatory to the last charge of the Imperial Guard.

A letter addressed to Lt Colonel Wilkins from Major General Adam, who commanded the brigade which document is now in possession of the Right Honourable The Secretary at War, confirms the most material part of this statement and the remainder is made known to Captain Smith who was then Adjutant to the battalion, now Barrack Master at Chatham.

Further note in the same hand:
Amos Norcott and Wilkins were both Lt Colonels when they commanded at Waterloo; the former was returned Lt Colonel severely wounded, the latter Major slightly, but who was from the great injury he had sustained obliged to retire from the service. This is named to guard Captain Siborne against being guided by the erroneous returns of the regiment. G.W.

1 The timing of Norcott's wounding would be near 5 pm, when the brigade moved into the front line. Wilkins therefore commanded the battalion until wounded himself at approximately 7 pm.

No. 127 From the same
Walton on Thames, 30 July 1839

ADD MS 34707, FO 101

Lt Colonel Wilkins has the honour to acknowledge the receipt of Mr Siborne's obliging note of the 26th instant, in reply to which he begs to state, that Major General Adam's Brigade being part of Lt General Clinton's division at Waterloo, was very early in the day posted considerably to the right. The division was well placed at this time in a map published by Heaven or Shand.

As the day advanced, say about 10 o'clock, the brigade was moved to the centre, when being in squares of battalions in rear of the British artillery and with a battalion of Hanoverians also in square close on the left, the whole were charged several times by the cuirassiers.

The guns being taken by the French and retaken by a charge of our cavalry, Adam's brigade advanced rapidly and when in front and below the guns which a slope in the ground admitted of, commenced with the artillery a most destructive fire on the confused mass below.[1]

Lt Colonel Norcott was at this time wounded and left the field, when the command of the battalion devolved on Lt Colonel Wilkins which he retained until, preparatory to the last charge of the Imperial Guard, the battalion being then in square to receive it and greatly reduced from the fire of the enemy's artillery.

Lt Colonel Wilkins and his horse were both felled to the ground, by, as Sir Walter Scott,[2] admirably describes it the 'Iron Shower'. Lt Colonel Wilkins has already exceeded the bounds of Mr Siborne's request and will for the present conclude, with a hope that should Mr Siborne return to London before the publication of his intended description of the battle of Waterloo, he will have the goodness to apprise him of it.

UNSIGNED

---

1 He means that the brigade and the re-manned British artillery brought their joint fire against the confused mass of French cavalry in the valley.

2 Sir Walter Scott, the great novelist, had written of the battle in his book on Napoleon.

No. 128 Captain George Miller[1]
Urquhart,[2] 2 December 1834

ADD MS 34705, FO 243

Sir,

I have to acknowledge the receipt of your letter and shall have much pleasure in communicating to you, such details of the battle of Waterloo, as I am enabled to do from personal observation. At the same time as your request, I shall purely make such observations as occur to me, with reference to the plan you propose.

In the first place then, the topography of your map appears to me so indistinct, more particularly that of the ridge occupied by the British army, that I cannot venture to mark the position of the 2nd Battalion 95th on it, without almost a certainty of leading you astray. The top of it is also towards the south; instead of the north, according to the usual custom, and there is no compass to it.[3]

No plan can ever convey so correct a notion of the ground as a model; but to confine yourself to one period of the battle, is to lose the point of your labour; and many regiments who bore a conspicuous part on that day, will be entirely left out. So complicated an action as that was, never can be represented by one plan. It occurs to me, that it would be much more satisfactory to yourself and also to the public, to place the respective armies in order of battle at its commencement on your model, accompanied by three separate plans, showing the progressive stages of the action. And if bits of wood on the model, representing battalions and squadrons were movable at first, and if you sent it to the United Services Club, you would find plenty of officers, to place them in the positions you require. Some of the German plans are very admirable specimens of that kind.

I shall now state the operations of the battalion to which I belonged, throughout the day. The 2nd Battalion 95th formed the left of Sir Frederick Adam's brigade, including the 52nd and 71st Regiments. The brigade was in reserve during the fore part of the day, in close column at regimental distance; and the troops were made to lie down, to be less exposed to the fire of the enemy's artillery. Shot and shells landing, a number of men were lost.

It was advanced about 3 pm and again formed squares; near the road to Nivelles. The enemy had then attacked our artillery on the top of the ridge, the brigade again advanced, and formed squares at the base of the ridge, when a cannon ball that passed through our square killed 7 men. The enemy's cavalry had then got possession of our guns, but fortunately had nothing to spike them,[4] and his trumpet sounded to form, which they did in very good order. Our artillerymen ran into the squares, the 10th Dragoons then charged from our left, towards the right in an oblique direction, and there was much sabre work for some time, within pistol shot of us. But when both parties retired, I did not see a single dead man on the ground.

As the enemy's skirmishers were close behind their cavalry, our brigade formed line, and we met them as they rose the hill. The left of my battalion reached exactly to the bend in the position, that you may take as a fixed point. We charged across the ridge and again formed squares; my battalion in the plain, the 52nd and 71st on the slope. The enemy then brought a number of guns to bear, so as to enfilade my battalion, (and one of Germans on the slope towards our left). Most of the shot passed over us and fell among the Germans who suffered severely.[5] They were forced to retire, leaving a square of dead on the ground.

The regiments of the enemy's lancers formed in our front, tending towards Hougoumont, within point blank shot of us, but as our ammunition was blown up a considerable time before, we had none to give for them. Two guns which played upon them from the ridge behind us, did considerable execution among them. The object of this movement I conceive, was to prevent any attack on that side, during the advance of the Imperial Guards.

At that period I was wounded, by a grape shot through the knee, fired from one of our own guns, which the enemy had taken between us and *La Haye Sainte*.[6] They fired it three times, loaded with grape shot, into our square, and did great execution.

Our brigade again formed line, and I had hardly retired to the rear of the position, to get my wound dressed, when I saw the Imperial Guards advancing in a heavy column along the ridge. That is the period you fix upon for your representation of the battle, and I am fortunately able to speak distinctly to it; as the setting sun shone full in the enemy's face, and on the backs of my own Regiment. The enemy advanced *to the bend of the position, and forced back the left of my Regiment, down the Eastern slope of the ridge and the right of the one to the left,*[7] *leaving an opening of between 1 and 200 yards in the line.* That appeared to me the most critical period of the battle; as there was only a line of Belgians behind, which would probably have made no great resistance, *all seemed lost.*

The advance of the Prussians on the other side however: the resistance he met with towards *La Haye Sainte,* and perhaps something of a panic, obliged the enemy to give way, when there was certainly no sufficient force in his front to oppose him. The whole

British line then advanced towards *La Belle Alliance*; and near that my regiment came in contact with a square of the enemy's infantry (from which it received a murderous fire). I was afterwards informed in France by General Foullert,[8] one of Bonaparte's aides de camp, that the Emperor himself was in that square, and that I believe was the last part of his army that remained formed.

During the day, my battalion lost as nearly as possible half its numbers. The crops appeared to be generally wheat and rye. I may add, that the only good plan I have seen of the battle is that published at Brussels.[9] I think you may almost depend upon its accuracy. The best accounts, the Prussian one by General Gneisenau[10] and a French one published at the time, the English ones decidedly the worst of all.

Yours sincerely,

GEORGE MILLER H P[11]

---

1 Miller joined the army as an ensign in 1804 and served in the Peninsula and was awarded a Gold Medal for the Nivelle. He was severely wounded in a skirmish in 1814. He received a CB and brevet lieutenant colonelcy for Waterloo. He went on the half-pay unattached list in 1826. He died in 1843.

2 Urquhart is approximately three miles west of Elgin in Scotland.

3 This has always been a problem with the field of Waterloo and attempts at portraying it. The valley between the two ridges is very deceptive, in plans it can appear quite inconsequential, but when actually stood on the valley floor, the land rises on both sides quite markedly.

4 This is a common criticism levelled at the French cavalry at the battle of Waterloo. However, it was certainly not normal practice to send the cavalry forward unsupported and I have discovered no evidence of such a tactic as cavalry spiking guns during the heat of battle ever having been employed. Certainly, such a venture would be highly dangerous with infantry squares positioned within pistol-shot of the guns. Any cavalryman tempted to remove a gun or spike it would have been singled out for special attention by the infantry. This would also probably explain why there is little evidence of the guns being turned upon the squares. The French cavalry felt more secure upon their horses and had no interest in the abandoned guns *per se*.

5 Probably a square of Kielmannsegge's Hanoverians.

6 This is an interesting reference regarding the use of some overrun guns by the French, but I have discovered no other statements of its happening.

7 The next unit to the left was the 2nd Battalion 1st Foot Guards which seems to have given way a little on finding the French on their flank. The 4th Battalion French Chasseurs found itself in a gap between the 2/1st Guards and the 2/95th. However assailed by cannon in front and the 2/95th and 1/52nd wheeling up on their flank, they retired.

8 Almost certainly the Master of the Horse, General of Division, Count Albert Louis Emmanuel de Fouler.

9 De Craan's map.

10 *The Life and Campaigns of Field Marshal Prince Blucher of Wahlstatt* by General Count Gneisenau published in English in 1815. Gneisenau had of course been Blücher's Quartermaster General.

11 Half pay.

No. 129 First Lieutenant John Charles Hope[1]
Halifax, 1 February 1835

ADD MS 34704, FO 211

Sir,
I have to acknowledge the receipt of your letter of the 6th November addressed to me in Jersey. I regret that it is not in my power to give you the information which you require, for although present and belonging to the 2nd Battalion at Waterloo, yet was attached to two companies of the 3rd Battalion on that day, also forming part of Lieut. General Adam's brigade. But I am quite positive that the 2nd Battalion at the period you mention, was formed in line four deep immediately on the left of the 52nd Regiment. Beyond this I can give you no information of the movements of that Battalion, neither can I at this distance of time bring to my recollection the description of crops then upon the ground, but the impression at this moment is that they consisted principally of wheat and rye, indeed these are the only two descriptions of grain that I have any distinct recollection of.

I have the honour to be, Sir, your most obedient servant,

J HOPE
MAJOR RIFLE BRIGADE

1 Born in Leytonstone, Essex in 1791, he joined the 95th as an ensign in 1807 and served at Copenhagen, the Corunna campaign, Walcheren and Cadiz including Barossa where he was severely wounded. He commanded the 3/95th after Waterloo until the capture of Paris. He was recommended to General Sir H. Clinton for gallantry at Waterloo. He served in Canada 1826–9 and eventually succeeded to the command of the 1st Battalion Rifles. He died on 12 October 1842.

No. 130 First Lieutenant Thomas Smith[1]
Jamsonstown,[2] 4 September 1835

ADD MS 34705, FO 334

Sir
I hardly know how to address you on the subject of the different papers which you did me the honour of forwarding for my opinion, I have in the first instance to apologise to you for detaining them as long and I fear you will be greatly disappointed on the receipt of this to find I have not entered into a lengthy detail of the operations of the 2nd Battalion 95th Regiment during the action and my only excuse for not doing so, I am not full equal to the task, you will naturally ask, why then did you not at once return the papers, because I was in great hopes that a very dear relation of my own would have put into good language the different observations I had given him and this enabled me to return you all the documents together but I have been sadly disappointed and excessively annoyed; I shall therefore now state that I have read over very attentively Lieut. Colonel Gawler's narrative and with the exception of one or two trifling remarks which I have made in pencil I think *perfectly correct.*

The regiments forming Sir F. Adam's brigade were the only troops who slept in the French position the night of the action, no other part of the army moved off the field of action with the exception of a few skirmishers of the 1st Battalion 95th Regiment.

I have no hesitation in stating that I firmly believe the 1st Brigade of Guards were in rear of the cross roads which runs along the ridge of the position and unites the two high roads upon this head I am positive for a short time previous to the crisis the battalion I belonged to being stationary in square I rode to the left for the purpose of looking at the 1st Brigade of Guards in action and they were then certainly in the rear of the road and neither as I think they ever crossed it, and as far from their having driven back the attacking column, they were very near being driven out of their own position and which would most decidedly have been the case had it not been for Sir F. Adam's brigade and a brigade of cavalry which charged on the moment of the former brigade moving to its left, and when the 2nd 95th Regiment gave their fire I do not think the final column could have been more than twenty paces from them and which fire well given in made most dreadful slaughter.

I beg to observe that Sir F. Adams brigade did not cross the road until it passed La Belle Alliance, whereas by Lieut. Colonel Gawler's plan of the field he has made the Brigade to cross before it reached Le Belle Alliance, this is incorrect.

I expect to be in Dublin about the end of the month when I shall do myself the pleasure of calling on you and any questions that you may wish to ask I will willingly answer them to the best of my recollection, and in conclusion I again beg to apologise to you for detaining the papers so long.

I have the honour to be Sir your most obedient humble servant

T SMITH

LATE ADJUTANT 2ND BATTALION 95TH REGIMENT

P.S. Please to acknowledge the receipt of the papers for I am most anxious to hear of their safe arrival.

---

1 Brother to General Sir Harry Smith. He joined the 95th as a 2nd lieutenant in 1808 and served in the Peninsula, being severely wounded at the Coa 1810. Sir H. Clinton, whom he served as adjutant, recommended him for promotion for gallantry at Waterloo, but he went on half pay due to ill health in 1819. Afterwards Principal Barrack Master at Aldershot. He received a special pension and was made a CB. He died on 6 April 1877 and was buried at the military cemetery at Aldershot.

2 I cannot identify this place, but the spelling is certain. Possibly a mis-spelling of Jamestown of which there are two towns so-named in Ireland, or, of course, Jamaica.

1st Infantry Brigade KGL

The 1st Line Battalion KGL

No. 131 Captain Baron Frederick Goeben[1]

Stade, 12 March 1835

ADD MS 34705, FO 42

Original in German

Dear Sir:

With regard to the request of the 27th of January of this year, which I had the honour of receiving from you, I will do my best to describe to you, exactly, if possible, the role played by the 1st Line Battalion, K G Legion, at the battle of Waterloo, to the best of my recollection. On the enclosed plan, I will also show the probable position of the battalion, as well as how the French Imperial Guard reached the level of our position at the time of their final attack. Nevertheless, I beg your forgiveness should I err with regard to the time, which I also beg, with regard to the positions and column movements designated on the plan, as I can in no way vouch for complete reliability because I never had the opportunity to view closely the battlefield, its heights, valleys, and roads.

The battalion belonged to the 1st Brigade K G Legion, under Colonel du Plat, which was part of the 2nd Division, under the command of Lieutenant-General Sir Henry Clinton. This division took the position that was assigned to it toward midday on the day of the memorable battle of Waterloo on the right wing, approximately diagonally from the Hougoumont farm at the level of the road from Brussels to Nivelle. The battalion marched out of this position between 2 and 3 o'clock in brigades and formed battalion squares. We crossed over the elevation that lay before us at the right wing of the position, which was occupied by several batteries. A cavalry skirmish was apparently coming to an end in the valley, which ran out to the left toward the Brussels to Genappe road, and the French cavalry quickly took cover behind an elevation. Having arrived at the level of the hedge belonging to the Hougoumont farm, the battalion took position at approximately *a* on the enclosed plan. We took very effective enemy rifle fire from the hedge, which they occupied. As a result, Lieutenant Colonel von Robertson,[2] who had until then commanded the 1st Line Battalion, was severely wounded, and command of the battalion now fell to me. In addition, Brigadier Colonel du Plat immediately suffered a fatal wound,[3] and only after repeated efforts were several disbanded battalion squares able to occupy a portion of the hedge, which mainly controlled our position.

This positioning of battalion squares close to the Hougoumont hedge had caused us constant losses. After several hours, however, this position was broken by an oncoming enemy infantry column,* made up of several battalions, which were supported by cuirassiers who followed at some distance. Thereupon, the battalion joined up with the 3rd Line Battalion, K G Legion,[4] and formed a square close to the level of the squares of the brigade under Major General Adam,[5] opposite the enemy, a short distance from the foot of the slope where we happened to be. A fierce skirmish developed, which ended a short time later with the partial destruction and complete dissolution of the enemy infantry column, which was partly the result of the penetration of the column by a regiment of English light dragoons. The enemy cuirassiers, advancing in two columns, now attacked both of the above-mentioned squares, but with complete lack of success. There was also a second attack by that body of cuirassiers on the square adjacent to us, which had been repulsed. The attack on the squares of the 1st and 2nd Battalions by the cuirassiers was repulsed with considerable losses, and hastened their retreat to *b*, which is where they had come from.

The enemy had retreated completely out of our sight, and because a re-formation of the square had become necessary because the troops in the two flanks of both battalions had been completely mixed, the square was ordered to *c* by current Brigadier, Lieutenant Colonel von Wissell,[6] where the formation took place. I believe that the

Letter no. 131

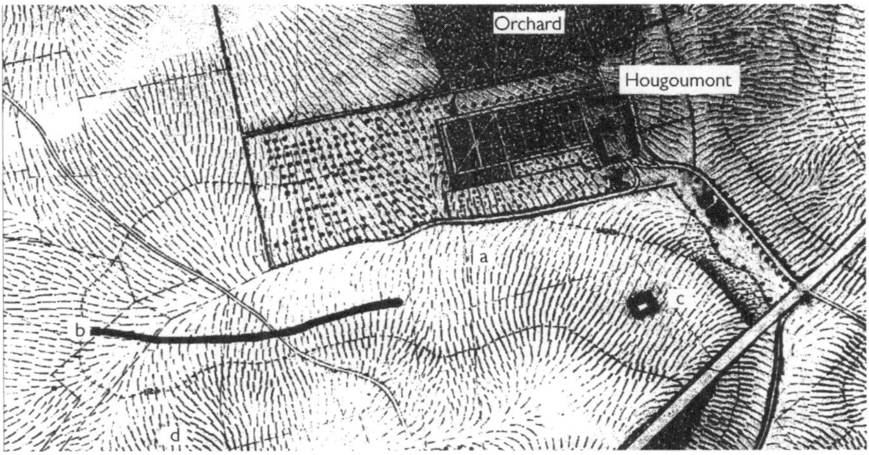

main attack by the French Grenadier Guard occurred just as the above-mentioned square was being re-formed here and was on the march. After some fighting, it was forced to retreat. Both the battalions united now comprised not quite 350 men under arms,‡ and they marched, formed in a single square, into a valley which was located in front of the right wing of the position, until it was ordered, approximately at *d*, to advance in a line 4 men deep, which took us, in a straight direction and without encountering any resistance to Belle Alliance. There, enemy artillerymen fired on us from several cannons, and then they rode after their fleeing army. We pursued the French fugitives until approximately the region of Rossomme, and then we bivouacked for the night on the left side of the road from Brussels to Genappe.

I have no reason to express doubts about the grain types and clover, etc., marked on the plan because as far as I can recall, the ground on which the 1st Line Battalion K G Legion was situated before and during the battle was completely covered with grain or clover, and no ploughed or fallow land particularly came to my attention in the region.

In accordance with your esteemed request, I send you the above remarks regarding the 1st Line Battalion KGL in the German language, and merely add that the battalion was positioned on low ground almost throughout the entire battle, or on somewhat higher land bordered by elevations when we manoeuvred, and therefore only little of the landscape could be seen in so far as we came close to it.

Dear Sir, I have the honour of being. your most obedient,

FREDI GOEBEN
CAPTAIN LATE OF THE
1ST LINE BATTALION, K G LEGION

* Designated as *b* on the plan.

‡ The rifle companies of the 4th Battalion of the 1st Brigade, K G Legion, were already separated from their battalions before the battle, and they formed their own rifle corps, which was attached to the brigade during the battle as well.

1 Goeben is listed in Beamish as number 381. He joined the corps in 1806, serving in the Baltic and the Peninsula in 1808–9 when he was severely wounded at Talavera. He received a

General Service Medal with one bar for Talavera. He did not see active service again until the north German campaign of 1814 and subsequently the Waterloo campaign. He became a brevet major on the retired list in 1816.

2 Lieutenant Colonel William von Robertson is listed in Beamish as number 376. He joined the Legion as a captain in 1803 and served in Hanover, the Mediterranean in 1806–7, the Baltic in 1807–8 and throughout the Peninsula, receiving a General Service Medal with nine bars for Talavera, Busaco, Fuentes d'Onoro, Ciudad Rodrigo, Salamanca, Vittoria, San Sebastian, Nivelle & Nive. He was severely wounded at Waterloo but made a lieutenant colonel on 18 June 1815, CB, KCH, and HGO2. He went on half pay in 1816, retiring to Hamburg.

3 Lieutenant Colonel George Charles Augustus du Plat, numbered 1017 in Beamish. He joined the Corps in 1803, serving in Hanover, the Baltic, the Mediterranean in 1808–12, the Peninsula and Southern France in 1812–14 and the Netherlands. He was severely wounded at Waterloo and died of his wounds on 21 June 1815. A Waterloo medal was issued, presumably to his family.

4 The 1st and 3rd Line Battalions were both part of the 1st KGL Brigade of Colonel du Plat in Clinton's 2nd Division.

5 The 3rd Brigade of Clinton's 2nd Division.

6 Lieutenant Colonel Frederick von Wissell, numbered 469 in Beamish. He joined the Corps in 1806, serving in the Baltic, the Mediterranean in 1808–12, the Peninsula and southern France 1813–14 where he fought at the crossing of the Nive. He became a member of the Guelphic Order and the Order of the Bath and a brevet colonel commanding the 2nd Battalion of Hanoverian Guards. He died in Nassau on 16 December 1820.

The 2nd Line Battalion KGL

No. 132 Captain Frederick Purgold[1]

Luneburg, 4 March 1835

ADD MS 34705, FO 11

Sir

In answer to your letter of the 27th instant, respecting the position of the late 2nd Line Battalion KGL at the battle of Waterloo about seven pm. I have the honour to reply that the battalion stood in a square, having the orchard of the farm of Hougoumont, which was enclosed with hedges and ditches, close to its right; the orchard was in possession of the enemy's skirmishers and we suffered much by their fire. In our front was the French cavalry drawn up and a short time after our arrival we were charged by them. I suppose they were cuirassiers. After their being beaten off, they retired, formed again and a short time afterwards they renewed the charge with the same effect. As the fire out of the orchard annoyed us very much, we formed a line behind the hedge, attacked them and drove them behind the second hedge in the said orchard, taking a position, *en debandade*,[2] behind the trees. Then the French attacked us and we were forced to give way. At this time we received an order to retake the orchard *a tout prix*[3] and our attack was crowned with success.

As I at this time was wounded and carried off from the field, I do not know what further happened.

The battalion – about 400 rank and file strong had at the beginning of the battle occupied a line between Braine l'Alleud and the high road from Brussels to Nivelles with its left close to the said road. At about five pm we marched off left in front, crossed the said road, passed over a deep trodden ground, which had been sown with wheat, but was now utterly devastated, formed in a square and halted at the orchard of Hougoumont, having the right wing of the brigade, although our post was the left.

I beg pardon for having erroneously marked the momentary position behind the hedge of the orchard upon the plan.

If errors or mistakes should have crept into my statement you will please excuse them, after so long an elapse of time they are almost unavoidable.

I have the honour to be Sir your obedient humble servant

FREDERICK PURGOLD

CAPTAIN, LATE 2ND LINE BATT KGL

---

1 Listed at number 427 in Beamish. He joined the Legion in 1804 and served in Hanover, the Mediterranean in 1806–7, the Baltic in 1808–9 and the Peninsula in 1808–14. He was severely wounded at Waterloo. He eventually became a lieutenant colonel on half pay and died at Luneburg on 3 March 1836.

2 French for 'helter-skelter'.

3 'At all costs.'

No. 133 Lieutenant and Adjutant Adolphus Hesse[1]

Hanover, 15 February 1835

ADD MS 34704, FO 255

Original in German

In reply to the kind letter written by Lieut. and Military Secretary Siborne of the 27th January 1835 in which I was requested to answer a few questions about my taking part in the battle of Waterloo with the former 2nd Line Battalion of the King's German Legion, I make the following remarks.

The battalion formed the left wing of Col. du Plat's brigade and moved to this position on the 18th marked *a*. To the right of us at *b* was the 4th, the 3rd at *c* and finally at *d* was the 1st Line Battalion. The whole brigade stood in marching columns in front of a hollow road[2] and quite parallel with the same, so that the right wing of the company (reverse flanks) of all the companies of the brigade touched it. It appears to me that according to the plan they could not have been at any other points but those that I marked *a, b, c* and *d*, partly because I remember that on the left wing of the 2nd Battalion this road was of a minimum depth and because they aimed at us cannon balls passing the hollow road practically at right angles. About 400 paces behind us stood Col. Halkett's brigade[3] of the Hanoverian infantry and approximately at *e* stood the 4 light companies of the battalion (*a b c d*) to cover the artillery; however I am not in a position to give the place accurately. As long as we remained at this position we saw nothing of the enemy because of a few bumps in the ground as well as due to the powder smoke caused by the artillery. However, it was at about 4 pm that the enemy appeared to have the advantage at *f*. At that moment I noticed that a brigade of English artillery took position at xxx but did not go into action.

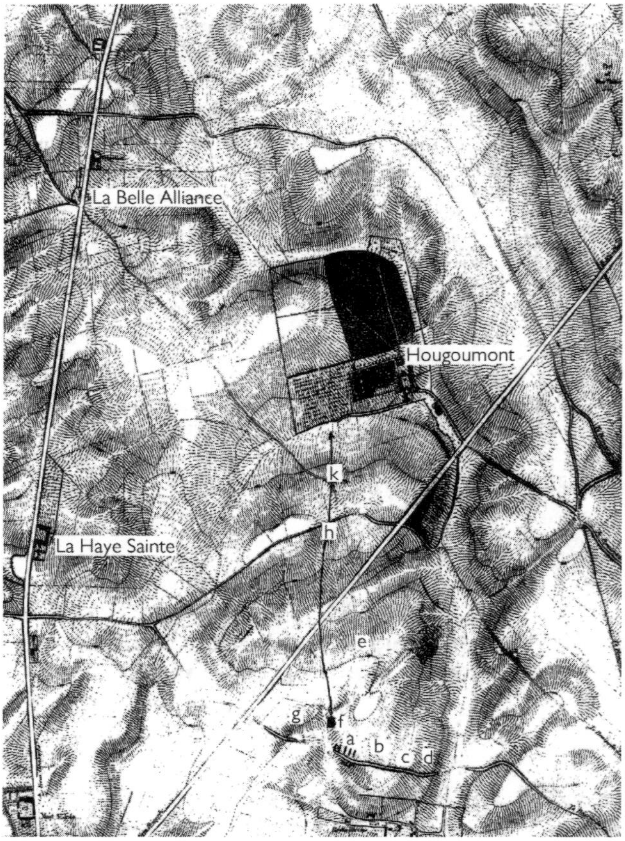

As the enemy, as I already said, about 4 pm, appeared to get the upper hand, there appeared suddenly on our left flank a regiment of the enemy cavalry which encountered at *g* a square of English infantry. I think they were highlanders and the attack, as I saw myself was defeated. This closeness of the enemy caused the column in front to change and stand close together at *h*.[4] Soon after that an adjutant rode along the front and shouted 'advance if you please!'

We formed a march formation and in the surroundings of *h* we met a battery of our artillery whereupon these troops withdrew through our midst while a column of enemy cuirassiers surprised us. At this moment about 150 paces right in front of us near 3 trees, the 4 light companies from the brigade were attacked.

We still had plenty of ammunition and produced an almighty fire aimed at the cavalry, whereupon the same turned around. We advanced again but arriving at *h*, our cavalry fled back through our intervals and a line of enemy cavalry appeared suddenly at the crest of a small height about 60 paces from our front. Capt. Sympher[5] who commanded a horse artillery troop at *m* rode with us and we showed front and advanced and made a few lucky shots causing gaps so that the cavalry turned back.

This happened as I said at *h* and I think at this time, about 7 o'clock that this was the moment that the French Guards won the position at the crest. Now, the enemy infantry opened a strong fire from the gardens[6] that we could not tolerate as we stood in a square. The Brigadier[7] was already killed and each battalion had to help itself. We fell upon the garden, chased off the infantry from it and captured at *I* the hollow road that bordered the garden from this side. Which battalions that stood to our left and our right from the time when we stood at *h* till the moment when we arrived at *I*, I no longer remember as the smoke did not allow me to have a view and one was very busy in the battalion. But I remember the 4 light companies of the brigade that stood at the 3 trees at *I* and who joined us in the attack on the garden. The enemy was repulsed from the garden and at 9 o'clock we met at La Belle Alliance.

ADOLPHUS HESSE
CAPT. HANOVERIAN RIFLE GUARDS
LT AND ADJ LATE 2ND LINE BATTALION KGL

---

1 Hesse is numbered 465 in Beamish. He joined the Legion in 1807 serving in the Baltic and the Peninsula in 1808–14. He was severely wounded at Burgos while leading the German forlorn hope and again at the crossing of the Bidassoa. He became HGO3 and HWC and received a General Service Medal with seven bars for Busaco, Fuentes d'Onoro, Ciudad Rodrigo, Salamanca, Vittoria, San Sebastian and the Nive. He later became a captain in the Hanoverian Rifle Guards.
2 This is the road to Braine l'Alleud.
3 The 3rd Hanoverian Brigade.
4 This indicates that the troops formed a solid square or column.
5 Captain Sympher commanded a KGL Horse artillery troop.
6 This refers to the gardens of Hougoumont.
7 Lieutenant Colonel George Charles Augustus du Plat.

The 3rd Line Battalion KGL

No. 134 Captain Albertus Cordemann[1]
Hanover, 2 March 1835

ADD MS 34705, FO 3

Original in German

Dear Sir,
With regard to your esteemed letter of 17th January of this year, including the layout of a plan of the battlefield of Waterloo, I acknowledge receipt thereof, and it is my great pleasure to return same to you enclosed, with such remarks as I, a participant in this noteworthy event, am still capable of disclosing after so long a time span.

With regard to your main question, I respond as follows.
What was the particular formation of the 3rd Line Battalion K. G. Legion at the moment—about 7pm, etc.?

The battalion formation at that moment – as it had been for a long time – was in square because especially there, we feared attacks by enemy cavalry, which we had to defend against.

What was the formation of that part of the enemy's forces in front of the battalion?

There was an especially large concentration of artillery and heavy cavalry, the latter of which had, toward 5 pm, already formed into columns behind this artillery in preparation for an attack on us and then toward 6 o'clock attempted, cost what may, to break through and destroy our battle line, particularly near our position.

Perhaps it will be agreeable to you if I report several facts to illustrate what happened between about 6 and 7 o'clock.

I must first note that the normal regularity that ensues after the command given by the commanding officer could not be observed with the usual precision, partly because it was not audible as a result of the uninterrupted thunder of the cannon and various other noises, making it incomprehensible, and partly because the battalion often did not know who the actual commanding officer was. The horses of these and of all saddled officers, had been shot, and so they served on foot. Our Brigadier du Plat[2] was mortally wounded, and our Colonel Wissell[3] followed him in the line of command; our Major Boden[4] likewise wounded, and Major Luttermann[5] was not able to carry out his duties in all places in the usual manner without a horse. The captains made every effort under these circumstances to inform the people of dangers and of enemy attacks, and to maintain order to the extent possible by means of constant attention. At the very moment when we expected a charge by the cuirassiers, we reminded the people again how they were to comport themselves: thereupon, the soldiers on their own loaded a second round and fired on the charging enemy at about 50–60 paces, independently, like hunters, so effectively that the same retreated with great loss, whereupon the legion's 1st Dragoons,[6] which were positioned behind us, burst forward through the gaps in pursuit of the same.

An artillery battery of the legion that we positioned in a gap on our left flank became engaged in a fierce fire, and answered the just-mentioned charge with case shot, nor did other squares and units spare their fire. Another column of cuirassiers immediately charged this artillery, which was supported by its subordinate infantry, and fired away until the enemy was between the cannon, whereupon the artillerymen with their side arms and their ammunition bags slung over their shoulders retreated in part into our square, in part some of them found protection among the trees.

Our people yelled loudly, 'We must retake the cannon!!' I was positioned on the *right* wing, which took up *the front* closer to the *Hougoumont* woods, and when I looked around to see where the call was coming from, I noticed that the left was firing their weapons at the enemy, who had just taken the cannons, then charged them with their bayonets, whereupon the enemy abandoned the cannon and hurried away. The artillerymen immediately made use of the cannon, discharging at the retreating enemy. In my opinion, this was an inspired, even outrageous manoeuvre, and I cannot say whether the order was given for it. I believe that it perhaps resulted from the impulse of those good men, or that of the artillerymen who had retreated into our square! After that, the enemy attempted two more charges against our square, both of which were unsuccessful, and by then it may have about been 6:30 pm.

On the plan you will find the approximate drawings with remarks, and I believe that I have fairly accurately marked the position of our squares because I remember quite clearly that we were positioned so close to the woods and bushes of Hougoumont that the enemy shells too often reached the ranks of the square and killed or wounded many. As a result, our Divisional General, Clinton finally felt the need to order a movement to the side far enough to be less exposed to this murderous skirmish fire. As a result I think they showed their loyalty, ...fulfilled their formations, etc., etc.

I add the remark that as far as I know, the British Guards claimed that the house and buildings of Hougoumont were like a fortress, the surroundings of which were full of Frenchmen, and that the enemy had such a well-covered position in the woods, the garden and the bushes that it was impossible for our 4 rifle companies,[7] which later joined with the 2nd Line Battalion, KGL,[8] to dislodge them, in spite of all their efforts. Captain Holle[8] of the 1st Line Battalion, Rifle Company was wounded here and died under the 3 trees that are drawn in on the plan. Captain Tilee of the 2nd Line Battalion was killed;[10] also shot was Captain Diedel of the 3rd Battalion Rifle Company.[11] Captain Heise of the 4th Battalion Rifle Company[12] was wounded and died in Brussels. Captain Beurmann of the 2nd Battalion Rifle Company[13] was slightly wounded.

With regard to the correctness of the terrain and of the fields that you drew in pencil on the plan, I must bemoan that I cannot give you even the slightest information. On the 17th, as we were returning from Quatre Bras, we passed by the region of the battlefield, and I do not recall having seen any thick vegetation there, as I saw everywhere else. Some of it had undoubtedly been taken into bivouac by friend and foe alike, and during the night of the 17th to the 18th, such a foggy rain fell that the heavy and clayey earth became very soft so that the low ground was somewhat inundated. As our Division was marching from the slope (plateau) of Waterloo through the plain and low land toward Hougoumont at about 2 pm, we found everything to be so trodden down that there was nothing to be seen of the beautiful vegetation. I regret that I didn't take special notice of it because so many more important and weighty matters occupied my eyes and my mind. I must admit that I took such care for my person in my current position that I knew little about the enemy or condition and circumstances of the opposing armies. It is true that we had heard that the Prussians had taken part in a skirmish on the 16th at Ligny, but of the result we learned only that Prince Blücher would join us during the battle on the 18th. We also learned that the French Army were marching from Quatre Bras, as we had a skirmish of the outposts on the 17th after we arrived at our bivouac late in the afternoon, which ended toward evening because of the rain and darkness.

The general order given by the Duke of Wellington on the 18th at 10 am made it clear to us that Napoleon faced us personally with superior forces, and that the Duke of Wellington had made a decision to fight a battle and to attack the enemy himself. The Duke explained that we could expect a hot day and a difficult battle ahead of us, and that he counted on the proven valour of the troops, etc., to fight hard and if possible to contribute to the honour of the day, etc.

We had already taken out and cleaned our loaded rifles, which had become wet, and returned the ammunition that had become unusable and received replacements, and then the signal was given to decamp. We marched away at 11 o'clock, and the division arrived at a line marked on the plan on the plateau of Waterloo with such regularity, as if, it had been, on a parade ground. From here we could look out over the magnificent

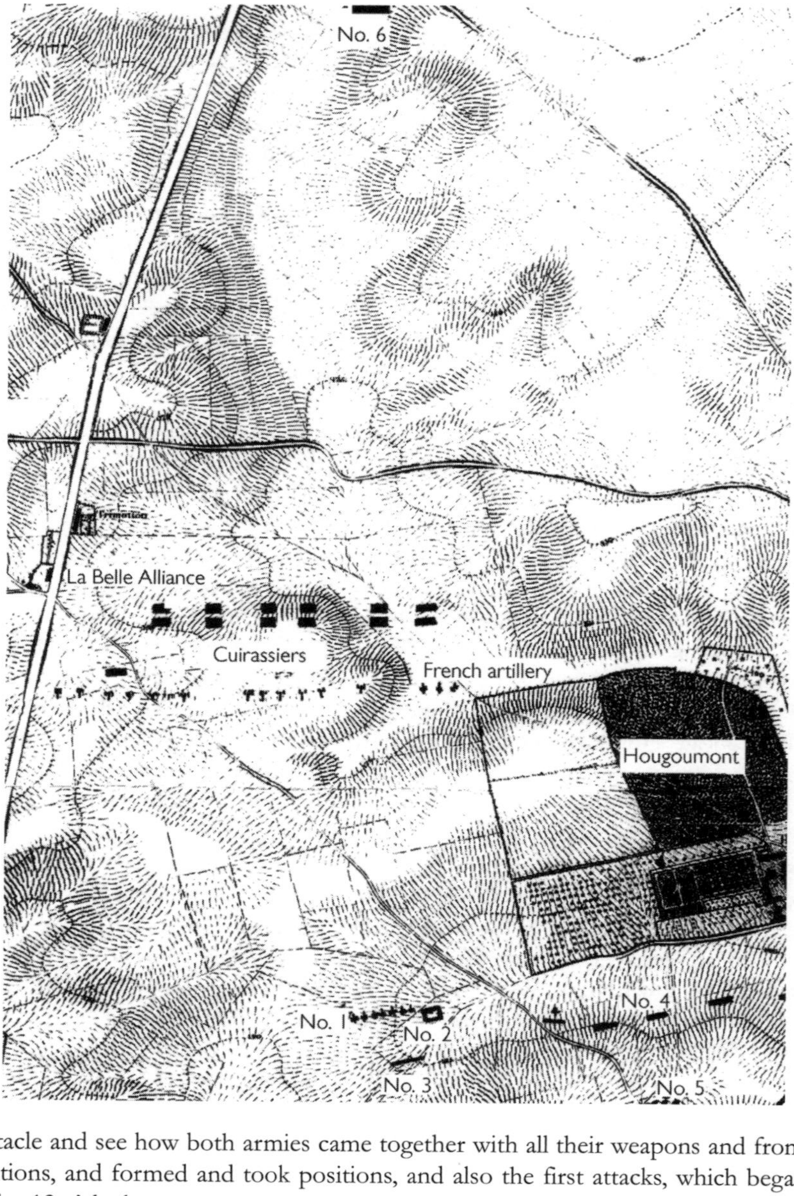

spectacle and see how both armies came together with all their weapons and from all directions, and formed and took positions, and also the first attacks, which began at midday 12 o'clock.

I ask you to consider how little we knew of the actual overall circumstances and conditions, and also to consider how fierce and desperate the enemy attacks were on ours and on the other positions of the British army between 6 and 7 pm. In so doing, you may perhaps have some concept of how great was our amazement when, after this serious strain, the sudden order came from the Duke of Wellington to all squares and corps immediately to 'Form line! Four deep and advance!!!'

Letter no. 134

In accordance with this order, this square, which had become smaller, was soon in line formation, we found such obstacles to our advance that at first we lagged behind, in part because the terrain was so soft and deep that the people could only get through with great difficulty, and some of them lost their shoes in the process; in part also because the field before us was so covered with killed and wounded enemy soldiers and cuirassiers, horses and weapons of all sorts that we could not keep our ranks closed, but continually had to split up to avoid humans and horse, the latter of which often kicked about with their hoofs. Their last remaining defence was the cuirassiers of the Guard and the 10th Regiment, as well as the grenadiers à cheval.

However, the concentration that now came into view and the sudden general flight from all positions by the enemy, who until a moment earlier had been so brave, and the abandonment of all who could not get away quickly – that gave the greatest encouragement to our soldiers to advance.

How important it was to the Duke of Wellington to pursue the enemy quickly and not to leave him any time may be gauged by the fact that whenever there was a momentary and even justified and excusable delay on the part of a battalion, he was there at a gallop with the order: 'Don't stop! Go on! Straight on!'

To see in this manner the rapid movement of the cavalry, artillery, and infantry—in a race – forwards, and to see the enemy fleeing in all directions, was and remains for me a pleasurable and unforgettable vision. For us at the time all the more so because we heard or perceived of no visible reason for it. Rather, this riddle was only solved for us toward 10 o'clock, when it was dark and we were in bivouac and we had met with a French officer who informed us that Marshal Blücher had arrived with his army via Wavre and had linked up with Wellington's left wing, and had attacked the enemy's right flank. The pursuit of the enemy ordered by the Duke of Wellington was also reinforced and made more mobile at this moment by his troops and horses, which had been less strained.

During the first half hour of our advance, between 50–60 abandoned enemy cannon lay behind us on the terrain that we had passed, and a large number of their men were running about leaderless. The rapid and irregular retreat was beyond description, which, as is known, resulted in the complete dissolution of the French army.

I have now disclosed to you everything concerning our battalion and its position, and I have passed over everything else to which I was not witness, as well as subsequent events and consequences of this battle which will be known from memoirs and the history of the time.

It would be a great pleasure to me if these lines of simple description and the enclosed plan of the Waterloo battlefield were of some use to you, but also extremely flattering if you were to mention the various corps of the K. G. Legion who were present with their positions, whose greatest pride it was and will continue to be to have had the outstanding good fortune and great honour to have served under the victorious banner of a great, noble, and magnanimous nation and under the command of such a one as the Duke of Wellington!

It is my honour to be Your Excellency's most obedient servant.

A CORDEMANN
CAPTAIN LATE OF THE 3RD LINE BATTALION
KING'S GERMAN LEGION

1 Cordemann is listed as number 479 in Beamish. He joined the corps in 1804 and served in Hanover, the Baltic, the Mediterranean in 1808–14 and the Netherlands. Afterwards a brevet major on the half-pay retired list in 1816.
2 Lieutenant Colonel George Charles Augustus du Plat.
3 Lieutenant Colonel Frederick von Wissell.
4 Major Anthony Eberhard Charles Boden, numbered 472 in Beamish. He joined the corps in 1803, serving in the Baltic, the Mediterranean in 1808–14 and the Netherlands. He was severely wounded at Waterloo and died at Gottingen on 19 February 1831.
5 Major Gottlieb Frederick von Luttermann, numbered 471 in Beamish. Joined the corps in 1803 and served in the Baltic, the Mediterranean in 1808–14 and the Netherlands. Made a lieutenant colonel on 18 June 1815. HGO3 and CB. He died at Gelliehausen near Gottingen on 15 September 1831.
6 The 1st Dragoons KGL commanded by Colonel von Dörnberg.
7 The rifle company of each line battalion must have been removed to form a rifle battalion.
8 2nd Line Battalion KGL commanded by Major George Muller.
9 Captain Charles von Holle, numbered 989 in Beamish. He had joined the corps in 1804 and served in Hanover, the Mediterranean, the Baltic, the Peninsula in 1808–14 and theNetherlands. He had been severely wounded at Talavera. He was killed at Waterloo; a Waterloo medal appears to have been issued to his family.
10 Captain George Tilee, numbered 984 in Beamish. He joined the corps in 1804, serving in Hanover, the Baltic, the Peninsula in 1808-11, northern Germany and the Netherlands. He was killed at Waterloo but a medal appears to have been issued to his family.
11 Captain Frederick Diedel, numbered 990 in Beamish. He joined the corps in 1804 and served in Hanover, the Baltic, the Mediterranean in 1808–14 and the Netherlands. He was killed at Waterloo but a medal was issued to his family.
12 Captain George Heise, numbered 1029 in Beamish. He joined the corps in 1803, serving in Hanover, the Baltic, the Mediterranean in 1808–12, the Peninsula in 1813–14 and the Netherlands. He was severely wounded at Waterloo and died on 27 June 1815. A Waterloo medal was issued to his family.
13 Captain Charles Beurmann of the 2nd Line Battalion, numbered 428 in Beamish. He joined the corps in 1806, serving in the Peninsula 1808–14 and the Netherlands. He had been severely wounded at Talavera and at Toloza but Beamish does not record his wound at Waterloo. The wound must have been slight as he is not listed as wounded in the London Gazette. He died at Waltzen, near Hoya in Hanover, on 26 August 1817.

The 4th Line Battalion KGL

No. 135 Major Philip Mejer[1]
Lauenburg, 14 February 1835

ADD MS 34704, FO 270

Original in German

The letter and the chart of the battlefield at Waterloo with which you honoured me was received and I will not miss the opportunity to reply to your letter and wish to report as follows.

I regret that I am not able to tell you the position of the 5th Battalion of the KGL on the 18th June I was employed as a major with the 4th Battalion and the 5th Battalion as far as I know was far removed from our position to talk about or see what was happening.

But as I, as previously mentioned, was acting as a major in the 4th Battalion and as I replaced Major Chüden who was killed at the beginning of the battle,[2] I am able to pass on what I saw as far as I remember, more so as I understand the Major Reh[3] and other staff officers of the 1st, 2nd, 3rd & 4th Battalions of the KGL have since died. As much as I want to fulfil your request, I wish to say that the length of the time since the day of the 18th June 1815 and the loss of my notes entered in my diary, make it impossible. To promise to give nothing more complete than what I remember is to limit myself to the fact that our brigade had 1,000 men.

On the 17th June, between 4–5 in the afternoon the brigade was placed at *A* I think, at least close to the village of Merbe la Leud[4] whilst villages on the left and somewhat to the right lay in front of us. On our right we saw on the horizon what appeared to be a large wood or forest. Behind us were Brunswick cavalry also bivouacking.

At the beginning of the battle the brigade was in position *B*; I reach this conclusion, because on the chart marked 'ravine' behind us was where many wounded were treated. The ground in the bivouac area as well as in front of us had fruit but I believe that this open space was a village green or a lawn.

On our left we had Scots and on the same side at a distance from us Hanoverians. On the right in Hougoumont were the English Guards, the 95th Regiment and 2 or 3 cannons firing at the enemy. On the horizon the French cavalry of two kinds was forming on the road from Nivelles to Brussels, as I clearly saw from the white and light blue coats. We ourselves were shot at by the artillery, which appeared to be stationed to our right and forward. A number of English pieces were attacked and were disabled.

We advanced further and had French light infantry in front of us and at the same time French cuirassiers formed in front of us on the height and the Battalion formed squares and were attacked by the cuirassiers 2 – 3 times, however without any gain for them because the ground was partly tilled – softened through the rain to such an extent that the horses stopped out of range of the rifles in front of the square, stood still and could go no further. At the retreat of the French they were pursued every time by the Brunswick cavalry till finally an English light dragoon regiment took on the chase and they disappeared from view. We moved in line until the hollow road, stopped there and were again attacked by the light infantry, which caused a number of deaths and injuries. The light infantry retired, we stopped for about ¾ hour. In front on our left was either a house – or La Belle Alliance – when suddenly, after hearing of the enemy withdrawal, we marched along the ditch on the left, crossed the chaussee and went into a very deep hollow road, well 20–30 feet, always moving straight on, crossed the chaussee from Genappe again and as it seems to me from the chart passed a wood or forest to the left.

With Le Caillou on the right, we marched straight through the fields and bivouacked in the grounds of a nearby farm. This farm was secured from the Prussians because Napoleon himself had supposedly spent the night there.

On the 19th we went straight across the fields to Nivelles, about ½ an hour later we made the chaussee and stayed the night on the other side of Nivelles on the right of the chaussee.

The ground on which we manoeuvred was mainly tilled and sown with either summer wheat or winter corn. I don't remember seeing meadows, just the mentioned

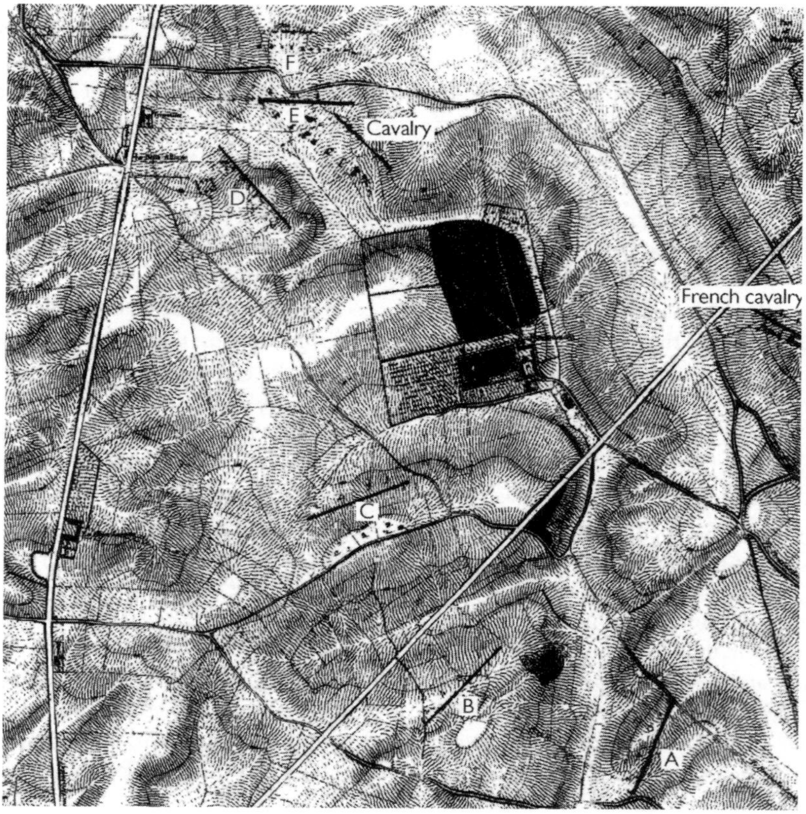

A Bivouac on the 17th
B Formation of the Brigade at the beginning of the fighting
C Position first night after forming of the Brigade
D Position in which the square was formed... NB I think these squares are given too far forward, as I did not see the Belle Alliance at that time to be so much to the side as with the squares indicated by me.
E Halt position of the Brigade after retreat of the cavalry, from here we went forward with Trimotion on the left
F Dangerous passage way through the hollow lane.
French cavalry marked black lines. The light infantry with dots.

lane leading toward Nivelles and the farm in whose vicinity we spent the night from the 18th to the 19th, the chaussee was on our right,

P H J MEJER
MAJOR HP 5TH KGL

These light infantry came towards us from the left over the lane.

1 Mejer is numbered 561 in Beamish. He joined the Legion in 1805, serving in Hanover, the

Baltic in 1807, the Mediterranean in 1808–12 and the Peninsula in 1812–14. He retired on half pay and resided at Lauenburg in Denmark.

2 Major George William Cyriacus Chüden numbered 1019 in Beamish. He had joined the Legion in 1803, serving in Hanover 1805, the Baltic in 1807 and northern Germany in 1813–14. Mejer is slightly mistaken as Chüden was severely wounded at Waterloo and died of his wounds on 19 June.

3 Major Frederick Reh, numbered 1173 in Beamish. He joined the Legion in 1803, serving in the Baltic in 1806–7, the Peninsula in 1808–11, the Mediterranean in 1812 and the Peninsula in 1812–14. He became CBO and HGO3, made a lieutenant colonel on 18 June 1815 and retired on half pay on 25 September 1815. He died at Osterode in Hanover on 24 July 1829.

4 This must be a mix up of names, the villages nearby were Merbe Braine and Braine l'Alleud, it is probable that they camped at Merbe Braine.

No. 136 Captain Conrad Schlichthorst[1]

Heufeld near Harburg, 26 February 1835

ADD MS 34704, FO 268

Original in German

Your letter of the 27 January addressed to Capt William Heydenreich[2] – who at the time when the battle of Waterloo took place, commanded as a Major a Hanoverian battalion[3] and so could not take part in the action of the 4th Line Battalion – was sent to me for reply. I have thus the pleasure in sending you my best recollection of all that took place on that memorable day, as far as it is possible for an officer to recollect who had plenty to do with the formations of the troops and so not being able to note everything that took place around him.

In order to be as accurate as possible, I am selecting the solution in the manner of a narrative, to inform you of the glorious 18th June and of all that is impressed on my memory.

Between 10:00 and 11:00 in the morning the division to which the 4th Battalion belonged[4] got ready. It formed in an open column and marched off some one hundred paces from the bivouac forward towards Merbe Braine. Here we were very inconvenienced by the enemy gunfire and lost besides Major Chüden,[5] Lieutenant and Adjutant La Fargue,[6] a number of sub-officers and troops. However, at the moment when on the ridge our firepower directed against the enemy started to act, the Battalion swung in a column of half distance forward towards the enemy and after passing the road towards Brussels and Nivelles, formed a square and marched down the valley, where we stopped and commenced an almighty small arms fire. While this was going on, our Hussars rode hard towards the enemy cuirassiers and pursued them through the gap between the 4th and 3rd Battalions and at this point and quite unexpectedly they broke towards the front of the 3rd Battalion. Not only did we have fire in the front but also on the left flank of the 4th Battalion which advanced some ninety paces and which flank the writer had that day the honour to command. As a consequence the enemy took flight. The enemy infantry stood – I believe – in a line in front of us with the Lancers behind on a ridge. After some time when the front became stabilized, the 4th Battalion moved sideways to the ridge and formed a line.

The Duke of Wellington came to the battalion at dusk and asked the commander of the same if the battalion, after its great performance, was able to do something else.

This was answered in the affirmative, the battalion reformed into a column of 4 men deep and rushed with rapid march in the direction of a small house that was nearly all destroyed in the proximity of the road from Brussels to Genappe. We were directed to the right and arrived at a position in a village whose name was unknown to us where we bivouacked all night alone. What I remember of this village is that it was full of enemy ammunition dumps and ordnance carriages and a shed filled with wounded.

I remarked that on our first attack there was on the right a high wooden structure. Whether the ground where the 4th battalion was located each time was waste/fallow or whether it was cultivated and what grew there I cannot recall at all and regretfully I cannot give any closer information in the same way as the marked positions of the 4th Battalion on the map are only approximate and I cannot vouchsafe their accuracy.

So, this is all that I can recollect of the memorable 18th June and I cannot add anything further.

Please accept my fondest regards and be assured of my deep respect.

I am your obedient servant

C SCHLICHTHORST, CAPTAIN
LATE 4TH LINE BATTALION – GERMAN LEGION.

---

1 Schlichthorst is listed as number 520 in Beamish. He joined the corps in 1806, serving in the Baltic, the Mediterranean in 1808–12, the Peninsula in 1812–14 and the Netherlands. He went on half pay in 1816. Little is known of his further career.

2 Captain William Heydenreich, numbered 516 in Beamish. He joined the corps in 1806, serving in the Baltic, the Mediterranean in 1808–12, the Peninsula in 1812–14 and the Netherlands. He was slightly wounded at Waterloo and retired as a major on half pay in 1816.

3 The statement that Heydenreich was absent from his battalion at Waterloo to command a Hanoverian corps, cannot be verified. He is not named as having commanded any of the Hanoverian battalions; indeed Siborne who received this statement has simply listed him as wounded under the 4th Line Battalion.

4 The 4th Line Battalion belonged to the 1st KGL Brigade in Lieutenant Colonel Sir H. Clinton's 2nd Division.

5 Major George William Cyriacus Chüden, numbered 1019 in Beamish. He had joined the corps in 1803 and served in Hanover, the Baltic, northern Germany in 1813–14 and the Netherlands. He was mortally wounded at Waterloo and died of his wounds on 19 June 1815. A Waterloo medal was issued to his family.

6 Lieutenant William Lewis de la Fargue, numbered 537 in Beamish. He joined the corps as an NCO in 1812, serving in northern Germany and the Netherlands. He was severely wounded at Waterloo and had a leg amputated. He died at Doesberg in Holland in January 1833.

THIRD DIVISION

No. 137 Captain James Shaw, 43rd Foot, Assistant Quartermaster General[1]

Kirkmichael House, 18 March 1842

ADD MS 34707, FO 350

My dear Sir

I have received your letter of the 14th asking me to give you such information as I may be able, to be considered strictly private and confidential, regarding the left battalion of Alten's division[2] at Waterloo.

So far the account which you have got seems to me to be correct, that the battalion,[3] from the severity of the fire from the French batteries, took shelter in the hollow of the crossroad. Several parts of the division were drawn back a little at the same time so as to find protection behind the slope of the ground. From the hollow in which the German battalion were thus placed, they no doubt gave their fire to the portion of cuirassiers who approached them, but that they should then have left this position and advanced across the road to attack the French infantry that were attacking Kempt's brigade is quite contrary to anything which I observed or had any idea of till I received your letter of the 14th instant.

I have not the least idea that the Duke of Wellington was there at that moment: I stood with General Alten very near to the Luneburg Battalion[4] and we were not aware that the Duke was there, and I do not see how he could have been without great danger of being made prisoner, unless he actually went into one of the squares of the division; for the whole ground was instantly covered with cuirassiers.

I really should think that the officers must be mistaken as to the time, and that their advance across the road, if at all, must have been at a subsequent period of the action. You will observe that my information to you on this subject is not direct: I was driven by the charge of the cuirassiers into one of our squares in the middle of the division, and therefore I could not say positively what occurred to the left battalion of the division.

It is within the realms of possibility that the Duke of Wellington may have rode up to them at that time and given the orders which you mention, but it is very difficult for me to suppose that such was the case. I do not know positively where the Duke was at that time, but my impression was that he then stood behind our Guards infantry, it is there I certainly would have looked for him had I been sent for orders: it is true that he was frequently in front of Alten's division and near to the left of its front, but I saw nothing of him or his staff when the charge of the cuirassiers took place, and I was then with Alten, on horseback, near to where the Luneburg Battalion stood.

It may be true that the attack by Somerset's and Ponsonby's brigades was a combined one and that Picton's division charged at the same time, which from my position in an infantry square I did not see. But that the attack by large columns of French infantry upon Picton's division entirely preceded the attack of cuirassiers upon Alten's division is quite certain, for Alten and I stood very quietly looking at that attack while Alten's division had no attack upon it whatever but from the French batteries; and moreover, a rush from Kempt's brigade, through the hedge, we distinctly witnessed, which irregular although it was, was very bold, and completely checked the French columns: all that *decidedly preceded* the attack on Alten's division by the French cavalry. Kempt's brigade, or indeed Picton's whole division, may have charged forward when our cavalry charged, and then the Duke might have rode forward to Alten's left battalion; but by this time the French were driven back, so that I don't see what would have been gained by Alten's left battalion crossing the road.

I am sorry that I cannot give you the precise information you require. I had the pleasure of seeing the model in London, it seemed to me perfection, and I am truly glad to find that we are to have an account of the action from your pen.

Believe me, yours very faithfully

J S KENNEDY[5]

---

1 Shaw joined the army as an ensign in 1805 and served in the Peninsula being slightly wounded at the Coa. He served as ADC to General Robert Craufurd though 1809–10 and received a General Service Medal with three bars for Ciudad Rodrigo, Badajoz and Salamanca. He became a brevet major for Waterloo and commanded at Calais during the three years of occupation. Later he organized the Constabulary force in Ireland and became a Lieutenant General, KCB and Colonel-in-Chief of the 47th Regiment. He was the author of the noted *Notes on the Battle of Waterloo,* published in 1865. He died on 30 May 1865.

2 Lieutenant General Baron Alten commanded the 3rd Division.

3 A handwritten note in Siborne's hand would indicate that the left battalion in question was the 1st Light Battalion, KGL commanded by Lt Col. Bussche of the 2nd Brigade KGL.

4 The Luneburg Battalion formed part of the 1st Hanoverian Brigade of the 3rd Division.

5 He assumed the name Shaw Kennedy on his marriage in 1820 (His name is often shown hyphenated, but the Army List and his own book show this as not the case).

5th Infantry Brigade

The 30th Regiment, 2nd Battalion

No. 138 Major Charles Albert Vigoureux[1]

War Office, 20 August 1840

ADD MS 34707, FO 183

Written on his behalf by Mr Alexander Tulloch[2]

Sir,

Colonel Vigoureux regrets, that owing to his continued illness, he is obliged to answer your letter through the medium of another, and that he cannot give the subject to which you refer that minute attention which it deserves.

Generally, however, he thinks you are quite correct as to the column in question having debouched from the security of La Haye Sainte and that Major Pratt[3] has been led into error by the circumstance, that as the column of the enemy was advancing upon La Haye Sainte, Colonel Vigoureux threw forward the light troops of the Brigade to meet it, whose fire proved so galling that the column immediately extended to the left, in the direction of Hougoumont, which may have had the appearance of a movement of the whole column from La Haye Sainte upon Hougoumont as described by Major Pratt. Colonel Vigoureux thinks this took place *after* the charge of cavalry, which was repulsed by the Household Brigade.

The Colonel thinks it better to answer your letter thus generally, than to attempt more minute details in his present state of health, indeed it was not until today that he has been competent to the fatigue even of dictating his recollections on the subject.

I return your enclosures together with your own letter in case you may wish to refer to the queries it contains.

I am, Sir, your most humble servant

ALEX M TULLOCH

1 Vigoureux joined the army as an ensign in 1793, serving in Holland in 1794 and 1799 and the Peninsula in 1810–13, receiving a General Service Medal with two bars for Fuentes d'Onor and Vittoria. Vigoureux was severely wounded at Waterloo where he commanded an ad hoc 'skirmishing battalion' comprising the light companies of 2/30th, 33rd, 2/69th and 2/73rd. Later he gained a CB and became Lieutenant Colonel of the 45th Foot in 1826. He went on half pay in 1839 and died as a colonel on the retired list on 24 December 1841.

2 This would appear to be Major Alexander Murray Tulloch, listed in the 1840 Army List as having served from 1826 until going on half pay (unattached) in 1838.

3 Lieutenant John Pratt of the 30th was wounded at Waterloo by a musket ball striking his chin and entering his mouth. He had joined the 30th as an ensign in 1811 and served in the Peninsula, being slightly wounded in the left leg at Badajoz. He transferred to the 28th Foot in 1819 and became a major in the 27th Foot in 1827. His letter is published in Siborne's *Waterloo Letters* (number 138).

No. 139 Captain Robert Howard[1]

Petersham, Surrey, 22 November 1834

ADD MS 37403, FO 317

Sir

Having been pretty much on the move I only received your letter yesterday. I will with pleasure give you every information in my power, but fear it will afford you very little assistance in the construction of the model so trifling is it. As to the formation of the 30th when the French Guards made the last attack my recollection is perfect. It was (forming one square with the 73rd) lying down to avoid as much as possible the artillery of the enemy which at that time was very destructive, under cover of which in our flank, or perhaps a little to our left in the direction of La Haye Sainte a very heavy column of French infantry advanced steadily with supported arms to almost if not quite within the range of musketry when it halted, having witnessed as we afterwards supposed the result of their attacks upon our right. This was the only body of the enemy that I remember seeing at the time.

Large bodies of British cavalry and some infantry now passed us from the rear to attack in their turn. We immediately formed line four deep and advanced, but were very soon halted as we had suffered severely and our men were completely exhausted.

It was so late on the evening of the 17th, when we got into our position under torrents of rain and the next morning so fully occupied in preparing for the battle that I cannot give you any information as to the nature of the crops, but the plain appeared to me to be pretty generally under cultivation, but perfectly flattened.

Nor can I speak as to the positions, movements and formations of the contending armies during the day, the only offensive movement of any consequence on that part of the field was an attempt to get possession of some guns the enemy had advanced which were playing upon us with terrific effect. It was at this time that General Sir Colin Halkett[2] was wounded in the face while with hat off he was encouraging the men to the attack, which was relinquished, and we endeavoured to fall back a little but were not allowed to do so, as we were immediately charged by cavalry. This was in my opinion (certainly with us) the most critical period of the day, it might be about four or half past four. The attacks we had to sustain were principally from cavalry aided by artillery which were frequent and desperate, driving in our light troops and artillery men who took shelter in the different squares on hands and knees to avoid the fire opened on them by the enemy. Their cavalry often passed to our rear without making the slightest impression upon any body of infantry. I wish Sir I had more satisfactory information to send you but I cannot at the present moment recollect anything beyond what I have already written.

I have the honour to be, Sir, your most humble servant

R HOWARD
MAJOR

Note on the envelope in the hand of Siborne:

General Halkett was twice wounded on that day therefore I am not quite certain as to which he received at the time above alluded to.

---

1 Howard joined the army as an ensign in 1803 serving in the Peninsula and the Waterloo campaign. He was made a brevet major for Waterloo and promoted to lieutenant colonel (unattached) in 1837. He died at Wigfair, St Asaph on 22 September 1856.

2 Major General Sir Colin Halkett commanded the 5th Brigade.

The 33rd Regiment

No. 140 Captain Charles Knight[1]
Haydock Lodge, 25 March 1835

ADD MS 34705, FO 103

Sir

I have the honour to acknowledge the receipt of your letter of the 23rd instant, accompanied by a plan of the field of Waterloo, which I found here a few days ago on my return from Lear's of Bristol. Major Harty[2] having shown me the plan which you sent to him some time back, we both had a good deal of conversation on the subject of the position of the 33rd marked upon it, as it showed us both to have been at the time the French Imperial Guards advanced to the attack about 7 pm. I think it therefore better to refer you to the plan forwarded by hand, and to return this without having any formations upon it fearing there might be some mistaken position there, I allow the remarks made both by Colonel Elphinstone[3] and Major Harty which shown to me, as far as my memory serves me, to be mainly correct; I was present during the whole of the action of the 18th of June but my recollection being not much good so great a length of time having since elapsed I fear I cannot give you any further information than had been already forwarded by these two officers.

In your letter you state the regiment to have been the 2nd Battalion 33rd Regiment instead of the 33rd Regiment in which I have to correct you, the 33rd never having had a second Battalion.

I have the honour to be, Sir, your most obedient humble servant

C KNIGHT LT COL
COMMANDING 33RD REGIMENT

---

1 Knight joined the army as an ensign in 1806, serving at the capture of Bourbon and Isle de France in 1810. He received a severe contusion at Waterloo but marched the regiment off the field. He became a lieutenant colonel in 1830 and succeeded to the command of the 33rd Regiment. He died onboard the SS *Pandora* at St Thomas's on 21 July 1841.

2 Captain Joseph M. Harty was slightly wounded at Waterloo. He had joined the army as an ensign in 1807 and served at the capture of Bourbon and Isle de France in 1810 and the campaign in Germany and Holland in 1814. Afterwards he became Colonel in 1854 and KH. He was still living in 1874. His letter was published by Siborne (number 141).

3 Lieutenant Colonel William Keith Elphinstone commanded the 33rd at Waterloo. Afterwards he was Major General CB, KSA and Commander-in-Chief in Bengal. Captured by Akhbar Khan in the retreat from Kabul, he died of his fatigues on 23 April 1842. His letter was published by Siborne (number 140).

No. 141 Lieutenant Arthur Hill Trevor[1]
United Services Club, London, 22 December 1842

ADD MS 34707, FO 537

My dear Siborne

We only require at present, one copy of your work, for the regiment – Master Harty is Colonel Harty's brother[2] – and you will find Joe in Geeles Street, there is a plate upon the door, I could read from this, if I could see it !!!

I am as sure about the colour as I am of anything that ever occurred and the General is mistaken.[3] He was wounded within two minutes of handing it back to the ensign.

Not a stand of colours of the brigade was sent to Antwerp that I can remember. I recollect that Mr Hart,[4] 33rd, tore off the King's colour and put it into his bosom when we were repulsed at Quatre Bras, but the silk was sewn on the staff again and it fluttered through the great fight and that there was something about a man of the name of Smith of the 33rd and a colour, Harty will remember. I think Smith[5] did go to the rear, but not to Antwerp, near the end of the action, with one of the colours, but he was up again immediately, there was a horrid scene at the time and I know I was all but done up having only returned from sick leave and being very delicate, which you will not believe, but you may depend that,

I am yours truly

A H TREVOR

I am here until the end of the month.

---

1 Trevor joined the army as an ensign in 1809, serving in northern Germany in 1813 and Holland in 1814. He became a captain on 27 July 1815, receiving a KH and went on half pay (unattached) in 1826.
2 Captain Joseph Mark Harty.
3 This most likely refers to Major General Colin Halkett who it appears has informed Siborne that all the colours of his brigade were sent to the rear on his orders.
4 Lieutenant James Hart is shown as killed at Waterloo in Dalton and in the London Gazette. However Siborne does not record Hart as killed or wounded.
5 Ensign Charles Smith became a lieutenant in August 1815 but left the army on half pay in 1817.

No. 142 Lieutenant Frederick Hope Pattison[1]
Buchanan Street,[2] 24 November 1842

ADD MS 34707, FO 481

From J. Pattison esq.[3]

Dear Sir,
I was duly favoured with your letter of the 16th and I immediately went to my brother Frederick who is in the country, very busy with his farming operations.

He has this morning sent me the enclosed – he says 'I have little time to spare, but if you think what I enclose is interesting, I could manage to give Captain Siborne a number of anecdotes of the such kind, some of them perhaps more interesting, but I am not accustomed to write for the press and if you forward the enclosed you had better make one of your clerks copy it'.

This I cannot well do with the hour to gain a post.

3 o'clock pm, bells ringing for the glorious accounts from China and India.[4] I am no judge either whether it can be of any use to you, if you think it can be of any service, I beg you will not hesitate to command both my brother and me.

Yours very much

J PATTISON

Anecdote illustrative of the fact that 'every bullet has its billet'.
It was at the termination of that fearful conflict that changed the fertile and beautiful fields of Waterloo into a complete desolation, having as if it were ploughed them from one end to the other and strewed them with the dead, the dying and the wounded, that a small coterie of officers belonging to Sir Colin Halkett's brigade – consisting of Lt Colonel Elphinstone 33rd Regiment;[5] Major Chambers of the 30th[6] Captain Knight of the 33rd[7] Captain Gore of the 30th[8] and Lt Pattison of the 33rd were talking over the splendid achievements of the day, and congratulating each other on their escape from so many dangers that their attention was attracted by a good deal of promiscuous firing,

in front: as it increased Lt Pattison left the circle saying, he would go and see what the fellows were about. In advancing 15 or 20 yards he got upon a small mound or rising ground, that he may be better able to see what was going on; he had not been there many minutes until several musket shots passed close by him, one of which he was soon aware had taken effect, for upon turning round he observed Major Chambers place his hand upon his breast, leave the party [to] look for a clean place to lie down, and in five minutes he was a lifeless corpse! The death of this distinguished officer was truly melancholy, as it happened when apparently all was over, and when a few minutes before he was expressing himself so confidently of getting promotion, which he fully deserved having gallantly commanded for many hours before the termination of the battle.

The following anecdote will illustrate in a striking manner the Duke of Wellington's extraordinary memory

In the summer of 1814, the 33rd Regiment of Foot which for many years was the Duke's own regiment, and in which he served as Lt Colonel and commanded at the storming of Seringapatam in 1799, was in garrison in the citadel of Antwerp. It will be remembered that the Congress that assembled at Paris after the termination of the war that year, and which was attended by almost all the Allied sovereigns, appointed His Grace to take charge and superintend the line of fortifications then proposed to be erected along the frontiers of France and Belgium to operate as a barrier against any intrusions of France and to maintain what was then termed 'the equilibrium of power', Belgium being then ceded and incorporated with Holland, to strengthen that Kingdom.

To accomplish this important undertaking, the Duke visited Antwerp in his way to the frontier in the month of August or September. In going into the citadel he met a part of his old regiment the 33rd coming out, amongst which there was an old soldier, who had served under him in India. His Grace immediately recognised him, called him by name, conversed with him for some time and when he left him, gave him a guinea. When it is considered that no less a period than [15] years had elapsed since the individual thus recognised was under the immediate command and observation of the Duke and that since that period the mind of Wellington had been occupied in accomplishing the most stupendous undertakings ever performed by man. This simple anecdote will sufficiently illustrate the excellence of his memory; but it will do more, it will also prove that he was Lieutenant Colonel, who like a good shepherd should always know his sheep, and be able to call them by name.

---

1 Placed on half pay as a lieutenant in 1821. His experiences were published privately in Glasgow in 1873 as *Personal Recollections of the Waterloo Campaign.* It is noticeable that the anecdotes differ in these letters from those of his recollections, which were written as a series of letters to his grand children much later in 1868.

2 Buchanan Street still exists in Glasgow.

3 John Pattison was his brother.

4 The news from China must have been the capture of Canton leading to the Treaty of Nanking on 29 August 1842, which ceded Hong Kong to the British and opened Chinese ports to British merchants. The reference to India must refer to the successful British invasion of Afghanistan by General Pollock, culminating in the capture of Kabul in September 1842. Stern reprisals were carried out in revenge for the more infamous

capitulation of General Elphinstone's army the previous year and their subsequent massacre whilst retreating.

5 Lieutenant Colonel William Elphinstone[9] commanded the 33rd at Waterloo.

6 Captain Thomas Walker Chambers, a major in the army, was killed at Waterloo as described.

7 Captain Charles Knight, his letter is published in this volume (number 140).

8 Captain Arthur Gore had joined the army in 1804 and was slightly wounded at Waterloo. He went on half pay as a colonel in 1826 rising to Lieutenant General, KH. He died on 23 June 1869.

9 This is the same Elphinstone who failed so spectacularly in Afghanistan some years later.

No. 143 From the same
Dalmuir, 6 December 1842

ADD MS 34707, FO 509

To John Pattison

My dear John,

I think the best way I possibly can answer Captain Siborne's query about the 33rd Regiment, is by giving him a short sketch of what came under my notice, at the battle of Quatre Bras. In doing so, it must be recollected, that I took no notes, and that since then twenty-seven years have elapsed; and therefore my statement is dependent entirely upon memory, and may not be so absolutely right in every particular, but will be found substantially correct.

As far as I remember, I think it must have been between 4 and 5 o'clock in the evening, that Sir Colin Halkett's brigade advanced to that spot which is intersected by four roads, and from which fact, the battle derives its name, being Quatre Bras, or Four Arms.

At this period, the Scotch division[1] under Sir Thomas Picton, was actively engaged a little in advance of the great road which leads to Charleroi. Immediately on getting there, orders were given for the brigade to move forward and to the right, and support the right of Picton's division. A movement agreeably to this order took place, each regiment advancing in open column of companies, preserving their respective distances, so as to deploy into line, when necessary. The ground through which we had to advance was much undulated, and in full crop of rye, which in that rich and luxuriant country grows exceedingly high, and on this account obstructed observation. As we advanced, the leading company of our regiment, reached a prominent part of the field, and observed the French cavalry advancing to the charge. Orders were then given to form square, to receive the enemy.

The enemy perceiving we were prepared for them, instead of advancing, made a movement to the left, broke in upon the open columns of the 69th Regiment, which being on a low part of the field had not observed them. The havoc that then took place was very great, and one of their colours, I think the regimental colour;[2] was carried off in triumph.

All this took place with amazing rapidity and despatch, and the 33rd was not left long to contemplate objects with indifference. As I have already observed we were made aware of the approach of the cavalry, and that by the grenadier company, it having reached rising ground; and having formed square upon that company, the whole regiment were placed as a beacon in presence of the enemy.

Immediately a park of artillery was opened at point blank distance upon our column, the destruction consequent upon this was fearful. At this time Captain Haigh,[3] having moved from the head of his company, to encourage the face of the square, fronting the enemy, was cut in two by a cannon ball; and poor Arthur Gore's brains were scattered upon my shako and face.[4] It was soon found necessary to deliver the regiment from this untoward situation, which was done by deploy[ing] into line, in an angular position.

Upon getting into this new position, we were supported on the right by a regiment of Brunswick cavalry, which behaved with great intrepidity.[5] In advance, near the corner of the wood a regiment or brigade of Brunswick infantry were fiercely engaged.

At this time, the 33rd moved toward them; but upon getting near the wood, a report being spread, that the cavalry were in the rear, the regiment entered it and dispersed. It was at this time, that Colonel Parkinson[6] was wounded. He with Captain Knight[7], Lieutenant Thane[8], and myself, went into the wood near the same place. Captain Knight formed the men near us, and advanced some distance, towards the place where we thought the enemy were; but soon being at a loss to know where we were going in the wood, we retrograded, and came out of it upon one on the intersecting roads, as already alluded to.[9]

Upon getting there we found a brigade of the Guards, which immediately advanced. The report of Sir Colin Halkett having seized one of our colours, and reformed the regiment may be true; and upon reflecting a vague impression of that kind fleets over my mind; but as the party with which I was connected consisting of the above mentioned officers and about fifty or sixty men, found the Regiment upon returning formed on the outside of the wood, if such a circumstance took place, none of us saw it.

By this time the Guards having advanced, and forced the enemy from the field, no other active movement took place with Sir Colin Halkett's brigade that evening; but we with the rest of the army, slept on the field of battle all night.

The Retreat

Early on the morning of the 17th the Brigade being under arms, was ordered to move from its position; and from the direction it took, we all were of opinion that an attack was to be made upon the right wing of the French, which rested upon a wood on a hill, a considerable distance from our left. Our conjectures however were fallacious; and I believe our apparent advance towards the enemy was intended as a feint to deceive them, as we no sooner crossed the road, which was contended for by Picton's division the previous evening, and had got between the wood and the enemy, so as to intercept from their view our movement, than we entered into a bye-road and retreated. We continued to retreat without any pause, until we reached the well known town of Genappe, where the brigade halted to get refreshment, no provision having been given out since it left the cantonments before day break of the 16th. However from the cowardice of the Commissariat, whose duty it was to make provision for the troops, but who in a panic fled, no refreshment could be obtained there, except what was got by the men individually, here and there.[10] After halting a considerable time, the retreat was continued and we were soon aware from constant firing of light troops and field pieces that the enemy pursued.

At this time everything appeared extremely disheartening, and the very elements of nature seemed to be frowning upon and contending with us. A dark fearful looking cloud arose above the direction of the enemy and approaching us, poured down such torrents of rain, and discharged such vivid lightning, accompanied with such tremendous peals of thunder, that though long in a tropical climate, I never beheld or heard the like before.

The army still continued to retreat, until it arrived at the place destined for its position. It was here that I saw Sir Thomas Picton for the first and last time, who ordered the 33rd to act as an advanced picquet, and which bivouacked that night in a field to the left of the great road of our position.

I am, dear John, yours truly

F H PATTISON

---

1 By 'Scotch Division' he means that the Scottish regiments were *in* this division. Picton's 9th Brigade commanded by Major General Sir Dennis Pack consisted of the 3rd Battalion 1st foot, the 1st Battalion 42nd and the 1st Battalion 92nd, all of whom were Scottish regiments, however the brigade also contained the 2nd Battalion 44th, the East Essex Regiment.

2 The 69th actually lost its Kings colour, not the regimental colour.

3 Captain John Haigh.

4 Lieutenant Arthur Gore.

5 This compliment is unusual and noteworthy. The Brunswick cavalry are usually dismissed in histories of the battle as having fled with the Belgian cavalry at an early stage of the battle.

6 Major Edward Parkinson.

7 See his letter above (number 145).

8 Lieutenant William Thain, who acted as adjutant and was wounded in the left arm at Waterloo. He had joined the army as an ensign in 1813, serving in northern Germany and Holland in 1813–14, becoming a captain in 1825 and brevet major in 1838 having transferred to the 21st Foot.

9 This would probably be the road running from Nivelles through Quatre Bras.

10 This is very harsh on the Commissariat department who had been ordered back to Waterloo to clear the road of impediments; they therefore could do nothing about feeding the troops at Genappe.

The 69th Regiment, 2nd Battalion

No. 144 Captain Charles Cuyler[1]
Henley Hall, Ludlow, 14 May 1835

ADD MS 34705, FO 263

Sir,

I have the honour to acknowledge the receipt of your letter requesting answers to certain questions relative to the formation and description of ground occupied by the 2nd Battalion 69th regiment in the battle of Waterloo, at the close of the day. Your letter was sent to the West Indies, and from there directed to me here, which I trust will account for the delay of my answer.

As far as my recollection serves me at this distant period of time, the 2nd Battalion 69th Regiment was formed in square about 7 o'clock on the evening of the 18th June 1815, upon the crest of the position.

The French Imperial Guard was in line immediately in front with artillery upon its right, supported by a heavy body of cavalry, by which the 69th were several times charged.

I have a very faint recollection of the different crops which were growing upon the fields in which the regiment was posted, but I think the last field in which it was formed previous to the Grand Advance, was standing rye, but of course very much trampled and trodden down.

Lieutenant Colonel Muttlebury[2] commanded the 69th Regiment at the end of the day, and may therefore be able to give a more minute detail of its movements, and the orders he received, than I was able to obtain as a Captain commanding a company. I do not know his direction, but he is residing very near to London, and I have little doubt that his address may be obtained at Mr Birkland's, 90 Pall Mall, and as I conclude you will wish to correspond with him upon the subject I shall return the plan untouched, with a view to its being submitted for his observations.

I have the honour to be, Sir, your very obedient servant

CHARLES CUYLER
LT COLONEL 69TH REGIMENT

1 Afterwards Sir Charles Cuyler, Bart., made Lieutenant Colonel of the 69th Regiment in 1826. He died on 23 July 1862. A short letter written by him to his father a few days after Waterloo is reproduced in Stephen Maughan's *With the 69th in the Waterloo Campaign,* The Napoleonic Archive (privately published, undated).

2 He had joined the Army as an Ensign in 1793. He was a major at Waterloo and received a CB; he became lieutenant colonel of the 69th in 1817. He died on 11 January 1854.

The 73rd Regiment, 2nd Battalion

No. 145 Lieutenant Colonel William George Harris[1]

Belmont, 23 January 1845

ADD MS 34708, FO 171

With respect to your question whether the 73rd entered the wood of Bossu on the 16th at Quatre Bras as stated by Captain Siborne. I can say most certainly that it did not, at the time that the 33rd was put into confusion and retreated to the wood, the 73rd *took up ground a little to the right of where it had been* at that moment, *but never* went into the wood, formed square on the move and then advanced to the front of the French position.

The only officer of the 73rd who was unhurt and remained with the Regiment till late in the day of the 18th[2] was a Lieutenant Stewart.[3] He continued in it for some years afterwards, but I have no idea whether he is still alive, as I have not heard of him for a long time.

I have the honour to be, Sir, your obedient servant

HARRIS

1 At Waterloo, the 73rd suffered dreadfully and at one time, when the men were slow to fill a

gaping hole in the square, he placed himself on his horse into the gap until his men recovered. He was wounded late in the battle; he gained a CB and KW for his services at Waterloo. Afterwards he became Lieutenant General Lord Harris KCH and Colonel-in-Chief of the 73rd Regiment. He died on 30 May 1845, only four months after penning this note.

2 Following the severe losses of the regiment, this statement is nearly true, but the records also show that Lieutenants Leyne and Dowling and Ensigns Hughes and Blennerhassett were also unwounded. There is nothing to indicate that these officers did not remain with the regiment throughout.

3 Lieutenant Robert Stewart went on half pay in 1818. He was restored to full pay in 1819 and in 1825 was promoted to captain in the 91st Foot. He was back on half pay unattached in 1826 and died on 5 November 1845.

No. 146 Lieutenant John Yuden Lloyd[1]

Exmouth, 6 February 1845

ADD MS 34708, FO 172

My dear Byers[2]

In reply to your letter containing questions about Waterloo and Quatre Bras, I hasten to answer those respecting the latter.

When the French cavalry charged the 69th Regiment, that corps was in line with the 2nd Battalion *73rd Regiment on its right, close to the wood*, which was in rear of the position.

The 73rd to give effective fire threw back its left a little, not however in perfect order, for there was not time. After the enemy had retired, the 73rd changed front to the right on the Grenadiers, observing all details in the formation, then proving that order was still maintained. Some of the men might have unavoidably entered the wood but any thing like a 'retreat' I cannot call to mind.

This communication will I trust be considered private as far as the public is concerned, for I do not wish to see my words in the papers. In regard to Waterloo, I have heard the particulars so frequently from brother officers, that I feel positive in saying you are correct in your statements.

Yours faithfully

J Y LLOYD

1 Lloyd is shown in Dalton as having been wounded; this was at Quatre Bras where he was severely wounded. He had joined the 73rd Regiment as an ensign in 1813, serving in Germany and the Netherlands. He later served in the Kandyan rebellion in Ceylon where he was mentioned in dispatches three times. He became a major in the regiment in 1828 and retired from the service in 1839.

2 I cannot discover to whom this letter could have been written.

Letter no. 147

2nd Infantry Brigade KGL

The 1st Light Battalion KGL

No. 147 Captain Frederick von Gilsa[1]
Eimbeck,[2] 9 December 1840

ADD MS 34707, FO 227

Original in German

My dear Sir!

I respond as follows in the matter of Waterloo: There were *at least* two other companies of the 1st Light Battalion including the 3rd under Lt Albert,[3] along with ours at the first French attack left of the chaussee.[4] He did the following:

When the French column was not yet at our height/level, he gave them to believe that he would not be able to penetrate them, and then marched his flank to the right. At this moment, I asked then Col. Lewis Bussche[5] for permission to break out of the ravine at *y*[6] with the company. I got it, with the remark that the Colonel wanted the other company to follow. I immediately had to push forward at point m.m. at a running pace to the left with my formations, and in a short time I was 30 to 35 paces from the left flank (or better said, at this moment to the rear) of the enemy column. We continued to follow at this distance, and fired away single shots as frequently as we could. Even if we performed no heroics, nonetheless, more than a few Frenchmen fell to our shots.

After we had continued this for some time, I heard cavalry behind me. I turned around and saw an English regiment, I believe one of the Guards, perhaps the Blues? I cried out to my men, 'Make room for them!' and they immediately hit the column without being fired on, and encircled it. At this moment I saw Albert with his company to the right of us. There seemed to be nothing more for us to do in the area at *o*, and our company closed ranks. But barely had we begun to do so than Albert cried out, 'Captain Gilsa, French cavalry!' and I turned around and caught sight on this side of la Haye Sainte; in other words not far from us, an enemy regiment coming up the chaussee. Things might have gone badly for us because we were not yet in formation, if at that moment cavalry had not burst forward from our side, whereupon the French immediately turned about. Albert marched back to the battalion with his company, but I remained on the left side of the chaussee with my right flank leaning against it at *p*. Shortly thereafter I was ordered to the La Haye [Sainte] farm *A* along with the 5th and 6th companies. General Lewis Bussche must also remember this incident – Lieut Kuntze[7] was also with my company.

I didn't see other companies of the battalion anywhere on the left side of the chaussee; in all probability *both* of these had retreated into the ravine. The fact that the 95th didn't see us may have been because as they were retreating from *x* they were on the right flank (now the front) while we were on the left flank (now the rear) of the French column. In addition, I myself saw nothing of the 95th at this time, which I find completely understandable given what I have just described. I saw only redcoats near the hedge at *p*. My persistence contributed most to the destruction [done] by the cavalry regiment that hit the column, because when it marched by us a short time later, every man was covered with blood from top to bottom.

More than this I don't know, and I hope that you will find in my writing what you are looking for.

Your friend

F VON GILSA

1 Captain Frederick von Gilsa, numbered 298 in Beamish, joined the Legion in 1804, serving in Hanover, the Baltic and the Peninsula in 1808–14. He was very severely wounded at Waterloo and received the HGO3 and HWC. He became a brevet lieutenant colonel half pay and commandant at Eimbeck.

2 Eimbeck lies some 40 miles south of Hanover.

3 Lieutenant Anton Albert, numbered 1008 in Beamish, joined the Legion in 1807. He served in the Baltic and the Peninsula in 1808–14, he was killed at Waterloo.

4 This describes the period of D'Erlon's attack on the left wing of the Allied line.

5 Lieutenant Colonel Lewis von dem Bussche, normally commanding the 5th Line Battalion KGL, commanded the 1st Light Battalion KGL at Waterloo. Numbered 558 in Beamish, he joined the Legion in 1804, serving in Hanover and the Peninsula in 1808–14. He received a Gold Medal for Vittoria and Nive and became CB and NWO3. He became a lieutenant general in the Hanoverian army, commanding the 1st Division of infantry.

6 This obviously refers to points marked on a plan that appears to be no longer extant.

7 Lieutenant John Frederick Kuntze, numbered 315 in Beamish, joined the Legion in 1813, serving in North Germany and Holland. He is last recorded by Beamish at Ratzeburg in Denmark.

No. 148 Captain Christian Wyneken[1]
Hanover, 24 November 1840

ADD MS 34707, FO 224

Original in German

My dear Heise,[2]

With reference to the letter which was sent to me from Captain Siborne on the 21st of the month, here is my response:

As in the battle of Waterloo, the first attack was from La Haye [Sainte], the 1st Light Battalion stood with two companies to the fore, next to La Haye Sainte in the narrow pass in a closed column.

The 95th Regiment behind the hedge, to the left of the roadway, at the point where there is a + marked on the map.[3] Immediately after the attack from La Haye Sainte or rather at the same time, a column approached on the right flank of the centre-left, which pushed the 95th Regiment back, this was in turn forced to retreat by General Kempt's Brigade, when I believe a large part were taken prisoners.

At this withdrawal of the 95th Regiment, they must have moved left because the road with the hedge, which was located opposite the narrow defile, was left unoccupied over a distance of some hundred paces and Colonel L. Bussche ordered the 5th and 6th companies under Captain Gilsa[4] to take it.

You know I was with both first companies in front of the Battalion and as I was thrown back by the cavalry or rather sent scattering, I found Gilsa with both the companies behind the hedge on the described road.

In the afternoon around 4 o'clock during one of the repeated attacks against the right flank of the centre-left, it was observed that there was an unoccupied stretch of roadway next to the hedge, which I was ordered to occupy with the remaining part of the 1st, 3rd and 4th companies. When I got there I found the English 32nd Regiment[5] left in front of me, behind a low hedge, rather only a low hillock, and the enemy by the hedge that was occupied in the morning by the 95th Regiment, the 95th must have been positioned elsewhere, at least at that moment I could not see it.

The 32nd engaged the enemy and threw him back, whereupon we returned to our battalion. Heroic deeds were not carried out by the 1st Light Battalion to the left of the highroad, at least we did not fire a single shot and I do not think that Gilsa was involved in shooting either.

What Captain Siborne of the 'Hedge on the high bank' should note about the highroad is that at every opportunity where the enemy was to be seen upon or to the left of the highroad, a position was taken there by the 1st Light Battalion. I know that for certain, I was there with the battalion and as I had the right wing, I know that the left was also posted there. I could name several people who fell there, Leonhart[3] and Adolph Heise[7] were wounded, the latter badly.

JOHN[8]

---

1 Wyneken, numbered 299 in Beamish, joined the Legion in 1803 and served in Hanover, the Baltic and the Peninsula in 1808–14. He was slightly wounded at Toloza in 1813, again at Bayonne in 1814 and again at Waterloo. He became a HGO3 and HWC and Lieutenant Colonel in the Hanoverian land Dragoons.

2 Probably Captain Kristofe Heise.

3 The map referred to does not appear to be extant.

4 Captain Frederick von Gilsa, see his letter (number 147).

5 The 1st Battalion 32nd Foot formed part of the 8th Brigade of Major General Sir James Kempt.

6 Lieutenant Harry Leonhart, see his letters (number 157–161).

7 Ensign Adolphus Heise, numbered 226 in Beamish, joined the Legion in 1814, serving in the Netherlands. He was slightly wounded at Waterloo. He became a Doctor of Law and advocate at Hoya in Hanover.

8 This letter appears to have been written by another on behalf of Wyneken. There are two possibilities, Lieutenants John Baumgarten and John Frederick Kuntze, but there is nothing to indicate which with any certainty but the latter is more likely having served in the same company with von Gilsa.

No. 149 From the same
Hanover, 2 December 1841

ADD MS 34707, FO 296

Original in German

At the moment that is indicated on the enclosed paper, I was with the 1st and 2nd companies of the 1st Light Battalion to the right of La Haye Sainte, where, as is well known, we were charged by French Cuirassiers. The 1st Lifeguards and 1st Dragoon Guards charged by us, as well as the 2nd Life Guards, which crossed the chaussee below

La Haye Sainte. When I came back and looked for the remaining four companies of the battalion, I didn't find them in the ravine nor behind it, until after a lengthy search on the left side of the chaussee, where they had – in crossing back – formed behind the road that goes in the same direction as the ravine. More than this I cannot say.

In the afternoon, at approximately 4 o'clock, a part of the 1st Light Battalion was again to the left of the chaussee, where we charged with the 32nd Regiment – during which I spoke with the Second Major of this regiment[1] – who had earlier been aide-de-camp to Lord Lynedoch[2] in Spain. We were speaking for only a short time because at that time the 5th and the 1st companies were ordered to La Haye Sainte.

According to the information given by the officer of the 2nd Life Guards who claims to have seen Captain Graeme,[3] he must have himself been in La Haye Sainte until the afternoon because the 2nd Light Battalion did not get out of La Haye Sainte, and Captain Graeme was within as well as wounded at about 4:30.

In everything else, I concur with the statement of Captain Leonhart.

C WYNECKEN
CAPTAIN WITH THE 1ST LIGHT BATTALION

---

1 This refers to Major Felix Calvert, second in command of the 32nd Regiment at Waterloo. He had joined the army as an ensign in the 98th Foot in 1807 and served in the Peninsula as Aide de Camp to Lord Lynedoch. He received a General Service Medal with three bars for Barossa, Vittoria and San Sebastian. He rose to colonel on the half-pay list unattached.

2 Thomas Graham, Lord Lynedoch, GCB, GCMG,. commanded the victorious British forces at Barossa and acted as Second-in-Command to Lord Wellington for much of the Peninsular war.

3 The statement referred to is in Lieutenant Waymouth's letter (number 20) in *Waterloo Letters.* He claims to have seen Lieutenant Graeme and a party of the 2nd Light Battalion KGL near a cottage to the left of the chaussee. This cannot be possible as Graeme was certainly within La Haye Sainte at this time. It is almost certain that Waymouth had actually seen a party of the 1st Light Battalion.

No. 150 Captain Kristofe Heise[1]

Hanover, 18 September 1837

ADD MS 34706, FO 373

Written to Captain Benne

My dear Benne,

When you write to Mr Siborne please to inform him that I have in the first instance forwarded his letter (addressed to General Baring) with Julius Hartmann[2] to Stade,[3] where Sir Julius will have an opportunity *personally* to obtain such information from the surviving officers of Captain Cleeve's battery[4] as I believe will clear up the first query. As for the second query I hope Sir Julius will be able to give the necessary information himself.

The third and last query I can fully ascertain through General Alten[5] and Colonel Wyneken.[6]

As soon as Sir Julius returns from his tour of inspection I shall forward Mr Siborne's letter to General Baring[7] in Switzerland. However I am afraid the General will not be able to add much on personal authority as he must have been so thoroughly occupied during his stay in the farm of La Haye Sainte that he had little inducement to attend to other parts of the field of battle.

I have this day written to Major Beamish, who by his last letter of the 4th instant informs me of his intention to leave home on the 20th for London, to forward to Mr. Siborne without delay the 2nd volume of the history of the Legion which contains a short but very clear, and as far as I can judge, a true account of the part which the Legion and the Hanoverians took in the battles of the 17th[8] and 18th June 1815. Should the volume not yet be ready for publication I have desired the Major to forward at all events the *sheets referring to those battles.*

As I know from experience, when collecting the materials for the Legion history for Major Beamish, how difficult it is to establish the real facts, and how remiss people are in giving information who are best able to do so, and how forward sometimes those who have none to give, I can well feel how anxious Mr Siborne must feel to see his queries properly answered.

You may assure him that I shall endeavour to have this done as early and as competently as it is possible after such a lapse of time since the battle was fought, and that I shall lose no time in transmitting the information received, through your medium.

Believe me, my dear Benne, ever your most humbly

KRISTOPHE HEISE

---

1 Christoph Heise recorded in Beamish as no. 305. He joined the Legion in 1810 and served in the Peninsula from 1811–14, being severely wounded at Tolosa in 1813. He was severely wounded at Waterloo and became a major in the Hanoverian Rifle Guards, HGO3 and HWC.

2 Lieutenant Colonel George Julius Hartmann, numbered 26 in Beamish. He joined the Legion in 1803, serving in Hanover, the Baltic and the Peninsula in 1808–14. He was slightly wounded at Talavera and again at Bayonne. He was made HGO2, HWC and KCB and he received a General Service Medal with three bars for Busaco, Badajoz and Salamanca and a Gold Cross and two bars for Talavera, Albuera, Salamanca, Vittoria, San Sebastian and the Nive. He became a lieutenant general in the Hanoverian artillery.

3 Stade is in northern Germany, close to the Danish border.

4 Captain Andrew Cleeve's Foot Battery of the KGL served as part of the artillery attached to the Third Division.

5 Lieutenant General Baron Charles Alten, Colonel Commandant of the 2nd Hussars commanded the Third Division at Waterloo. He is listed as number 208 in Beamish. He had joined the Legion in 1803 and had served in Hanover, the Baltic, Sicily and the Peninsula, being severely wounded at Salamanca. He became HGO2 and Inspector General of the Hanoverian service and Minister at War. He died at Osnabruck as a Lieutenant General in 1820.

6 Captain Christian Wyneken, of the 1st Light Battalion KGL at Waterloo. See his letters (number 148–149)

7 See Major Baring, 2nd Light Battalion KGL for his letters (numbers 168–170).

8 This is a mistake for the 16th when the battle of Quatre Bras was fought.

No. 151 From the same
No date[1]

ADD MS 34706, FO 435

Written to Captain Benne

My dear Benne!
Enclosed I transmit to you for Mr Siborne some statements in answer to the queries which were contained in his letter to General Baring.[2] From the latter I have only to day received an answer, and this will account for the delay.

Regarding Mr Siborne's query about Captain Johnstone K.G.[3] I have written to Darmstadt, and hope to be able to procure the necessary information.

Relative to the queries about General Cambronne[4] I shall speak to General Halkett[5] and will not fail to communicate to you the particulars.

Yours most truly

KRISTOPHE HEISE

Saturday morning

---

1 Although there is no date, a note signed by Benne indicates that he received the letter on 10 February 1838.

2 See his letters under 2nd Light Battalion KGL (numbers 163–5).

3 K.G. is presumably King's Germans but I can find no officer of this name listed in the KGL.

4 General Pierre Jacques Etienne Cambronne, the defiant officer in the last square of the French Imperial Guard, who supposedly reacted to calls to surrender with either '*Merde!*' or 'The Guard dies but never surrenders', the latter being the great rallying cry by Napoleonist sympathizers in post-Waterloo France. General Halkett however claimed that he had captured Cambronne, when separated from the square and thus could not have been the officer who uttered the immortal words, if indeed they were ever said. Wellington backs Halkett's story by stating that on his return to his Headquarters in Waterloo, Cambronne was among the group of captured French officers there, whom he snubbed for their disloyalty to King Louis.

5 Lieutenant Colonel Hugh Halkett of the 7th Line Battalion KGL, number 646 in Beamish. He joined the Legion in 1803 and served in Hanover, the Baltic and the Peninsula. He received a Gold Medal with bars for Albuera and Salamanca and KStA, SwOS, HWC, CB and KCH. There is much evidence to confirm his claim that he captured General Cambronne. He became a lieutenant general in the Hanoverian service, commanding the 2nd Division of infantry. His letter was published by Siborne (number 130).

No. 152 From the same
11 February 1838

ADD MS 34706, FO 438

Written to Captain Benne

My dear Benne!
I have just seen General Halkett and enquired of him about the capture of General Cambronne at Waterloo, and I beg you will forward to Mr Siborne the following statement in answer to his queries on the subject:

It was from General Cambronne *himself* that General Halkett was informed of his

(Cambronne's) name, when he took him prisoner. General Halkett did *not* hear him make use of any expression similar to that of 'La Garde meurt et ne se rends pas', and lastly the French General was taken prisoner by General Halkett *before* he reached La Belle Alliance.

In fact the General says there was nothing extraordinary in Cambronne's conduct on the occasion, and that the circumstances attending his capture are correctly stated in the 2nd volume of the Beamish's *History of The King's German Legion.*

As for the lists of wounded of the Hanoverians you can easily procure them for Mr. Siborne from the Adjutant General's Office here; the principal loss at Waterloo and at Quatre Bras was however borne by Kielmannsegge's[1] and Halkett's[2] Brigades, already in Mr. Siborne's possession; the loss of the other Brigades being very inconsiderable.

Believe me, my dear Benne, yours very truly

KRISTOPHE HEISE

---

1 Major General Count Kielmannsegge commanded the 1st Hanoverian Brigade at Waterloo.

2 Lieutenant Colonel H. Halkett commanded the 3rd Hanoverian Brigade at Waterloo.

No. 153 From the same
4 December 1840

ADD MS 34707, FO 229

Original in German
Written to Captain Benne

The memorandum of Capt. Siborne raises the question whether the 1st Light Battalion of the KGL took part in repelling the initial enemy attacks on their rear and left wings, such that it proceeded from the right side of the Genappe chaussee to the left side of same and thereby contributed to repelling the enemy column, which dispersed their main thrust against General Kempt's brigade. Of the officers still living of the 1st Light Battalion who were present at this action I have, because of the shortness of time, only been able to ask three to tell you the opinions of the point in question; this is contained in nos. 1, 2, and 3.[1]

As far as my own person is concerned, I am able to tell you about my opinions in a few words and with whatever certainty there may be after 25 years.

When the enemy attack in question began, the 1st Light Battalion was emplaced in the ravine at *h–y*[2] with four companies. Two companies were forward to our right, closer to La Haye Sainte. The Duke of Wellington was positioned with his staff directly behind our four companies, and he himself gave us the sign to advance with the words, 'Now it is your time, my lads.' My functions then as acting Adjutant did not tie me to any single company so that I was able to survey the entire operation. Once the company under Captain Gilsa had broken out of the ravine to the left, it was followed by the company under Lieutenant Albert, which I myself joined. Whether more of the Battalion followed us I cannot say with certainty, as I didn't take notice in the heat of the moment. The company under Albert ran at a swift pace across the chaussee, and I also mention here in passing the circumstance that we marched past both pieces of artillery that Captaine Siborne marked as being on the chaussee in his memorandum, and that for the moment these had been abandoned by their crew.[3] On the other side of the chaussee at *m–m*, this company formed itself in the same way as Captain Gilsa's company, and advanced with it at approximately the same time. The front of the enemy column was attacked by Kempt's brigade, while we shot into the enemy column's left flank and rear. The enemy column turned about in great confusion, and we followed it closely at a few paces distance, firing into the dense masses as fast as we could reload. I received a serious leg wound that prevented me from continuing on my own at the spot that I have marked with †. One of our people brought me back along the path marked with x–x, or in any case in this direction, to the *right* side of the chaussee; however, he was forced to leave me at the bottom of the steep bank while he himself sat down approximately 10 feet above me on the high bank where he was at least safe from individual enemy cavalry who were roving about. During the time I was lying there, I observed a number of enemy cuirassiers in this segment of the chaussee. I estimated their number at about half a squadron. I must have lain there for about ten minutes, perhaps it was only five, when several detachments of Life Guards and Dragoons from our position came chasing down the chaussee, driving the enemy cavalry before them. The French cuirassiers now took to the left shoulder and tried to hold up our allied cavalry by closing off the chaussee, but after some resistance they made way for our forces. An opening was thus made free for me for the moment, and with the help of my trusty assistants I was able to make my way to the other wounded at the little house that was behind our position.

The fact that the 95th regiment claims to have seen nothing of our Battalion is not surprising because the uniforms we wore were so similar.[4] I am certain that our good old comrades have collected such a rich store [of credit] from Siborne that they don't really need to look at some of the few pages on which we took the opportunity [to tell our story], particularly as we accomplished it together.

KRISTOPHE HEISE
MAJOR IN THE KGL
FORMERLY CAPTAIN IN THE
1ST LIGHT BATTALION OF THE KGL

1 These are the statements of von Gilsa (number 147), Wyneken (number 148) and Leonhart (number 157).

2 This refers to a map that appears to be no longer extant.

3 It is generally agreed that these were from Ross's troop, but see the letters of Whinyates troop (numbers 72–80).

4 These statements are not incompatible with those made by those of the 95th. The 1st Battalion 95th who manned the sand pit and knoll were driven back to Kempt's brigade by the French advance. From this position, they would not have seen the German Light infantrymen crossing the chaussee and attacking the flank and rear of the column. When the 95th advanced again, the Germans had retraced their steps and those that remained could easily have been mistaken for their own men.

No. 154 From the same
Hanover, 24 January 1841

ADD MS 34707, FO 241

Original in German
Written to Captain Benne

After Captain Siborne was kind enough to show me the correspondence, including his concluding remarks, which derived from his memorandum, I showed it to my friend, Captain Leonhart, who is presently here; I have not sent it on to the other two gentlemen, Colonel Gilsa and Wynecken because I am convinced that neither of them will have anything of substance to add.

I agree completely with Captain Leonhart's remarks. It is and remains *fact* that a portion of the light Battalion of the King's German Legion advanced from the right side of the chaussee out of the ravine in the manner described by Captain Leonhart at the particular time and in the direction noted, to attack the enemy column with their bayonets; that this part (at least two companies) crossed the chaussee, that units of the same followed the enemy column at a close distance at least a hundred paces; and that I can give an affidavit at any time that I was wounded at the spot marked by me. More than that I cannot state, and again I agree completely with Colonel Leach's[1] opinion that it basically makes no difference on which side of the chaussee one fought on the day of the battle of Waterloo, which every good soldier was duty-bound to do.

Furthermore, I wish to thank both of our comrades-in-arms from the old 95th Regiment for the kind and comradely sentiments that they expressed for us, and Captain Siborne for the extraordinary way in which he has treated both sides.

I know from experience (from the earlier gathering of information for the history of the King's German Legion) what a difficult task it is to reconcile the contradictory reports of otherwise trustworthy and competent eyewitnesses, and to ascertain the true course of a particular matter. Often the chronicler must simply be satisfied that the opposing sides do not pounce on *him*.

I think and hope that we the green boys[2] of the old Wellington army will have said our piece for now and for ever about the case in question, and that we now leave it to the esteemed Captain Siborne to set out the individual roles in the great drama that unfolded on 18 June 1815, insofar as we participated in them.

KRISTOPHE HEISE

---

1 Captain Jonathan Leach, 1st Battalion 95th Regiment at Waterloo. He assumed command of the battalion when the two senior officers were wounded. He was eventually wounded himself and made CB. In 1831 he wrote *Rough sketches of the life of an old soldier.* He died as a lieutenant colonel at Worthing on 14 January 1855.

2 The two light battalions KGL and the 95th Regiment were all equipped with green uniforms.

No. 155 From the same
Wednesday, 3 November 1841

ADD MS 34707, FO 294

Original in German
Written to Captain Benne

My dear Benne!
Only yesterday when I returned from Bamischen hunt, I found your letter of 31 October with the memorandum from Captain Siborne. Because I am departing again this day, and because your trip to England is set for tomorrow, I have lacked the time to show the memorandum in question to other still-living officers of the 1st Light Battalion of the King's German Legion who were present at Waterloo and who were visiting (except for Captain Leonhart and Colonel Wyneken, who were both here). In addition, I am of the opinion that such a procedure would not gain Captain Siborne greater clarity, and so I think that no one will take it amiss if I spare myself the inconvenience of informing my comrades for the third time that he 'does not believe their unanimous statement regarding their participation in the charge on the enemy column to the left of the chaussee, nor even their crossing of this chaussee.' I am far from doubting Captain Siborne's good intentions, but I do find it a hard stroke that he wants to render my comrades and me blind with his seeing eye. His memorandum demonstrates that his compatriots enjoy greater credence than do we. The episode of Lieutenant Graeme of the 2nd Light Battalion, who is mentioned by the officer of the Lifeguards at the moment in question at the battle of Waterloo, is important insofar as Graeme really was the brave defender of the small building *inside the wall of the farm at La Haye Sainte*, and was sometimes called by his friends Commander of the Pigpen, which stood above it. However, it is giving the barn too great an honour to elevate it to a horse stall, even though it might sound better. But to place it outside the wall of La Haye Sainte, on the *left side* of the chaussee is truly a grave error. None of the maps of the battle of Waterloo that I have seen, even that of Capt. Siborne, indicate this small building. In Part II of the history of the KGL published in 1837,[1] there is in Table 5 a ground plan of the farm at La Haye Sainte. It contains the building in question – precisely on the *right side* of the chaussee. It is designated as a *piggery* on the ground plan. I only mention this in order to show that one can easily make mistakes in the heat of battle, and that not everything is gospel that is said and claimed about the details of each moment by individual participants at the battle of Waterloo after a quarter of a century.

I have neither been able to move both my comrades who live here to mark with red on the sketch the position of the 1st Light Battalion as Captain Siborne has requested, nor am I myself able to mark the disposition of the troops on this sketch. The configuration of movements is such that there is little or no room left to sketch in the 1st Light Battalion of the KGL. However, if Kempt's brigade had not at that moment charged forward as on a parade ground, but had instead, which is the nature of things, *immediately undertaken to charge by the right shoulder*, I believe that the 1st Light Battalion would still have had sufficient room available, and filing out of the ravine and crossing the chaussee, between the right wing of Kempt's brigade and which was occupied by the 95th Regiment, in order to be able to participate in the charge in question. I know this to be the case as a personal participant and eyewitness. If one is not willing to grant credence to the unanimous statements of my still living comrades and myself, which are of such a positive sort, then I must console myself and refer to the panorama of the battle that was published and presented to the public in London in 1817 on which not a single individual from my battalion was to be seen, and that the painter who happened to be there justified himself saying that he believed that our green Germans had been killed or wounded by friendly fire, knowing that the Lifeguards who took up our positions would have had an easy time of it sitting before him to have their portraits taken.

Well, my dear Benne, I have to hurry to conclude, as the carriage is already at the door. In the future I am prepared obediently to render any service to your friend, Siborne, but in the matter of Waterloo, I hope that I will now have heard the last of it. I explained once that I consider it a matter of complete indifference to the few individuals still living who participated in this charge, whether they are positioned on the right or the left side of the chaussee on the model of the battle. It is enough that you yourself can say where you were in the actual battle, and that you fulfilled your duty.

Sincerely yours

KRISTOPHE HEISE

General Bussche was at the moment in question attached to two companies of the 1st Light Battalion in front of the ravine and to the right behind La Haye Sainte. Thus, he cannot report about the charge as an eyewitness.

1 This refers to Beamish's *History of the King's German Legion.*

No. 156 From the same
Hanover, 29 January 1842

ADD MS 34707, FO 347

Original in German
Written to Captain Benne

My dear Benne!

I feel very badly for Captain Siborne, who is making such an effort to reconcile the various statements by eyewitnesses to the charge of Kempt's brigade at the battle of Waterloo, and I must express my conviction that he will never be able to achieve what he has set out to do. In a word, he is attempting the impossible! May his compatriots have the firm intention of telling the truth, the whole truth, and nothing but the truth, and may they also tell only what they know from personal experience and leave out of it everything that they know from hearsay. Otherwise there will be such a confusion of time and sequence of the individual movements that he who collects and orders the data will be faced with insurmountable difficulties.

I am enclosing the statement of Captain Leonhart[1] regarding the battalion's firing on the enemy cuirassiers, and I can with certainty state from my own memory that this occurred within a short time of the charge that we made left across the chaussee.

I must repeat that this charge took place under the eyes of the Duke of Wellington and his staff, who gave our battalion the sign to break out of the ravine by waving his hat. We ourselves had wanted to move forwards a minute or a half a minute earlier, but the Duke kept immediately behind the left wing of the Battalion and called out to us, 'Not yet. I will tell you when it is your time.' And shortly thereafter he said with a friendly smile, taking off his hat, 'Now go my lads, hurrah!' – I repeat that during the charge we went several hundred paces across the left side of the chaussee, as I have already represented the spot in one of my earlier submissions on Captain Siborne's plan. Our opponents were not enemy cavalry men, but rather a column that at first advanced with some order, but which soon dissolved into a rabble that turned about, and which we shot at with impunity at a short distance in that we reloaded and fired as quickly as we could as we advanced.

Now my friend, I have written this several times to Captain Siborne, and I cannot do more than to repeat the truth.[2] I may err in small details, but in the main thing, *that we supported the charge of Kempt's brigade on the left side* of the chaussee, and that we supported them *with vigour*—in that I do not err. Nor do I gladly admit that I received a serious wound and that such a one that I took no further part in this event.

Yours ...

KRISTOPHE HEISE

---

1 This refers to letter 157 published in this volume.

2 Siborne does fleetingly refer to the 1st Light Battalion crossing the chaussee to engage the column on p. 254, but this mention is of the briefest and does not clarify their role. He obviously felt unable to completely reconcile the alternative statements on this subject.

No. 157 Lieutenant Harry Leonhart[1]

Hanover, 1 January 1840

ADD MS 34707, FO 226

Original in German

As you requested, my dear Heise, and in accordance with Captain Siborne's memorandum, I enclose the following:

When the first royal attack[2] was made on the centre-left and the left flank of the allied army in the course of which, or immediately beforehand, both of our companies of tirailleurs were scattered by the French cuirassiers; then the brigade on the left next to us (General Kempt's) attacked the royal infantry column with bayonets; the 1st Light Infantry went out of the narrow defile,[3] across the highroad and joined up with this bayonet attack. We passed the hedgerow coming out at A where our cavalry undertook further pursuit of the returning members of the French forces who had been scattered. We then retreated across the highroad to the point opposite.

The battalion's fire on the cavalry directly in front of us, and therefore to the right of the highroad, ceased immediately before the bayonet attack from the narrow defile. During the bayonet attack itself, the battalion was not on the same level with General Kempt's brigade, but was some way back because we could only debouch from the narrow defile in single file and then begin the advance up the incline on the left side of the highroad, which naturally resulted in a delay.

The order for us to advance came, incidentally, directly from the Duke of Wellington, who arrived at that precise moment from the right flank.

Truly yours

LEONHART

1 Leonhart, numbered 226 in Beamish, joined the Legion in 1812, serving in northern Germany. He was severely wounded at Waterloo. He became a captain in the 2nd Light battalion and adjutant to the 1st Division of Hanoverian infantry, and HWC.

2 The translation is definitely correct, however it would appear that he used the wrong term, he means the French Imperial infantry.

3 This can only refer to the sunken road.

No. 158 From the same
24 January 1841[1]

ADD MS 34707, FO 239

Original in German

Captain Leonhart's statement

The position of the battalion before the beginning of the battle (or rather the 3rd, 4th, 5th and 6th companies), though – as Captain Siborne says – in closed columns behind the hollow road, the road was about ten paces from them and the left wing were about the same from the chaussee.

The losses due to an almighty cannonade at the beginning were immediately so great– Captain Holtzermann[2] and certainly 10–12 dead – that the battalion made full use of the hollow road to take cover.

Shortly after their fire was directed against the cuirassiers, the leading troops ran over the lane and joined the bayonet attack. If the French cuirassiers then retreated by the hollow lane we could not confirm it, but it appears that it was not improbable, as they were present in the lane during our crossing, they arrived before us and were mingled with some of our people. The point of our crossing of the lane is confirmed from the following:

The moment of our break out from the hollow lane was when the brigade next left to us were already in front and had advanced admirably.

Naturally Captain Kincaid, who went forward at the same time, did not see that a Battalion of troops emerged from the hollow lane on the right of him. He saw that prior to that the Cuirassiers were driven off, but we did not notice it.

H LEONHART

1 The statement is undated, but this date is written on it in Siborne's hand.

2 Captain Gottlieb Thilo Holtzermann, numbered 987 in Beamish. He had joined the Legion in 1804 and served in Hanover, the Baltic and the Peninsula in 1808–11 and 1813–14. He was killed at Waterloo but Beamish states that a Waterloo medal was issued to his family.

No. 159 From the same
Hanover, 27 February 1841

ADD MS 34707, FO 247

Original in German

The part of the French cuirassiers which attacked our battalion and on whom we fired, turned immediately and disappeared behind the high ground; they could still pass between the square as well as on the right and a few cuirassiers found themselves in the chaussee while we ran across. These last could have well been those that were broken by General Kempt's brigade; because it appears impossible for the French cavalry to have escaped as the width of the chaussee was just that of a coach.

Equally, any other reason is unacceptable for us leaving the hollow lane, for our attack on the enemy's infantry on special order, as in the hollow lane we prepared ourselves for all eventualities and a few troops on the right wing were sufficient to repulse the cavalry should they enter the hollow lane.

With regard to the questions posed by Captain Siborne at the end of his memo, I would like to comment that the answer to the first one is given at the beginning of my statement, I did not personally see the fire of the squares on my right as well as the possibility our guns[1] being on the right of the lane. As the cuirassiers entered the lane our battalion must have been already on the left side of the lane.

H LEONHART

1 There was some suggestion that some KGL guns also fired on D'Erlon's troops, but this appears to be incorrect.

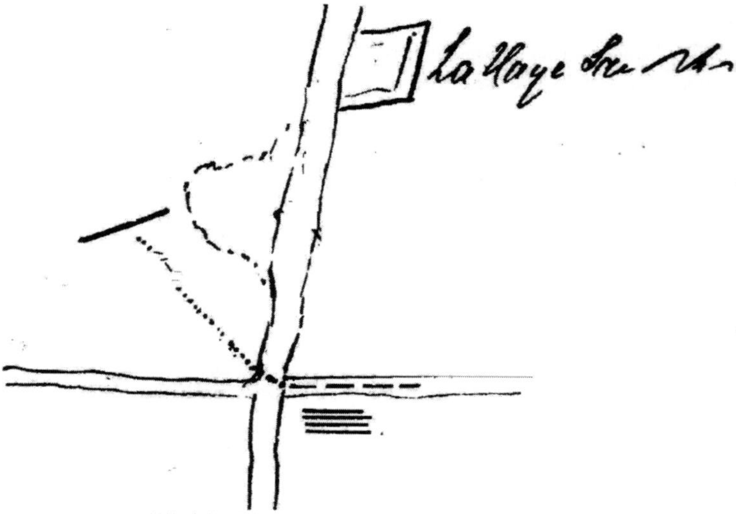

Movement of the 1st Light Battalion KGL across the road

No. 160 From the same
Hanover, 28 January 1842

ADD MS 34707, FO 346

Original in German

It appears to me that at the moment selected for the model, the 1st Light Battalion was formed to a large extent in a line (somewhat to the right and rear of General Kempt's position in line and the brigade was advancing) and were possibly considering in the last instance to form [with] the troops. The French cuirassiers and the 2nd Lifeguards had to pass on the right of the battalion.

As the battalion passed the lane there were no French skirmishers lining the hedge on the way to Wavre, I doubt that they arrived at these points as the 2nd Brigade[1] was intending to occupy the hollow. The battalion had actually fired on the French cuirassiers from the right of the lane just at the crossing; these cuirassiers had preceded the infantry column on the left of the chaussee.

The reason the battalion attacked the infantry on the left of the chaussee was due to a special order of the Duke, besides we were not expecting any problems in our deep hollow road.

The cuirassiers on whom we were firing turned round and dispersed on the right; they could not come over our part of the hollow road and it was not advisable for them to remain in their position due to the fire of the battalion.

During the charge of General Kempt, we never came to the front of his brigade but stayed on the right wing and somewhat back. The attack was directed on the columns and not on the skirmishers.

H LEONHART CAPT

---

1 The 2nd Brigade KGL commanded by Colonel Ompteda of which the 1st Light Battalion formed a part.

No. 161 From the same
Hanover, 2 November 1841

ADD MS 34707, FO 297

Original in German

At the given moment, the 4th company of the 1st Light Battalion was partly on the left side of the lane, partly perhaps engaged in crossing. General Kempt's brigade had moved left, as it appears quite natural from the positioning of the French columns. If after all a number a number of officers of one battalion unanimously agree they were on a particular spot and a number of officers of another battalion state they could not see the spot, one quite reasonably does not assume that the statement of the first was wrong.

H LEONHART CAPT

No. 162 Ensign and Adjutant William Buhse[1]
Hanover, 24 February 1835

ADD MS 34704, FO 264

Original in German

1st Light Battalion, Kings German Legion
Its disposition and movement during the battle of Waterloo on 18 June 1815:

The battalion was the right wing battalion of the 2nd Brigade of the KGL under the command of Colonel von Ompteda, consisting of the 1st and 2nd Light and the 5th and 8th Line Battalions, which formed the left brigade of the 3rd Division under Lieutenant General Count von Alten.

The brigade was behind the road that led from Wavres to Braine L'Alleud, on the morning of the 18th they were formed in close columns with its left wing based on the chaussee. The 2nd Light or the left wing battalion had occupied the farm of La Haye Sainte the night before, for which reason the 1st Light Battalion was placed by the Brigadier on the left wing and took position in a hollow lane. The tree marked does not stand on the other side but on this side of the hollow road.

At the beginning of the battle and the enemy attack on Hougoumont, the 3rd Division marched in column on the right of the battalion. The battalions sent both the first companies right of La Haye Sainte in groups towards the left wing of the garden. Both these companies were engaged in the first attack by a number of enemy cavalry squadrons on the left flank, whilst fired upon by skirmishers and due to the untimely interventions of a number of Hanoverian light infantry and mix ups, they could not regroup and were over-ridden and broken up. The rest of these companies as well as a part of the 2nd Light Battalion, which occupied the gardens of the farm then abandoned them, joining the battalion that occupied the hollow lane.

After the enemy cavalry were so bravely repulsed and the French columns captured, the whole 2nd Light Battalion was taken in [to the farm] and the 1st Light Battalion occupied mainly the hollow road from which position, it fired on the enemy columns which were attacked by the 5th Division as well as by those in La Haye Sainte.

Around 2 o'clock, both the left wing companies of the battalion were sent over the chaussee to assist the 1st Battalion 95th Regiment and the remaining four companies occupied a small height between the hollow road and La Haye Sainte where for quite some time they forcefully resisted the attacking columns.

Later, both companies that were sent to the left to support the 2nd Light Battalion in La Haye Sainte [who] left the farm between 5 and 6 o'clock whereupon the 1st Light Battalion reoccupied the hollow road. The attacks of the enemy cavalry and infantry became so severe and followed each other so very quickly that our losses were very large and the battalion melted away.

Immediately after 6 o'clock the weakened 5th Line Battalion was attacked in line formation by an enemy column coming from La Haye Sainte, they were overrun in their flank by French cavalry and broken up, so the whole 3rd Division withdrew somewhat and the weak remainder of the 1st Light Battalion successfully occupied the house behind the hollow road in the direction of Mont St Jean.

The battalion remained in this position until after 7 o'clock, after the said attack of the French Guards on the right wing of the British army. As the enemy suffered a total defeat, the battalion advanced again to the hollow road and took its position there.

The Allied army now went onto the attack, the weak remainder of the Battalion moved to the ground between La Haye Sainte and La Belle Alliance, later it was pulled back and stayed, with the whole 3rd Division and spent the night on the battlefield close to La Haye Sainte with the exception of the 8th Line Battalion which advanced to La Belle Alliance.

I cannot describe the formation of the enemy in our front quite accurately as the infantry stood first in a line and then changed to a column. Our defence in the centre and on the left wing stood firm; the ground was softened by the rain, which did not allow any movement of the cannons in our line with the exception of the late arrival of a British battery from Brussels,[2] which moved very effectively in the lane.

W BUHSE CAPT
ADJUTANT OF THE FORMER 1ST LIGHT BATTALION KGL

---

1 Buhse is numbered 328 in Beamish. He served in the Legion in the Baltic in 1806–7, the Peninsula in 1808–14 with a short spell in Sicily in 1809. He was severely wounded at the crossing of the Bidassoa. He became a captain and quartermaster in the Hanoverian Rifle Guards, HGO3 and HWC.

2 This can only refer to the arrival at the front of Captain Sinclair's foot artillery battery, which was the only late movement of fresh artillery in this area. This battery had actually remained in reserve all day near Mont St Jean rather than arriving late from Brussels as described. This battery proceeded along the chaussee until near the crossroads, when it moved across the rear of the slope and moved into the front line to the right of the KGL at approximately 4.30 pm.

The 2nd Light Battalion KGL

No. 163 Major George Baring[1]
Hanover, 12 March 1835

ADD MS 34705, FO 48

Original in German

Sir,

I find myself almost unable to execute the task your letter of the 27th January last imposes on me, on account of the variety of circumstances which occurred to the battalion under my command on that memorable day, .

In the year 1816 I complied with the request of a friend and wrote down, for him only, all the different things that happened to me and the battalion before and during the battle. This narrative fell into the hands of some other gentleman who, very much against my own will, inserted the same in the [Hanoverian] *Military Journal*; a copy of which I take the liberty of enclosing, hoping you'll take it as a proof of how willing I am to contribute to your undertaking, and not look upon it as a mark of selfishness and boasting.

As to the different queries your letter contains respecting the nature of the ground, I cannot possibly give a decisive answer: when I came to the spot everything was already completely trodden down, but I believe the fields all around the farm La Haye Sainte were cornfields.

In order to find the different corps mentioned in my narrative in their then situation, I have marked them in the same as well as on the plan with corresponding numbers.

In regard to the moment when the Imperial Guards charged the position, I believe it was that marked thus T in the narrative.

I shall feel most happy to answer any further question you should think proper to make, as far as my recollection will lead me;

and have the honour to be, Sir, your most obedient humble servant

GEO BARING
M GENERAL

The narrative of the participation of the 2nd Light Battalion of the King's German Legion in the battle of Waterloo[2]

The narrative was translated and published in English in Beamish's *History of the King's German Legion*, volume II, page 453. This translation is accurate, but has some passages removed from the original German version. In this new translation of the original German account; the text not printed by Beamish is shown in italics.

Preface of the Editor[3]

In the days of Quatre Bras and Waterloo, the Colonel and Brigade Commander George Baring acted as a major in the 2nd Light Battalion, the King's German Legion. In response to the request of the editorial staff he expressed his willingness that the following narrative, which he wrote a few weeks after the remarkable days as a private undertaking, be made available to the general public. It is written in a simple and unadorned language, which style is here maintained and the actions do not require any elaboration. The Colonel wished expressly that the reader be reminded that he writes in the first person. The editors preferred to keep the original form as any change in the wording would contradict the wishes of the Colonel.

The anticipation of the troops was very high, due to the return of Napoleon and the subsequent movements in France. The order of the day, 16 June 1815, instructed the battalions of the 3rd Division under the command of General Carl von Alten, to be moved from their quarters near Esscaussines[4] *and march to the village of Braine-le-Comte and at the same time move towards Nivelle.*

The English and Hanoverian brigades[5] *marched to Quatre Bras, while the 2nd German Legion moved under Colonel von Ompteda one hour away on the road to Mons and took position there.*[6] *In the afternoon we heard a tremendous fire to our left without knowing its meaning. Before we knew the outcome, an order in the evening called us to join the division at Quatre Bras, where we arrived at 12 midnight. At daylight, we saw the enemy opposite on the battlefield of the previous day.*

A few shots marked the beginning of the new day, 17 June, otherwise both armies appeared to be inactive and we expected at any moment the order to attack. About 7o'clock in the morning, I was called to General Alten[7] *and was told that the Prussian army to the left had been beaten the night before and consequently we were to fall back. At the same time I received an order to form a rearguard. I arranged that all forward positions would reduce their forces, formed a concentric position with the remainder and when the division had marched back far enough to lose visual contact with us, I started my own withdrawal*

Beside the battalion, I had under my command some Brunswick cavalry. Should the enemy break

out in force, we would certainly lose in such open terrain, for which eventuality I was quite prepared.

Against all expectation, the enemy did not attack and I rejoined the division at Genappe, without firing a shot. After a short break, we started again at about 2 pm and at that moment the weather suddenly changed, there came on a tremendous storm with an unusually heavy rain and in a few minutes, the troops that were in the streets stood up to their knees in water. Everyone marched towards Brussels on the wide road and the troops were often stopped because of the congestion. It transpired that my battalion and the 95th English Regiment were the last infantry.

The French attacked our men with power and had great success,[8] *as they managed to throw our regiment over the hillock. I saw the enemy at a few hundred paces behind me and marched my battalion from the lanes into the fields to be ready to receive the enemy in a quarry. Colonel Barnard did the same with his 95th Regiment on the other side. We marched thus till half an hour before 8 [pm], to our position at Waterloo, without being attacked by the enemy's cavalry.*

I was sent to the farm of La Haye Sainte in order to occupy it. We built defensive positions during the remainder of the daylight hours and as far as the rain allowed us and laid down in expectation of an attack the next morning.

The farm of La Haye Sainte lies, as is well known, close by the side of the high road which leads from Brussels to Genappe, in the centre of the two positions, and about midway between them.

The dwelling-house, barn, and stables were surrounded by a rectangular wall, forming a court in the interior. Towards the enemy's side was an orchard, surrounded by a hedge, and in rear was a kitchen-garden, bounded by a small wall towards the road, but on the other sides by a hedge. Two doors and three large gates led from the court to the exterior; but of these, that of the barn had been unfortunately broken and burned by the troops.

The battalion consisted of six companies, which did not number 400 men; I posted three companies in the orchard, two in the buildings and one in the garden.

Important as the possession of this farm apparently was, the means of defending it were very insufficient, and besides, I was ordered, immediately on arriving there, to send off the pioneers of the battalion to Hougoumont, so that I had not even a hatchet; for unfortunately the mule that carried the entrenching tools was lost the day before.

As the day broke on 18 June, we sought out every possible means of putting the place in a state of defence, but the burned gate of the barn presented the greatest difficulty.[9] With this employment, and cooking some veal which we found in the place, the morning was past until after eleven o'clock, when the attack commenced against the left wing.

Every man now repaired to his post, and I betook myself to the orchard, where the first attack was to be expected; the farm lies in a hollow, so that a small elevation of the ground immediately in front of the orchard, concealed the approach of the enemy.

Shortly after noon, some skirmishers commenced the attack. I made the men lie down, and forbad all firing until the enemy were quite near. The first shot broke the bridle of my horse close to my hand, and the second killed Major Böseweil,[10] who was standing near me. The enemy did not stop long skirmishing, but immediately advanced over the height, with two close columns, one of which attacked the buildings, and the other threw itself on mass into the orchard, showing the greatest contempt for our fire. It was not possible for our small disjointed numbers fully to withstand this furious attack of such a superior force, and we retired upon the barn, in a more united position, in order to continue the defence: my horse's leg was broken, and I was obliged to take that of the adjutant.

Colonel von Klencke[11] now came to our assistance with the Luneburg Battalion. We immediately recommenced the attack, and had already made the enemy give way, when I perceived a strong line of cuirassiers forming in front of the orchard; at the same time Captain Meyer[12] came to me and reported that the enemy had surrounded the rear garden, and it was not possible to hold it longer. I gave him orders to fall back into the buildings, and assist in their defence. Convinced of the great danger which threatened us from the cuirassiers, in consequence of the weak hedge, so easy to break through, I called out to my men, who were mixed with the newly arrived Hanoverians – to assemble round me, as I intended retiring into the barn. The number of the battalion which had come to our assistance, exceeded, by many degrees, that of my men, and as, at the same time, the enemy's infantry gained the garden – the skirmishers having been driven out by a column attack – the former, seeing the cuirassiers in the open field, imagined that their only chance of safety lay in gaining the main position of the army. My voice, unknown to them, and also not sufficiently penetrating, was, notwithstanding all my exertions, unequal to halt and collect my men together; already overtaken by the cavalry, we fell in with the enemy's infantry, who had surrounded the garden, and whose fire the men were exposed in retiring to the main position. In this effort a part succeeded. Notwithstanding this misfortune, the farmhouse itself was still defended by Lieutenants George Graeme[13] and Carey,[14] and Ensign Frank.[15] The English Dragoon Guards now came up – beat back the cuirassiers – fell upon the infantry, who had already suffered much, and nearly cut them to pieces.

In this first attack I lost a considerable number of men, besides three officers killed, and six wounded; on my requisition for support, Captains von Gilsa and Marschalck[16] were sent to me, with their companies of the 1st Light Battalion, I gave the defence of the garden, leaving the buildings to the three officers who had already so bravely defended them: the orchard I did not again occupy.

About half an hour's respite was now given us by the enemy, and we employed the time in preparing ourselves against a new attack; this followed in the same force as before; namely, from two sides by two close columns, which, with the greatest rapidity, nearly surrounded us, and, despising danger, fought with a degree of courage which I had never before witnessed in Frenchmen. Favoured by their advancing in masses, every bullet of ours hurt, and seldom were the effects limited to one assailant; this did not, however, prevent them from throwing themselves against the walls, and endeavouring to wrest the arms from the hands of my men, through the loop-holes; many lives were sacrificed to the defence of the doors and gates; the most obstinate contest was carried on where the gate was wanting, and where the enemy seemed determined to enter. On this spot seventeen Frenchmen already lay dead, and their bodies served as a protection to those who pressed after them to the same spot.

Meantime four lines of French cavalry had formed on the right front of the farm; the first cuirassiers, second lancers, third dragoons, and fourth hussars, and it was clear to me that their intention was to attack the squares of our division in position, in order by destroying them to break the whole line.[17] This was a critical moment, for what would be our fate if they succeeded! As they marched upon the position by the farm, I brought all the fire possible to bear upon them; many men and horses were overthrown, but they were not discouraged. Without in the least troubling themselves about our fire, they advanced with the greatest intrepidity, and attacked the infantry. All this I could see, and confess freely that now and then I felt some apprehension. The manner in which this cavalry was received and beaten back by our squares, is too well known to require mention here.

The contest in the farm had continued with undiminished violence, but nothing could shake the courage of our men, who, following the example of their officers, laughing, defied danger. Nothing could inspire more courage or confidence than such conduct. These are the moments when we learn how to feel what one soldier is to another – what the word 'comrade' really means – feelings which must penetrate the coarsest mind, but which he only can fully understand, who has been witness to such moments!

When the cavalry retired, the infantry gave up also their fruitless attack, and fell back, accompanied by our shouts, and derision. Our loss, on this occasion, was not so great as at first; however, my horse was again shot under me, and as my servant, believing me dead, had gone away with my other horse, I procured one of those that were running about.

Our first care was to make good the injury which had been sustained; my greatest anxiety was respecting the ammunition, which, I found, in consequence of the continued fire, had been reduced more than one half. I immediately sent an officer back with this account, and requested ammunition, which was promised. About an hour had thus passed when I discovered the enemy's columns again advancing on the farm; I sent another officer back to the position with this intelligence, and repeated the request for ammunition.

Our small position was soon again attacked with the same fury, and defended with the same courage as before. Captain von Wurmb[18] was sent to my assistance with the skirmishers of the 5th Line Battalion, and I placed them in the court; but welcome as this reinforcement was, it could not compensate for the want of ammunition, which every moment increased, so that after half an hour more of uninterrupted fighting, I sent off an officer with the same request.

This was as fruitless as the other two applications; however, two hundred Nassau troops were sent me.[19] The principal contest was now carried on at the open entrance to the barn; at length the enemy, not being able to succeed by open force, resorted to the expedient of setting the place on fire, and soon a thick smoke was seen rising from the barn! Our alarm was now extreme, for although there was water in the court, all means of drawing it, and carrying it were wanting – every vessel having been broken up. Luckily the Nassau troops carried large field cooking kettles; I tore a kettle from the back of one of the men; several officers followed my example, and filling the kettles with water, they carried them, facing almost certain death, to the fire. The men did the same, and soon not one of the Nassauers was left with his kettle, and the fire was thus luckily extinguished – but alas, with the blood of many a brave man! Many of the men, although covered with wounds, could not be brought to retire. 'So long as our officers fight, and we can stand,' was their constant reply, 'we will not stir from the spot.'

It would be injustice to a skirmisher named Frederick Lindau,[20] if I did not mention him: bleeding from two wounds in the head and carrying in his pocket a considerable bag of gold which he had taken from an enemy officer, he stood at the small back barn door, and from thence defended the main entrance in his front. I told him to go back, as the cloth about his head was not sufficient to stop the strong flow of blood; he, however, as regardless of his wounds as of his gold, answered: 'He would be a scoundrel that deserted you, so long as his head is on his shoulders.' This brave fellow was afterwards taken, and lost his treasure.

This attack may have lasted about an hour and a half, when the French, tired from their fruitless efforts, again fell back. Our joy may well be imagined. With every new attack I became more convinced of the importance of holding the post. With every attack also, the weight of the responsibility that devolved upon me increased. This responsibility is never greater than when an officer is thus left to himself, and suddenly obliged to make a decision upon which perhaps, his own as well as the life and honour of those under him,- nay even more important results,- may depend. In battles, as is well known, trifles, apparently of little importance, have often incalculable influence.

What must have been my feelings, therefore, when, on counting the cartridges, I found that, on an average, there was not more than from three to four each! The men made nothing of the diminished physical strength which their excessive exertions had caused, and immediately filled up the holes that had been made in the walls by the enemy's guns, but they could not remain insensible to the position in which they were placed by the want of ammunition, and made the most reasonable remonstrances to me on the subject. These were not wanting to make me renew the most urgent representations, and finally to report specifically that I was not capable of sustaining another attack in the present condition. All was in vain!* With what uneasiness did I now see two enemy columns again in march against us! At this moment I would have blessed the ball that came to deprive me of life.But more than life was at stake, and the extraordinary danger required extraordinary exertion and firmness. On my exhortations to courage and economy of the ammunition, I received one unanimous reply: 'No man will desert you, we will fight and die with you!' No pen, not even that of one who has experienced such moments, can describe the feeling which this excited in me; nothing can be compared with it! Never had I felt myself so elevated; but never also placed in so painful a position, where honour contended with a feeling for the safety of the men who had given me such an unbounded proof of their confidence.

The enemy gave me no time for thought; irritated by the opposition which they had experienced, attacked with renewed fury. The contest commenced at the barn, which they again succeeded in setting on fire. It was extinguished, luckily, in the same manner as before. Every shot that was now fired, increased my uneasiness and anxiety. I sent again to the rear with the positive statement that I must and would leave the place if no ammunition was sent me. This was also without effect.[21]

Our fire gradually diminished, and in the same proportion did our perplexity

* It must be observed that the battalion were armed with rifles, and, therefore could not make use of the ordinary infantry ammunition. This circumstance explains what occurred; but at the same time, shows how dangerous it may prove to have firearms of different calibres. *Note of the editor of the Hanoverian Military Journal.*

increase; already I heard many voices calling out for ammunition, adding 'We will readily stand by you, but we must have the means of defending ourselves!' Even the officers, who, during the whole day, had shown the greatest courage, represented to me the impossibility of retaining the post under such circumstances. The enemy, who too soon observed our wants, now boldly broke in one of the doors; however, as only a few could come in at a time, these were instantly bayoneted, and the rear hesitated to follow. They now mounted the roof and walls, from which my unfortunate men were certain marks; at the same time they pressed in through the open barn, which could no longer be defended. Inexpressibly painful as the decision was of giving up the place, my feeling of duty as a man overcame that of honour, and I gave the order to retire through the house into the garden. How much these words cost me, and by what feelings they were accompanied, he only can judge who has been placed in a similar situation!

Fearing the bad impression which retiring from the house into the garden would make upon the men, and wishing to see whether it was possible still to hold any part of the place, I left to the before-mentioned three officers the honour of being the last. The passage through the house being very narrow, many of the men were overtaken by the enemy, who vented their fury upon them in the lowest abuse, and the most brutal treatment. Among the sufferers here was Ensign Frank, who had already been wounded: the first man that attacked him, he ran through with his sabre, but at the same moment, his arm was broken by a ball from another; nevertheless he reached a bedroom, and succeeded in concealing himself behind a bed. Two of the men also took refuge in the same place, but the French followed close at their heels, crying *'No pardon for you bastard greens!', and* shot them before his face: Frank had himself the good luck to remain undiscovered until the place again fell into our hands. As I was now fully convinced, and the officers agreed with me, that the garden was not to be maintained when the enemy were in possession of the dwelling house, I made the men retire singly to the main position. The French, pleased, perhaps, with their success, did not molest us in retreat. The men who had been sent to me from other regiments, I allowed to return, and with the weak remnant of my own battalion I attached myself to two companies of the 1st Light Battalion, which, under Lieutenant Colonel Lewis von dem Bussche, occupied the hollow road behind the farm. Although we could not fire a shot, we helped to increase the numbers. Here the combat recommenced with increased fury, the enemy pressing forth from the farm, and I had the pain to see Captain Henry von Marschalck fall – a friend whose distinguished coolness and bravery on this day I can never forget; Captain von Gilsa also had his right arm shattered; Lieutenant Albert was shot, and Lieutenant Graeme, as he swung his cap in the air to cheer on the men, had his right hand shattered; neither would go into the hollow road, not withstanding all my persuasions, but remained above upon the edge. On the retreat from the buildings Captain Holtzerman[22] and Lieutenant Tobin[23] were taken, and Lieutenant Carey was wounded, so that the number of my officers was very much reduced. I rode a Dragoon horse, in front of whose saddle were large pistol holsters and a cloak, and the firing was so sharp that four balls entered here, and another the saddle, just as I had alighted to replace my hat which had been knocked off by a sixth ball.

The 5th Line Battalion which stood on our right, were now ordered to attack the enemy with the bayonet. *The battalion made it with the greatest courage. In the moment when a certain disorder was inevitable, a regiment of cuirassiers came from the rear and gained terrible revenge for the decimation that their comrades had just suffered.*[24]

The cuirassiers thought this a good opportunity to break through the line, not, perhaps, being aware of the presence of our men in the hollow road; however when they had arrived within about twenty paces, they received such a fire that they wheeled about in the greatest disorder, well marked by our men; at this moment the 3rd Hussars[25] advanced.

The cuirassiers reformed with unbelievable speed and faced again. Both corps appeared not to trust each other, however they enticed the hussars in and the encounter about 200 paces from us was short but very bloody. After about a quarter of an hour of intense fighting both sides withdrew; the hussars were mixed amongst our infantry.

A strange incident took place here. A corporal from the hussars was surrounded by the cuirassiers, he managed to find a way between them; one cuirassier had the same fate between the hussars. Both wanted to rejoin their corps and met about half way, although the hussar was bleeding a lot, they attacked each other. All this was happening in full view of their respective comrades, nobody went forward to stop the fight. I feared for the hussar as I saw him bleeding; however, all his training showed above the strength of his opponent, and managed to get on his left side, gave a mighty blow to his face which laid him on the ground and he then rode calmly back to his side while his comrades were cheering and congratulating him.

Fresh columns of the enemy again advanced, and nothing seemed likely to terminate the slaughter but the entire destruction of one army or the other. My horse, the third which I had had in the course of the day, received a ball in his head; he sprung up, and in coming down again, fell on my right leg, and pressed me so hard into the deep loamy soil, that, despite of all exertion, I could not extricate myself. The men in the road considered me dead, and it was not till after some little time that one of them came out to set me free. Although my leg was not broken, I lost the use of it for the moment: I begged most urgently for a horse, offering gold upon gold, but men who called themselves my friends, forgot the word, and thought only of their own interest! I crept to the nearest house behind the front. An Englishman was charitable enough to catch a stray horse, place a saddle upon him, and help me up; I then rode again forward, when I learned that General Alten had been severely wounded. I saw that the part of the position, which our division had held, was only weakly and irregularly occupied. Scarce sensible, from the pain which I suffered, I rode straight to the hollow road, where I had left the rest of the men; but they also, had been obliged to retire to the village in consequence of the total want of ammunition, hoping there to find some cartridges. A French dragoon finally drove me from the spot, and riding back, in the most bitter grief, I met an officer, who gave me the above information of the battalion. I directed him to bring my men forward, if there were only two of them together, as I had hopes of getting some ammunition. Immediately after this, there arose throughout the whole line, the cry of 'Victory!' 'Victory!' and with equal enthusiasm 'Forward!' 'Forward!' What an unexpected change! As I had no longer any men to command, I joined the 1st Hussars,[26] and with them followed the enemy until dark, when I returned to the field of battle.

The division, which had suffered dreadfully, remained, during the night, on the field. Out of nearly 400 men, with which I commenced the battle, only 42 remained effective.[27] Whoever I asked after, the answer was 'Killed', or 'Wounded'! I freely confess that tears came involuntarily into my eyes at this sad intelligence, and the many bitter feelings that seized upon me. I was awakened from these gloomy thoughts by my friend Major Shaw,[28] Assistant Quartermaster General to our division. I felt myself exhausted to the greatest degree, and my leg was very painful. I lay down to sleep, with my friend, upon some straw which the men had collected together for us: on waking we found ourselves between a dead man and a dead horse! But I will pass over in silence the scene which the field of battle, with all its misery and grief, now presented.

We buried our dead friends and comrades; amongst the rest Colonel von Ompteda, the commander of the brigade, and many brave men. After some food was cooked, and the men had, in some measure, refreshed themselves, we broke up from the field to follow the enemy.

Return of the officers of the 2nd Light Battalion, two companies of the 1st Battalion, and the skirmishers of the 5th Line Battalion of the King's German Legion, who were present at the defence of the farm of La Haye Sainte, 18 June, 1815.

2nd Light Battalion

		Majors	
George Baring	…	A. Bösewiel	… Killed
		Captains	
E. Holtzermann	… Taken prisoner	W. Schaumann[29]	… Killed
		Lieutenants	
F. Kessler[30]	… Wounded	T. Carey	… Wounded
C. Meyer	…	E. Biedermann[33]	…
O. Lindam[31]	… Wounded	D. Graeme	… Wounded
B. Riefkugel[32]	… Wounded	S. Earl[34]	…
A. Tobin	… Taken prisoner		
		Ensigns	
F. von Roberston[35]	… Killed	L. Baring [36]	…
G. Frank	… Wounded	W. Smith [37]	…
Lieutenant and Adjutant W. Timmann [38]		… Wounded	
Surgeon G. Heise [39]	…		

1st Light Battalion

		Captains	
Von Gilsa	… Wounded	Von Marschalck	… Killed
		Lieutenant	
Kuntze	…		
		Ensign	
Baumgarten[40]	…		

Skirmishers of the 5th Line Battalion

		Captain	
Von Wurmb	… Killed		
		Lieutenants	
Witte[41]	… Wounded	Schläger[42]	…..
		Ensign	
Walther[43]	… Wounded		

1 Baron George Baring, numbered 335 in Beamish, became eternally famous for his defence of La Haye Sainte. He had joined the Legion as a captain in 1803 and served in Hanover, the Baltic, the Peninsula in 1808–9, Sicily, northern Germany and the Netherlands. Made HGO1, PTS, HWC, KCH and CB. He received a General Service Medal with nine bars for Albuera (slightly wounded), Ciudad Rodrigo, Badajoz, Salamanca, Vittoria, Pyrenees, San Sebastian, Nivelle, Orthes and Toulouse. He became a major general in the Hanoverian service, commanding the 1st Brigade of Infantry and became Commandant at Hanover.

2 This is the narrative forwarded under cover of Baring's letter dated 12 March 1835.

3 This narrative was first published in the *Hanoverian Military Journal,* part II, 1831.

4 Esscaussines is to be found approximately eight miles from Nivelles.

5 The 5th Brigade of Major General Sir Colin Halkett and the 1st Hanoverian Brigade of Major General Count Kielmannsegge.

6 It appears from a number of officer's memoirs of this brigade, that they were ordered to cover the road from Mons to Brussels at Nivelles. This fact seems to have been overlooked by all British historians of the campaign. These troops would have been of immense value to Wellington at Quatre Bras, but he chose to leave them guarding this position, further indicating that he strongly feared a flank march by the French on this road.

7 Lieutenant General Charles Count Alten commanding the 3rd Infantry Division.

8 This comment refers to the French cavalry pushing the rearguard hard.

9 It has never been adequately explained why, although the garrison commenced preparations for the defence of La Haye Sainte as soon as they arrived in the evening, no effort was made to save the barn door or to seal the entrance with farm equipment and why no reserves of rifle ammunition were stockpiled in the farm.

10 Captain Adolphus Böseweil, numbered 975 in Beamish, joined the Legion in 1804, serving in Hanover, the Baltic, the Peninsula in 1808–11, Sicily and Holland before he was killed at Waterloo.

11 Lieutenant Colonel von Klencke commanding the Luneburg Battalion was wounded at Waterloo.

12 Captain George Meyer, numbered 343 in Beamish, joined the Legion in 1809, serving in Sicily and the Peninsula in 1811–14. He was severely wounded at Bayonne and slightly wounded at Waterloo. He died in Ottendorf in Hanover on 16 March 1832.

13 Lieutenant George Drummond Graeme, numbered 354 in Beamish, joined the Legion in 1812, serving in the Peninsula in 1813–14. He received a General Service Medal with three bars for Vittoria, Nivelle & Nive, and became HGO3 and HWC. He became a captain in the Hanoverian Grenadier Guards. His letters were published by Siborne (numbers 179 & 180).

14 Lieutenant Thomas Carey, numbered 351 in Beamish, joined the Legion in 1811, serving in the Peninsula in 1811–14. Made HGO3, he became a captain on the retired list in 1816.

15 Ensign George Frank, numbered 361 in Beamish, joined the Legion in 1814 and was made HGO3. He retired on half pay as a captain in 1816 at Liebenburg in Hanover.

16 Captain Gustavus von Marschalck, numbered 300 in Beamish, joined the Legion in 1805, serving in Hanover, the Baltic, the Peninsula in 1808–13 and northern Germany. He received a General Service Medal with six bars for Albuera, Salamanca, Vittoria, San Sebastian, Nivelle & Nive. He became HGO3 and HWC, and a lieutenant colonel in the Hanoverian 7th Line Battalion.

17 This would appear to be the moment when the French cavalry were preparing for their great assault on the centre of the Allied position.

18 Captain Ernest Christian Charles von Wurmb, numbered 981 in Beamish, joined the Legion in 1804 and had served in Hanover, the Baltic and the Peninsula in 1808–14 before being killed at Waterloo.

19 These were men of the 1/2nd Nassau Regiment.

20 I have not been able to clearly identify this soldier. The only private with a similar name recorded in the Waterloo Medal Roll in the 2nd Light Battalion was Frederick Lindemann, but there is no evidence to prove that this is our man.

21 It is a singular fact that although their own rifle ammunition was not available, the 95th Rifles were posted across the road and used the same Baker rifle, but it seems that no one thought to request ammunition from them.

22 Captain Ernest Augustus Holtzermann, numbered 340 in Beamish, joined the Legion in 1804, serving in Hanover, the Baltic, and the Peninsula in 1808–14. He received a General Service Medal with six bars for Albuera, Salamanca, Vittoria, San Sebastian, Nivelle and Nive. Made HGO3 and HWC, he eventually became a lieutenant colonel in the 2nd Hanoverian Line Battalion.

23 Marius T. H. Jobin (Tobin in text), numbered 349 in Beamish, joined the Legion in 1810, serving in the Peninsula in 1811–14). He had previously been slightly wounded before Bayonne and again at Waterloo. He died at Surinam in 1825.

24 The 5th Line Battalion KGL was ordered by the Prince of Orange to La Haye Sainte and advanced in line. They were caught by the cuirassiers when still in line and rapidly rolled up. Some sources claim up to 93% casualty rates for this battalion, but Beamish records losses of 168 officers and men from a total of 471, a casualty rate of 36%.

25 The 3rd Hussars KGL with the 13th Light Dragoons formed Arenschildt's 7th Cavalry Brigade.

26 The 1st Hussars KGL commanded by Lieutenant Colonel Wissell, belonged to 6th Cavalry Brigade of Major General Sir Hussey Vivian, therefore Baring was probably involved in their great charge at the end of the battle.

27 This is probably the most misquoted sentence *ever* by British historians, who regularly use this to indicate that only 42 defenders escaped from La Haye Sainte and the carnage within; this is *certainly wrong*. Baring makes it clear that the defenders from the other Battalions were returned to their own units and that his figure of 42 only applies to his Battalion alone, and that for the actual number of men with him at the end of the battle some three to four hours later. This was after much further severe fighting around the cross roads and when many of his men had dispersed in search of ammunition and did not return that night. The number of men escaping from La Haye Sainte would have been a much higher figure in total. This is confirmed by the casualty totals for the 2nd Light Battalion, which shows that they actually lost 16 officers and 195 men killed, wounded and missing from an original total of 33 officers and 398 men (47%). This is still a major loss, but more realistic than the over 90% losses some historians would have us believe. It should also be noted that only 79 are recorded as killed or missing, therefore some 132 of these losses were wounded, who must either have been taken to the rear before the French overran the farm or more likely that the French were less ruthless to those wounded remaining in the buildings than is generally portrayed, and they were made prisoner until the farm was recaptured.

28 Captain James Shaw of the 43rd Foot, see his letters (number 137)

29 Captain Frederick Melchior William Schaumann, numbered 988 in Beamish, joined the Legion in 1805 and served in Hanover, the Baltic, the Peninsula, Sicily and northern Germany before being killed at Waterloo.

30 Captain Frederick Theodore Kessler, numbered 342 in Beamish, joined the Legion in 1807, serving as an NCO until 1809. He served in the Baltic, Sicily and the Peninsula in 1811–14. He was slightly wounded at Tolosa in 1813 and again at Waterloo. Made HGO3 he died at Hanover as a brevet major half pay on 28 January 1833.

31 Lieutenant Ole Lindam, numbered 347 in Beamish, joined the Legion as an NCO in 1810 and served in the Peninsula from 1811–14. He received the HGO3 and a General Service

Medal with five bars, for Albuera, Ciudad Rodrigo, Salamanca, Vittoria and Nivelle. He became a brevet major on the retired list and was last known living in Devon.

32 Lieutenant Bernhard Riefkugel, numbered 348 in Beamish, joined the Legion in 1807 as an NCO, serving in the Baltic and the Peninsula in 1808–14. He was slightly wounded at Nivelle in 1813 and again at Waterloo. He received a General Service Medal with nine bars for Talavera, Busaco Fuentes d'Onoro, Albuera, Salamanca, Vittoria, San Sebastian, Nivelle and Nive. He received the HGO3 and HWC and became a captain in the Hanoverian Rifle Guards.

33 Lieutenant Emanuel Biedermann, numbered 252 in Beamish, joined the Legion in 1811, serving in northern Germany in 1813–14. He died at Steinhütte in Switzerland.

34 Lieutenant Salomon Earl, numbered 356 in Beamish, joined the Legion in 1813 and served in the Netherlands before Waterloo.

35 Ensign Frederick von Robertson, numbered 1013 in Beamish, joined the Legion in 1813, serving in Holland in 1814 before being killed at Waterloo.

36 Ensign Lewis Baring, numbered 365 in Beamish, joined the Legion in 1814, serving in the Netherlands. He later became a lieutenant in the Hanoverian Rifle Guards.

37 Ensign William Smith, numbered 363 in Beamish, joined the Legion in 1814, serving in Holland.

38 Adjutant William D. Timmann, numbered 370 in Beamish, joined the Legion in 1805 as a Private. He served in Hanover, the Baltic and the Peninsula in 1808–14. He died in Hanover in 1818.

39 Surgeon George Heise, numbered 1204 in Beamish, joined the Legion in 1805, serving in Hanover, the Baltic and the Peninsula in 1808–14. Made HGO3 and HWC, he later became Staff Surgeon to the Hanoverian Grenadier Guards.

40 Lieutenant John Baumgarten, numbered 308 in Beamish, joined the Legion in 1805, serving in Hanover, the Baltic and the Peninsula in 1808–14. He retired as a captain to Lubeck.

41 Lieutenant Charles von Witte, numbered 574 in Beamish, joined the Legion in 1807 as an NCO and served in the Baltic, Sicily and the Peninsula in 1808–14. He was slightly wounded at Burgos in 1812 and severely wounded at Urugne in 1813. Made HGO3 he became a captain on half pay in Hanover.

42 Lieutenant Charles Schlaeger (spelt Schläger in text), numbered 576 in Beamish, joined the Legion in 1805 serving as a bombardier in the artillery. He served in Hanover, the Baltic, the Peninsula in 1808–13 and Holland. He was slightly wounded at Burgos in 1812. He received a General Service Medal with five bars for Talavera, Badajoz, Fuentes d'Onoro, Salamanca and Vittoria. Made HGO3 he became a captain in the Hanoverian Grenadier Guards.

43 Adjutant William Walther, number 597 in Beamish, joined the Legion in 1811 in the ranks. He served in the Peninsula in 1811–14 and Holland. He received the General Service Medal with five bars for Salamanca, Vittoria, San Sebastian, Nivelle and Nive. Made HGO3 he was afterwards captain and quartermaster on half pay at Stade in Hanover.

No. 164 From the same

Nice, Kingdom of Sardinia, 24 January 1838

ADD MS 34706, FO 427

Sir,

I am truly sorry your letter of the 28th August last should have remained so long unanswered, having however travelled about ever since that period, and not staying any length of time at the same place, it did not reach me before this very day. The delay will however be of little consequence to you, for to my great regret I am unable to give a satisfactory answer to the questions your letter contains.

In regard to the French column of 4 to 5,000 men which should have been debouching from the Genappe chaussee close to the southern extremity of the orchard of La Haye Sainte; I must contradict this fact in so far, that no column of 4 or 5,000 men did debouch from the chaussee in the neighbourhood of the orchard of La Haye Sainte proceeding towards La Ferme Hougoumont. I never perceived such a column, and it could not then possibly have escaped my noticing it. If this fact existed, it *must* have *taken* place *farther* away on the other side of the height next to the orchard in question where I could not see it.

As to the Dutch brigade and battery, I did not see neither the one nor the other, and I am perfectly confident that they never came upon the ground to the left of General Halkett's brigade. Even at the general advance I did not see them there; they may have followed in the rear, which I cannot say.

What concerns the Brunswickers, I confess I never saw them in the first line of the position we held. In the evening, when my horse was shot and fell on my right leg, I fell much hurt and with great difficulty moved from the front line somewhat to the rear endeavouring to get another horse; it may have lasted half an hour before I succeeded, and riding up again I met my friend Colonel Shaw, who will remember our conversation. Shaw then made off in search of the Duke, and I was informed, that during my absence the enemy had brought up some guns close to the position in the fields on the right of La Haye Sainte, and there being no guns in our line to answer their fire, they had badly treated General Kielsmansegge's brigade and thrown it into confusion. Colonel Shaw and myself, we saw neither troops nor guns on the left of Halkett's Brigade, nor did I see any afterwards until the moment of the general advance.

Should Colonel Shaw still be in Dublin I beg you will have the goodness to remember me most kindly to him, and tell him, that your letter had given me the first news of him; that I had written to him several years ago, but receiving no answer I had suspected that he had left Scotland, and that all my enquiries after him had remained fruitless.

I have the honour to be, Sir, your most obedient humble servant

GEO BARING
M GENERAL

No. 165 From the same
Undated[1]

ADD MS 34707, FO 159

Sir,

I beg to acknowledge the receipt of your note of the 26th instant which reached me this very day, and Major Benne having left Hanover yesterday I send this by the post as directed.

I sincerely regret that I cannot give you the desired answer in regard to the rocket troop that was employed near the farm La Haye Sainte during the battle of Waterloo, my attention being at that time so much engaged to the front that I did not observe what passed in the rear; however I perfectly recollect, that during the second and third, I believe, of the enemy's attacks on the farm, rockets passed near and over us, some of which reached the enemy's columns and did great execution; but where the battery was placed I could not possibly tell.

I have the honour to be, Sir, your most obedient humble servant

GEO BARING
MAJOR GENERAL

---

1 Although undated, the letter clearly indicates that it was sent from Hanover and a pencil mark in Siborne's hand indicates that it was written in 1839.

The 5th Line Battalion KGL

No. 166 Lieutenant Colonel William von Linsingen[1]
Undated[2]

ADD MS 34704, FO 237

Original in German

On the 18th June 1815 at the advance of the enemy, the 5th Line Battalion of the King's German Legion, which belonged to the Brigade of Col. von Ompteda was stationed behind a hollow path near the road, which went off right from the Brussels chaussee just before reaching La Haye Sainte. The 5th Battalion stood in close column and closer to the lane stood the 8th Battalion of the legion in a field of barley. To the right of the 5th Battalion was the Hanoverian Battalion Grubenhagen[3] on the field mentioned. Over the road on the right, stood some cannons belonging to the battery of Major Cleeve[4] of the legion.

Under the lively cannon fire a few close columns of the enemy appeared who made as if to attack us. The 5th Battalion of the legion whom the undersigned had the honour to command, was forced to deploy but during the deployment enemy cavalry rode forward from behind the columns of enemy infantry and the 5th Battalion hardly had time to form a square. Although the enemy Cuirassiers received the fire of the 5th and of the Grubenhagen Battalion, they managed to break into the square but were here engaged by a number of squadrons of the 3rd Hussar Regiment[5] of the legion and were beaten back with substantial losses.

The enemy infantry had during this time moved nearer to La Haye Sainte, which was now attacked powerfully, whereupon the light company of the 5th Battalion under the command of Captain von Wurmb[6] was sent there as reinforcement. The enemy cavalry made further attempts to break through the squares but were always beaten back.

So the matter stood, the cannon fire was murderous and directed mainly on La Haye Sainte and at the squares stationed there. As the enemy infantry attacked La Haye Sainte, the 2nd Light Battalion of the legion, the light company of the 5th Battalion of the legion and some companies of Nassau infantry in spite of brave resistance, were forced to abandon the buildings of the farm to the enemy as they were on fire and the ammunition had run out. A part of the enemy infantry came from La Haye Sainte and the rough hedge on the other side of the hollow road allowed them to attack our squares with skirmishers, upon which Col. von Ompteda received the order to advance a battalion of his brigade over the hollow road to remove the enemy, following which I received the order to advance the 5th Battalion into the hollow road. When the 5th Battalion was deployed in line to cross the road, we started at a light jog with a loud Hurrah to throw the enemy back. The enemy gave way and looked for the hedges of La Haye Sainte to regroup. The 5th Battalion pursued them, but before they were able to reach the hedges the enemy regiment of cuirassiers broke out on the right wing and as there was no chance to reform the square and as the battalion had no reserves, they were over ridden and beaten. The few unwounded, approximately 30 men and a few officers gathered by and by in the rear of the hollow road and as a result could only take partial action in the battle. After this occurrence a few officers remained, 3 died, 8 were wounded and 1 was missing.

The reason why only a comparatively few officers were casualties was because at that time they were in command of other positions and a few were ill.

The places are marked on the attached plan where the 8th, the 5th and the Battalion Grubenhagen stood during the course of the whole action.[7]

W VON LINSINGEN
FORMER COMMANDER AND LIEUT COL
OF THE 5TH LINE BATTALION KGL

---

1 Linsingen is numbered 559 in Beamish. He joined the Legion in 1803 and served in Hanover in 1805, the Baltic in1807 and the Mediterranean in 1808–14 with a short period in the Peninsula in 1812–13. He received the CBO and HGO2. He later became a lieutenant colonel on half pay living in Hildesheim.

2 Almost certainly written in early 1835.

3 Field Battalion Grubenhagen formed part of the 1st Hanoverian Brigade of Major General Count Kielmannsegge.

4 Captain A. Cleeve's Foot Battery KGL.

5 The 3rd Hussars KGL formed part of 7th Cavalry Brigade of Colonel Arenschildt.

6 Captain Ernest Christian Charles von Wurmb. He was killed during the defence of La Haye Sainte.

7 This plan does not appear to be extant.

No. 167 Captain Eberhard Von Brandis[1]
Harburg, 12 February 1835

ADD MS 34704, FO 235

Sir,

In answer to your letter of the 27th instant, I beg to state to you, to the best of my recollection, the following details regarding the positions and movements of the 5th Line Battalion K. G. Legion[2] during the battle of Waterloo.

At about 7 o'clock pm the 5th Battalion was posted in the formation of a square, behind the hollow road in the rear of La Haye Sainte, which position I have marked upon the plan as desired.[3]

The troops of the enemy opposed to the battalion at this time appeared to be a close column of infantry with *cavalry* in the rear of them.

At the beginning of the action I myself counted at least twenty-four pieces of artillery of the enemy posted opposite to the 5th and 8th Battalions,[4] and I believe that this artillery still maintained their position at 7 o'clock pm.

Till at about 5 o'clock pm the 5th Battalion occupied a position some hundred yards in front of the before mentioned hollow road, at this time the battalion was ordered to deploy in line and to attack a column of French infantry which were advancing upon La Haye Sainte, the enemy were driven back in disorder, but at this moment the battalion was charged unexpectedly by a regiment of cuirassiers in their right flank and sustained a most severe loss, among which was Colonel Ompteda commanding the brigade, who was leading the 5th Battalion to charge the French infantry.

The remainder of the 5th Battalion was then posted at the spot which I marked upon the plan and retained this position till the whole of the British line advanced upon the enemy.

At an earlier period of the action when the enemy attacked the centre of the British position, the 5th Line Battalion sustained several charges of French cuirassiers, which were always repulsed with great loss to the enemy.

The light company of the 5th Battalion was sent to reinforce the 2nd Light Battalion posted at La Haye Sainte, soon after the commencement of the action.

With regard to the crops you marked with pencil on the different fields, I beg to observe, that most of the fields in front of the brigade appeared to me to be ploughed land at that time. As I was acting as aide de camp to Colonel Ompteda,[5] I had often to pass from one battalion to the other as well as in front of the line, and well remember the difficulty I experienced in getting through the swampy fields, which were so softened by the heavy guns. The fields with crops were much easier to pass on account of the long straw which was quite trodden down and mixed with the ground.

In remitting to you the above-mentioned circumstances occurred on that memorable day, I beg you will excuse any involuntary error which these notices may contain, and I shall be happy if they will prove of any use to your understanding.

I have the honour to be, Sir, your most obedient humble servant

E DE BRANDIS

CAPTAIN LATE 5TH LINE BATTALION KGL

---

1 Brandis is numbered 570 in Beamish, joined the Legion in 1807 and served in the Baltic and throughout the Peninsular war in 1808–14, being slightly wounded at Talavera and Salamanca. He received a General Service Medal with nine bars for Talavera, Busaco, Fuentes d'Onoro, Ciudad Rodrigo, Salamanca, Vittoria, San Sebastian, Nivelle and Nive. He became HGO3 and HWC. He became a captain in the Hanoverian 12th Line Battalion and was resident at Celle.

2 Commanded by Lieutenant Colonel William B. von Linsingen.

3 This plan appears to be no longer extant.

4 The 5th and 8th Line Battalions were brigaded with the 1st and 2nd Light Battalions in the 2nd Brigade KGL commanded by Colonel Baron Ompteda.

5 Colonel Commandant Christian von Ompteda, numbered 972 in Beamish, killed at Waterloo. He had joined the Legion in 1803, serving in Hanover, the Mediterranean, Baltic and the Peninsula in 1813–14. His diary was printed in English in 1894 entitled '*In the King's German Legion*'.

Letter no. 168

The 8th Line Battalion KGL

No. 168 Captain Frederick Marburg[1]

Hermannsburg,[2] 12 February 1835

ADD MS 34705, FO 248

Original in German

I regret very much that I cannot accede to the request of Mr Siborne to give information about the battle of Waterloo, as on the march to France my luggage with my diary was stolen which was very unfortunate, but I will try to remember as much as possible that concerns the 8th Battalion.

On the 18th June 1815 the Battalion was positioned on the right side of the Brussels chaussee formed in square and had on the right flank the 5th Line Battalion of the Kings German Legion and on the left the 73rd Regiment and in front of the lane a farm, the name of which I do not remember but I think it was called La Haye Sainte.

The enemy attacks were undertaken mainly by cavalry and skirmishers. The battalion received the order to form line – probably for the purpose of taking the farm - but Colonel von Ompteda[3] was afraid the enemy cavalry would cause a lot of damage, but it was forbidden for the Lieutenant to follow his orders. The Battalion had hardly formed into line when it was attacked by the Cuirassiers and before it could form a square again it lost a flag, which the battalion recovered, as the enemy did not take it. There were many wounded officers – amongst them the battalion commander Col. von Schroeder[4] and quite a number of men.[5]

The battalion maintained this position the whole day while the enemy attack took place only through cannon fire and cavalry and they only had the opportunity once to fire as the enemy cavalry tried to attack the Duke of Wellington in their front.

After the battle described, the battalion pursued the enemy for a number of hours then bivouacked and rested. On the morning of the 19th, the battalion went back over the battlefield and started the march to Paris. Due to my advanced age my memory is weakened and as I am not able to copy the plan I had to limit myself to these notes.

With high regard, most obediently

F MARBURG, CAPTAIN
8TH LINE BATTALION OF THE FORMER KGL

---

1 Marburg is numbered 701 in Beamish. He joined the Legion in 1806, serving in the Baltic and the Mediterranean in 1808–14, before serving in the Waterloo campaign. Nothing is recorded of his later life.

2 Hermannsburg is some 60 km north of Hanover.

3 Colonel Ompteda commanded the 2nd KGL Brigade.

4 Lieuenant Colonel John Christopher von Schröeder of the 2nd Line Battalion KGL numbered 1018 in Beamish, commanded the 8th Line Battalion at Waterloo. He joined the Legion in 1803, serving in the Baltic, the Mediterranean in 1808–14 and the Waterloo campaign. He died on 22 June 1815 from wounds he received at Waterloo.

5 It is often stated that the 8th Battalion was decimated in this attack. This is clearly a gross exaggeration as Beamish records that the battalion received casualties of 31 officers and men killed and 84 officers and men wounded from an original total of 489 (24%). This is far from a crippling loss when compared with many other units in the battle.

No. 169 Captain Christopher Bernhard Bertram[1]
Burgwedel, 25 February 1835

ADD MS 34705, FO 250

Original in German

Dear Sir
I have the honour to respond to your esteemed letter and the enclosed plan.

I have noted along the plan approximately where the 8th Line Battalion KGL was situated at 7 o'clock in the evening, as well as the position of the enemy cavalry, which may have been approximately two to three squadrons in strength. Of these I have only noted two squadrons on the plan. I am not able to give you information about the strength of enemy artillery and infantry, as they would have been at 7 o'clock, because the trees hid them.

At the commencement of the battle at Waterloo, the enemy cavalry/cuirassiers emplaced themselves at the corner of the garden of the farm La Haye Sainte.

We formed a square.

Soon thereafter, they commenced to attack our square, which was answered with well-placed gunfire, and they were forced to retreat with losses, where upon they regrouped in their previous position. They made a second attempt sometime later, but met with the same fate as the time before.

The farm of La Haye Sainte was occupied by the 2nd Light Battalion. How the farm was attacked by the enemy I cannot say, except that in my opinion it was at about 5 o'clock that the enemy took the farm, whereby the 2nd Light Battalion fired all its munitions. We thereupon received orders from His Royal Majesty, the Crown Prince of Orange, if I am not mistaken, who commanded the 1st Corps, to retake the farm. We formed a line and advanced rapidly.[2] As soon as we had advanced somewhat, the enemy cuirassiers attacked our right wing at a gallop, too quickly for us to form a square, and they inflicted a considerable defeat on us. But soon thereafter the English Horse Guards arrived and drove them back, when they once again took up their position at the corner of the garden. The English cavalry again took their position behind us. We had retreated somewhat, and we reformed, and took up our previous position once again. However, we had lost so many men that we were only able to reform a square at 7 o'clock made up of two files/ranks,[3] and we were very exposed to enemy fire from the farm and the garden. At 7:30 we received orders to form a line and to advance – as soon as the enemy cuirassiers saw this, they charged in full gallop. We advanced only as far as the garden and drove the enemy before us as far as Belle Alliance, where we bivouacked for the night.

I would very much like to say more about the movements, etc., of the enemy, as well as about our own, that took place during the battle in the proximity of the 8th Battalion, but the farm lay between us, which makes that impossible; and then again, I cannot say much about our side because I was only a lieutenant, and as the Captain von Westernhagen[4] was killed, I commanded a company, and so I was unable to pay attention to other troops.

Nor can I give you information about how the ground and fields near the house were planted and farmed, because it was so devastated that one could not even tell whether the land had been ploughed, was lying fallow, or had been planted. Nor did I pay much

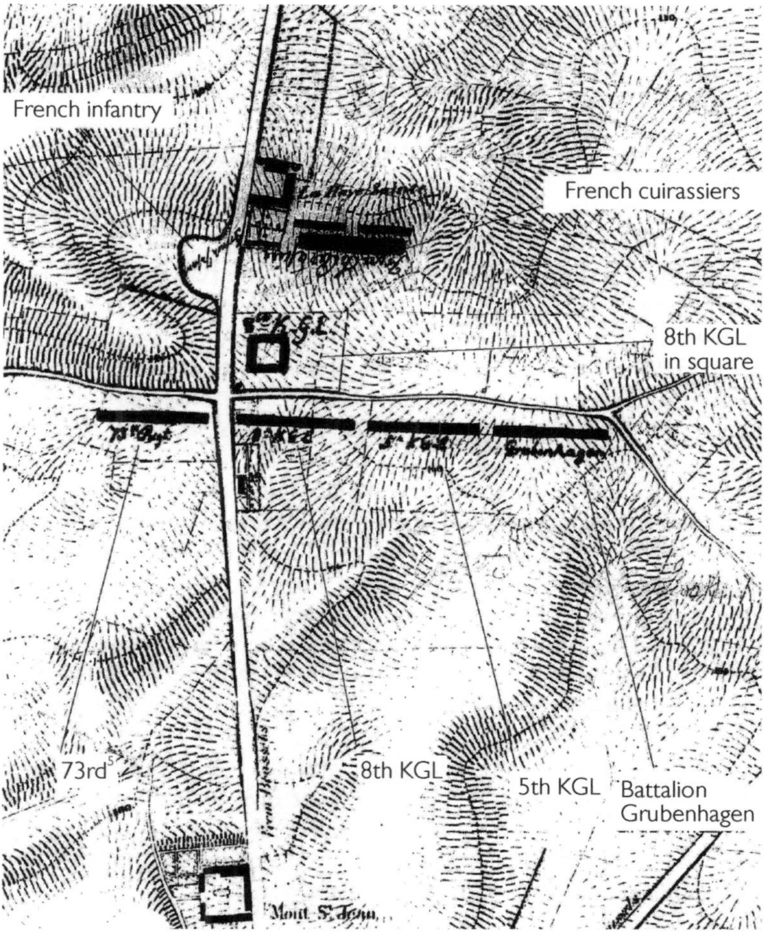

attention that day to such things, and almost 20 years have passed, and so much has been forgotten.

It has been my honour, respectfully, Your Excellency, obediently yours,

C B BERTRAM, CAPTAIN

---

1 Bertram is listed as number 716 in Beamish. He had originally joined the KGL as a cadet or NCO in 1811 and had served with the 8th in the Mediterranean and then the Netherlands. He went on the retired list as a brevet captain.

2 This is the second occasion on which the Prince of Orange ordered a battalion forward in line to retake La Haye Sainte. This attack, just like the earlier one of Ompteda with the 5th Battalion was rolled up by a flank attack by waiting cuirassiers. It is noticeable that the German troops also blamed the Prince for these catastrophic orders.

3 The squares were usually formed four men deep; the losses of the battalion forced them to form a much weaker two deep formation.

4 Captain Thilo von Westernhagen listed as number 992 in Beamish. He had joined the

regiment in May 1806 and had served in the Baltic, the Mediterranean and Netherlands. He was killed at Waterloo.

5 This is a mistake; it should be the 79th.

No. 170 Ensign Frederick Dorndorf[1]
Osnabruck, 4 May 1835

ADD MS 34705, FO 247

Original in German

Memorandum regarding the position of the 8th Line Battalion KGL at the battle of Waterloo.

The 8th Line Battalion originally stood behind the post road that runs in front of La Haye Sainte and branches from the road that runs from Brussels to Genappe and then to the right to Hougoumont and Braine L'Alleud. The battalion had its left wing touching the Brussels road, and the 5th Battalion KGL to its right; to its left on the other side of the road was the 73rd Regiment.[2]

After this initial deployment and after the battalion had crossed the post road in order to drive back the enemy infantry,[3] which pushed forward from La Haye Sainte, it was run down by enemy cuirassiers and driven back across the post road, where it gathered itself together and took up its original position.

On the plan,[4] all designated battalions are in their positions as of 7:30 in the evening, where the attack by the French Guards on the English right wing was repelled, remained there, and only then pressed forward with the entire army in order to drive the enemy to the other side of [La] Belle Alliance, where it remained when the Prussians took over the pursuit.

The model goes up to the moment of the battle, the four Battalions marked on the plan were formed as shown, just as the position of the enemy infantry and cavalry is correctly given at the time mentioned near La Haye Sainte. The square that is drawn in on the plan in blue pen is not to be removed from the right centre.

The 8th Battalion was situated in a barley field.

F DORNDORF

1 Dorndorf is numbered in Beamish as number 722. He joined the Corps as an NCO serving in the Baltic and the Mediterranean until 1812. He seems to have received a commission and transferred to the Peninsula in 1812. He then served in the Netherlands in 1814 and the Waterloo campaign. He received the King William Cross. He became a captain and quartermaster in the 2nd Hanoverian Dragoons.

2 This is a mistake, the 79th was stationed across the road; the 73rd was actually further to his right beyond the 5th KGL.

3 This refers to a question that Siborne found difficult to reconcile and thus he sent many enquiries to officers to clarify the event. The claim by the KGL troops that they joined the attack on D'Erlon's Corps is difficult to knit with the statements of the cavalrymen, who stated that no German infantry were in their front, but here again Dorndorf states that they did cross over. No clear answer has been achieved.

4 The plan no longer appears to be extant.

FOURTH DIVISION

4th Infantry Brigade

The14th Regiment, 3rd Battalion

No. 171 Captain William Ross[1]
Manchester, 18 January 1836

ADD MS 34706, FO 1

Sir,
In acknowledging the receipt of your letter of the 3rd instant, the plan of the field of Waterloo is herewith returned.

I have marked thereon with pencil the position I occupied with the Light Company 14th Regiment from an early hour until the close of the action – having been thus detailed from the battalion under the command of Lt Colonel Keyt 51st Light Infantry.[2] I suggest that I have not the means of giving answers to your questions.

I am Sir, your most obedient humble servant

W ROSS
MAJOR 23RD FOOT

---

1 Ross had joined the army as an ensign in 1804 and served in India from 1805–09. Afterwards he became a lieutenant colonel in the 23rd. Two other letters of his were published by Siborne (numbers 133 & 134).

2 Keyt was born in Wendlebury, Oxfordshire and joined the 51st as an ensign in 1800. He served in the Kandyan War (Ceylon 1803), in the Peninsula in 1808–9, Walcheren in 1809 and the Peninsula again in 1811–14. He received a severe wound in the arm on the height of Lezaca. Dalton confirms that Captain Keyt commanded the Light Companies of the 51st, 14th and 23rd at Waterloo. For this command he became a brevet lieutenant colonel and CB. Appointed Lieutenant Colonel of the 84th Foot in 1828, he died in Jamaica in 1835.

The 23rd Fusiliers

No. 172 Major Thomas Dalmer[1]
Paris, 27 December 27 1834

ADD MS 34704, FO 104

Addressed to First Lieutenant Enoch[2]

Dear Enoch,

After a lapse of nearly twenty years I find the enclosed application of Lieutenant Siborne to be rather out of date and having left in England such notes as I had made relative to Waterloo I really cannot venture to offer him my assistance in a direct manner through fear that my memory may prove treacherous. I therefore refer the matter to you in the probability that you may have preserved documents that may enable you to elucidate the subject in question.

With respect to the query No. 1 – the general answer may be that the 23rd Royal Welch Fusiliers was formed in square, having a Brigade of infantry (composed of I know not at this moment what regiments[3]) between it and the Guards in Hougoumont on its right, and close on its left a brigade, or more, of artillery.

The 3rd Battalion 14th Regiment, and the 57th Regiment were detached, as I believe, to support the light companies of the brigade which had been sent to the right of Hougoumont to oppose the enemy in that direction, so that the Welch Fusiliers was the only regiment of the brigade in the position that I have described.

As Mr Lindsay, the friend of Lieut. Siborne, appears to be in the Commander in Chief's office you will in all probability be in acquaintance with him, therefore you can readily communicate to him your ideas on the matter for the information of Mr. Siborne.

Believe me to remain, dear Enoch, very faithfully yours

THOMAS DALMER

Although in France I take the opportunity of adhering to a good old English custom of wishing you much happiness and all the usual compliments of the season.

1 Dalmer joined the army as an ensign in 1797 and served in Egypt and the Peninsula. He received a General Service Medal with two bars for Egypt and Corunna and a Gold Medal with bar for Salamanca and Vittoria where he commanded a light battalion. Dalmer had a horse shot under him at Waterloo and would have assumed command of the regiment following the severe wounding of Lieutenant Colonel Sir Henry Ellis during the battle. Afterwards Lieutenant General, CB, and Colonel-in-Chief of the 47th Foot. He died on 25 August 1854.

2 First Lieutenant John Enoch, Adjutant of the 23rd born in Camarthen, had joined the army as a 2nd lieutenant in 1809 and served at Walcheren and in the Peninsula in 1810–13. He received a General Service Medal with four bars for Albuera (slightly wounded), Badajoz, Ciudad Rodrigo and Salamanca (severely wounded). Afterwards he rose to colonel half pay in 1854 and died in London on 13 July 1855.

3 Probably Colonel du Plat's 1st Brigade of the King's German Legion.

The 51st Regiment

No. 173 Captain James Campbell[1]

Belfast, 25 August[2]

ADD MS 34706, FO 1513

My dear Sir

Having had a consultation with all the Waterloo officers present with the regiment. I send you our answers and opinions as to the points of your note, *to the best of our belief.*

Letter no. 173

I shall be most happy at any time to answer any question as far as my recollection goes.

Believe me, yours very truly

J CAMPBELL

1st Question	*Answer*
Whether, when the General advance took place, the 51st in extended order moved forward along with a portion of the Guard and Brunswickers, 'by *the right of Hougoumont*, and if so whether you met with any and what kind of resistance. Whether any Allied troops, Infantry or cavalry passed you, how far you advanced and such.	If by the General advance is meant that which took place about 7 o'clock in the evening. The 51st moved by the right of Hougoumont into the orchard where it bivouacked for the night. At that time it met with no resistance, the enemy having retired. Small parties of Prussian cavalry passed us in pursuit of the enemy, supposed to be the advance of a body of cavalry which passed afterwards, moving upon the Nivelles road.
I am doubtful about the position of the 14th Regiment but think it must have been near where I have placed it.	As far as we can form an opinion, the 14th Regiment appears to be placed in its proper position, but of this we cannot speak with certainty, as we advanced and left them early in the day.
With respect to the place of the Abatis.[4]	There being a difference of opinion with respect to the actual place of the abatis, we cannot answer this question, but we are inclined to think it was not *so* far in the rear as where it is placed.

1 Campbell joined the army as an ensign in 1799, serving in Ceylon in 1803 and the Peninsula in 1809 and 1811–15. He received a General Service Medal with five bars for Corunna, Vittoria, Pyrenees, Nivelle and Orthes. He was promoted to Major in 1821 and Lieutenant Colonel in 1831 and retired on half pay in 1838, becoming KH and Major General in 1854. He died at Breslington on 8 May 1856.

2 No date, but probably between 1836 and 1838.

3 The questions and answers unusually precede the short introductory letter which is the one listed by the British Library as F152.

4 This alludes to the position of the abatis placed on the Nivelles road, not the ones usually referred to at La Haye Sainte.

FIFTH DIVISION

No. 174 Colonel H. Mansel[1]

Limerick, 9 December 1842

(Not at Waterloo)

ADD MS 34707, FO 515

My dear Siborne

After writing to you by the last post, I met Price of the Horse Artillery,[2] whose brother was ADC to Sir Thomas Picton at Waterloo[3] and he at once stated that Sir Thomas was wounded on the 16th[4] and referred me to Robinson's *Life of Picton*,[5] an extract from which I enclose.

I really have not the most distant recollections of ever hearing any of his family mention this circumstance and if you wish it, I will still write for further information on this subject, or if you like, I will send on [to] you the book, 2 vols., Robinson's *Memoirs of Picton*.

Most truly yours

H L MANSEL

1 The identity of this officer is problematical. The initials seem certain, but there is no officer of this name listed in Hart's Army List for 1840. There is however a Lieutenant Colonel John Mansel listed, who served in the West Indies, including the captures of St Lucia and Trinidad, and in the Peninsula in 1811–12 and in 1814. He was involved there in the reduction of the forts at Salamanca, and the battles of Salamanca and Toulouse. I cannot however bring these two together.

2 Probably First Lieutenant Edward Price RA.

3 Captain B. Price of the 50th Foot. He was evidently on half pay in 1815, but served at Waterloo as an extra aide de camp. He was not recorded as having been wounded but died soon afterwards in London on 21 January 1816.

4 This establishes with certainty that Picton was wounded at Quatre Bras but concealed his wound to continue in command until his death at Waterloo.

5 H.B. Robinson's two-volume work was published in London in 1836, entitled *Memoirs and Correspondence of General Sir T. Picton.*

No. 175 Captain The Honourable Charles Gore, 85th Foot, Aide de Camp to Sir James Kempt[1]

Montreal, 23 September 1842

ADD MS 34707, FO 426

Sir

I enclose three sketches of the ground and positions occupied by Kempt's brigade.

Letter no. 175

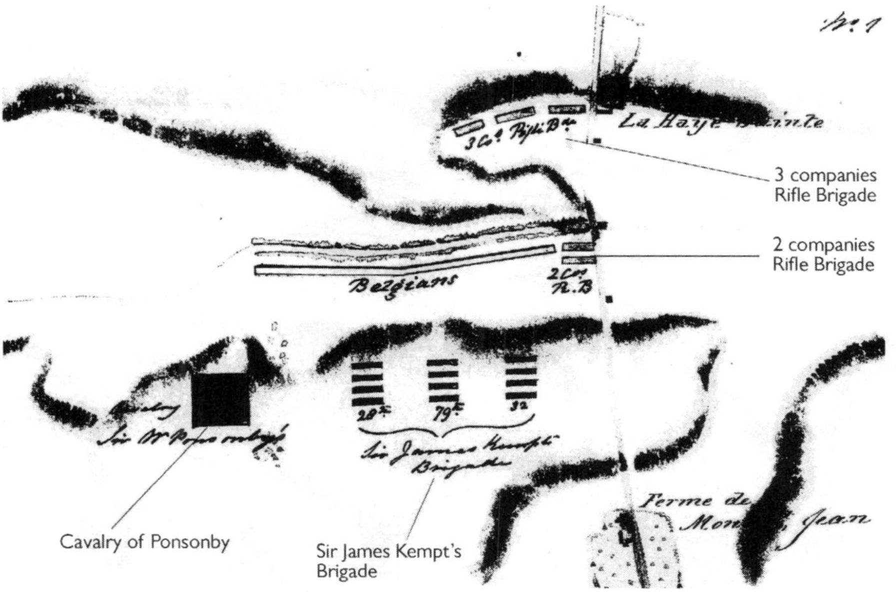

In no.1 the Belgians under General Perponcher[2] were in line by the hedge but ere the first grand attack they gave way – when Sir James Kempt's brigade let them through, formed line, advanced to the hedge as in no. 2, arrested the French column and drove them down the slope and formed squares, returned to their position and formed line as in no. 2.

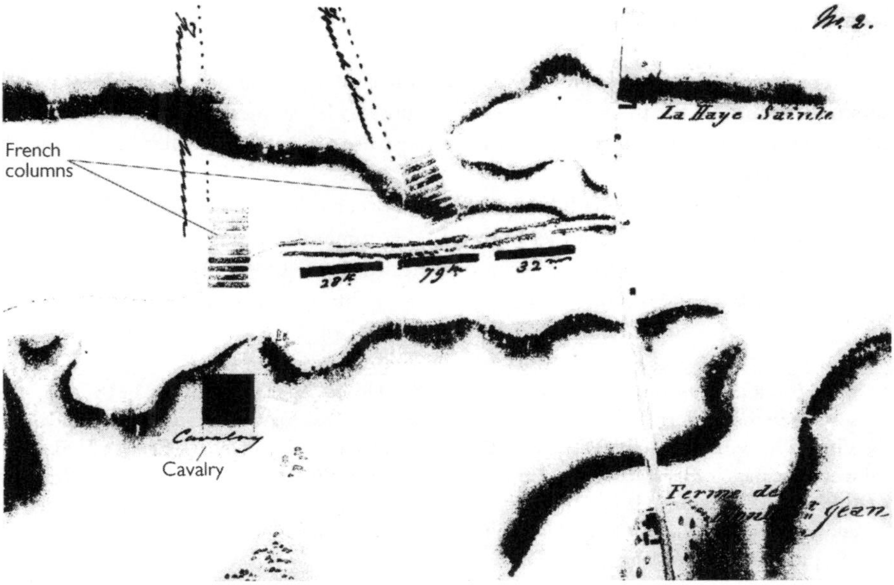

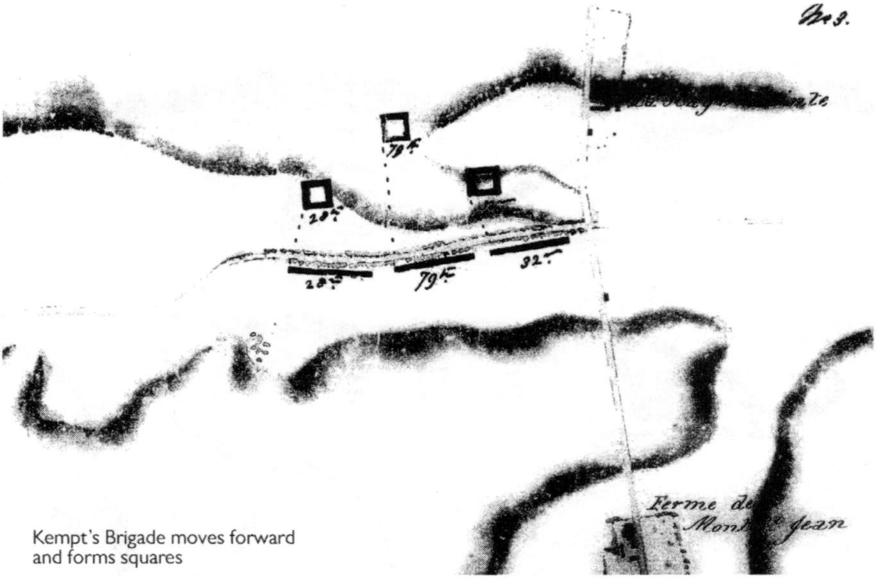

Kempt's Brigade moves forward and forms squares

A French column had passed the road just after the column opposed to Kempt's brigade were defeated and marched direct to Sir William Ponsonby's brigade of cavalry, which charged into them and drove them back.[3]

Pack's brigade had formed line and were also advancing but being more retired than we were did not reach the road so soon. Kempt's brigade was commanded by Sir William Belson[4] of the 28th, as General Picton was killed in attempting to rally the Belgians, which was immediately reported to Sir J. Kempt as he directed line to be formed from column and to advance, so that we reached the hedge at the same time as the enemy.

Kempt's brigade had its right within a few yards of the road not on it. The ground was not favourable for them and we had only time to form line and advance, I cannot recollect the exact position of the 95th after they were driven in[5] but when we advanced they did so also.

The 1st and 6th Battalions KGL[6] was on the other side of the road and I am quite sure from what I know of Colonel Baring who commanded them, that he would have let no opportunity slip of doing mischief to the attack of the enemy upon us.

I have the honour to be, Sir, your most humble servant

CHARLES GORE

---

1 Gore had joined the 6th Foot as an ensign in 1808. He exchanged to the 43rd in 1811 serving in the Peninsula. ADC to Sir Andrew Barnard at Salamanca and to Sir J. Kempt at Vittoria he remained in this capacity until Waterloo. He received a General Service Medal with nine bars for Ciudad Rodrigo, Badajoz, Salamanca, Vittoria, Pyrenees, Nivelle, Nive, Orthes and Toulouse. He had three horses killed beneath him at Waterloo. Made GCB, KH and afterwards General, Colonel of the 6th Foot and Lieutenant Governor of Chelsea Hospital, he died on 4 September 1869.

2 Lieutenant General Baron Perponcher commanded the 2nd Dutch Division, only the 1st

Brigade of Major General Bijlandt was stationed in line in front of Picton's troops, the 2nd Brigade was stationed further to the left at Papelotte. This is particularly interesting as it shows that Bijlandt's Belgians *were* formed behind the hedges at the time of the attack rather than on the forward slope, which remains a persistent claim. Secondly and more importantly, it shows the Belgians forming a long line at the hedge with Kempt's Brigade forming in reserve. This gives the Belgians adequate room to deploy (see John Hussey's article 'Bylandt's Brigade at Waterloo' (*The British Army Review* 129, Spring 2002, pp 78–86) regarding their frontage appearing to be too small for the number of troops). It also ties in perfectly with British memoirs which describe the Belgians falling back through them, which could only happen if they were deployed *behind* them.

3 This is a notable statement as it infers that the column passed the road before being charged by the cavalry, however, all other witnesses state that they did not reach the road. If this statement were correct, it would immediately pose the question as to how the French columns were caught unprepared and ridden over, as Gore's testimony would have put them firmly in the rear of the crest, where the advance of the cavalry would be clearly observed.

4 Lieutenant Colonel Sir Charles P. Belson KCB of the 28th Regiment took command of the 8th Brigade following Picton's death with Major General Sir James Kempt taking command of the 5th Division. Belson had served throughout the Peninsular war with the 28th. Afterwards he became Lieutenant Colonel of the 56th Foot and a major general in 1819. He died at Blackheath on 5 November 1830.

5 They were pushed back from the sand pit and knoll to the sunken road.

6 This is a mistake by Gore, the 1st Battalion was in Colonel du Plat's 1st KGL Brigade and the 6th Battalion was not at Waterloo at all. Colonel Baron Ompteda commanded the 2nd KGL Brigade which as part of Alten's 3rd Division was stationed just to the right of the cross roads. The KGL units here would have been the 1st Light Battalion and the 5th and 8th Line Battalions. Major Baring with the 2nd Light Battalion and other detachments commanded the defence of La Haye Sainte and was occupied there at the time of the cavalry charge. See his letters (numbers 163–165).

Eighth Brigade

The 28th Regiment

No. 176 Captain Charles Cadell[1]

Edinburgh, 30 April 1835

ADD MS 34705, FO 217

Sir,

I am sorry to state that when your letter with the plan of Waterloo came here, I was in London busying with the narrative of the 28th[2] and was expected to return any day, and when I did come I found my brother was from home who had charge of all my letters and I only got the plan the day before yesterday. I have traced the position of the 28th as well as my recollection will admit after so long a period, imperfect as it is I hope it will be of use to you, but really a platoon officer can make very few observations, as the face of our position changes every moment, perhaps you may be able to get some truer information than mine.

I have the honour to be, Sir, your most obedient servant

CHARLES CADELL
LIEUTENANT COLONEL

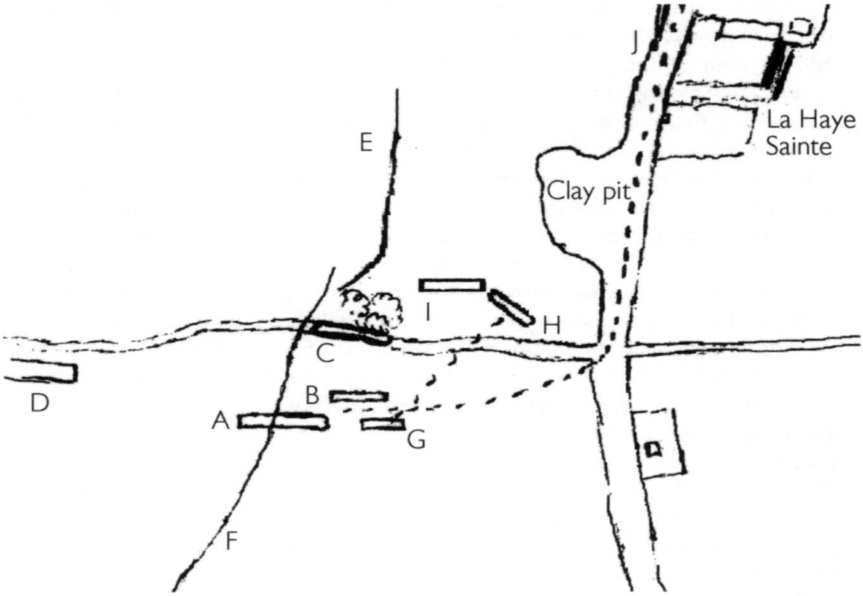

Notes to Sketch

A Night of the 17th in a cornfield or wheat.

B Position at the beginning of the action.

C About 1 or ½ past 1 – when the 28th in the rear of La Haye Sainte, checking with the bayonet and musketry, a heavy French column that was charged shortly after by the heavy cavalry. After which they moved to the rear of the hill and lay down to avoid the heavy cannonade, with the skirmishing in front. Which was maintained until the last advance of the enemy at about 7 pm, when we were moved up across the lane in front of La Haye Sainte and forming obliquely on the right of the 79th, threw in a flank fire on their advancing columns on the other side of the Grand Chaussee, and after their total defeat wheeled up into line and moved forward with the general advance.

D 2nd Brigade 5th Division.

E Route of French column attacking.

F Charge of Heavy cavalry.

G Retired and laying down, under cover of the hill, and sending out skirmishers in front.

H About 7 pm pouring in a flank fire on the enemies last advance.

I 79th

J Final advance.

1 At the close of Waterloo, Cadell commanded the regiment as the major and all of the seven other captains were killed or wounded. Cadell had been born near Edinburgh in 1789 and joined the 28th as an ensign in 1804. He served at Copenhagen, the Corunna campaign, Walcheren, Gibraltar (including Barossa), and in the Peninsula in 1811–14. He received a General Service Medal with eight bars for Corunna, Barossa (slightly wounded), Vittoria, Pyrenees, Nivelle, Nive, Orthes and Toulouse. He became a major in 1826 going on half pay in 1833, eventually becoming a lieutenant colonel on the retired list in 1866.

2 Cadell was completing his *Narrative of the Campaigns of the 28th Regt. From 1802 to 1832* which was published in London in 1835.

No. 177 From the same
Longniddry,[1] 28 March 1837

ADD MS 34706, FO 282

Sir,

I beg to acknowledge your letter of the 3rd and should have answered it long since but I have been endeavouring to find some plans and a circular of interesting memorandum I left at home in '29. I am sorry to say, I can't find them, if I had they might have been of some use to you.

The sketch you enclosed of Quatre Bras is very imperfect, the cross roads is too near the village. Where we went off the road to the right the corn was so high that the only points we had to direct us were the horses of the mounted officers. I shall do anything I can to recover the papers when I will write you.

With regard to Waterloo, I think that the 79th[2] was to our left, after the attack of D'Erlon's, I am certain the Cuirassiers attacked the 28th, I think it was to the close of the fight that the 28th brought up their left also marching to throw a flank fire into a Column that was opposing us. I expect to be in Dublin the beginning of May when I may be able to find you some information. I will keep the sketch in case I may find the lost papers.

I have the honour to be, Sir, your most obedient humble servant

CHARLES CADELL

LT. COLONEL UNATTACHED

1 Longniddry lies approximately 5 miles east of Edinburgh.

2 The 79th Foot were in the 8th Brigade with the 28th.

No. 178 Ensign Thomas William Blewett Mountsteven[1]
Undated

ADD MS 34707, FO 109[2]

Battle of Waterloo, 18th June 1815

The rain continued to fall in torrents until a little before 8 o'clock am when the weather began to clear up. About half past 10 o'clock, the enemy were observed falling in, and soon after in movement to commence the attack. To wait his approach the regiments of the 5th Division (Picton's) were ordered to form into close columns at deploying distance. The enemy continued to advance in columns, under cover of a tremendous cannonade, which was answered by our *artillery* with great spirit. A body of Belgian infantry[3] which had been posted some distance in front fled on the enemy's approach and were *honoured* with hisses and cries of shame in passing our troops. The 8th Brigade (Kempt's consisting of 95th Rifles, 32nd, 79th and 28th Regiments) then deployed into line and advanced close to the division guns, lined a road which ran along the summit of the ridge having a hedge on each side. The 9th Brigade (Pack's consisting of the 1st, 42nd, 44th and 92nd Regiments) were in reserve in the second line. The light companies descended into the valley and maintained a severe contest against superior numbers, being at last obliged to retire by the advance of a strong column of the enemy towards the left of the 79th and right of the 28th, a close engagement followed with the line, of warm and obstinate duration, but of lasting honour to the 8th Brigade. The enemy were charged and routed; and a Brigade of cavalry (Ponsonby's consisting of 1st, 2nd and 6th Dragoons[4]) coming up, intervals were made for them, they *gallantly* charged past us, surrounded the flying column and took the whole prisoners, it was at this period of the action that General Picton was killed. A body of the enemy's cavalry which had come to the support of their infantry having now been perceived in our front, the 79th Highlanders advanced about fifty paces and formed square. The enemy having been repulsed, the 79th were soon after ordered to retire to this former position, and again lined the hedge nearest the enemy, and were sufficiently occupied by his advanced troops in front.

UNSIGNED

---

1 Mountsteven is recorded as being wounded at Waterloo. He became a lieutenant in 1820, captain in 1835 and then paymaster of the 79th Highlanders in 1836. He went on half pay in 1847.

2 The British Library records Lieutenant Riach of the 79th Foot as the author of this letter. However, the handwriting is clearly not that of Riach. The covering letter of Riach (not printed) mentions enclosing material from Mountsteven. I have therefore assumed that this is the author of the memorandum. Mountsteven also has a letter printed in Siborne (number 151).

3 Major General Graf van Bijlandt's 1st Netherlands Brigade. There has been a myth in existence ever since the battle that this brigade remained on the front slope and suffered heavily for this error. There is much evidence that the brigade was actually moved back in the morning to line the hedge on the road, where they lay down to avoid suffering too heavily from the fire of the grand battery, until the French columns approached. It would appear that the part of the brigade directly in front of the column fired raggedly then broke, but adjoining units appear to have stood and poured in a withering fire from the flanks.

4 The Union Brigade.

The 32nd Regiment

No. 179 Captain John Crowe[1]
Bideford, Devonshire, may 10th 1837

ADD MS 34706, FO 320

Sir

In reply to your letter of the 1st instant I beg leave to state as well as my recollection can assist me, the situation of the 32nd Regiment at Quatre Bras on the 16th June 1815 during the time I was with it.

The 5th Division to which the 32nd Regiment was attached was halted on the Brussels side of Quatre Bras close to the village about 3 o'clock on the 16th June - soon afterwards it moved to the front of the village keeping the Lasne road.[2] Upon this road the 32nd Regiment was halted and remained in line with its rear to [the] hamlet for at least half an hour, in its front was corn fields and rather hilly.

Sir James Kempt appeared from the highest part of the Brigades front and called out for the marksmen of the 32nd. I moved my company, being the light company, to the rising ground where the General was. He said pointing to his rear 'Here they are Sir, extend your company as fast as you can and drive them back.'

I led the advance close up to the hedge which was thickly lined with their light troops and we were forced to retire for a few minutes, we again advanced and drove the enemy through the gaps in the hedge but they were so numerous that we were again compelled to retire. In the rear of this hedge there were several columns of the French and clouds of light troops. Sir James Kempt's brigade was in our rear about 500 yards and the 32nd was ordered to send out detachments of sections to reinforce my company, almost as soon as they arrived I was wounded and obliged to leave the field. When I moved my company to the front the 32nd Regiment was the only one upon the road. At the time it detached sections to reinforce me it was in our rear as I have before stated about 500 yards in column of quarter distance, with the other regiments of the brigade.

I hope that this feeble attempt of mine at this distant period of time may be of service to you in the arduous task you have undertaken. Wishing you every success.

I have the honour to be, Sir, your most obedient servant

JOHN CROWE
LT COLONEL

---

1 Crowe joined the army as an ensign in 1800. He served in the Peninsula from 1811 and received a General Service Medal with two bars for Salamanca and Orthes. Afterwards he went on half pay in 1826 and became a lieutenant colonel in 1837 and KH. He died at Fairlea Villa, Bideford, in March 1860.

2 The road towards Ligny and the Lasne stream.

The 79th Highlanders

No. 180 Lieutenant Colonel Neil Douglas[1]

Broughty near Dundee, 22 November 1834

ADD MS 34703, FO 309

Sir

I have the honour to acknowledge the receipt and to thank you for your letter of the 17th instant containing a plan of your model of the field of Waterloo.

In reply I beg to inform you that the particular formation of the 79th Regiment about 7 o'clock on the 18th of June 1815 when the French Imperial Guards made their attack, was in line, and that in this order the regiment charged a column, which from all the evidence I have been able to obtain was comprised of that description of troops,[2] and which being already broken and in confusion was again charged by Sir William Ponsonby's brigade of heavy cavalry, the 79th in the mean time wheeled back into column of companies to allow them to pass through.

As you invite remarks I take the liberty also of mentioning that the 79th was the only one of the Highland regiments that was in the front line during both the actions of the 16th and 18th, and that this circumstance will account for their having more killed and wounded than any other battalion.[3] I herewith return your plan but I do not observe upon it the pencil marks you describe, this is however of the less consequence, as from my having been severely wounded on the 16th, I was not present on the 18th consequently I could not be of much use in ascertaining the correctness of your information with regard to the troops, but what I do give you on the other side must be significantly correct as I received it a few days after the battle from officers of the Regiment who were actually present and fully confirm their disorder.

I have the honour to be, Sir, your most humble servant

NEIL DOUGLAS, COLONEL

---

1 Born in Glasgow in 1783, Douglas joined the 21st Foot as an ensign in 1801 and rapidly advanced through a number of regiments (9th Foot 1802, 42nd Foot 1803, 95th Foot 1803), before becoming a captain in the 79th having raised a quota of men. He served at Copenhagen, the Corunna campaign and the Peninsula and received a General Service Medal with two bars for Corunna and Busaco (wounded by balls through the left shoulder and arm) and a Gold Medal for The Pyrenees, Nivelle, Nive and Toulouse. He was wounded in the right knee at Quatre Bras. Afterwards he became Lieutenant General Sir Neil Douglas, KCB, KMT, KStV and KCH. Colonel-in-Chief of 78th Highlanders, he died in September 1853.

2 He describes troops of the French Imperial Guard, which is obviously a mistake.

3 Losses at Quatre Bras are listed as 1 officer and 28 men killed, 16 officers, 10 sergeants and 248 men wounded. Losses recorded for Waterloo are 2 officers, 2 sergeants and 27 men killed and 11 officers, 7 sergeants and 126 men wounded or missing. A total of 478 casualties over the three days, from an effective strength of 703 men; a casualty rate of some 68%, confirming the 79th as a serious candidate for the highest losses by any British regiment in the campaign.

The 95th Rifles, 1st Battalion

No. 181 First Lieutenant John Gardiner[1]

Boyle,[2] Saturday 14 May 1842

ADD MS 34707, FO 361

By J. Slater Esq.[3]

My Dear Siborne

Many thanks for your kind note forwarding on the official confirming the exchange.

I shall be happy in being able to afford you any information for your history of Waterloo. Gardiner (who is a nice old fellow) will call at your office when he goes up to Dublin where he proposes remaining for a week with his brother who is in the 8th.[4]

However the little information I have got from him I here give you.

He tells me he was with the companies of the 95th in advance on the knoll[5] behind the sand pit but was drawn in before Picton's division was attacked; that when Picton's division was attacked by the French columns of infantry the 95th were on the right of the 32nd, the right flank of the 95th resting on the great road.

The 95th charged in line with Kempt's brigade, Kempt leading the 32nd. Gardiner appears perfectly conversant in all your enquiries and will be of service in giving you information for your work which I feel assured will be a most valuable one.

Believe me, yours very sincerely

J SLATER

---

1 Gardiner had served in the Peninsula and was wounded at Badajoz. He received a General Service Medal with six bars for Vittoria, Pyrenees, Nivelle, Nive, Orthes and Toulouse. He was severely wounded at Waterloo. Afterwards a captain and brevet major in the 82nd Regiment. He died at Jock's House, Kinnoull, on 18 June 1852.

2 Boyle is approximately 10 miles south of Sligo in Ireland.

3 Possibly John Slater who had joined the army as an ensign in 1814 and served in the Peninsula.

4 Captain David Gardiner, who had joined the Army as an Ensign in 1811 and rose to Captain in the 8th Foot in 1837.

5 A small rise near the crossroads.

9th Infantry Brigade

The 1st or Royal Scots Regiment, 3rd Battalion

No. 182 Lieutenant John Stoyte[1]

Kinsale, 19 November 1834

ADD MS 34703, FO254

Sir,

I beg to acknowledge the receipt of your letter requesting information respecting the particular position occupied by the 3rd Battalion 1st Foot about 7 pm 18th June '15. The length of time which has passed; not having been on the ground since, and having been at the time, from the evening of the 16th on a detached duty, render it impossible for me to afford you the information you desire with the precision I could wish. I have also lost by shipwreck my journals and notes by which I might refresh my memory. The battalion suffered so heavily on the 16th, that it was much injured on the 18th[2] – and on the morning of the 19th when leavers[3] and all others were collected we could only muster 120 men.

As well as I can recollect the ploughed land on the right, and a little in rear of La Haye Sainte was the position of the battalion at 7 pm being in line the 28th Regiment on the left, the line advancing. The enemy retiring rather in confusion, but not very hurried.

I shall make every enquiry to afford you any information likely to assist in the interesting work you have undertaken.

Lieutenant Symes[4] on half pay, late of the 1st Foot now residing somewhere in the Co. Wicklow, will, if you can discover his address, afford you much assistance. Lt. Lane[5] Barrack Master, Clonmel, might also afford assistance, he was wounded but whether on 16th or 18th I cannot say, but I think Mr Symes would be more likely if you can find him, to afford assistance than *any other individual.* Captain Ingram[6] and Black[7] 1st Foot Regiment if at home could also.

I have the honour to be, Sir, your most humble servant

J STOYTE
CAPTAIN 24TH FOOT

---

1 Stoyte was born at Carlow in Ireland in 1795 joining the 1st as an ensign in 1811 and received a General Service Medal with two bars for Badajoz and Salamanca. He was severely wounded at Salamanca while carrying the colours, the staff being broken; he lost a finger on his left hand and was injured in the breast. He was wounded in the right hand and taken prisoner at Bergen-op-Zoom in 1814. He was shipwrecked in 1830 but survived to become a major in the 24th Foot and died at Bath on 13 December 1854.

2 Stoyte states that he was on detached duty from the 16th, but was back with the regiment on the 18th as he was wounded at Waterloo.

3 Those absent with leave.

4 Joseph Symes is recorded as being wounded at Waterloo; he was reduced with the battalion in 1817.

5 George Lane is recorded as being wounded at Waterloo; he was reduced with the battalion in 1817.

6 John Ingram was a lieutenant at the time of the battle and is recorded as having been wounded at Waterloo. He remained with the regiment and was made a captain in 1825. No records of him exist after this date.

7 John Lewis Black had joined the army as an ensign in 1813 and had been called off the half pay list of the 49th Foot to serve with the 1st at Waterloo, where he was slightly wounded. Afterwards he became a lieutenant colonel in the 53rd Foot and died on 3 February 1859.

The 44th Regiment, 2nd Battalion

No. 183 The Reverend Edward T. Gregory, Rector and Vicar of Kilmore-Meath[1]

Paget Priory, Post Town Kilcock,[2] 8 November 1842

(Not at Waterloo)

ADD MS 34707, FO 460

Sir,

I have this moment had the honour of receiving your letter of yesterday.

I have not seen the statement to which you allude and am ignorant as to what paper it appeared in;* but the colours of the old 2nd Battalion 44th[3] being in my possession is a matter of notoriety as they are unfurled in front of my house (which is commanded by the high road from Dublin to Summerhill and from Kilcock to Dunsgaughlin) on the anniversary of every action in which either that corps or the 38th[4] were engaged, and on the birthdays of my sovereign and her royal issue.

They were presented to me by his widow,[5] who has died within the last few weeks, as a gift in keeping with my unconcealed attachment to my original profession, having in early life had the honour of serving as ensign and lieutenant in the 38th under the command of my recent departed friend, the gallant Colonel Charles Greville, and being present in every affair (including the storming of San Sebastian) in which they were engaged from my joining, to my reduction by the peace, and had frequently the pleasure to stand piquet with your relative Captain Siborne[6] of the 9th, who I particularly remember; the 1st, 9th, 38th and 47th with the Corps of Brunswickers being brigaded together.[7]

My uncle Lt Colonel Edward Gregory died on the 12th July 1834, in London, from the consequences of a musket ball, received many years before in action, having worked up from the abdomen to the spine; owing to this wound, he sold out of the service of the regiment, being ordered to India, maintaining the rank of Lieutenant Colonel on the continent of Europe.

Illness prevented me seeing your far famed model when on exhibition in Dublin and I'm happy to find a new opportunity will be afforded me of doing so.

The history of which you have so obligingly forwarded me a prospectus, is a [dedication? sic] in the annals of our country. It should be in the library of every man who by the honours of the British army is now enabled to own 'Such a joyful testimony'.

I have the honour to be, Sir, your most obedient servant

E TIGHE GREGORY

* Should it chance to be in your office, perhaps you would have the kindness to forward it.

---

1 Gregory had served as an ensign in the 38th Foot throughout the latter years of the Peninsular war, receiving a General Service Medal with three bars for San Sebastian, Nivelle and Nive. It appears that following the Wars he, like many other veterans took holy orders.

2 Kilcock is approximately 10 miles west of Dublin.

3 The 2nd Battalion 44th was present at Quatre Bras and Waterloo, very nearly losing its King's colour at the former battle when attacked by lancers. It is pretty certain that it was not this colour, but the regimental colour that he possessed. See note 5 below.

4 The 38th did not serve in the Waterloo campaign remaining on garrison service in Ireland. This is somewhat surprising as the regiment had fought with some distinction throughout the Peninsula campaign and could have contributed many much needed battle hardened veterans to Wellington's line.

5 I have yet to discover who this officer was who had the colours from the campaign. The records of the regiment claim that the King's colour was held by Major General G. O'Malley CB who took command of the regiment when Colonel Hamerton was wounded at Quatre Bras. However O'Malley did not die until 1843 whereas the letter was written in 1842, therefore the colours given to the Reverend Gregory must have been the regimental colour. The only officer of the 44th who left a widow before 1842 was Captain Adam Brugh, the senior captain, who died in 1825. Presumably it was his widow that passed the colours on.

6 Captain Benjamin Siborne 9th Foot, his father. He had served with the regiment in the Corunna campaign, Walcheren and the Peninsula from 1810. He was severely wounded at

the Nivelle and these wounds led to his ultimate death. He initially recovered enough to serve in the defence of Canada, returning to Europe too late for Waterloo, but serving in the occupation of France. The regiment was then ordered to the West Indies, where he died at St Vincent on 14 July 1819.

7 Gregory's memory is slightly awry. All of the regiments he mentions were in the 5th Division, but formed different brigades. The 3/1st, 1/9th and 1/38th formed Hay's Brigade; the 1/4th, 2/47th and 2/59th formed Robinson's Brigade, these with two companies of Brunswick Oels and Spry's Portuguese Brigade formed Leith's 5th Division.

The 92nd Gordon Highlanders

No. 184 Lieutenant James Kerr Ross[1]
7 Windsor Street, Edinburgh, 25 November 1834

ADD MS 34703, FO 341

Sir,

I have been favoured with your letter and enclosure. If any communication I can make relative to the battle of Waterloo will tend to be of the least service to you in the praiseworthy undertaking in which you have embarked, it would afford me immense satisfaction, but I cannot promise to suppose any thing I can impart to you, can be of consequence, as per my rank, you will have received invaluable information from officers of more exalted ranks than I on that most memorable day told. Being quite a farming man and lieutenant in command of a company, I however after marching to Paris and after recovering from a wound in my right arm, took a few notes of the three days proceedings commencing from Quatre Bras on the 16th, and I shall then fully impart to you extracts from them relative to the 18th: as it is to that day you refer. My notes were taken with a view to impress on my mind sufficiently what the 92nd actually did, that I might be enabled (without fearing contradiction) to mention anything it formed during the action which I conceived reflected on it or the characters of the regiment. I did not take notes of its different movements which however were not numerous as the regiment was fully much stationary during the day, or those of the enemy.

I find from my notes, that we reached our position at Waterloo on the afternoon of the 17th, it was on, almost the extreme left of the line in a ploughed field, where we lay until 12 o'clock in the forenoon of the 18th: when we were ordered to stand to with the army, the enemy being in motion to attack. They were posted on a ridge of heights or marked rising ground parallel in a great measure with our army, the cannonade began at twenty minutes past 12, and lasted till the conclusion of the action with the greatest fury. The French infantry began their attack on the right and centre at half past twelve or one o'clock, and on the left about two, when also his cavalry were hotly engaged. Everything in front of the 92nd had been forced to give way about three o'clock, when General Sir Denis Pack[2] came up to Major Macdonald[3] commanding the regiment and told him, 'Everything now depends on the 92nd, as all in front of you have given way'. Previous to detailing the movements consequent on this intimation from Sir Denis Pack, it may be of use to mention as much as possible the ground the regiment stood on at that ground, we were formed in our columns some way down the slope of the hill. In our position, being in square, and I think – there was a ploughed field, or one of trodden down crops of some sort immediately contiguous. We were at all events some way down the slope from the crest of the position, with the view, to our avoiding the cannonade as much as practicable, having been a very weak battalion after the severe loss we had sustained on the 16th.[4]

In consequence of Sir Denis Pack's intimation we advanced in close columns up the hill, on our ascending which, we encountered a strong column of French infantry forming on the top of our position, whose leading files gave us their fire which our men did not return, but advanced steadily to the attack, and when we got within a very short distance of the enemy (at perhaps not thirty yards) they broke up and ran back in great confusion. Our fire now was very destructive and on our charging the enemy's column which was *now* in flight in all directions.[5] The Greys were marched from our rear toward their flanks, and got into and round this part of the enemy, which on attacking was estimated by us to consist of about 3,000 men and out of which, I believe the French lost two thirds in killed and prisoners. The conduct of the Greys and the rest of the heavy brigade regiments were very gallant, and as the Greys marched round our flank, in charging the column of French infantry, their men called out to ours, 'Scotland for ever'.

The enemy supported this attack by another column of I should imagine of great strength and which we found, on charging the one down the hill, which had gained the crest of it,[6] formed in the hollow of it. This column seeing the fate of the others, and the cavalry and us charging down the hill, threw itself into squares, the regiment halted and marched back to nearly where we advanced from and the heavy cavalry charged the square alluded to in most gallant style, but I believe could not break it. The 92nd some time after this retired a little ground to its right and advanced up the hill where we remained till the general order to advance. We were generally formed in column, sometimes in square against cavalry, but to the best of my remembrance, at the period the French Imperial Guards attacked the right of the British forces, about 7 o'clock, the 92nd stood in line, the enemy in its immediate front formed in column with a great many skirmishers in *its* front. In fact assuredly there is 20 officers in Edinburgh that served with the 92nd at the battle of Waterloo with whom I would have talked the subject over, with the view of refreshing my memory and sounding for more information, than I find from the long period that has elapsed since the battle, I dare venture to do, and I have been induced to communicate this little information I have given, from your invitation not to withhold any thing I would say, for the fear of committing mistakes, feeling assured that nothing but the best use will be made by you of such communications. I have stated nothing but what my recollection leads me to believe is correct, but my data may be at variance with that of others you may have received, the time I took from my own watch, but there is one thing I do most positively recollect and of which you are desirous viz, the existence of ploughed land. The 92nd were posted on a ploughed field for many hours, and I think you have been correctly informed as to its locality by the farmers as laid down in your plan so far as I can thank my memory, but I may add, all my attention was given to the men under my command and from the trodden down state of the crops I should now fear to trace the movements of the regiment lest fearing it be incorrect. I have notes relative to Quatre

Bras, and I think I could give a much more minute detail of that action or rather the movements of the enemy and the 92nd, as there were fewer troops of the British engaged in that battle, and the 92nd on that day traversed more ground, as its movements were more various than on the 18th, being charged with the protection of much more ground.

I have a justification in my mind that it was the Young Guard that the 92nd charged and broke at three o'clock on the 18th, but I cannot say definitely at this distant period that it was.[7]

I have the honour and remain, Sir, your most obedient servant

JAMES KERR ROSS
MAJOR UNATTACHED

---

1 Ross joined the army as an ensign in 1807 and served in the Peninsula as ADC to General Sir John Buchan. He received a General Service Medal with six bars for Vittoria, the Pyrenees (slightly wounded), Nivelle, Nive, Orthes and Toulouse. He was wounded at Waterloo. Afterwards Major General, KH. He died at Edinburgh on 26 April 1872.

2 Major Sir Denis Pack KCB commanded the 9th Brigade of which the 92nd was a regiment. He was made Colonel-in-Chief of the York chasseurs for Waterloo but died on 24 July 1824.

3 Major Donald Macdonald commanded the 92nd after Lieutenant Colonel Cameron was killed and Major Mitchell was wounded at Quatre Bras.

4 The 92nd suffered 39 killed and 247 wounded at Quatre Bras.

5 This account agrees with many others published by officers of this corps, that the French were in retreat *before* the Greys struck.

6 The transcription is correct but confusing. The 92nd having driven the first column off the ridge discovered a second column in the hollow below and proceeded to charge down the hill toward them, but left the heavy cavalry to press the attack.

7 Ross is mistaken; it was part of D'Erlon's Corps that had been driven off.

No. 185 From the same

Nisbet house, near Dunse, Berwickshire, 10 March 1837[1]

ADD MS 34706, FO 252

Sir

I have been favoured with yours of the 4th instant and very willingly do I sit down to communicate to you any little information it may be in my power to supply you with, relative to the show the 92nd had in the actions of the campaign of 1815.

In the first place I shall narrate to you our proceedings on the evening of the 15th; from the time we got under arms, till the close of the action on the 16th at Quatre Bras, and afterwards I shall answer your question relative to the enemy's cavalry and Picton's division at Waterloo.

You will be aware that the 92nd was brigaded with the 3rd [Battalion] Royals, 2nd [Battalion] 44th and 42nd under Sir Denis Pack, Picton's division.

About seven o'clock on the evening of the 15th, I understood that the troops, *that night*, were to move in consequence of the enemy being in motion. We accordingly about 11 o'clock pm, assembled on our parade, and shortly afterwards proceeded to the park where we found the rest of the division assembling and where we remained till about 4 or five o'clock on the morning of the 16th, when we advanced on the road to Quatre Bras. We reached the Forest of Soignies about 9, when we halted for about two hours, when we continued our march in the same direction. We arrived at the Quatre Bras about 3 in the afternoon, when the regiments of the division moved down to the plain consequently as they came up, and got in the action immediately. The French attacking with great fury at this moment, the 92nd were ordered to form in line on the road that ran to our left at the farm of Quatre Bras, the right of the regiment resting on the road to Brussels. On taking up our position now (which I believe we did by orders of the Duke himself) we observed the enemy had a heavy column of cavalry (cuirassiers) formed at some distance on the plain to our immediate front, formed as we imagined, with a view to making a dash to carry the road leading to Brussels. A corps of Belgian (mixed with some Brunswick cavalry if I don't much forget) were ordered to attack this corps of the enemy's cavalry, for which purpose they entered the plain by a gap that was in the field at our right, and to the left hand side of the road. The attack completely failed on the part of the Allied cavalry, the French having charged them and drove them back upon the 92nd, who retained its fire till the last moment, when it fired in a deliberate and well directed volley against the cuirassiers, causing them very great loss, and effectually checking them. They were from the destructive consequences of our fire thrown into confusion, but reformed and retired steadily and retired only to where they advanced from. Perhaps I may as well mention now, that the cuirassiers having in their charge got amongst the Belgian cavalry, it was out of the power of the 92nd to refrain from firing one moment longer than it did, its own safety depending on its steadiness and effects of its volley, as its formation at the time was a critical one to be charged in, viz. in line. Indeed the men were in the ditch that ran along the side of the road, having been ordered to take advantage of it before the cavalry came on, and having been exposed to a severe cannonade and the enemy not being near enough for musket shot, some of the Allied cavalry did fall at the time we gave the volley to the cuirassiers. These same cavalry were ordered again to attack the cuirassiers and for which purpose they entered the plain again with no better effect, only they retired sooner, charged by the cuirassiers, to whom we gave a second fire, again causing them much loss and completely driving them back. This second repulse seemed to have made them abandon the idea of taking possession of the road to Brussels, as though they made a short advance as if intending to try it again, but our front being clear on this occasion, we opened a fire at a longer range and they did not attempt to charge.

About this time the enemy sent forward a body of infantry which took possession of those houses which lay down the road leading to Gemioncourt (which we had just had, near our line) and some time after, they sent forward another column of infantry to support the first. Just at this moment the Adjutant General Sir Edward Barnes[2] rode up to the right of the regiment, and observing this second column of the enemy's infantry marching towards these houses, said 'What have we got here?' when we informed him they were enemy infantry, and that they had got another body who had possessed themselves of the houses and ground immediately about them, he then took off his hat, and said '92nd follow me', when we instantly charged down the road and received a very destructive fire from the enemy at the houses, we however drove them out, and when we had claimed this post, we received a second fire from the column that had been advancing up to the houses at the time we charged. This column also fell away and retired, after crossing the ditch to their left of the road on the side of the Bois de Bossu, they disputed the ground with us, but we drove them back a long way, and maintained all the ground we had gained, although we were opposed to a falling fire of shot, shell, grape and musketry and sustained a very severe loss both in officers and men. Indeed we had to occupy and defend ourselves on ground, that it surprised me how we were not cut to pieces, as we were frequently as a battalion extended! Acting as skirmishers, now and then throwing ourselves into squares to repulse cavalry, by which we were threatened, and when we were sure to suffer severe loss from the enemy's guns, as they took every opportunity of bringing them to bear upon us, whenever they could, with any chance of annoying us. I take the liberty of mentioning this, with the view of doing justice to my old friends the 92nd, who I can safely say upon this hard fought bloody day, behaved with a coolness, steadiness and gallantry that could not be exceeded, and they received their honourable reward by being particularly mentioned by the Duke in his Despatches.

Towards the close of the action on the 16th,we found ourselves acting in consort with some of the Guards and Brunswick infantry. At night we were recalled to the farm of the Quatre Bras where we remained till next forenoon when we retired on Waterloo between 10 and 11 o'clock. I should mention, the ground in front of our first position where we drove back the cavalry was to the best of my recollection pasture, when we were engaged with the French infantry, principally corn, wheat or rye, hay in both.

In relation to your questions about the French cavalry charging or threatening to charge any part of Picton's division after the attack made by D'Erlon's columns about 2 o'clock. I should say, that certainly the enemy's cavalry did advance to the crest of the hill and threatened part of Picton's division, for unless my memory deceives me very much, they threatened the 92nd more than once, and that we threw ourselves into square to resist them, but I cannot recollect their having actually charged any part of the division; this must have been later than two.

I received a wound in my right arm, which prevented me writing down my remarks for a few weeks after Waterloo, but the period was so short my memory must have been quite fresh. You must recollect, they are remarks and impressions of, at the time, a young man, and I commit them to your keeping, feeling in true confidence in the use you will make of them, and if they prove of any use to you, it will afford me sincere pleasure in being instrumental through your history to seeing the share my old regiment had in those glorious actions recorded.

The many of the officers who fell, and the entire loss of the regiment on the two days, will be supplied you by the Horse Guards, indeed the lists are, *I think*, correctly stated by Stuart in his history of the Highlanders and Highland regiments. Colonel Cameron who took the regiment at Quatre Bras into action, fell at the house when we first received the enemy's fire from infantry, and I think we had a succession of six or at all events five commanding officers at Quatre Bras.[3]

I have mentioned that I heard on the evening of the 15th, that we were to advance, purposely, as I think all historians of that campaign would only be doing justice to the Duke of Wellington and his army, in doing away an impression that still exists in the memoirs of many in civil life, that he was surprised while he was at the Duchess of Richmond's ball. His arrangements were all made before he went there, I believe beyond doubt to be the fact. Wishing every success to your praiseworthy undertaking.

I have the honour to remain, Sir, your most obedient servant

J KERR ROSS

---

1 This must be Duns, some 15 miles west of Berwick.

2 Major General Sir Edward Barnes KCB, who was indeed the Adjutant General. He is recorded as being wounded at Waterloo. He became Governor of Ceylon in 1824, then Commander-in-Chief in India in 1831–33. MP for Sudbury, GCB and Colonel-in-Chief of the 78th Foot, he died in London on 19 March 1838.

3 The figure possibly should be five. *1st* Lt. Colonel John Cameron was killed; *2nd* Lt. Colonel James Mitchell was wounded; *3rd* Dalton states that Major Macdonald was absent so the command went to Captain George Holmes who was soon wounded; *4th* Captain Dugald Campbell who was also wounded; *5th* Captain Peter Wilkie who remained unwounded at Quatre Bras. This would have been the succession if they were wounded in the same order, a questionable hypothesis. It could also have been six if the absent Major Donald Macdonald had arrived near the close of the battle, for he would have assumed command as senior to Captain Wilkie. There is however no evidence for this actually happening.

No. 186 Lieutenant James Hope[1]

ADD MS 34703, FO 18

Extracts from the military memoirs of an infantry officer 1809–16[2]

About 5 o'clock another attempt was made to wrest Quatre Bras out of our hands, but with no better success than the former. Soon after this, the Brigade of Guards, under Major General Maitland,[3] and the 3rd Division commanded by Lieutenant General Sir Charles Alten, arrived to our assistance. Never did troops receive a more seasonable reinforcement. The Guards were thrown into the wood of Bossu, on the right of the village, and the 3rd Division moved along the road leading to Ligny, till they passed the Royals, then they halted, and formed the left of our line. As each battalion hurried past us, it was loudly cheered by every man in the Highland corps. Yes, tears of joy bade them welcome to share our perils and our glory, and our best wishes followed but too many of them to their last and silent abode. Leaning against a bank when the 73rd Regiment approached us, and unconscious at the time that I had the pleasure of being known to any member of that corps, I felt something like surprise when Lieut ____,[4] a genuine Irishman, jumped out of his place, and grasping my hand as firmly as a vice, said 'James, how are you my boy?' In an hour he was no more.

As the 3rd Division proceeded along the road to their destination, the enemy were not very sparing of their shot and shell.

Under cover of a heavy cannonade, they pushed forward 2 columns of infantry; one by the high-way leading from Charleroi to Quatre Bras, and the other by a hollow, or kind of ravine, in front of the wood of Bossu, towards the same point. On the left of, and fronting the road to Charleroi, 200 yds in front of Quatre Bras, there was a house of 2 floors, from the rear of which ran a thick hedge, a short way across a field. On the right of the road, and immediately opposite to the house, there was a garden, surrounded with a thick hedge. In the face fronting the road there was a small gate, from which a gravel walk led to a similar one on the opposite side. The house and hedge were occupied by the enemy's advanced guard, and their main body, 12 or 1,500 in number, had taken post about 100 paces from the rear of the garden, when the Field-Marshal[5] gave us orders to charge.

The order was no sooner given, than every man of the 92nd Regiment, about 600 in number, appeared in front of the bank, behind which they had reposed for 4 hours. Colonel Cameron[6] accompanied by General Barnes,[7] the Captain General, advanced by the highway, at the head of the Grenadiers and flank company. The other companies by an oblique movement to their right, directed their march upon the same points, the house, garden, and hedge; the enemy pouring on us a deadly fire of musketry from the windows of the house, and from the hedge on the left of it, till we succeeded in driving them from both, which was not accomplished without a severe loss. Amongst the officers who fell at this time, was the brave Cameron, who, on receiving his mortal wound, retired.

But although we had forced the enemy to relinquish their hold of the house and hedge on the left of it, the principal part of our duties remained to be performed. Although their advanced guard had been driven back, the main body showed no disposition to retire. On the contrary they poured on us showers of musketry, sufficient to appal soldiers of more experience in these matters than one half of those who fought on the plains of Quatre Bras. In fact it required no little exertion to keep some of the young soldiers in the ranks; for, perceiving the French as much more numerous than themselves, and that the garden-hedge, though very thick, afforded them no protection, the danger appeared to some of them as very great, that but for their veteran companions, and the attention of the officers to their duties, they might have been induced to retire. But from this disagreeable situation we endeavoured to extricate ourselves in the following manner. The only obstacle between us and the enemy being the garden, it was proposed to move a portion of the battalion round between it and the wood of Bossu, another division round the left, or lower side of the garden, and a third to open a passage for itself through the garden, by entering at the front gate. Being of this party, we accomplished our task of forcing the gates with some little difficulty, for the fire of the enemy was truly dreadful; and we could not take any steps to render it less effective, till the whole battalion could be brought to bear upon the enemy. At length, however, all the 3 columns arrived at their appointed stations. Seeing our friends on the right and left ready, we moved out at the rear gate, and quickly formed in front of the hedge. On this formation being accomplished, the signal of readiness was given, when the whole joined in 3 hearty cheers, and then, with the irresistible bayonet in their hands, advanced to the work of death.

Suffice it, therefore, to say, that for a few seconds the French appeared quite seduced to await our assault; but on perceiving that we really intended to close with them, they wheeled to the right-about, and attempted to escape by a hollow in front of the wood, along which their left column had previously advanced. As soon as they turned their backs, we poured in upon them a volley of musketry, which did great execution. Never was the fire of a body of men given with finer effect than that of the 92nd, during the pursuit of the enemy, which continued for fully half a mile, and until the advance of a corps of French cavalry rendered it prudent to retire into the wood of Bossu. In fact, before we parted, their column, at first so formidable in numbers, was reduced to a skeleton.

This was the last serious attempt made by Ney[8] to obtain possession of Quatre Bras, but he continued to dispute the wood, and various portions of the ground on the left, till after 9 o'clock, when every prospect of victory having vanished, he withdrew his troops, and left us in possession of the ground which they occupied at the commencement of the engagement.

On the left side of the road leading from Quatre Bras to Ligny, a bank rose 8 or 10 feet above the crown of the highway, which trifling circumstance was occasionally the means of placing a few of our men in jeopardy. For on hitting the bank, the shells frequently came dancing across the road to their own music, till they arrived in the ditch among the Highlanders.

Waterloo

About one o'clock he (Napoleon) opened a most horrendous fire upon our Division, from numerous artillery planted along the ridge on which his army was posted. Under cover of this cannonade, he pushed forward 3 columns of infantry, each from 3 to 4000 strong, towards the heights we occupied. With loud shouts of ' Vive L'Empereur' the left column attacked the farmhouse of La Haye Sainte, while the right column, supported by the 3rd, moved against the Belgian troops assailed with terrible fury, returned the fire of the enemy for some time with great spirit.[9] But on the approach of the French, they shifted their ground, and retired behind the hedge, which, although it afforded them no shelter from the enemy's fire, yet concealed them from their view. Hence, on seeing themselves well supported, they showed a little more courage, and although exposed to a heavy fire, they maintained their ground with considerable fierceness, until the enemy having gained possession of La Haye Sainte, by putting every one of the garrison to the sword,[10] increased the numbers of the assailants.

Under cover of his artillery, Bonaparte caused the right and left columns formerly mentioned, supported by the 3rd column, to move forward and attack the heights on which our division was posted. With drums beating, colours flying, and eagles soaring above their huge headdresses, the enemy advanced in solid column to the attack. Their progress was considerably retarded by the fire of our artillery, and volleys of musketry from the Belgian infantry, till the enemy having almost gained the summit of the ridge, our allies partially retired from the hedge. At the entreaty of their officers, the greater part of them again returned to their posts, but it was merely to satisfy their curiosity, for they almost immediately again retired without firing a shot. The officers exerted themselves to the utmost to keep the men at their duty, but their efforts were fruitless and at length the whole corps took fairly to their heels.

The post thus abandoned by *Les-Braves-Belges*, was instantly re-occupied by the 3rd Battalion the Royals, and 2nd Battalion 44th Regiment. Those two weak Battalions poured on the assailants a heavy fire of musketry, but the latter continued to advance with unflinching courage, till they succeeded in compelling our friends also to retire from the hedge.[11]

Everyone was now convinced that our affairs had approached an important crisis, and that an attempt to resist the torrent must instantly be made, or the heights, and with them the victory, yielded to the enemy. The Belgians had left us; the Royals and 44th had also retired to our rear, and the 42nd Regiment being posted on an important spot considerably to our left, from which they could not move, the hazardous attempt devolved upon the 92nd Regiment, then about *230 strong.*

On arriving at the hedges, the enemy formed in close column, opposed to us a front not longer than our own, but then they had ten similar fronts to support the one in view. In fact their numbers were *3,000*, ours *230*. Perceiving the urgent state of affairs, and the absolute necessity that existed of adopting some decisive measures, Sir Denis Pack, said, with much earnestness '*Ninety Second, you must charge! All the troops in your front have given way!*' To this not very encouraging address, the Regiment responded with cheers, and then advanced to measure bayonets with their enemies. For some time the latter appeared resolute to give us a meeting, but in arriving within 30 paces of them, the whole column completely panic struck, wheeled to the right about, and in the utmost confusion, attempted to escape. But it was now too late; for on perceiving the disorderly manner in which the French infantry were retiring, Sir William Ponsonby rushed forward with the 1st, 2nd (Scots Greys) and 6th Regiments of heavy dragoons, cut his way through them as far as the valley – killed and wounded an immense number – captured 2 eagles, and took 2000 prisoners. The Scots Greys being the centre regiment, advanced directly upon the French column, and charged past our flanks. On approaching us, the Scots Greys cried, as with one voice 'Hurrah, 92nd, Scotland for ever'. This charge was made about 3 o'clock.

The result of this attack must have deranged the plans of Napoleon dreadfully, for an almost total suspension of hostilities on this flank took place, from ¼ past 3, till about 20 minutes from 4. During this time, our rocket brigade attempted to break the French columns of support, while the Scots Greys hovered on its flanks, to take advantage of any opening that might occur. But their efforts were fruitless, the enemy remained firm as rocks.

About 4, two Prussian officers passed in front of us at full gallop, eagerly enquiring for the D. of Wellington. On delivering their message, they returned by the same route, cheered, and cheering all the way. Soon after this, we perceived the French, but as each Prussian Battalion arrived it took part in the battle, so that by 6 o'clock, ample work was carved out for Bonaparte in that direction. Finding himself attacked by the Prussians in a much more serious manner than he had anticipated, Bonaparte caused his right to be reinforced. Between this portion of the French army, and the Prussians under General Bülow,[12] a dreadful conflict took place, and continued till 7 o'clock, by which time, all the Prussians moving by the pass of St. Lambert, had arrived at the scene of active operations, and the head of General Ziethen's[13] column, accompanied by Blücher,[14] made it's appearance about the same time near Ter-la-Haye.[15] To prevent the junction of the 2 armies, Napoleon sent several considerable bodies of troops towards the extreme left of the allied army. These columns were attacked with great spirit by Blücher, who on leaving Ohain, marched directly upon Papelotte, leaving Ter-la-Haye on his right. By this movement, the junction of the two armies was effected, and Bonaparte's object completely defeated.

1 Although named James in all of the records, he uses the name of Isaac in his 1829 statement of service. He joined the 92nd at the age of 20 and went on the Walcheren expedition of 1809 as a volunteer. He became an ensign that November and served in the Peninsula, being severely wounded at the Pyrenees. He became a lieutenant in 1813 and received a General Service Medal with three bars for Vittoria, Pyrenees and Nivelle. He is shown in Dalton as being wounded at Waterloo. He was placed on half pay on 25 March 1817 and died in Kensington on 18 March 1860.

2 Hope's memoirs were published anonymously in 1819 entitled *Letters from Portugal, Spain and France, during the memorable campaigns of 1811,1812,1813; and from Belgium and France in the year 1815 by a British Officer*, recently republished as *The Iberian and Waterloo Campaigns*, Naval and Military Press, Uckfield, West Sussex, 2000. However, Hope published a rework of his memoirs in 1833, it was again anonymous and privately published, entitled *The military memoirs of an infantry officer 1809–16*. Siborne was obviously privy to a copy of the latter, as these notes are in his hand. The book is extremely rare and describes the events in far greater detail than the earlier version; I have therefore felt that its inclusion in this book was justified.

3 Major General of the 1st Brigade.

4 Probably Lieutenant Matthew Holles (spelt Hollis in Dalton, but a letter published in *The 2/73rd at Waterloo* by Alan Lagden and John Sly, privately published, Brightlingsea, 1988, p. 104, proves the spelling). Lieutenants Holles and Strachan were the only two officers of this rank in the regiment killed in the Waterloo campaign. Holles was the only Irishman, Strachan hailing from Plymouth.

5 The Duke of Wellington.

6 Lieutenant Colonel John Cameron, was originally buried in a hastily dug grave in a quite lane, by his foster brother Ewen McMillan who served as a private in the regiment. The body was later re-interred in Kilmallie churchyard, where stands a tall obelisk inscribed by Sir Walter Scott.

7 Major General Sir Edward Barnes, KCB Adjutant General.

8 Marshal Michel Ney commanded the left wing of the French Army of the North, which was launched against the Duke of Wellington's Allied forces.

9 This passage is rare in British memoirs of the battle, in its allowing the Belgians to have fought well until eventually forced to retire. It would appear that the Belgians did not just run away as some historians would have us believe.

10 This is a mistake; the capture of La Haye Sainte should not appear at this stage of the description, it happened at a much later hour. The garrison was also far from annihilated.

11 It is rare indeed for a British officer to admit that British troops were also repulsed by the attack of D'Erlon's columns. This puts the retreat of the Belgians moments earlier in a far better light.

12 General Count Friedrich Wilhelm von Bülow commanded the Prussian IV Corps attacking Plançenoit.

13 Lieutenant General Hans Ernst Karl, Graf von Ziethen, commanded the Prussian I Corps, which formed a junction with Wellington's left flank.

14 Field Marshal Gebhard Leberecht von Blücher, commanded the Prussian army.

15 Small village on the left flank of Wellington's army.

No. 187 From the same
Liverpool, 3 September 1840

ADD MS 34707, FO 193

It was with very sincere regret that I learned from your note of the 14th instant that so little have your countrymen appreciated the pecuniary and other sacrifices which you have made in preparing for their gratification the beautiful model of the battle of Waterloo that not more than one hundred thousand of them, have, either from gratitude or curiosity been carried to pay a visit. Failure to this extent I really did not anticipate, although from *various causes* I never thought your remuneration would be very ample. Three thousand guineas is a large sum, but were the model mine, I should not owe them a farthing one year hence. If errors have been committed in the plans for having the model before the public, it is not yet too late to correct them.

To do so with effect, some little increase in the daily expenses would have to be submitted to, but that would be compensated ten fold by the vast increase in the number of visitors to that model. The remedy is in your own power, therefore you have only to will and it is done. John Bull is a strange sort of a fellow, for though fond of sights, he likes to have value for his money. By this remark I do not by any means intend to convey to you an idea that the entrance money is too high, on the contrary, I should, were the model mine, rather increase the entrance money, but on terms which would prove *alike beneficial to the payer and receiver.*[1]

It is a very general complaint, that, notwithstanding the explanatory remarks of those in attendance, nine out of every ten take leave of the model, without having added anything to their previous store of information respecting that memorable event.

Last November an officer of very considerable talent assured me that he paid the model three very long visits before he could comprehend the various details. This you may rest satisfied is the great cause of failure, for the hundreds and thousands who have quitted the model under similar circumstances – have no doubt been the means of deterring thousands of their friends from visiting it – by assuring them that they would [not] gain any information from seeing the model.

When I visited last November, there were *four* of the Household Brigade there at the time, all of whom told me that they could not comprehend the various parts of it, and begged I would describe that part of the field where their regiment was stationed – which I did – adding a little more information respecting other corps, which seemed to give them pleasure.

I am very glad to hear that you are preparing a model to represent what you seem pleased to term 'A Glorious Scene'. Many were of opinion that you ought to have selected this stage of the battle for your model in preference to the one you did, it proving that the *latter was not a truly British scene.*[2] Doctors will disagree. Had there been fewer of Father Blücher's children in the distance, the model would undoubtedly have had more [the look of a] British victory.[3]

I am like wise quite delighted to hear that you are proposing for the book, a narrative of the campaign of 1815. It will afford me, pleasure to render you all the service I can on this occasion. With regard to the formation of the 92nd Regiment at the period of the battle alluded to by you, the battalion was *not* in *Column, but in line four deep.*

Seven or eight years ago, I published a little work under the title of 'Military Memoirs of an Infantry Officer' – to which I beg to refer you for information respecting that charge – as also the whole of the operations of the 5th Division on the 16th, 17th and 18th June.

It was published in Dublin by a Mr Brakeman of D'Olier Street, no copy of the work are now to be had, but it is possible you may find one at some circutatious *[sic]* Library in Dublin.

I sincerely trust that your venture will be a straightforward *British one* – and that no delicacy towards our neighbours[4] will prevent you from clothing your little work in a truly British dress. If so decorated, it will sell – if not – you will have it for some time in your hands.

A war with that country would at this moment be popular with a very large majority of the population of these realms.

Believe me, my dear Sir, very faithfully yours

JAMES HOPE

1 It is clear that William Siborne got himself into a financial mess over the model, which was compounded by what appears to be a complete abdication of control of the exhibition to a manager. As his financial future relied solely on the success of the venture, is it not strange that he did not retain a tight hold on the project? This would appear to indicate poor business sense.

2 By this time the Victorian public had embraced Waterloo as a thoroughly 'British victory' and his audience would be looking to have this shown clearly on the model. The model was however more indicative of an 'Allied victory'.

3 This was a serious complaint by many visitors including officers, regarding the model. The Prussian advance was shown as being close to cutting the road and therefore detracted from the defeat of the Imperial Guard in the model. It is to Siborne's credit that he insisted on maintaining historical accuracy and positioning the Prussians in such an advance position, despite the criticism.

4 Almost certainly the French, where Thiers' very one-sided *History of the Consulate and Empire* was all the rage.

No. 188 From the same
Liverpool, 4 January 1842

ADD MS 34707, FO 336

My dear Sir

In reply to your note of the 2nd instant I regret to state that the officers of the 42nd, 79th and 92nd did *not* wear plaid on the memorable field of Waterloo – neither did any of the men.[1]

During the Peninsula campaign the dress of the officers of my own corps, the 92nd, were scarlet jacket, two silver epaulettes, blue artillery web pantaloons, boots or shoes and gaiters, highland sword, sash thrown over the shoulder, bonnet and feather, and a very bad dress it was for full purposes, for the men being in *kilts*, we were of course but too good marks for the enemy riflemen. At Quatre Bras 35 officers went into action with the 92nd, six of whom were killed or died of their wounds, seventeen were severely and two slightly wounded, and all in our charge which the regiment made about 7 o'clock.

In the military papers of last week I observed your forthcoming work advertised for

February. I hope you may be fully remunerated for your trouble. It is with pleasure that I now look forward to a period when justice will be done to individual corps, and the garbled statements of interested or mercenary writers exposed to public view. Maxwell[2] has committed a sad blunder regarding the movements of various bodies of troops at Waterloo and such. If not too late I could furnish you with proofs of his incorrectness I hope you will steer clear of the rack on which he has been stretched.

Most truly yours

J A HOPE

1 He refers here to the fact that the regimental officers did not wear kilts or plaid trousers, but wore the plain grey trousers issued to most other British regiments. The men wore kilts.

2 Probably W. H. Maxwell's *Stories from Waterloo,* the date of its first publication is unknown. However he published another book entitled *Peninsula Sketches* in1844. I must thank Richard and Rosalind Brown of Ken Trotman Limited for this information.

No. 189 From the same
Liverpool, 8 September 1842

ADD MS 34707, FO 409

My dear Sir

Believe me that it will at all times afford me pleasure to give you such information regarding the memorable events of the 16th, 17th and 18th June 1815 as my very limited knowledge of them will permit. As to the formation of the 92nd Regiment on the 18th, it was told off in *ten divisions*,[1] but on the following day I believe it was reduced to six, there being only five or six company officers remaining.

I cannot speak positively to the formation of the other regiments of the brigade but I am inclined to think that all the others mustered their ten divisions on that eventful day.

With respect to the *halberds*[2] – the 42nd, 79th and 92nd Regiments carried that *splendid* and *most useful* weapon on the 18th.

I trust you will write on the eve of starting [to] print the book. I have been expectantly looking for it – in hopes that you may correct the errors into which several writers have fallen regarding the strength of the hostile armies, the periods at which the various attacks were made, by whom, and the different corps by which these actually were defeated.

Maxwell is completely wrong on this point. He makes it appear that seven regiments of infantry were present when the eagles were captured, when there were one only – the 92nd.

Very truly yours

J A HOPE

1 The division equates with a company, a regiment normally consisted of ten companies. Because of heavy losses, the men were reformed into six companies following Waterloo.

2 The halberd was officially no longer carried after 1792, when a half-pike or spontoon had been introduced to be carried by all sergeants except those in the Light infantry. It is certain that the old terminology was simply retained for the new version. They were generally

useful laid across the men's backs by the sergeants to push them back into line if their formation appeared to be buckling, from Hope's description it also appears that because of their reach; they proved very useful against cavalry.

No. 190 From the same
18 Winchester Place, Claremont Square, 3 March 1846

ADD MS 34708, FO 260

My dear Sir,
I thought that some friend of the Royals, 42nd or 44th, would have replied to your letter in the *United*[1] for the present month. I have delayed until now returning an answer to your note.

The statement you published in last months United M[agazine], proves satisfactorily, that none of the three corps named took any part in the charge.

'The 44th formed the left of the brigade and during the attack, had its front covered by Best's Hanoverians,[2] and remained in support upon the summit or knoll immediately above.'

Now supposing your information correct (which as I have often told you is undoubtedly correct), as to the station of the 44th, it follows that it could not have taken any part in the charge. And with regard to the Royals, you say they make no claim to having attacked the column, being stationed on the right of the brigade. This reduces the number of competing regiments to two, 42nd and 92nd, and what does the claim of the former amount to, absolutely nothing, as you know. Therefore if it is maintained that the French column was attacked and broken by a regiment forming part of Pack's brigade, that regiment must be the 92nd, none of the others having by their own statements had any thing whatever to do with that actual charge.

Nor is it at all likely, that if the 42nd could have claimed *even the half* of the credit of beating the French column, they would have omitted to notice the share which they had in it, for the half of the honour assumed on that occasion by the least battalion engaged, would not have been beneath the acceptance of even so distinguished a corps as the Royal Highlanders.[3]

As to the retreat of the Royals and 44th past our flanks, I have in my little trifle[4] stated the facts as they really occurred, and therefore have nothing to add, nothing to retract. If my statement had not been perceived as fact, would not some one of the *eighteen* officers of the Royals who were kind enough to purchase copies of the memoirs, have challenged my veracity?

I have no doubt but the Staff and other officers mentioned by you, believe to be facts all that they stated to you regarding the charge, and therefore without in the least degree questioning their veracity, I beg to claim your attention to the following statement quoted from a letter written by the Duke to Sir W. Scott, the 17th August 1815.

'Just to show you how little reliance can be placed even on what are supposed the best accounts of a battle, I mention that there are some circumstances mentioned in General ____'s account, which did not occur as he states them. He was not on the field during the whole battle, particularly not during the latter part of it.'

Now, although the Staff officer[5] may have been on the field, he could not possibly have been present when that charge took place. First, for none of the *Duke's Staff* were present on the occasion, and secondly, because many things stated by him did not occur at the place where, and the time when, the charge was made.

I perfectly agree with you that in the circumstances, you could not do less than take the statements of the officers of these regiments in preference to the statements of myself and other officers. But this does not do away with the injustice done to the '*Old Gordons*'[6] *by your informants*, who have led you to conclusions which go to deprive them of the laurels which they nobly won on the plains of Waterloo. Laurels for which fifteen or twenty years after that desperate engagement, no individual, not even one officer of Pack's Brigade, betook themselves, or any one member of the Allied army, ever attempted to defend them. Laurels, which they will now share with any other corps, they being the individual property of the 92nd, and the 92nd alone.

I deeply regret to hear that your models are giving you so much unhappiness, limiting the place of deposit to the places mentioned in your prospectus has much impaired your prospects. Had you at once named the *National Gallery* or the *Museum,*[7] *and no other*, you would have secured twenty subscribers for one you have raised. It is too late now I fear, for you to make any alteration, but if such alteration could be made *known* to a certainty, that your subscription list would be greatly increased.

Ever truly yours

JAMES HOPE

---

1 The *United Service Journal.*
2 The 4th Hanoverian Brigade of Colonel Best.
3 The 42nd were titled The Royal Highland Regiment of Foot.
4 Hope's memoirs were published anonymously in 1819 entitled '*Letters from Portugal, Spain and France, during the memorable campaigns of 1811,1812,1813; and from Belgium and France in the year 1815 by a British Officer*'.
5 This possibly refers to Major General Sir Edward Barnes, Adjutant General, whom Siborne records on p. 91 of his history as having ordered the 92nd forward.
6 The 92nd Foot was also known as the Gordon Highlanders.
7 The British Museum. In fact the model was purchased by the United Services Institute in 1851.

5th Hanoverian Brigade

Landwehr Battalion Hameln

No. 191 Captain Augustus Hartmann[1]
Hildesheim in the kingdom of Hanover, 9 February 1835

ADD MS 34704, FO 227

Sir!

In reply to your letter, which I had the pleasure to receive on the 7th, I beg leave to state, that having been at the time of the battle of Waterloo detached from the 2nd Line Battalion of the K. G. Legion[2] to the Hanoverian Landwehr battalion Hameln as Brevet

Major, I am very sorry, not to be able to afford to you the desired information, referring to the 2nd Line Battalion of the K. G. Legion.

But presuming that instead of it, it might be agreeable to you to get acquainted with the particular position and formation of any other corps, which got a share in that memorable victory, I shall feel great pleasure, to communicate to you, as much as relates the brigade I served in, according to my best remembrance, the Hanoverian Landwehr battalions Hameln, Giffhorn, Peina and Hildesheim formed the 5th Hanoverian Brigade and was commanded by Major General Vincke.[3] This brigade engaged to the 5th Division under Sir Thomas Picton, afterwards Sir James Kempt.

At 7 o'clock the brigade was posted in the 2nd line behind its division, forming two solid squares of which the battalions Hameln and Giffhorn constituted the one, the other two battalions were some time before ordered away to take up another position, but I do not know where they were gone.[4]

Our square was posted about fifty paces (at 2' 8") to the left side from the high road, leading from Brussels to Genappe, and distant about 300 paces from the farm Mont St Jean, and 700 paces from La Haye Sainte, as marked down in your model, which I herewith do remit. The ground we occupied was to my best recollection a slanting one, sloping down to form a small height, levelling to the high road, and was fallow land.

With regards to the different positions of the enemy in front of us, during the designed moment, I am quite unable to tell anything about it; our view being of course obstructed by the first line; to get a view of it, was not sooner granted to me, than about at a quarter past seven, when we were ordered to break into column, and to form into line four deep, on the right of the mentioned high road, near the small house, situated between Mont St Jean and La Haye Sainte, but this further ought not to be placed here.

Hoping that you will be kind enough, accept this short and perhaps incomplete sketch of mine.

I have the honour to be Sir! your most obedient humble servant

AUGUSTUS HARTMANN
LIEUTENANT COLONEL
CAPTAIN IN THE 2ND LINE BATT OF THE LATE KGL

---

1 Hartmann, numbered 426 in Beamish, joined the Legion in 1804 and served in Hanover, the Mediterranean, the Baltic, the Peninsula in 1808–12 and northern Germany. He received a General Service Medal with three bars for Talavera, Ciudad Rodrigo and Salamanca and retired as a lieutenant colonel on half pay at Hildesheim after the wars.

2 The 2nd Line Battalion KGL was in the 1st Brigade KGL of Colonel du Plat.

3 Colonel von Vincke at Waterloo.

4 It is not clear where if indeed these battalions went. No history of the battle notes this movement, although it is conceivable that these troops were moved nearer to the crossroads as the Prussian troops arrived to bolster the centre. This however seems unlikely as the two battalions stated as having moved elsewhere, actually received much lower casualties than the two that remained.

SIXTH DIVISION

10th Infantry Brigade

The 40th Regiment, 1st Battalion

No. 192 Captain Sempronius Stretton[1]

Lenton Priory, Nottinghamshire, 7 February 1837

ADD MS 34706, FO 224

Replies to Lieutenant Siborne's enquiries on the subject of the battle of Waterloo, by Colonel Stretton then brevet major 40th regiment, in charge of the left wing of this corps.

The regiment went into action on the morning of the 18th June about 720 rank & file, commanded by Major Heyland, their loss on this day was Major Heyland killed, 12 other officers and 180 men killed and wounded.

The formation of the enemy's force immediately in our front was a double line of Tirailleurs, supported by a heavy column of infantry. The former had possession of a rising ground on the opposite side of the road to the farm of La Haye Sainte, who whilst laying down, appeared to shoot their objects with great precision. It appeared to me that this force formed the French line which supported as above, charged our front that evening as some of them were bayoneted *close* to our front rank.

The field immediately about the 40th was thickly scattered with horses and men of the French cavalry who repeatedly charged our squares (without making any impression) and who passing and returning between the squares of the 40th, 27th and 4th Regiments, suffered severely from the fire of each.

On the left of the 40th at the commencement of the action were, a rocket brigade, and one of artillery,[3] the tumbril of the latter was blown up by a shell from the enemy and both were silenced before the close of the action, by the numerous artillery of the French.

The formation of the 40th at the period when the French Imperial Guard advanced to attack the right of the British force, was in line, having previously repulsed the enemy's cavalry in square.

When the British line moved forward, the 40th drove the Tirailleurs from the rising ground in its front and occupied it at the same time the 27th Regiment with the rest of the 40th took possession of the farm of La Haye Sainte, in which they made prisoners of a General officer and a party of the enemy.

Towards the evening whilst the regiment was in open column, a round shot from the enemy, took off the head of a Captain (Fisher[2]) near me and striking his company on the left flank, put hors de combat *more* than 25 men; this was the most destruction that I ever witnessed during a long period of service.

The 4th regiment was upon the left of the 40th, the 27th upon its right, part of the right wing of the latter was upon the main road.

The accompanying plan of the field of Waterloo appears to me to be perfectly correct.

S STRETTON COLONEL HALF PAY
LATE MAJOR 40TH REGIMENT

---

1 He joined the army in 1800 and served in the Peninsula from 1812–14 being present at Vittoria, the Pyrenees, Nivelle, Nive, Orthes and Toulouse then New Orleans. He retired on half pay in 1824 and became a lieutenant colonel half pay in the 84th Foot and CB. He died on 6 February 1842.

2 Captain William Fisher; his death is also described in *The Autobiography of Sergeant William Lawrence,* edited by G. N. Bankes, London 1886.

3 These would be Whinyates' and half of Bijleveld's Dutch horse artillery batteries

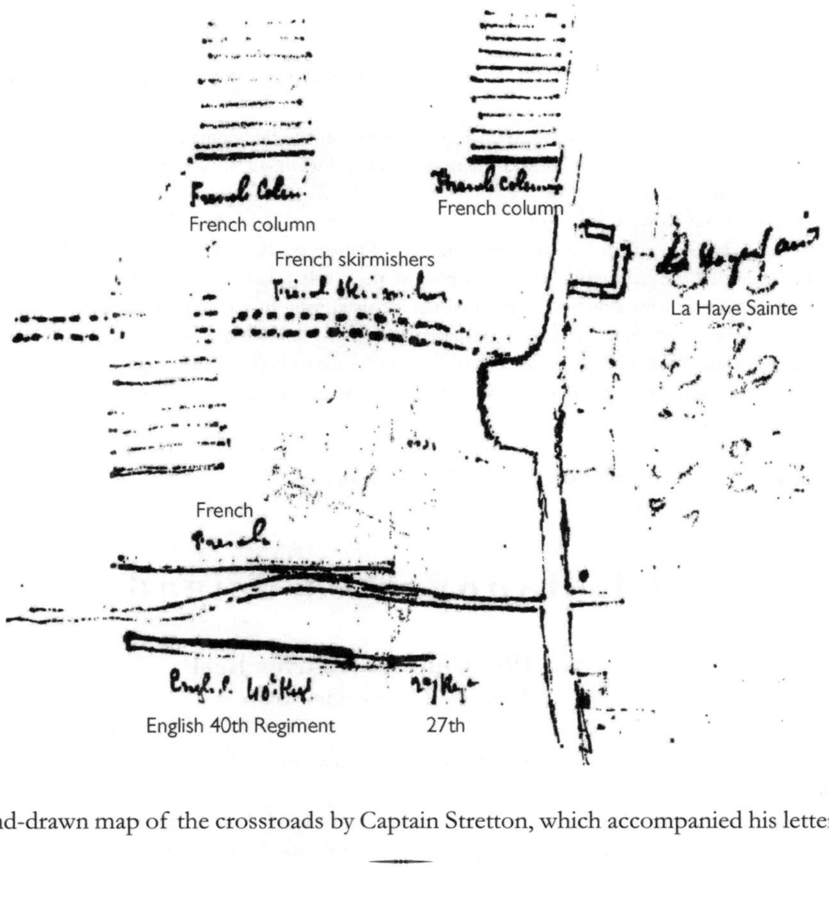

Hand-drawn map of the crossroads by Captain Stretton, which accompanied his letter.

No. 193 Captain Peter Bishop[1]
Leamington Spa, 30 April 1835

ADD MS 34705, FO 213

Sir,

I should have replied to your letter of the 20th March, before now, but was from home, when it reached this place. I now do so with pleasure, as well as my recollection of the battle of Waterloo will enable me, but from the great length of time that has elapsed and my not having left any memoirs I fear I cannot give you all the information you wish. I think about 7 o'clock on the evening of the 18th, the 40th Regiment had formed into line, after having first charged the enemy, in which we lost several officers and men, and amongst them (Major Heyland[2]) our then Commanding Officer. The Duke of Wellington came up to us at the moment and we gave him three hearty cheers; I was from circumstances in command of the regiment at the time.[3] We were in Sir John Lambert's brigade[4] and Sir Lowry Cole's division,[5] and upon the right[6] of the road leading from Brussels to Genappe and nearly in line with Hougoumont. I am sorry I cannot charge my memory with any further particulars of that memorable event, or I should have had much pleasure in communicating them to you.

I am, Sir, your very obedient servant

P BISHOP

MAJOR UNATTACHED LATE 40TH REGIMENT

---

1 He joined the army in 1803 as an ensign; he served in the Peninsula and was severely wounded at Nivelle. He became a major in 1828 and went on the unattached list in 1829, and was made KH.

2 Major Arthur Rowley Heyland.

3 There is some confusion about this statement. Dalton states that Major Feilding Browne commanded the regiment in the latter part of the battle following Major Heyland's death and this is confirmed by Sergeant Lawrence in his autobiography. There is no record of Browne being wounded and indeed there were six Captains senior to Bishop of which only one was killed and two wounded. Four officers senior to Bishop therefore survived without wounds, making it very unlikely that he took command of the regiment that day.

4 10th Brigade.

5 6th Division.

6 This is an error, the 40th stood on the left of the highroad.

4th Hanoverian Brigade

No. 194 Colonel Charles Best[1]
Verden, 27 February 1835

ADD MS 34704, FO 278

To Captain Lewis Benne KH[2]

Dear Sir,

In order to comply with the contents of your letter of the 13th instant, I will endeavour to satisfy Lieutenant Siborne's demands, by stating as far as memory will admit, the formation of the 4th Hanoverian Infantry Brigade, 6th Division of the British Army. At the moment when the French Imperial Guards advanced to attack the right of the British forces about seven pm on the 18th June 1815 at the Battle of Waterloo, as the period chosen by Lieutenant Siborne for the representation on his intended model.

The 6th Division was formed on a height between La Haye Sainte and Papelotte, behind a hedge of bushes running along these heights, intersected in its immediate front by a deep gutter (ravine). Consequently the 4th Brigade with a company of Hanoverian foot artillery[3] were in the same line as I have marked with a pencil on the plan, in the following order.

The *1st Battalion Verden* on the *left* of the guns formed in line.

The *3rd Battalion Osterode* also in line on the *right* of the guns; to which the *2nd Battalion Luneburg* closed and formed in line. The *4th Battalion Minden was kept in rear of the whole as a Reserve.* This formation will appear rather singular, as the Battalions are formed so irregular, out of their proper order in the Brigade, but as the previous attacks of the enemy had caused the defence or aid of one or the other Battalion, had caused this irregularity.

As the Prussians had at this moment begun their attack on the enemy's right, there was little danger for our left, except in the event of our right being repulsed. Our left was therefore only to be considered as steady spectators of the struggle, merely exposed to the enemy's cannonade.

In addition to this I will endeavour to relate as far as I can recollect, what is required in the sequel of Lieutenant Siborne's letter.

The British army, or rather part of it, having retreated from Quatre-Bras on the 17th joined the rest, and assembled near Mont St Jean, where they bivouacked for the night. On the morning of the 18th the Army was formed in line of battle on the height already described, which was most judiciously chosen by the Duke of Wellington, to ensure his Army a strong position of defence, and the result had warranted his foresight. During our retreat from Quatre-Bras the preceding day, the enemy had pursued us with some cavalry and horse-artillery as far as La Haye Sainte, and then withdrew, and assembled during the night and morning of the 18th and formed opposite to us also on some heights on this side Plançenoit, on the right and left of the high road from Waterloo to Genappe.

The rain which had fallen the latter part of the preceding day and incessantly fell all night, had softened the ground particularly cornfields to such a degree, that it was very difficult to move upon, especially for cavalry. The troops had hitherto moved on the high road, but the forming in line of battle required the disregard to cultivated ground, and most of the corn fields, which were at this time of the year, in full growth, in the neighbourhood of the Army, were soon trodden down, by the different movements of the troops, and more so during the conflict in the course of the day. About 11 we could clearly perceive with our glasses the French Emperor passing down the line from right to left haranguing his soldiers by whom he was received with loud shouts of *'Vive L'Empereur'*. The cannonade now began on both sides, and as part of the enemy's cavalry on their right seemed to indicate an attack on our left, I ordered the brigade to form Battalion Squares four deep (Note A).[4] A most furious attack on our left now ensued by a strong Corps of Infantry followed by a Reserve of Cavalry, by which the

Brigade of Highlanders suffered much (Note B), I ordered the 1st Battalion Verden to support them, and a most serious conflict took place. At the beginning of this attack I had ordered the 2nd and 3rd Battalions to form *into line* in order to meet the enemy, who contented himself merely to harass us with his numerous Tirailleurs, as his main object seemed to be to turn our outermost left. The enemy's attack (Note C) was however repulsed with great loss on both sides, and Sir Thomas Picton killed (Note D). In return an attack was made on our side on the right of the French where a hard contest took place between the cavalry on both sides, by which Major General Ponsonby lost his life (Note E). About one o'clock a strong corps of French infantry attacked our centre at La Haye Sainte, near part of the 5th and 6th Division, by which the 2nd Battalion Luneburg became strongly engaged, after a hard conflict the enemy was repulsed (Note F) and pursued by General Vandeleur's cavalry, which was however obliged to withdraw, on account of meeting a superior force. Whilst our centre and right encountered the enemy's attacks – about 3 o'clock pm – at La Haye Sainte (Note G) and Hougoumont, the 3rd Battalion Osterode withstood a furious attack from a much superior corps of Infantry, which induced me to order the 4th Battalion Minden for its support, and the enemy was soon brought to retire. The cannonade had all this time continued without interruption on both sides; but Major Heise[5] having spent all his ammunition except three rounds, which he intended to keep for the support of the Brigade at the event of any sudden attack, had withdrawn his guns to the rear, and to repair the damages sustained.[6] At about 6 o'clock pm we descried the heads of columns of a Prussian corps under General Bülow defile through the wood from the village Smohain (Note H), their artillery soon began to cannonade the right of the enemy's position. The rest of the Prussians under old Blücher soon followed, their cavalry forming behind our left to be at hand when required. Major Heise having received the ammunition resumed his former position, and firing wherever an advantage offered.

The French Emperor perceiving the danger that threatened him by the arrival of the Prussians, resolved as his last effort to turn our right. It is said that he took the Prussians on their appearance for the detached corps of Grouchy, whom Blücher had kept in check at Wavre, but soon perceiving the mistake, took recourse to an attack with his Guards (Note J); about 10,000 men, who had not as yet partaken of any of the engagements, but were kept as a Reserve in rear of his army for some brilliant exploit.[7]

The result of this attack is already described at the beginning of the narrative, and I can only add that it wholly failed in its intention, and decided the day. The Duke of Wellington now ordered a general attack on the whole front of the French line, whereupon all corps of infantry left their positions and formed in line and advanced, colours flying, drums beating and music playing, the cavalry following in second line. This was one of the finest military sights ever beheld, as the troops not only kept their proper distances but were also dressed in one uniform line as on a field day. At this moment the enemy fled in great confusion and in all directions towards Genappe, leaving a great part of his artillery behind, most of which was either disabled during the action, others deserted by their men. However a few shot were fired during this confused retreat or rather flight by them, one of which carried off the leg of the Marquess of Anglesey. A corps of Prussian cavalry and infantry [Note K), and some British cavalry pursued the flying enemy towards Genappe, whilst the British army halted and took their bivouac on the field of battle and on the very spot where the hottest contest had taken place during the action, the ground being covered by dead and wounded from both sides.

Thus ended that most glorious day, and decided the fate of Napoleon and stopped all further bloodshed, where British arms show in their brightest lustre, and where the utmost bravery and steadiness of our troops withstood the furious attacks of a much superior enemy in number for nearly ten hours, till the arrival of the Prussians and the defeat of the Imperial Guards decided our victory. Had the battle been lost before the Prussians came to our aid, the consequences cannot well be calculated, for it would have opened the Belgian country and its resources to Napoleon's forces, which no doubt would have been also augmented by the desertion of the Belgian auxiliary troops.

In addition to this, and with a desire of aiding Lieutenant Siborne in forming his model with the most possible accuracy I have thought proper to annex the following notes to the foregoing narration. As Lieutenant Siborne has himself been on the spot to take up the ground as is represented on his plan, he will no doubt have observed the unevenness of the same, especially that part on which the British army had been formed at the commencement of the battle, which had been so judiciously chosen by our experienced and able commander, as the most proper one for defence, securing at the same time the communication with the Prussians at Wavre. He would therefore have been very desirous, had Lieutenant Siborne more distinctly marked the different hedges; trees, ravines etc. etc. that run over the ground here and there, to facilitate the state of formation of the 4th Hanoverian Brigade with due correctness; unless the road so marked on the plan, which runs from Smohain to the highroad (chaussee) from Bruxelles to Genappe is meant to represent this hedge that runs along it, and which I have accordingly taken for such. As to the nature of the ground on, and near which the 4th Brigade was generally posted on the 18th June, is impossible for me to recollect precisely as all vegetation on it had been devastated and trodden-down the preceding evening, by our troops marching across it, and I consider the information the farmers residing on the spot have given, to be quite correct.

Note A The squares were formed in the following manner [see diagram overleaf].
Note B On the right of the 4th Hanoverian Brigade, the 9th British Brigade commanded by Major General Sir D. Pack consisting of the 1st Battalion 42nd, 1st Battalion 92nd and 2nd Battalion 44th Regiment was stationed. A corps of Nassau under the Prince of Saxe Weimar was stationed on our left, consisting of two battalions of Orange-Nassau and two battalions of Nassau-Usingen. This corps repulsed the enemy's attack in a very gallant manner.
Note C The attack on our left was made by a French Corps under Count d'Erlon consisting of 4 Brigades of infantry, 1 Brigade of cavalry with 80 pieces of cannon, they reached Smohain unperceived, from where they made their attack.
Note D After Sir T. Picton being killed, Sir J. Kempt took the command of the 6th Division, and Sir J. Lambert that of the 5th which they however exchanged on the 19th June, till the arrival of Sir L.Cole.
Note E This corps consisted of General Ponsonby's brigade, viz. the regiment of Scots Greys; and Inniskilling, and General Vandeleur's brigade of two regiments of

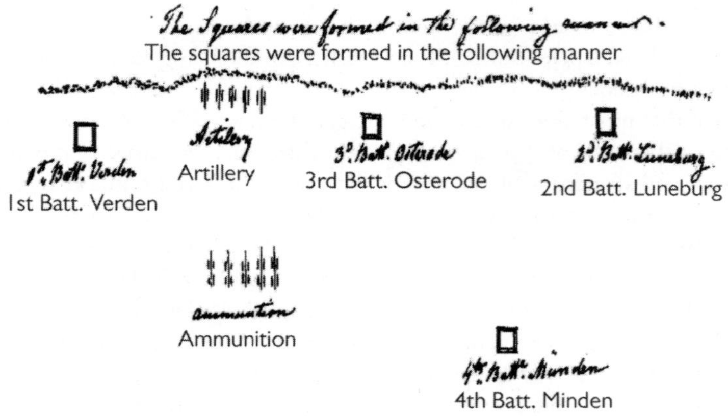

Light Dragoons. The latter retreated on the 4th Hanoverian Brigade.

Note F The 9th British Brigade was furiously attacked by a much superior corps of French infantry, but driven back by this brigade at the point of the bayonet.

Note G Lord E. Somerset's brigade and the 2nd Light Battalion KGL defended La Haye Sainte.

Note H It was the 4th Corps of the Prussian army that defiled; from St Lambert, and in conjunction with the corps of Nassau from our left brought the enemy to retire from Smohain and Papelotte, which he had occupied.

Note J These guards suffered much by our musket and grape shot and although it is said they had sworn not to retreat, they soon changed their promise into a precipitate flight.

Note K The pursuing Prussians were headed by General Gneisenau, they made a great number of prisoners, took 60 pieces of ordnance besides part of the enemy's baggage along with the Emperor's travelling coach and horses.

The forces of the French army consisted on the 18th June of 63,000 infantry and 15,000 cavalry total 78,000 men, besides the Corps under Marshal Grouchy 36,000 strong. The British allied army estimated at 53,000 infantry, 13,000 cavalry, and the detached Corps under Lord Hill, total 65,000 men.

Having thus complied with your wishes, I conclude with the hope that the foregoing relations, however imperfect, considering the period that has elapsed since the battle took place, may contribute something to the perfection of the model, Lieutenant Siborne intends for the representation of the field of battle of Waterloo.

I have the honour to be, dear Sir, your most obedient humble servant

CHARLES BEST
MAJOR GENERAL

---

1 Colonel Best, numbered 695 in Beamish, joined the 8th Line Battalion in 1803. He served in Hanover, the Baltic, the Peninsula in 1808–9, Sicily, and northern Germany. He commanded the 4th Hanoverian Brigade at Waterloo, which along with Major General Lambert's 10th brigade formed the Sixth Division. HGO2, he became a major general on half pay and died only a year after this letter, at Verden on 5 December 1836.

2 See Benne's letters (numbers 12–14).

3 This must refer to Captain von Rettberg's battery.
4 The highlighted sections and separate notes are as in the original manuscript.
5 I presume he refers to Major Heise whom Dalton shows as commanding Major Roger's battery, Royal Artillery and Captain Braun's Hanoverian artillery battery. However the comments in the letter regarding Heise refer only to the Hanoverian battery of Braun, which was brought into the front line at approximately 2 pm. He could however be referring to Lieutenant Heise of Rettberg's battery.
6 The removal of artillery units from the line to replenish, was a major cause of Wellington's disapproval of the artillery at Waterloo and their sparse mention in the Waterloo despatch.
7 The wording almost indicates that the 10,000 Guards were launched at the Prussians. This is not intended; this represents the attack of the Guards on Wellington's centre, most estimates however number the attackers at about 6,500.

No. 195 Captain Frederick Christian Baron von Heimburg, Brigade Major[1]

2 March 1839

ADD MS 34707, FO 32

Original in German

It is my honour, in accordance with your wishes, dear Colonel, to clarify the position of General Best's brigade[2] at Quatre Bras. That this brigade must have been positioned behind General Picton's Division appears to have been a mistake, because we only had, on this occasion, the Brunswick Division in front of us.

Your respectful and obedient servant

HEIMBURG

---

1 Heimburg is listed as number 4 in Beamish. He joined the KGL in 1804 and served in Hanover, the Baltic and the Peninsula in 1808–14. He received a General Service Medal with two bars for Nivelle and Nive. HGO3 and HWC, he retired on half pay in 1816 and became a brevet major in the Hanoverian army and town major at Hanover.
2 Colonel Best commanded the 4th Hanoverian Brigade in the 6th Division.

The Corps of Engineers

No. 196 Captain John Oldfield, Engineer Brigade Major[1]

Commanding Engineers Office, Liverpool, 12 March 1845

ADD MS 34708, FO 181

Sir,

From the perusal of your *History of the War in France and Belgium in 1815*, I find in the list of officers given in attendance and present in the actions of the 16th–17th and 18th June or in formation at Hal on the latter day is not correct as far as my corps is concerned. You give the staff of the Artillery, but not of the Engineers. Lieutenant Colonel Carmichael Smyth[2] was commanding engineer with the army, Major Sir George Hoste KT[3] was commanding engineer with the 1st Corps. I was Major of Brigade and Lieutenant

Sperling, Adjutant.[4] Captain Harris was *not* present with the army in the field, nor was he attached to a division *until* the 20th of June; having been employed at Ghent.[5]

I am in possession of the Commanding Engineers orderly books from the landing in Holland in 1813 to the breaking up of the army of occupation in 1818, with various letter books and other documents connected with that period.[6]

I have the honour to be, Sir, your obedient servant

J. OLDFIELD
COLONEL ROYAL ENGINEERS

---

1 Oldfield joined the Engineers in 1806 and served in the 1814 Holland campaign and throughout the occupation of France. He made a number of observations of the country-side and a map of the Waterloo area was produced from them (Dalton credits Lieutenant Colonel Smyth for the map). This map was given to Lieutenant Waters to take to Wellington at Quatre Bras on 16 June. Waters was nearly captured and his horse with the map was lost. Luckily Waters recovered his horse and got the map to Wellington. Using this map, Wellington discussed his plans to retreat to a new position. The map was handed to his Quartermaster, Sir William De Lancey who preceded the army to mark out its positions. There is some evidence that De Lancey initially considered the Belle Alliance ridge but decided it was too extensive to defend, before settling on the La Haye Sainte ridge. The map still exists, marked heavily with De Lancey's blood when he was mortally wounded and is now at the Royal Engineers Museum. It measures some 3 feet by 4 feet and still bears the pencil marks made on the map near La Haye Sainte. Oldfield died as a General and KH on 2 August 1863.

2 Lieutenant Colonel James Carmichael Smyth received the CB for Waterloo. At the commencement of the action he had the unfortunate duty of placing the officer in command of the sappers and miners detachment at Braine l'Alleud under arrest for failing to construct the field fortifications ordered to strengthen this position. Afterwards he was Governor of Guiana, where he died on 4 March 1838.

3 Hoste was a captain in the corps at Waterloo. He had joined the Engineers in 1802 and served at Maida, Scylla in 1806, Alexandria in 1807, the Ionian Islands in 1810, two attacks on Antwerp in 1812 and he led the Guards in the assault on Bergen-op-Zoom. Afterwards he became a brevet colonel in 1838 and CB. He died in 1845.

4 Lieutenant John Sperling had led the forlorn hope at Bergen-op-zoom in 1814. He retired on half pay as a lieutenant in 1824 and died on 14 February 1877.

5 Harris would have been employed in repairing the defences of the city in case of defeat.

6 It is notable that the staff of the engineers was completely new to Wellington, not one of those that had served with him in the Peninsula served at Waterloo.

No. 197 Captain Charles White[1]

Chateau de Chokier, 31 July 1845

(Not at Waterloo)

ADD MS 34708, FO 202

Parts of original in French

My dear Siborne

Your form of the 24th followed me to this place, whence I shall proceed into Germany in a day or two. I was led to suppose from not receiving a reply to my last letter, that it had not reached its destination. You were right in not creating jealousy by inserting names in your preface. Although I might perhaps, not have exceeded just limits in expecting a copy of your first or second edition, a copy of your third edition will be satisfactory, as it will prove that the book finds numerous purchasers.

As to the assistance you now require, in your discussion with the *Quarterly*,[2] I much fear that my powers cannot keep pace with my inclination. Agreeable to your request I forthwith applied to the Belgian 'Bureau Topographique' at their War Office and found that no plans have been made – no levels taken of the fields of Ligny and Quatre Bras or the intervening ground. Consequently *no documents* exist where from the necessary data may be positively extracted.

You say that you have referred to a letter of mine (written I believe in 1839) wherein I stated that 'even the mill of Brye or Bussy could not be seen from Quatre Bras or from any spot within ½ a mile of the latter.' I have no copy of that letter or notes – but I decidedly recollect that, whilst occupied in superintending the engineers employed in taking the levels, where from you modelled your plans of Ligny and Quatre Bras, I most carefully examined the two fields of battle, and it is fresh in my memory that I could not possibly distinguish either the above mentioned mill, or any contiguous position of the Ligny position from any of the highest points within 3200 metres (2 miles) of Quatre Bras. The highest points according to the levels, of which a sketch is before me, are

No. 1 the eminences right and left of the Namur chaussee south and south-east of Pireaumont and Thyle (45 metres)

No. 2 those intersected by the cross road from Reves to Bauterlet north of Quatre Bras (50 metres).

No. 3 Those in front of the wood of Pampouch (50 metres).

No. 4 Those contiguous to the wood and farm of Bordeaux south of the Ahyle rivulet (at the extreme south east edge of your plan (50 metres).

Brie as well as the extreme right of the Prussian position, up to the Roman road, was concealed either by the eminences or by the trees in front and around Marbais and the former village.

I may be in error but I nevertheless hold it *physically* impossible for any person *to see* the movement of troops moving round Brye, or even Wagnelé, from any spot occupied by the British troops during the combat of Quatre Bras, or to speak more positively from any spot within the distance of two miles to the east, west or north and 1½ miles to the south of Quatre Bras. It would be however be easy to ascertain the effect of a battle terminating as did that of Ligny from the vicinity of Quatre Bras by the sound of musketry and artillery – whose sounds must naturally have become more distant in proportion as the French pushed forward their centre and gained ground upon their left flank.

I have reason to believe that you are in error as to the writer of the article in the *Quarterly* to which you allude. I chanced to meet Colonel Gurwood[3] one evening (some fortnight past) at Brussels and understood from him that Lord Egerton had written an article on the subject[4] and that he intended to proceed on the following morning to Waterloo, Quatre Bras and Ligny – with Lord Egerton. Their object was probably to verify the statement to which you object. If this be the case Lord Egerton will have verified with his own eyes the correctness of his own observations.

Have you met with a book on the campaign of 1815 written by a Prussian officer

(Damitz) which has been done into French? I have seen neither translation or original, but a friend to whom I wrote on the subject of the levels has sent me the following extracts applicable to the subject before you.

Battle of Ligny

'The Field Marshal remained in constant contact with the Duke of Wellington: nearly every half hour he received news… Communications with the English were not broken at any time.

Between 7 and 8 o'clock in the evening the enemy were only maintaining themselves in a defensive formation at St Armand… certain sections of the Army were already exhausted (before the attack of the Imperial Guard).

It was half past eight and the day was going to finish without either of the warring armies having to admit defeat. Napoleon, with the aid of the darkness, managed to penetrate the line at Ligny on the eastern side.'

Therefore it was dark when the charge of the Prussian cavalry took place and still darker when they were defeated between Brye and Ligny – which renders the possibility of such disaster having been *seen* from the Quatre Bras field still more problematical.

In speaking of Quatre Bras Damitz observes:

'At half past eight in the evening the Duke of Wellington had received from Prince Blücher a letter in which the Prince expressed his hope to be able to hold the battle (at Ligny). He did not have to make a subsequent report to the Duke. The officer who was supposed to inform him of the retreat of the Prussian army to Wavre was taken by surprise and was captured by the enemy in the *darkness*.'

Had my time and engagements permitted I might have been enabled to settle the point at issue by a second or rather by a *intensive* examination of the country between Quatre Bras and Ligny – but this is impossible.

Should you have any further communication to make do me the favour to address your letter 3 Place de Waterloo whence it will be forwarded as my movements are very uncertain.

I am very sincerely yours

WHITE

The copy of your work when it comes out can be addressed to my son (Coldstream Guards)[5] 59 [indecipherable] st, St James.

---

1 The identification of this officer is a little problematical, Siborne has written simply 'Captain White' on the letter and the British Library simply states 'Charles White'. It cannot be Andrew White, the only engineer named White who served in the campaign, as he died at Paramatta, New South Wales on 24 November 1837. The only other potential candidate is Major Edward Philip White who went on half pay in 1839 from the Royal Staff Corps, although I have nothing to verify this hunch.

2 The *Quarterly Review*, a magazine.

3 Captain John Gurwood, 10th Hussars. See his letters (numbers 54–56).

4 This refers to the *Quarterly Review* article of June 1845 by Lord Francis Egerton, later Earl of Ellesmere entitled 'Marmont, Siborne and Alison' reprinted in his *Essays on History, Biography, Geography, Engineering* printed by J. Murray in 1858. I must thank John Hussey for this information.

5 This would be ensign Charles H. White; he had joined the Coldstream Guards in 1839.

FOURTH DIVISION AT HAL

No. 198 Lieutenant General Sir Charles Colville GCB[1]

Manchester, 13 December 1842

(Not at Waterloo)

ADD MS 34707, FO 520

Sir Charles Colville returns compliments to Captain Siborne and in acknowledging the receipt of his note of the 8th instant has the pleasure to agree with him that his information is correct 'that a staff officer (Lieutenant Colonel Woodford of 2nd Brigade of the 4th Division, now Major General Sir John Woodford[2]) was sent by him early on the 18th June 1815[3] to the Duke of Wellington for orders, was detained by His Grace about his side at the battle of Waterloo in order that he might be prepared to return to Sir Charles with every information which circumstances might render necessary.'

That officer did not rejoin the division until the next day, nor did Sir Charles receive any information from the Duke on the 18th or through any other channels, but the order to fall back at Hal[4] (quoted by Colonel Gurwood) written by Colonel De Lancey[5] the evening before and delivered to him by Lieutenant Colonel Jones,[6] at an early hour of the 18th with the Brunswick contingent[7] just after the two brigades had been ordered to pile their arms and were already in the streets, after roll call at day break.

The two brigades having with them two brigades[8] of 9 pounder artillery marched immediately in the direction of Hal and falling in at Tubize near Hal in front of Lembeek,[9] with the division of Prince Frederick of Orange's Dutch corps[10] halted there; it being the point of junction with the road leading by Braine le Chateau and Braine l'Alleud to the field of battle. It was there that Colonel Woodford was dispatched to the Duke to report the arrival of the brigade at that point, at which His Grace reposed his satisfaction and gave the directions to the Colonel before mentioned.

Sir Charles Colville would with much pleasure communicate to Captain Siborne 'any circumstances connected with his detached position and those which are likely to be deemed useful to him in the completion of his work,' but in fact he knows of none, but to the last singular [fact?], that though at so short a distance from the cannon fire to indicate a battle, not a shot was heard by the 4th Division,* therefore remaining on the open ground, with piled arms the whole of the day and night, securing means of forage on those of the country.

Nor was any thing known of the momentous affair that had been going on, until a letter was received by means of an officer of the Belgian Garde Dragoons,[11] from his first remarks complimenting Sir Charles Colville on our glorious victory, and directing him to march immediately to Nivelle.

Reply by hand

* Probably owing to the intervening wood.

Note in same hand

Sir Charles Colville requests that Captain Siborne will include his name, on his list of subscribers to his *History of the War in France and Belgium 1815.*

---

1 Colville commanded the reserve which Wellington left at Hal, this consisted of part of the 4th Division (the 4th Brigade had been detached). This force of approximately 6,000 men was left here by Wellington to prevent any turning movement around his right flank, it would also have been useful as a rallying point behind which the army could reform if defeated. It is therefore strange that Wellington did not think to put this corps on alert, he may have assumed that the noise of battle would have warned him, a dangerous assumption as is shown. Colville is often forgotten in this campaign, but he had shown himself to be a good divisional commander in Spain and this was potentially a very important post. Wellington would have only given this command to an officer he rated highly. He had joined the army as an ensign in 13th Regiment in 1781 and served in St Domingo, Egypt, Martinique, Fuentes d'Onor, Badajoz (severely wounded in left thigh and lost a finger), Vittoria (wounded) and Nivelle. Afterwards GCB, GCH, KTS, Colonel of the 5th Foot, General and Governor of Mauritius. He died at Hampstead on 27 May 1843. For more on this man read his biography *The Portrait of a General* by John Colville (Salisbury, Michael Russell, 1980).

2 Lieutenant Colonel John George Woodford, 1st Foot Guards, Assistant Quartermasters General. Woodford joined the Army as an Ensign in 1800, he had acted as DAQMG at Corunna where he was wounded. He received a General Service Medal for Corunna and a Gold Cross for Nivelle, Nive, Orthes and Toulouse. Having reported to Wellington he acted as an Extra ADC to Wellington throughout the battle. Afterwards Major General, CB, KCB and KCH. He died on 22 March 1879.

3 Dalton states that Woodford was sent on the 17th but agrees that he did not arrive until just before the battle. Hal is no more than a two-hour ride from Waterloo and Colville's statement that he was sent in the morning makes more sense.

4 The dispatch is to be found on p. 476 in vol. 12 of Gurwood's *The Duke of Wellington's Dispatches 1799–1815.* This message was penned before it was fully clear to Wellington that Blücher would come to support him the following day but clearly indicates to Colville that Hal must be held firmly, which again highlights Wellington's concerns for his right flank and the Mons-Brussels road. It is clear however, that a major criticism can be levelled against Wellington and his staff for failing to inform Colville of later developments, such as the decision to offer battle or any updates during the day of battle. They were not to know that Colville was unable to hear the noise of battle and was not fretting over his situation desperate for information.

5 Colonel Sir William Howe De Lancey, KCB, Deputy Quartermaster General, who was mortally wounded at Waterloo.

6 There is some doubt over this name. The only Jones on the staff was a Captain Charles Jones on half pay of the 15th Hussars, who acted as Major of Brigade to the 5th Cavalry Brigade. There is some doubt as to why he would be employed on this duty and no indication that he attained the rank of Lieutenant Colonel. I have however failed to find any other suitable candidate, as the only Lieutenant Colonel Jones at Waterloo was Major Arthur Jones of the 71st (Lieutenant Colonel in the army) but again there is no obvious reason why he would have undertaken such a task.

7 Colville is mistaken in this statement, attached to the 6th British Brigade was the 6th Hanoverian Brigade, commanded by Major General Lyon and which consisted of raw Militia troops, they were certainly not Brunswick troops. The 4th Brigade had marched to Waterloo and did participate in the battle.

8 Colville is again mistaken. He did have two artillery batteries within the 4th Division, Major Brome's foot artillery and Captain von Rettberg's Hanoverian artillery battery. Von Rettberg's battery had been detached with the 4th Brigade and fought at Waterloo. Therefore, Colville only had Brome's battery of five 9-pounders and a 5.5 inch howitzer.

9 The village of Lembeek is approximately one mile north of Tubize.

10 The Dutch corps commanded by Prince Frederick of Orange consisted of the Indian Brigade and 1st Netherlands Division totalling approximately 10,000 men.

11 Probably the Belgian Carabineers.

OTHERS NOT AT WATERLOO

No. 199 Baron Ernest Knesbech, Hanoverian Army

Travellers Club, 27 July 1845

(Not at Waterloo)

ADD MS 34708, FO 200

Sir

Referring to our conversation the other day with respect to a new edition of the Waterloo campaign you are proposing. I am sorry to say that time does not allow me to enter into many particulars of your interesting work. But I take the liberty to direct your attention to some objects of little consequence no doubt, but which I think you would better alter in a new edition.[1]

The Hanoverian battalions of infantry were divided into field battalions and Landwehr battalions. You will do better therefore to mention General Kielmannsegge's brigade,[2] 3rd Division, as field battalions Bremen, Verden, York, Luneburg and Grubenhagen, instead of 1st Battalions, which refers to a later denomination.

General Lyon's brigade,[3] 4th Division, consisted of the field battalions Lauenberg and Calenberg and of the Landwehr battalions Nieuberg, Hoya and Bentheim. You made all of these to Landwehr battalions.

Some printing facts require correction viz.

Lieutenant General Count Alten should be Lt. General von Alten, as Alten was only a Count in 1816 or 17.

Colonel Bruckmann... must be Colonel Brückmann[4]

Major von Ranschenplatt... Major von Rauschenplatt

Colonel von Baderken... Colonel Boderken[5]

Landwehr Battalion Ottendorf... L. B. Otterndorf

You never mention Lt. Colonel Julius Hartmann,[6] though he was present at the battle and commanded the whole of the Hanoverian and Legionary artillery present there.

The loss of the 8th Battalion KGL was not so heavy, as is described here, having only one wing cut down and dispersed.[7]

The reason of Major Baring not being supplied with ammunition was that there existed only one cart with rifle ammunition for the two light battalions KGL and this cart had been involved in the scandalous retreat of a great part of the baggage on the Brussels road and thrown into a ditch.[8]

On the plan of the battle of Waterloo, if I am not mistaken, for I have not the plans before me, Prince Bernhard of Saxe Weimar is called Prince Edward of Saxe Weimar.

There, Sir, are the small alterations[9] I take the liberty to suggest to you. On the whole I only can repeat what I told you verbally already, that my brother officers, who were present at the battle of Waterloo, all agree that your description of it is very lively and interesting, full of details and impartial, and if there is some difference of opinion regarding the views you take of a few military matters and some important facts connected with the general history of the campaign, yet every one is satisfied with the fair part you allow for the Hanoverian army.[10]

I have the honour to be, Sir, your most obedient servant

BARON ERNEST KNESBECK

---

1 These corrections were made in the third edition.

2 Major General Count Kielmannsegge commanded the 1st Hanoverian Brigade.

3 Major General Sir James Lyon KCB commanded the 6th Hanoverian Brigade. This Brigade formed part of the reserve at Hal.

4 Lieutenant Colonel F. Henry Brückmann of the Legion artillery. He joined the Legion in 1803 and served in Hanover, the Baltic, northern Germany and Holland. Made HGO2 and RStVO4, he died as a major general half pay at Stade on 27 October 1834.

5 Almost certainly Lieutenant Colonel Rudolphus Bodecker (as spelt in Beamish) of the 1st Line Battalion. He joined the Legion in 1803 and served in Hanover, the Mediterranean, in the Baltic and in the Peninsula in 1808–14. He received a Gold Cross for Talavera, Salamanca, Vittoria and Nive. CB and HGO2, he became a major general and Colonel Commanding the 10th Regiment of infantry and died at Emden on 17 January 1831.

6 Sir Julius Hartmann.

7 This refers to the moment when the 8th Line Battalion KGL was caught in line by cuirassiers. Siborne still indicates in his third edition that the battalion was so roughly handled that they took no further part in the battle. Beamish states their losses in killed, wounded and missing at 131 from a total rank and file of 388.

8 This gives a reason for the garrison of La Haye Sainte, led by Major Baring, running out of ammunition, which directly led to the loss of the farmhouse. It is still a mystery why the nearby 95th were never approached for a supply as they used the same Baker rifle.

9 The only omissions I have made from this letter are to remove the innumerable page references, which do not aid the reader.

10 This is very notable. It is more normal to hear claims that the German contribution in the battle is understated by British historians, Siborne in fairness does not fall into that trap.

No. 200 John Paulet, Earl of Wiltshire[1]

Paris, 7 December 1835

(Not at Waterloo)

ADD MS 34705, FO 362

Original partly in French

My dear Siborne,

Chermside[2] and myself went on Saturday to the Bureau de la Guerre to see the Chief Secretary and confidential persons of General Petiet[3] and questions most pointed were put to him as to whether or not a series of answers were prepared in reply to the questions you sent over here some months back. However as usual in France we met with their *national shrug* of the *shoulders* and cry [of most] infinite servility possible. All we could extract from these diplomatic links with the War Office was an acknowledgement that the orders of Marshal Soult[4] would have been received by this date, but that General Durrieu had returned to his command at Montpellier and that

General Petiet was back in the countryside because of his injuries sustained on the 20th July. However, they would probably be returning to Paris for the reconvention of the Chambers and the Fieschi[5] case, which will begin at the start of the month of January. So you see by this the strategies come of the burnings and I fear that the case will drag on till January and perhaps even then you'll not get the satisfactory information you require for the completion of your model. 'I *recommend*' you strongly coming yourself. You talk of the expense which after all is but a trifling consideration now you have already expended so much *money* on the *model* and as it is so nearly finished it would be a pity to ruin it merely for the trifling reasons you give. I am convinced you'd get leave if properly applied for *should* I not be able yet to do anything for you, however, you must have patience until after the opening of the chambers when all these great Generals who are also peers will be in Paris.

The battle of Waterloo is and always will be a sore subject with the French and as consummate vanity is the leading feature in their character, particularly as regards the deeds of arms, you must make some allowances for their weakness on this point, however much interest you may take in your own *model* and however much *they* vaunt their Austerlitz, Wagram, Borodino, Jena and Friedland to be, it's a subject one never likes to broach here. Chermside has tried through Flahaut[6] to get some information on certain points and no answers were given to the questions he wrote down. In short the idea of a model to commemorate a victory gained over them is decidedly not agreeable. Marshal Soult and Lobau[7] have been the most civil I understand when Chermside has had an interview with them but then it has always ended in a reference to others such as *Petiet* and *Durrieu,*[8] one of which acted as Chef d'Etat Major to the Corps of Lobau and the other I think latter, as Chef d'Etat Major to Soult,[9] who was Major General of the field. I should rather be inclined 'as boney you are' to believe Lt. Col. Batty's account[10] and for the simplest reasons.

First of all before that last *attack* was made, '*Napoleon's*' attention was much called to his right, by the taking of Plançenoit and the *arrival* of the Prussians *under Blücher* just above 'Papelotte' on our extreme left and on the road of *Ohain* to *Wavre*. This naturally was unexpected by *Him* and must have called for a *reinforcement* on that side of the field. Therefore I am inclined to think the last attack on *our right* was made by the *two columns* in question[11] as a last serious effort in a moment of desperation on finding the Prussians arrived *under Blücher* and that it was made [rapidly?] without any support *whatever* or reference to the general charge of French jackets, as the advance of Sir Fred. Adam's Brigade *proves* as he would not have ventured to have wheeled left into line or formed to his left and *exposed his right flank unprotected.*[12] *This* is the *strongest proof* you can have there was no *support* to the *attacking French columns.* Of cavalry, there was *little* at the end of the day and certainly on this occasion there could have been none. There are not *if I recollect right* – inequalities of ground sufficient to have concealed a *supporting* body of cavalry. Therefore it enabled Sir Frederick Adam to make his movement with confidence which under no other circumstances he would have undertaken. I shall yet see what is to be done after Soult, Petiet, Durrieu are to arrive. So you can get on with those other parts of your model and as the question of the last attack seems to be the only one you required a satisfactory answer. I am in hope it may be obtained from some means or another, but let me remark it's no [good] your attempting to threaten to publish or make a *demand*, your object is information and you had better get it smartly and on *good terms* even should it be slower than you anticipated, or written in haste.

Believe me, yours very truly

WILTSHIRE

---

1 Born in 1801, he became 14th Marquess Winchester in 1843. The records do not show that he held any diplomatic post in France.

2 Assistant Surgeon Chermside of the 7th Light Dragoons, see his letter in this volume (number 47).

3 Colonel Auguste-Louis Pétiet served on Marshal Soult's staff at Waterloo.

4 Marshal Nicholas Jean de Dieu Soult acted as Chief of Staff to the French Army of the North.

5 On 28 July 1835 during a review of the National Guard at the Boulevard de Temple there was a great explosion caused by an infernal machine designed to kill Louis-Phillipe. An ardent Corsican Nationalist Joseph Fieschi produced the machine, which comprised of a battery of 25 linked rifle barrels. The attack missed its intended target but wounded 22 and killed 18, including Marshal Mortier who had risen to fame under Napoleon.

6 General de Division Comte Flahaut de la Billarderie, was Aide de Camp to Napoleon at Waterloo.

7 Marshal Georges Mouton, Comte de Lobau had commanded the VI Corps at Waterloo.

8 Marechal de Camp Baron Durrieu served on Lobau's staff at Waterloo, where he was wounded.

9 It should read 'former', see notes 3 and 9.

10 Robert Batty, who served as an ensign in the 1st Foot Guards published a short account, entitled *Campaign of 1815*, in 1820.

11 This indicates that the Imperial Guard advanced in two columns.

12 Adam's 3rd Brigade, consisting of the 52nd, 71st and 95th, wheeled onto the flank of the column of the Imperial Guard. See the letters of officers belonging to these regiments for details.

PRUSSIAN ARMY

No. 201 Captain Wagner, Prussian Staff[1]
Berlin, 15 March 1837

ADD MS 34706, FO 281

Original in German

There exists neither in the German nor the French language a work that contains more details about the fighting in the village of Plançenoit than the description signed by you which I received.[2] The main purpose therefore was to examine everywhere the most precise details of the fighting, and if anything was left unmentioned, it is surely a sign that nothing outstanding was found about it.

That which has been said about the various attacks upon the village of Plançenoit has been taken word for word from the reports of the corps involved. Any reporter who has failed to use them in like manner is not capable of writing comprehensively about it. For this reason, there can be no other work that contains further details.

Naturally, no one paid sufficient attention to the placement of the French artillery to be able to give an authentic account; only a careful observation of the terrain allows us to find the points where the cannons could be advantageously placed, and the celebrated skill of the French artillery officers allows us to assume that they probably used the same. Should one or several cannon not have stood at such a place, it is improbable now that anyone is now available who could set the record right. In this case, where precise information is lacking, there is nothing else to do but to fall back upon the probability that the rules and dictates of tactics were applied.

The General Staff expresses its most obliged thanks for the information, especially for the map of the battle on the Boyne river.[3]

WAGNER, COLONEL

---

1 Wagner served at Waterloo as a volunteer on the Prussian staff.

2 This statement is a further testimonial to the accuracy of Siborne's history relating to the Prussian involvement in the battle. Wagner would know, as he was the author of *Plane der Schlachten und Treffen 1813, 1814, 1815 (Plans of the Battle and Engagements),* vol. 4, published in 1825.

3 Fought on 11 July 1690, between the forces of William III and James II. It was an indecisive affair, but it caused James to flee precipitately to France and is therefore seen as the end of the war, although it rumbled on until 1692.

No. 202 Christian Charles Josias de Bunsen, Prussian Ambassador to Britain

4 Carlton Terrace, 14 January 1848

(Not at Waterloo)

ADD MS 34708, FO 265[1]

Not one moment do I lose, my dear Captain Siborne in forwarding to you the papers received by this days courier from Berlin.

As to the *printed papers*, they will speak for themselves, as you read our language so well.[2] But as few foreigners read our written character, I give you here an *extract*. As to this *written Official Report of Major Gerwien* of the General Staff of the Prussian Army, I see he contains first (pp 1–3) the direct and indirect proofs, that the Duke received the intelligence of the advance of the French, through General von Ziethen[3] at nine on the morning of the 15th.

The dispatch was sent on 15th June by *4 o'clock in the morning* (3:45) by a *Feldjäger* to the Duke, at Brussels. General Ziethen wrote a letter *on this subject, on the 21 Jan 1819*, at the particular request of General von Grolman, which letter is preserved in the archives of the Staff.

According to this letter, the Feldjäger arrived at Brussels *early at 9 o'clock of the same day*. There exists *no copy* of the report of General de Ziethen. The General in the letter alluded to, explains this by the circumstance that having no officer with him who could write French well enough, he, the General was obliged to carry on himself the whole correspondence with the Duke, and therefore there was no time to take a copy. The courier was dispatched at 3:45 in the morning precisely.

That the letter arrived *by 9 o'clock,* at Brussels is proved by the Duke's own despatch of that day to the Duc de Feltre (of 15th June 10 o'clock in the evening).[4] (See p 3 of the report.)

The intelligence received *from Charleroi* by the Duke, according to his own letter, that day *at 9 o'clock*, *can* be no other than General Z[iethen]'s letter. *Damitz*[5] therefore is not *quite accurate* when he says, the letter arrived *at 11*.

The other intelligence 'that the enemy had attacked the Prussian posts' came *from Blücher*, and was sent by him from Namur at 12 o'clock at noon. According to Müffling's account[6] it arrived at Brussels at 4:30 pm. There follows (p. 4) extracts from the Gerwien journal, as a proof that there were on the fifteenth of June, *two* communications from the Prussian Staff to the Duke. The difference as to the *time* of these two communications is to be explained thus, *either* by a not quite accurate recollection of the writer, or *by some accident*, the intelligence of the fight of the Vanguard arrived only at 3 o'clock pm at *Tirlemont hotel*, after having been known many hours before elsewhere, by some other accident, the two Prussian Aide de Camps were really *only* met at 6,[7] but after they had some time fulfilled their commission.

p. 6 contains following remarks on Captain Siborne's account of the events alluded to:

1 There is no account of Ziethen's courier, although both Wagner[8] and Damitz mention it.

2 Nor is there an account of General Steinmetz's communication to the Commanding officer of the English (Dutch) vanguard, respecting the events on

the Sambre, mentioned by Damitz.[9]

3 It is *assumed*, that these events ought to have been known at *Binche*, at the latest, at 5 o'clock in the morning.

4 Upon this assumption is founded the reproach to the Dutch troops, acting there with the Prussians, for not having been in the Brigade Quarters at 8:30 in the morning. But, as to the *assumption of no. 3*, it is to be observed that the Prussian troops in Binche had no intelligence of those events before 8 o'clock in the morning. They had in consequence of the wind being against them, not heard the cannonade at Maladries, at h[alf] p[ast] 4 o'clock in the morning. As to the real attack, they were only apprised of it by the general officer sent to the Dutch General van Merlen (at St Symphorien), when that officer[10] [Major von Arnauld] passed through Binche. Thus the reproach founded upon such assumptions falls to the ground.

Finally it is said (p. 7) that certain numbers of the *Military Weekly Journal* of the Prussian army contain much authentic information which may prove to be of interest for a new edition of Captain Siborne's work.

Baron Canitz has given order in consequence; that the numbers quoted by Major Gerwien should be added to the expedition *[sic]*.

These are the numbers enclosed.[11] As to Major Gerwien, he is the Chief of that sector of the General Staff, which, presides over the documents relative to the history of the wars.

Hoping the communications may still come in time I have only to add, that I am at all events most anxious to know what your definitive opinion on this interesting subject will be. If you pass by Carlton Terrace any hour before 1 or after 4, I should be then most obliged to you, for a call, as I am almost bound to my room, in consequence of the *influenza*.

Ever yours faithfully

BUNSEN

---

1 Letters 201–5 have recently been published by Peter Hofschröer in *Age of Napoleon* magazine, no. 25.

2 This is an important comment. It destroys the claims of David Hamilton-Williams in his *Waterloo – New Perspectives* (London, Arms & Armour Press, 1993) that Siborne could not read German and ignored the role of the German contingents at Waterloo.

3 Lieutenant General Count Hans von Ziethen commanded the I Corps of the Prussian Army, it was his troops that had initial contact with the French invasion and was forced to draw back.

4 This refers to a major discussion point to this very day. This letter states correctly that there were only two communications from the Prussian army to Brussels on 15 June. Bunsen relies upon Ziethen's unfortunately vague remarks made to General Grolman and upon a phrase in the Duke of Wellington's letter to the Duc de Feltre which may be interpreted in two completely different ways. Although William had considerable doubts about parts of the Prussian submissions, he was eventually persuaded to adopt their conclusions in his 3rd edition. The interested reader should study the argument over these points: Peter Hofschröer sets out the case for accepting the Prussian claims in *1815 The Waterloo Campaign – the German Victory* (London, Greenhill, 1999); John Hussey provides the counter-argument in the *Journal of the Society for Army Historical Research* (1999, pp 250–68) and *War in History,*

(1999, pp 84–116, 2000, pp 465–80) and more recently has quoted the Prussian historian Pflugk-Harttung (1848–1919) in his support.

5 Carl von Damitz, author of *Geschichte des Feldzuges von 1815 in den Niederlanden und Frankreich (History of the Campaign from 1815 in the Netherlands and France)*, 2 vols, published in 1837–8.

6 Müffling's *History of the Campaign*, written in late 1815. In his later memoirs, written in 1844 and published 1851, he states the time as 3 pm.

7 This refers to the article 'Operations of the Fifth or Picton's Division in the Campaign of Waterloo' in the *United Services Journal* of 1841 (recently reprinted by Ken Trotman, Military Monograph 1, Cambridge, 2001), where the writer describes meeting two Prussian ADCs who had brought Blücher's message warning of the attack in Brussels at about 6 pm (see also letter 204). In this letter Bunsen seeks to assure Siborne that the meeting must have occurred hours after they had delivered their despatches. If they had only just delivered their despatches at this time, it would destroy the Prussians claims against Wellington.

8 See his letter (number 201).

9 Here he takes Siborne's statement in his history of the campaign to task. It had been shown in *The Weekly Military Journal* of 1846 from General Rebeque's journal, that Steinmetz *had* sent a warning message to the neighbouring Dutch force under Van Merlen at approximately 8 am.

10 This was at about 8 am; the information was directed to Mons and from there to Braine Le Comte and on to Brussels for the Prince of Orange. He advised Wellington of the message at approximately 4 pm. When Ziethen's and Blücher's letters also arrived later, Wellington ordered the army to concentrate. The Prussian troops at Binche learnt of the fighting from this officer and hence could not have warned the Dutch forces earlier.

11 Letter 202, together with copies of the weekly military journal no longer traceable, from Major Gerwien is the attachment.

No. 203 From the same

4 Carlton Terrace, 8 February 1848

ADD MS 34708, FO 280

My dear Captain Siborne

I loose *[sic]* not a moment to transmit to you Major Gerwien's further communications,[1] in reply to the observations which you entrusted to my care.

I add General von Canitz, my Chief's, original dispatch to me, which accompanied that memoir, for your inspection and occasional return.

I am most anxious to know the result of the impartial historian's and officer's meditation.

It appears to me that G[erwein] acknowledges the force of your argument, that Ziethen could not report at 3:45 what happened at 4:30. But, his argument seems to be this, 'There *must* have been, according to the documents and facts which are incontestable, a mention of *begun hostilities* in Ziethen's report, because there was no occasion for reporting early on the 15th what he had reported on the *14th*[2] … ergo &c i.g.e.d.[3] Then comes the force of the argument from Muffling's evidence. Am I right in stating it so? I remain my dear Captain Siborne.

Ever yours faithfully

BUNSEN

1 This refers to letter 205 from Gerwien and letter 206 from von Canitz.

2 This continues the argument over Ziethen's message to Wellington. If it had been sent at 3.45 it could not have mentioned the French attack as it had not started then. If written at 4.30 he would have mentioned the French cannon commencing the attack. Although Ziethen remembers sending the message at 3.45 the argument for a later time does have much strength.

3 The meaning of this is roughly the same as QED.

No. 204 Major Gerwien, Department Chief on the Prussian Staff

Berlin, 13 December 1847

(Not at Waterloo)

ADD MS 34708, FO 269

Original in German

Concerning the reports of 15 June 1815 that were sent by the Prussians to the Duke of Wellington in Brussels in the early hours of this day

From the files referring to the campaign of 1815 regarding the message in question from the then commanding General of I Army Corps, von Ziethen, to the Duke of Wellington on the attack of the French on the Prussian outposts on the Sambre on 15 June 1815 the following is beyond doubt:

'That this message sent from Charleroi at about 4 am on 15 June was handed over in Brussels to the Duke of Wellington by a courier.'

General von Ziethen confirmed this in writing in a letter (contained in our files) to the now deceased General von Grolman[1] dated 21 January 1819. The latter specifically requested this after he had already been informed of this verbally, learning at the same time that:

The courier (on 15 June) arrived at 9 am[2] in Brussels.

No copy of the message in question exists.[3] General von Ziethen apologizes for this in the above mentioned letter to General von Grolman, writing:

> 'As all correspondence with Field Marshal the Duke of Wellington had to be in the French language, and as in 1815 I had no officer who had mastered French so well that he could write it, I had to conduct all correspondence with the Field Marshal the Duke of Wellington myself. This is why no copy of the letter that I sent by a courier whose name I do not recollect to Brussels at *3:45 am* on the morning of 15 June 1815. I take this opportunity Your Excellency to reply to the letter of 30th of this month.'

As you can see, General von Ziethen made no comment about the time that this courier arrived in Brussels. It is not known where General von Grolman got the information that:

'The courier arrived in Brussels at 9 am.'

However, nobody can doubt this information, because in Gurwood's *Despatches*, vol. 12, p. 473, the letter from the Duke of Wellington to the Duke of Feltre dated 15 June 1815, states the following:

'Brussels 15 June 1815 10 pm
My Lord Duke,

I have received news that the enemy has attacked the Prussian outposts at Thuin on the Sambre this morning and appears to be menacing Charleroi. I have received nothing from Charleroi since 9 am.'[4]

From whom other than General von Ziethen could the information have come which the Duke knew from Charleroi at 9 am? *

The later 'News that the enemy had attacked the Prussian outposts, etc.' came from Prince Blücher, passed on to the Duke of Wellington by General von Müffling who was attached to the English headquarters. They were dispatched at 12 noon from Namur and according to General von Müffling's work *History of the Campaign of the Anglo-Dutch Army in 1815, arrived in Brussels at 4:30 pm.*

The *United Services Journal* 1841, part II, pp 170 ff, contains an essay regarding the 'Operations of the Fifth or Picton's division in the campaign of Waterloo' where, on p. 172, the writer states:

'About *three o'clock of the afternoon* of that day, our officers were sitting at dinner at the Hotel de Tirlemont, where we had our mess, when we heard of a commotion, or greater stir than usual, having arisen in the City; presently some Belgian gentleman came in and told us, that there had been 'an affair of outposts' on the frontier, and that the French suffered a repulse. This was the piquet affair of the Prussian General Ziethen, who had gallantly resisted the enemy's advanced guard, coming in the direction of the grande chaussee to Brussels, but was driven back, or in fact he fell back as all outposts do, as a matter of course.

After dinner we strolled, as was our custom in the afternoon, into the park, where the great world promenaded every evening. *Towards six o'clock* sauntering about the walks, I encountered two Prussian aides-de-camp, who had come from Blücher with intelligence of the advance of the French army, pointing towards Brussels, or in that direction; we were instantly ordered to hold ourselves in readiness to march to the front in the morning.'

The above confirms the arrival of *two* messages:

1 A message from General von Ziethen in the first half of the day.

2 A message from Field Marshal Prince Blücher in the second half of the day.

The differences in the apparent times of arrival of the messages can be explained either by a mistake or poor memory by the English writer, or it could be that the rumour of a skirmish at the front, after it had been circulating for hours, actually did only reach the Hotel de Tirlemont as late at 3 pm, being circulated for several hours before; and that this meeting did actually take place with the Prussian couriers at *6 pm*, who had completed their tasks. It should be noted here that Captain Siborne, who, in his description of the Prussian part in the campaign of 1815 otherwise follows the works of Wagner and Damitz very closely.

1 He completely ignores the sending of a courier from General von Ziethen to the Duke of Wellington *which both works mention.*

2 Does not mention the message from General von Steinmetz to the commanding officer of the Anglo-Dutch outpost at Binche regarding the events on the Sambre and furthermore

3 Assumes that these events must have been known in Binche by 5 am at the latest.

4 Believes the criticism of the Dutch troops who were in close contact with the

Prussians is justified, not to have assembled at brigade headquarters by 8:30 am.[5]

Concerning the first two points nothing more can be added. On the third point however it should be noted that the Prussian troops in Binche did not have knowledge of the mentioned events until 8 am as, due to opposing winds, they did not hear the firing at Maladries, where at 3:30 am, the enemy opened the attack with four cannon, thereby alarming those elements of the 1st Brigade near there. The news of the attack which had taken place was first received by the Dutch General van Merlen (at St. Symphorien) from the Staff Officer of 1st Brigade (Major von Arnauld), as he passed through Binche. The accusation covered under 4 is thus not sustainable.

If, by the way, Captain Siborne has the intention of publishing a third edition of his work, then he would be able to take into account what is contained in nos 1–8 and 15–35 of the 1845 volume of the *Military Weekly Journal*, in nos 3–11 of the 1846 volume and in nos 34–38 of the 1847 volume. It is all the more desirable and all the more unavoidable as these contain a documented explanation of many events which even in the works of Wagner and Damitz are either not clarified or not mentioned.

Main Headquarters General Staff
Department of War History

GERWEIN
MAJOR IN THE GENERAL STAFF

* In Damitz's work, the time of its arrival is given as *11 am*. That this is an error can be seen from the above.

---

1 General Major Karl Wilhelm Georg von Grolman (1777–1843). Grolman joined the Prussian Army in 1791 and fought at Auerstadt in 1806 following which he served on the Military Reorganization Committee. However in 1809 he joined the Austrian service and then served with the Spanish army until captured by the French in 1812 at the fall of Valencia. He escaped and returned home. Promoted to major on the General Staff in 1813, he came under Blücher's command in 1814. In 1815 he served at headquarters as Quartermaster General.

2 This is slightly misleading as no one has been able to establish beyond doubt that the message arrived at 9 am; however, rumours of a French attack did abound at Brussels on the 15th. It seems certain however that whatever time the note arrived, it provided insufficient information to convince Wellington that this was anything beyond a mere skirmish or probe.

3 It is unfortunate that the note no longer exists as it would clear up this vexatious question.

4 This comment wishes to show that the Duke's statement that he had received nothing from Charleroi since 9 am refers to Ziethen's letter which must therefore have arrived at 9 am in Brussels. The counter argument is that the Duke meant that he had not heard any news since 9 am timed at Charleroi, which would have then reached Brussels around 4–5 pm. The argument continues to rage to this day.

5 This lists the contentious issues with reference to Siborne's first edition of his *History*. It should be noted that these letters convinced Siborne to change his version in the third edition to agree entirely with this Prussian version of events. There is much evidence now that the Prussian version may have been flawed.

No. 205 From the same
Berlin, 29 January 1848

ADD MS 34708, FO 284

Original in German

Reply to Captain Siborne's doubts about the message regarding the commencement of hostilities by the French the day that General von Ziethen sent to the Duke of Wellington in the morning of 15 June 1815.

If Captain Siborne believes that the despatch sent in the morning of 15 June 1815 by General von Ziethen from Charleroi to Field Marshal the Duke of Wellington in Brussels contained no other news than the assembly of the enemy in great strength before the Prussian front line and of the probability of a coming offensive, then this office is not in a position to refute that by producing a copy of this message as proof. The reasons for this are given in Ziethen's letter of 21 January 1819. There is however another proof:

On the morning of the 15th, the time is not given, but it was probably *before 5 am*, General von Ziethen sent a despatch to Prince Blücher in Namur that read:

'On the right flank there are cannon shots and now also (thus for the first time) small arms fire, but reports from there have yet to be received. As soon as they are received, he, General von Ziethen, will not fail to forward them. Meanwhile, he has arranged to move everything into position, and, if necessary, will concentrate at Fleurus.'

What makes it probable that this report was sent off at before 5 am (perhaps at 4:45 am) can be deduced from the fact that Prince Blücher's reply had already been sent at *9 am*, saying:

'He, the Prince, had received the report of the artillery and small arms fire that morning. That night, orders for the 2nd, 3rd and 4th Corps to concentrate, the 2nd at Onoz and Mazy, the 3rd at Namur and the 4th at Hannut had already been issued, and they were expected to be in position this *evening* (i.e., the 15th). It is most important that General von Ziethen observes most accurately every enemy movement, its direction and the strength of his columns, particularly in the direction of Binche and the Roman road. In all further reports, the General is to note the time at which they are despatched'.

The distance between Charleroi and Namur via Sombreffe is five geographical miles.[1] To cover this distance would have taken about 3½ hours. Thus, if this despatch as assumed had been sent before 5 am, and it is certain it arrived in Namur between 8 and 9 am. It is safe to assume that this time was needed to cover that distance.

From the *two original documents in our files here*, it is evident that:

'General von Ziethen, as Captain Siborne assumes, was not waiting for a report from Lobbes via Fontaine L' Eveque before reporting the commencement of hostilities, but, rather he made that report as soon as he heard the artillery and small arms fire in Charleroi.'

The following can also be deduced from these documents:

'*That General von Ziethen reported this situation to the Duke of Wellington at the same time.*[2] Because the enemy had concentrated on the right flank of the Prussian army between Maubeuge and Beaumont and placed strong forces at Lobbes and Thuin, pushing forward strong detachments to Merbes le Chateau. The information being obtained by spies and deserters was that an attack was expected with certainty on the 14th or the 15th.'

As General von Ziethen had already reported this not only to Prince Blücher but also to the Duke of Wellington on the 14th, then why should he *repeat this report* on the morning of the 15th?

That General von Ziethen sent such a report on the 14th can be confirmed by a letter in the archives here from General von Müffling, who was attached to Wellington's Headquarters, to General Count Gneisenau on the morning of 15 June which states at the beginning:

'....the reports from General von Dörnberg and of General von Ziethen of yesterday's date are confirmed. It is confirmed from French newspaper reports of the 12th that Napoleon had left Paris. His current whereabouts are unknown. *It appears that as we were not attacked yesterday*, it would seem that the enemy wants to deceive us and mask his front to hide the movements that he has in mind...'

Here, there is mention of an attack on the 14th which General von Ziethen foresaw and which he certainly expected.

As mentioned above, he had, on the 14th, also sent such a message to Prince Blücher, *so the message of the morning of the 15th could be none other than to report the firing that he had heard to convince the two commanders that hostilities had indeed begun.*

That General von Ziethen's despatch to the Duke of Wellington arrived in Brussels before 9 am is beyond doubt as the Duke himself sent a letter at 10 pm on 15 June to the Duc de Feltre as has already been mentioned.

That the report in question *mentions the commencement of hostilities*, even if the above evidence were insufficient, it should be repeated that at Brussels at noon on the 15th, rumours of a battle on the Sambre were already circulating and came to the ears of English officers from Picton's Division in the Hotel Tirlemont.

Who else other than the Prussian courier could have brought this news and been the cause of its circulation?

Captain Siborne, if he wishes to be fair, will now not be able to raise any more objections, or reproach General von Ziethen that he, the General, failed to send to the Duke of Wellington a report of the enemy attack on the Prussian outposts on 15 June.

Even if the time given by General von Ziethen, 3:45 am, appears impossible and supports Captain Siborne's view that such a report could not have been made, then this evidence is in no way irrefutable. Basically it is down to the fact that in General von Ziethen's letter to General von Grolman of 21 January 1819, *4:45 am* was meant and not 3:45 am, the latter time being a failure of memory. *This can indeed be proved.* In the message from General von Ziethen to Prince Blücher mentioned above, he explains that:

'There has been cannon fire since *4:30 am...*'

As is known, at 4:30 am, the enemy attacked Maladrie with four cannon.

At about 5 am (perhaps at 4:45 am, we conjecture), General von Ziethen reported to Namur that he had heard shots, etc., on his right flank. It is beyond doubt that General von Ziethen reported this to the Duke of Wellington around *5 am (4:45)*.

But even if this message had been sent to Brussels later than 4:45 am, *it still arrived there at 9 am, and, as it was reporting the commencement of hostilities*, this was then the most important point and is here the most important point which is of concern and remains so.

Main Headquarters General Staff

Department of War History

GERWEIN
MAJOR IN THE GENERAL STAFF

---

1 Five German miles equalled approximately 35 kilometres.
2 It has to be said, that this evidence does *not* prove that Ziethen wrote to Wellington as stated. Just because he *should* have done does not mean that he *did*.

No. 206 General von Canitz

Berlin, 30 January 1848

(Not at Waterloo)

ADD MS 34708, FO 283

Original in German
Written to Chevalier Bunsen

Your Excellency's helpful letter of 19th of this month arrived on the 24th and I have passed it on the General von Krauseneck, along with its enclosures from the General Staff.

General von Krauseneck does not doubt that this refutation based on official documents contains everything necessary to lay to rest all the doubts that Captain Siborne had, and refutes his accusation against General von Ziethen that the latter had neglected to report to the Duke of Wellington in good time the attack of the French on the Prussian outposts. He also expressed to me the wish that I too have that the respected author of the *Waterloo Campaign* now no longer has any objections to take over the defence of General von Ziethen.

GENERAL VON CANITZ

FRENCH ARMY

No. 207 General of Division Georges Mouton, The Count Lobau[1]

Paris, 13 September 1834

ADD MS 34703, FO 217

Original in French

Printed heading on paper: National Guard of the Department of the Seine

The Marshal Commandant to Mister W. Siborne, Lieutenant of the 47th British Regiment, Military Secretary, aide to the Commanding General in Ireland.

Sir,

Your letter from Dublin dated 1 August was handed to me on the 7th of this month by a doctor of the English Embassy at Paris.[2] I would thank you for forwarding a copy of the letter you addressed to the Duke of Dalmatia,[3] on the same date, as well as a copy of the plan you mentioned. I am very flattered by the attention you give me.

I regret that I am not able to satisfy your wishes immediately. As much as I would like to help you, I cannot find the documents you need and unfortunately, my memory is failing. However my Lieutenant General at Waterloo, Durrieu,[4] will come here, hopefully in the middle of this month or at the beginning of next month. As soon as he arrives, all the pieces required will be given to him. I will make sure that he does everything to answer your wishes as soon as possible and as efficiently as he can.

You must believe that I will do everything that I possibly can do, in order to provide you as much help as I can. Especially in this matter, all the information we can produce for you will be a priority.[5]

I have the honour, Sir, to offer my salutations

LOBAU

---

1 Mouton, the son of a baker rose rapidly after joining the army in 1792. He served with distinction in the wars in Italy and was seriously wounded at Genoa. He became an Imperial Aide in 1805 and served as such at Jena-Auerstadt, Eylau and Friedland where he was again badly wounded. He became famous at the bridge at Landshut after which Napoleon coined the phrase '*Mon Mouton est un lion*'. He served with distinction again at Aspern-Essling and was granted the title Comte de Lobau. He served in Russia and Germany. In 1815 he commanded the VI Corps which held the Prussian advance back for many hours until wounded. Following the Restoration, he became a member of the Chamber of Deputies, Commander of the Paris National Guard and in 1831 Marshal of France. He died in 1838 when his old chest wound from his days at Genoa burst open again.

2 This would be Surgeon Robert Alexander Chermside, see his letter in this volume, number 47.

3 Marshal Soult, Duke of Dalmatia

4 Marechal de Camp Baron Durrieu served on Lobau's Staff at Waterloo, where he was wounded.

5 This is the only recorded reply from the French officers at Waterloo. The typically flowery phrasing of this Gallic letter indicates that despite the promises of help it contains, there was little intention of supplying any information whatsoever. The letters of Surgeon Chermside (letter 47) and the Earl of Wiltshire (letter 200) show the growing frustration at the lack of information provided by the French marshals, despite the most extravagant promises.

APPENDIX A

Correspondence regarding the models

No. 1 Letter from Lieutenant Colonel Sir Charles Routledge O'Donnell[1]
Horseguards, 20 August 1833

ADD MS 34703, FO 134

My dear Siborne,

I have this day attended Lord Fitzroy Somerset's[2] house with the sole view of inducing his Lordship to decide the question of your circular. Lindsay[3] has endeavoured as much as possible to bring your papers before his lordship and succeeded as far as to give one a hope that I should be enabled to obtain a final answer this morning, but I am sorry to tell you that your patience must again be put to the test for Lord Fitzroy requires a little longer to consider of it and tells me that he will in a few days let me positively know.

I think he wishes to refer to the Quarter Master General's Department for the names of those officers now in existence who are most competent to give the detailed information, and it strikes me that he is apprehensive- the conflicting statements are such, sufficient regularity will not be given to the representation. Such however is my own private opinion. I told him *again* if he was to only suggest the names of those officers to whom you could apply I was confident you would not only attend to but be obliged for the suggestion.

I like your postscript to the circular and should like it better if it went further back to the commencement of the affair, but that can be done hereafter if you should think better of it and if hereafter you find that the later publications respecting 'the Crisis' produce sufficient matter. Bye the bye Major Gawler's reply to Sir Hussey Vivian will appear in the *U.S.J.* for next month.[4]

Many thanks to you (and offer the same with my compliments to Sir Hussey) for your [assistance?] about the leave for my young friend in the 76th. I communicated the intelligence respecting embarkation immediately to his mother who has taken the necessary steps to let him know. He is at the moment in Scotland so that some time will necessarily elapse before the information reaches him, in the reaches of the north. But I have no doubt that as soon as it does he will return with all expedition.

I have just received, very opportunely a very handsome present and very complimentary letter from Prince William (the 2nd son of the King) of Prussia. It is no less than a book of lithographic drawings, coloured, of all the Prussian Army of 1830, so that if what I sent you from [Col. Nash?] are not complete I can send you over the book altogether, there being little or no difference as I am informed in their [appointments?] since 1815.

Believe me my dear Siborne very truly yours

C R O'DONNELL

---

1 O'Donnell had joined the army in 1813 as an ensign and rose quickly to lieutenant colonel by 1826 when he went on half pay unattached. It is unclear why he was involved in this issue as he is not named on the staff.

2 Lord Fitzroy James Henry Somerset, Military Secretary to Lord Hill, General Commanding-in-Chief and Colonel of the 53rd Foot. He had joined the army as a cornet in 1804 and served throughout the Peninsular war and Waterloo campaign as Military Secretary to Wellington. He received a Cross with five bars for Busaco (wounded), Fuentes d'Onoro, Badajoz, Salamanca, Vittoria, Pyrenees, Nivelle, Nive, Orthes and Toulouse. He was wounded and lost his right arm at Waterloo. He became Baron Raglan and Field Marshal, commanding the army in the Crimea. He died of dysentery at Sebastopol on 28 June 1855.

3 I believe the British Library catalogue to be correct, which states that Mr F. H. Lindsay was Chief Clerk in the Commander-in-Chief's office.

4 There is some confusion over this statement. The date of the letter is certainly correct but Gawler's 'The Crisis at Waterloo' was published in the July edition of the *United Service Journal* as was Vivian's account. Gawler's reply to Vivian was not published until 1835.

No. 2 Letter from Major General Sir James Charles Dalbiac[1]
34 Cavendish Square, 5 March 1834

ADD MS 34703, FO 147

My dear Siborne,

Since the receipt of your letter, I have had several conferences with Lord F. S.[2] and Mr Lindsay – indeed the former has put into my hands the papers regarding your proposal, requesting as he is so much hurried, that I will for the present communicate with you thereupon.

It was suggested that the latter part of the 1st paragraph after 'Secretary at War' should be omitted.[3]

We are all of opinion that the minimum subscription should be set at £10 – there are many persons who would subscribe ten that would not subscribe twenty.

We also think that it would greatly increase your difficulties rather than tend to elucidation to write a circular for information to the different general officers who commanded Brigades etc and who from a variety of circumstances must have such very different versions of what happened before their eyes. I understand Sir P. Maitland does not admit the reminiscences of Major Gawler.

We also think that it would be well to insert in the prospectus, that it is the intention of the subscription fees after the model shall have been duly exhibited in some of the most principal cities and towns in the U. Kingdom to present the same to the Duke of Wellington.

Lord F. S. has promised to speak to Lord Hill[4] on the subject, and I shall hope to write to you again in a few days.

Yours faithfully

J CHS DALBIAC

1 Major General Sir James Charles Dalbiac KCH. He had joined the army as a cornet in 1793 and served in the Peninsula in the 4th Dragoon Guards at Talavera, Campo Major, Llerena and Salamanca. He became Colonel of the 3rd Foot Guards in 1839. It is unclear why Somerset passed these proposals to him as he does not appear on any staff list.

2 Fitzroy Somerset.

3 This section was indeed removed from the circular.

4 General Commanding-in-Chief 1828–42, General Lord Rowland 'Daddy' Hill GCB, GCH, KC, Colonel of the Royal Regiment of Horse Guards. He joined the army as an ensign in 1790, serving in Egypt (wounded) and receiving a Cross with four bars for Rolica, Vimiera, Corunna, Talavera (wounded), Vittoria, Pyrenees, Nivelle, Nive Orthes and Waterloo.

No. 3 Letter from W. Siborne to Major General Sir James Charles Dalbiac
Dublin, 8 March 1834

ADD MS 34703, FO 149

My dear General
I have been favoured with your communication of the 5th inst., by which it appears that the papers regarding my proposals to complete my model by raising a subscription have been placed in your hands by Lord Fitzroy Somerset.

At the time I communicated to Lord Fitzroy an explanation of the manner in which I proposed to carry on the work, I did not for a moment anticipate that by so doing, I was likely to give so much trouble, as now appears to be the case, either to his lordship, or to any other individual: but the Lords of the Treasury having been pleased to make over to me the benefit of the £400 already advanced upon the condition that I should carry on the work upon my own account I felt it my duty, as Lord Hill had, from the first sanctioned and approved of my undertaking, to make known to his lordship the position in which I was placed by that decision, and which enforced upon me the necessity for such of the requisite funds, of having recourse to some mode of raising them, and in presenting to him a prospectus of the plan I had adopted. I solicited the continuance of that sanction and support which he had extended to me when the work was carried on by aid of funds from government.

With respect to the different points adverted to in your letter, I trust I may be excused the liberty I venture to take in offering a few remarks upon them.

It is suggested that I should omit the latter part of the last paragraph after the words 'Secretary at War'. I must confess I do not see what objection can be made to the part in question, as it states most explicitly the circumstances which led to my being left to complete the work on my own account and at my own risk.

With regard to the minimum subscription being fixed at £10 instead of £20, I must respectfully beg leave to adhere to my original plan – my object being to endeavour to obtain the sum required by the aid of as *small* a number of subscribers as possible-indeed I was much inclined at first to make £50 the lowest sum. In support of my own view of this point I may observe that the only two officers in this country to whom I mentioned my proposed plan of subscription, immediately desired me to put down their names for £100 each, (thus making up nearly a seventh of the whole amount[1]) and one of them remarked that he was certain I could raise the money through 15 or 20 subscribers, principally among those who were on the General Staff at Waterloo. At all events I am disposed to try the experiment of £20 being much the minimum subscription.

I cannot consent to insert in the prospectus 'that it is the intention of the subscription after the model shall have been duly exhibited in some of the principal cities and towns in the U. Kingdom, to present the same to the Duke of Wellington' – conceiving that such an insertion tantamount to an acknowledgement that the model would be the property of the subscribers, instead of which, I only *borrow* the money from them such money to be repaid with interest, nor can I, above all, thus deliberately deprive myself of the honour and gratification, of presenting in my own name, as the author, the result of my labours after having reaped the benefit of them either to the Duke of Wellington, or to the Government to be preserved as national property.

You observe in reference to my 'Circular for information to the different general officers who commanded brigades, etc.' that the latter ' from a variety of circumstances must give such very different versions of what passed before their eyes'. I must readily admit the possibility, if not probability, of an officer giving a very different version of what occurred to a brigade or regiment to which he was *not* attached, as with compared with that given by an officer who really belonged to it – indeed this is fully attested by recent discussions, and is borne out by your remark that Sir Peregrine Maitland does not admit the reasoning of Major Gawler: but surely it will be conceded that officers may be able to give a very good version of what passed before their own eyes, *as far as related to themselves and their own corps.* Had Major Gawler strictly confined to his statement to an account of what was done by the *52nd*, he would not have laid himself open to the recriminations of those officers, the movements of whose corps he had ventured to comment upon.

Fortunately, there still exists a considerable number of eyewitnesses of the Battle of Waterloo, and it appears to me that the principal utility and advantage of constructing a model of the action at the present day, is to secure before the favourable opportunity is gone for ever, a well authenticated representation and record of the positions and movements of the troops engaged, and that the only mode of arriving at accurate conclusions essential for such a purpose, is to weigh and compare the statements of those eyewitnesses-to become convinced of the actual position or movement of any particular regiments only when the concurrent testimony of two or more of its surviving officers coincides with the disposition of the brigades as deposed to by the Brigadier General and Staff, and in this manner to arrange the difficult positions of the machinery (if I may use the term) with all the accuracy which such data will admit. I cannot proceed upon any other principle – it would be useless to trust to the very imperfect first hand history accounts that have hitherto been published, which though they might serve the purpose of the general historian, or of the designer of a battle-piece, become of little or no value to the modeller, who, from the nature of his work, especially when that is constructed upon an unusually large scale, can make no progress without correct data – *accuracy*, *not effect*, being the sole object of his labours.

I remain, my dear General, your very faithful servant

WS

1 He required £1500 in total.

No. 4 Memorandum from Colonel Charles Grene Ellicombe[1] Royal Engineers

84 Pall Mall, 29 October 1834

ADD MS 34703, FO 192V

I fear this office cannot assist Lieutenant Siborne in any of the points referred to except it be from two printed sketches and a general plan by W. B. Craan in French which appears to be very detailed showing the position of all the corps engaged but as for the 'Crisis' I don't know how the information is to be got at and I fear the answers to the proposed circular would only bring a mass of information that never could be got together with any degree of accuracy.

The plans in this office could not of course be parted with except by the Master General's sanction.

C G ELLICOMBE

1 Colonel Charles Grene Ellicombe CB, Brigade Major to the Royal Engineers, had joined the Royal Engineers as a 1st lieutenant in 1801 (never having served as a 2nd lieutenant). He served in the Peninsula from 1811 until the end and received a Military General Service Medal with five bars for Ciudad Rodrigo, Badajoz, Vittoria, Nivelle and Nive. He also received a Gold Medal for San Sebastian. He died in 1871.

No. 5 Sir James Willoughby Gordon[1] to Lord Fitzroy Somerset

Horseguards, 1 November 1834

ADD MS 34703, FO 192

Private

My dear Lord Fitzroy,

I return herewith all the papers you gave me from Lieutenant Siborne.

There is in this office a very good plan of the field of Waterloo and of the position of the two armies as they respectively stood at the commencement of the action, and of which Mr Siborne may take a copy if he pleases to send any one here for that purpose, as I have not help enough to offer to make one for him.

If Mr Siborne persists in his intention of representing upon his model 'The Crisis of the Battle', I do not see any prospect of his being enabled to obtain any information that can be depended upon.

The commanding officer of each regiment could certainly say where his regiment was posted at any period of the day, but to require such information for the purpose of a plan or model, would in my opinion lead to anything but an accurate exposition of the battle.

Two, three, or more regiments might be, and probably were, posted exactly on the same spot, within a few minutes each after the other and this could not be clearly represented either on a plan or model, but on the contrary would lead to a scene of indistinctiveness and confusion in the mind of any spectator whether civil or military:- besides as each commanding officer may be expected to attach great importance to the achievements of his own corps, and which his reflection during a period of 20 years has not perhaps tended to diminish in his own estimation, no very great reliance could be placed on information to be obtained from such a variety of sources, each enhancing (without an intention to mislead from) the truth.

It appears to me that the clearest point of view under which both armies could be represented on a model upon a large scale, would be that of their position at the commencement of the action, when each successive movement could best be followed up by an attentive study of the Duke's despatch – whereas if the action is to be represented as it stood at the close, and the information to be obtained from each commanding officer, or perhaps from others even less informed, this must in great measure tend to weaken the high authority of the Duke's despatch and to substitute in its stead divers minor accounts and those too not detailed at the time but after a lapse of 20 years.[2]

This is the way in which the matter strikes me, and I merely throw it out for the better judgement of those who have thought more about it.

Yours faithfully

J W GORDON

---

1 Sir James Willoughby Gordon GCB, GCH, Quartermaster General to the Forces. He had joined the army in 1783 as an ensign and rose to lieutenant general by 1825. He became Colonel of the 23rd Foot.

2 Gordon does seem to be very keen to avoid any diminution of the authority of the Duke's despatch.

No. 6 Lord Fitzroy Somerset to Mr F. H. Lindsay
Dover, 3 November 1834

ADD MS 34703, FO 192

My dear Lindsay,

I beg your attention to Sir W. Gordon's letter and to the memorandum by Colonel Ellicombe. You will see that they both concur with me in objecting to the circular and in thinking that it would lead to the production of a mass of contradictory information.[1] You had better communicate to Mr Siborne what they say, telling him at the same time that I am certain that Sir James Kempt will allow him to have access to the sketches and plan to which Colonel Ellicombe refers.

Yours faithfully

FITZROY SOMERSET

---

1 Again, there is clear evidence of a concerted effort to avoid any evidence that would prove contradictory to the Duke's despatch.

No. 7 From William Siborne to Lord Fitzroy Somerset
Dublin, 7 November 1834

ADD MS 34703, FO 193

Remarks upon Sir W. Gordon's letter of November 1st 1834 to Lord Fitzroy Somerset[1] *and Colonel Ellicombe's memorandum of 29th October*[2] *respecting the Waterloo model*

The model which I am constructing is not merely one of the *field* but also of the *battle* of Waterloo. Had I limited it to the former, a very small scale would have answered the purpose, similar to that which I adopted in my model of Borodino, and the positions of the troops might have then been represented by means of raised lines. Considering the number of accounts that have been published of Waterloo and the number of plans that have been drawn of the field, I must confess I do not see what novelty or interest a model would possess if intended only to represent the positions occupied by the respective armies at the commencement of the action. At all events this was not the object I had in view when I undertook the work. My idea was that so long as a sufficient number of remaining eyewitnesses of, and participators in the battle remained in existence an excellent opportunity was afforded for the construction of a model which by the grandeur of its scale, the minuteness of its finish, and the accuracy of its representation, should be at once novel and attractive, and which by its depicting more particularly the eventful crisis of the battle upon the issue of which hung the destiny of Europe, should at the same time possess that national interest and importance which we are accustomed to attach to works of art associated with deeds which constitute the glory of the Empire. It is considered that to effect this, I shall 'not be able to obtain any information that can be depended upon,' great stress being at the same time laid upon 'the lapse of 20 years.'

Upon this I trust I may be allowed to remark with all due submission that I cannot persuade myself that there are not to be found, among the mass of surviving Waterloo officers, more particularly among those who held important commands on the day, many, who even supposing then not to retain a vivid recollection of *all* the distinguishing features of *the last great action in which they were engaged*, are fully able to answer the simple question – 'What was the formation and position of the division, brigade, regiment or battery, at the moment the French Imperial Guards reached the crest of the right of our position.' – a moment so definite, so distinct, and so critical. The other question 'What was the formation of the enemy's troops opposite the division' and such may not be so easily answered, and many an officer may say 'The smoke was so thick I could not observe them with sufficient distinctiveness' – then I must endeavour to procure the information from others who had a better opportunity of observation as also perhaps from the French themselves, but failing in all this I can with the greatest ease represent the thick smoke upon the model. It is also argued that 'two, three, or more regiments might be and probably were, posted exactly on the same spot within a few minutes each after the other, and this could not be clearly represented either on a plan or model, but on the contrary would lead to a scene of indistinctiveness and confusion.' There can be no doubt that the same spot of ground was occupied by different regiments during the day, and at very short intervals of time, but it must be recollected that there was a considerable pause previous to the attack of the Guard, that with the exception of the 5th and 6th Cavalry Brigades coming into position from the extreme left, as also a portion of the reserve from the right, the troops were all formed and ready for the coming storm, and that the ground on which they were posted was greatly limited in extent. Some commanding officers may recollect what particular regiments were on the flanks of their own or in their rear, and very few I should imagine would be unable to say what kind of force was in their immediate front, and at all events, it is not very likely that general officers in command of brigades, already forget in what manner the regiments under their orders were disposed in brigade. I do not anticipate my circular producing a mass of contradictory information, but am inclined to think that as every officer is made aware by that circular that he is not the only one from whom information on some particular point is requested, he will be very guarded in his statements, particularly with reference to the plan – indeed the few answers I have already received justify this opinion; nor can I conceive how an attempt to illustrate more in detail the main features of the battle, 'must in a great measure tend to weaken the high authority of the Duke of Wellington's despatch,' for it will contain nothing at variance with one syllable of that document, and moreover, I do not intend to fasten a single figure upon my model, until I shall have submitted for His Grace's approval and correction, a plan of the action, showing the manner in which I propose to distribute the troops at the moment in question.

After all, however, should this explanation not be deemed satisfactory still there are insurmountable obstacles to an abandonment of my original design. More than a hundred of my circulars have already been issued, and I continue issuing them daily. I have made application to the French and to the Prussian military authorities for information with respect to the 'Crisis'.

I have made and have in hand, houses represented as on fire, others as shattered with shot and shell, I have several thousands of figures, representing men in the act of firing and such, and as any alteration *now* would be attended with incredible inconvenience, immense sacrifice of labour, great loss of precious time and very heavy expense, I trust that in expressing my earnest wish to complete my work upon the plan with which I at first set out, I may not be deemed deficient in proper deference and submission to the military authorities, or undeserving of a continuance of their favourable continuance and support.

P.S. Since writing the above I have received the accompanying letter from Sir Hussey Vivian, giving his *decided* opinion that it is *preferable* to place the troops as they stood at the *Crisis*.[3]

SIBORNE

---

1 Letter number 5.
2 Letter number 4.
3 Letter number 8.

No. 8 From Sir Hussey Vivian
Royal Hospital, 7 November 1834

ADD MS 34703, FO 194V

My dear Siborne,

I regret much your continued indisposition and especially as it prevents your coming to me, as I was desirous of having an opportunity of saying a few words to you on the subject of your model and in reference to Sir Willoughby Gordon's remarks on your proposition to place the troops as they stood at the crisis, and his own proposition to place them as they stood at the commencement of the battle. My opinion decidedly is that that it is preferable to place them as they stood at the crisis – my reasons are as follows:

1st You will exhibit an infinitely more interesting part of the day than if you showed the two armies before a shot was fired and the scene itself as described by the distribution of the troops will convey some notion of the glorious victory obtained, which would not be the case if the two armies were simply posted on their original ground.

2nd In reply to those who doubt your being able to obtain correct information I would say that in no plan which has ever yet been published have I seen the different corps posted precisely as they stood even at the commencement of the battle. I say this from my own knowledge and personal observation. Craan for instance (and his plan I believe is one of the best) is incorrect as to the position of Vandeleur's brigade and mine, and I think you will have no difficulty in placing the armies (the British at least) at the Crisis as correctly on the ground as if you adopted the suggestion of the Q. M. General and made the time the commencement, and as to the information you may obtain, all I can say is, speaking from my own recollection; (if others have the same of what happened to the troops under their orders) I will undertake to say I could ride over the ground and make the different movements of my brigade and not diverge fifty yards to the right or left of the ground on which the regiments stood on that over which they passed, and I see no reason why others should not have just as perfect a recollection of the occurrences.

3rd It is urged by the Q. M. General that at the crisis 'two or three or more regiments might be posted exactly on the same spot within a few minutes each after the other and that this could not be clearly represented', the same might almost be said of the disposition of the troops at the commencement, but the fact is that immediately before the crisis, that is immediately before our advance, the British army had for the most part been steadily fighting for some time in position; the part of Lord Hill's corps which had come from the right and the two cavalry brigades from the left having moved into their places in line at an earlier period, so that supposing officers commanding divisions, brigades and regiments are prepared to state where their corps stood immediately before the advance, I see no reason whatever why as correct a position of our Army at least might not be exhibited as if the time chosen were that before the first shot was fired.

4th Sir Willoughby Gordon speaks of following up the movements from the commencement by the Duke's despatch, and fear that attempting to describe the position at the crisis may 'tend to weaken his high authority'. I am sorry to differ from Sir Willoughby, but must on this occasion be permitted to say that I think it will be more interesting and moreover that it will fully as much be in conformity with the despatch and the Duke's authority to follow up the movements from the commencement by that despatch until you place the troops in position as they stood immediately before the advance.

Lastly And it is of all the most important consideration and which does not appear to have occurred to Sir Willoughby if you describe the commencement of the battle or rather the period before the fight commenced, what are you to do with the Prussians? The advance of the Prussians and their attack on Plançenoit and on the right flank and rear of the French was one of the most important features, if not the most important, in the whole day, if your model has the troops placed as at the commencement, *the Prussians must left at home*, this is in my mind *conclusive* and I am sure will be in Sir Willoughby's and Lord Fitzroy's also.

In haste, ever yours very faithfully

H VIVIAN

No. 9 From Mr F. H. Lindsay

Horseguards, 15 November 1834

ADD MS 34703, FO 233

Dear Siborne,

I will answer your letter of the 13th when I have consulted Maling[1] – that of the 8th with its enclosures, I gave Lord Fitzroy to read – his remark upon the corner is pithy – 'Then let him issue his circular and the Lord give him a safe deliverance.'

I return Chermside's letter – and rejoice that in my haste to assist, the blunder I have committed has done no harm – you may make whatever use you like of me.

You will be surprised with the news.[2]

Yours truly

LINDSAY

1 Lieutenant Colonel Maling, 2nd West India Regiment, Assistant Military Secretary.

2 This probably refers to the shock resignation of Melbourne and the Whig government on 15 November. The offer of forming the government was made to Wellington, he declined and Peel was called. Peel was on tour in Europe and could not return from Rome for three weeks, in the interregnum the Duke stood in as caretaker.

No. 10 From Mr Algernon Greville[1]

Apsley House,[2] 10 April 1836

ADD MS 34706, FO 74

Mr Greville presents his compliments to Captain Siborne and in answer to which he regrets much to inform him that he can find no trace of the plans to which he refers. If they can be found he may rely upon being informed of it.

Mr Greville has mentioned Lt. Siborne's wish to the Duke of Wellington; His Grace says that he knows nothing of the plans. Mr. Greville is very much afraid therefore that they cannot be in his Grace's possession.

1 Algernon Frederick Greville secretary to Wellington 1827–42.

2 Apsley House, the London home of Lord Wellington, No.1 London.

No. 11 William Siborne to Lord Fitzroy Somerset
6 September 1836

ADD MS 34706, FO 153

My dear Lord,
At length I am enabled to transmit to your lordship a plan carefully prepared according to the result of the information in my possession and to the best of my judgement of the disposition which I propose to make of the troops upon the Waterloo model; and I shall feel greatly obliged by your having the kindness to submit it with the enclosed explanatory memorandum to the Duke of Wellington for any corrections or alterations which His Grace may feel disposed to make, and in particular to bring under His Grace's notice the '*doubtful points*' which I have enumerated and which without the Duke's gracious assistance I feel myself quite unable to clear up in a satisfactory manner.

At the same time I trust I may be pardoned the liberty I take in remarking that it is of the utmost consequence as regards the progress of the work that the plan should be returned to me with as little delay as may be compatible with His Grace's consideration.

I am Sir

W SIBORNE

No. 12 Mr F. H. Lindsay
Horse Guards, 26 October 1836

ADD MS 34706, FO 173

Confidential

My dear Siborne,
Lord Fitzroy Somerset appears to have placed your papers in the hands of D of W[1] – and from what I can gather, it is clear he is solicitous to converse with you upon some points which are very material to the perfect accuracy of your plan. Especially touching the share the Prussians actually had in deciding the battle. I therefore write – *earnestly* – to press your coming here – and as it may lead to your having an interview with the Duke, it will be as well that you should be prepared accordingly.

Let me hear by return of post that it is convenient for you to come – and the sooner the better, as you may catch the Duke either on his way through town[2] – or at Walmer[3] where you might have the assistance and advice of Lord Fitzroy beforehand.

Keep the object of your journey quiet – but believe me, you will do well to come.

LINDSAY

---

1 The Duke of Wellington.

2 London.

3 Walmer Castle was a favourite residence of the Duke whilst he held the post of Warden of the Cinque Ports.

No. 13 Reply from W. Siborne to Mr F. H. Lindsay
Commander-in-Chief's office, Horse Guards, 29 October 1836

ADD MS 34706, FO 174

Appendix A

My dear Lindsay

Be assured that I am most fully sensible of your kindness and of your continued attention to my interests evinced by your urgent advice that I should immediately proceed to London for the purpose of entering into some explanation with Lord Fitzroy Somerset concerning certain points very materially affecting the accuracy of my work, but you will I fear scarcely believe me when I tell you that it is quite out of my power to do as simply from my want of means. The truth is I am so completely *ruined* by my undertaking that it is very doubtful whether the small sum I have remaining in hand will suffice to enable me to transport the model to London when completed. Indeed I may safely say it will not – and how I am to get money to rent a temporary building for its reception (no exhibition room would be large enough) I know not. I have expended upon it upwards of £2,000, out of which I borrowed £1500, and this latter sum costs me in interest £10 a *month* including insurance on my life. At the lowest calculation 4 or £500 more will be required to enable me to *bring out* the work in London, but I see no prospect of obtaining that sum. It has also been the means of depriving myself and family of every comfort and I have lived in the utmost seclusion as you may probably have heard from others. So much for my starving to complete a work commenced under the authority and sanction of Government, without which *I* should have never ventured to have undertaken it in *the first instant.*

These circumstances added to the numerous impediments and vexatious delays of all kinds with which I have had to contend, and crowned by the severe disappointment I am made to feel by the rejection of any claims to promotion for the performance during as long a period of the most high and important duties, they confer distinctions upon my superiors, have, as you may easily conceive, made sad havoc with my health, which indeed had already been sufficiently impaired by my close confinement and occupation. It is with regret I must confess, that I am at this moment writing to you suffering with extremely ill health and the utmost depression of spirits.

Although my going to London is quite out of the question, I think it right to remark that I am most ready to supply answers to any questions respecting the proposed disposition of the troops on the model. With respect to the Prussians I must observe *in justification* that the distribution of the 4th and 2nd Corps which was in support coincides generally with best French accounts, and that the disposal of the 1st Corps (Ziethen) is strongly confirmed by corroborative records in my possession.[1]

Believe me Lindsay

PS More especially as regards the most advanced Prussian cavalry regiment *in rear* of the British left wing, *before* the general advance of our line.[2]

---

1 This clearly shows that the disposition of the Prussians on the plan had raised concerns within Wellington's circles.

2 The Prussian cavalry of Ziethen's corps was indeed closing in on the extreme left of Wellington's army at the time of 'the crisis', but had not reached the rear of that wing. Siborne *was* mistaken in placing the Prussian cavalry so close.

No. 14 Lord Howick[1]
War Office, January 5th 1837

ADD MS 34706, FO 199

Copy of letter Written to Sir Hussey Vivian
Private

Dear Sir Hussey
I received your note of the 3rd enclosing Lt. Siborne's letter, and it would have given me great pleasure if in consideration of the strong recommendation you have given him I could have complied with his request, but I have no authority to do so, and it would have been quite in vain for me to recommend the application to the Treasury where the case has already been decided. I cannot conceive that if the work is really so good and if Lt. Siborne has just grounds for expecting that he could repay the advance he wants, he would have any difficulty in obtaining a loan to this amount from private individuals.

I am Sir.

HOWICK

1 Lord Howick served as Secretary at War 1835–39; he succeeded as the 3rd Earl Grey in 1845. He died in October 1894.

No. 15 From E. Marshall
War Office, 9 January 1837

ADD MS 34706, FO 207

Sir,
In reply to your letter of the 2nd instant, requesting an advance of money to enable you to complete the model undertaken by you of the field of Waterloo, I am directed to acquaint you that Lord Howick very much regrets that he does not feel himself authorized to comply with your request.

I am, Sir, your most obedient servant

E MARSHALL

No. 16 From Lord Fitzroy Somerset
Horseguards, 7 March 1837

ADD MS 34706, FO 250

My dear Sir,
I return the confidential memorandum you sent me on the 28th ultimo. I am very much obliged to you for letting me see it as also for the details which your letter affords.

Knowing how much time and labour you have bestowed on the model of Waterloo, how ably you have executed the work and how important it is to your interests that no time should be lost in exposing it to view I feel great reluctance in acknowledging to you that I continue of the opinion I before specified and that I still think that the position you have given to the Prussian troops is not the correct one as regards the moment you wish to represent, and that those who see the work will deduce from it that the result of the battle was not so much owing to British valour and the great generalship of the chief of the English Army, as to the flank movements of the Prussians.

I have not leisure to go into a consideration of the different authorities quoted in your memorandum, but I must observe that the time of the advance of the Prussians varies very much in the different accounts, and that I cannot help thinking that if as early in the afternoon as is advanced by some of the extracts you have given, a forward movement had been made by them in large numbers, the Duke of Wellington would have been immediately apprised of an event of such primary importance and yet certainly as long as I remained with him no such intimation was received notwithstanding that the point of the road from which the Prussians must have branched to their left could not have been a quarter of an hours ride from the part of the field where His Grace was to be found. I have always understood that the Duke's movement in advance arose from his observing the confusion of the enemy after the failure of their last attack upon his position, and that he then put everything in motion to his front, but I have never before heard that he came to this resolution from any other causes.

Colonel Egerton[1] will write to you or Colonel D'Aguilar[2] on the subject of Lord Hill's subscription. I regret to say that it would be very inconvenient to me to subscribe at this moment and I am therefore obliged to relinquish the idea of assisting in the completion of the work.

Believe me very faithfully yours

FITZROY SOMERSET

---

1 Colonel Richard Egerton, CB, half pay unattached, Aide de Camp to Lord Hill. He had served in the Peninsula and Waterloo.

2 Colonel George Charles D'Aguilar, CB, unattached, Deputy Adjutant General for Ireland. He had served in India with Lake, at Walcheren, Ciudad Rodrigo, Badajoz and Salamanca.

No. 17 From Sir Hussey Vivian
19th April 1837

ADD MS 34706, FO 312

My dear Siborne!

I sincerely rejoice to find that your prospects are so bright and as truly hope they may never again be clouded.

I care not what any one may say to depreciate the importance of the Prussian aid. My own opinion always has been and always will be that but for that aid our advance never would have taken place. We might have held our ground (but then we should not have done had Grouchy[1] been available for the attack on our left where we were weak) but as to advancing, we could not have thought of it had not the Prussians carried Plançenoit and had not the enemy in consequence begun to leave. I saw some part of their force [move?] towards the rear, which was observed by the D. of Wellington (I apprehend) before he gave the order to move. I know not what high authority may object to giving due credit to the Prussians, certainly not the D. of W. I should think. As to what Freemantle[2] may say, he must be dreaming when he speaks of the Prussians being engaged on the 17th and Plançenoit being at a distance of a march and such.

There are two facts for that I can vouch that settle the point. First, when the 18th Hussars attacked and pursued the enemy beyond La Belle Alliance, they found Prussian troops in the high road from the Belle Alliance to Genappe and on the Brussels side of the latter village *considerably*. They mistook them for French and some blows passed, and if the truth was told some Prussians were cut down by men of the 18th. Now these must have been part of those who had been attacking the French right in and about Plançenoit. 2ndly when I rode up to the D. of Wellington after the last attack of my Brigade and having reformed it on the ground beyond La Belle Alliance, I said I was ready to go on in pursuit. The Duke ordered me 'No, put up your brigade, the Prussians have undertaken the pursuit, I have settled it with Marshal Blücher'. How, if the Prussians were at a march distant, how happened it the Duke could at this time have seen Blücher? This may speak for itself.

I have no desire to take from the merits of the British, but I cannot be blind to the advantage, the important advantage, the attack of the Prussian force was of to us, and it's not fair not to give it its due weight and the Prussians their due credit. The Duke's despatch however speaks for itself and shows what were his feelings on the subject.[3]

From there, as to your question as regards the first advance of the Prussians. If I mistake not, it was between Papelotte and Frischermont (entering part of the former) that it occurred, but I could show you on the plan I think, I am sure I could on the model. There had been some skirmishing there about all day between small bodies of the French and the Nassau troops (I believe) who occupied Papelotte. I have no recollection that the advance of the Prussians occasioned any much greater fire, it appeared to me they were not resisted until they had crossed the hedge and formed, then as I have before described the French threw out a body against them and they at once retired under cover of the village and the farms, nor was this followed by any serious conflict. The French appeared to be satisfied and I do not think they even completely after this occupied the village. I was so much at times occupied with my own duties that I could not of course attend to every thing that occurred, it was some considerable *time after this* that any large body of Prussians *were seen advancing and extending away to their left towards Plançenoit.* (Still I presume this was seen by him before he quitted the left[4]).

The Major thank God is much better. Send a letter to me for Major Rudyerd[5] and I will send it to him, that will be your shortest way whom to.

Ever my dear Siborne yours most faithfully

HUSSEY VIVIAN

---

1 This statement is a peculiar one. The detachment of Grouchy's corps was meant to prevent the junction of Blücher's army with Wellington. If Grouchy's corps had been at Waterloo, then Napoleon would have faced the prospect of the whole of the Prussian army converging on him and presumably would have needed to use such a force to hold the Prussians back rather than using it against Wellington's flank.

2 Lt. Colonel unattached John Freemantle CB, Aide de Camp to Queen Victoria. He had joined the 2nd Foot Guards in 1805, serving in Germany in 1806, South America in 1807 the Peninsula (Vittoria and Orthes) and Waterloo where he was an aide de camp to Wellington, with the rank of lieutenant and captain.

3 The Duke made clear his view in his Waterloo despatch of 19 June 1815, quoted in

Gurwood's *Despatches* vol. 12. On p. 482 he states 'These attacks were repeated until seven in the evening, when the enemy made a desperate effort with cavalry and infantry, supported by the fire of artillery, to force our left centre, near the farm of La Haye Sainte, which, after a severe contest, was defeated; and having observed that the troops retired from this attack in great confusion, and that the march of General Bülow's corps, by Frischermont, upon Plançenoit and La Belle Alliance, had begun to take effect, and as I could perceive the fire of his cannon, and as Marshal Prince Blücher had joined in person with a corps of his army to the left of our line by Ohain, I determined to attack the enemy, and immediately advanced…' And on p. 484 'I should not do justice to my own feelings, or to Marshal Blücher and the Prussian army, if I did not attribute the successful result of this arduous day to the cordial and timely assistance I received from them. The operation of General Bülow upon the enemy's flank was a most decisive one...'

4 Lord Wellington.

5 This is probably Lieutenant Colonel Samuel Rudyerd, Royal Artillery (he became a lieutenant colonel on 10 January 1837, hence Vivian referring to him as a major is a mistake). He had joined the corps in 1803, serving in bomb vessels off the coast of France in 1804 and then served in the East Indies. He served at Waterloo as Second Captain in Major Lloyd's battery.

No. 18 From Lord Fitzroy Somerset KCB
Horseguards, August 28th 1837

ADD MS 34706, FO 352

My dear Sir,

I return the memorandum which you sent me on the 14th instant and regret to say that it is not in my power to afford you any information upon the several points to which your enquiries are directed.

It appears to me that the Duke of Wellington could not fairly be called upon to speak to any separate or specific operation of the battle without going at the same time with the whole question and having his opinion received as entirely conclusive.[1]

Very faithfully yours

FITZROY SOMERSET

---

1 From 1815 onwards, Wellington avoided all attempts to engage him publicly in the various discussions regarding the battle of Waterloo as he did not wish to convey any criticism of his subordinates, which must surely have happened if he had openly pronounced his honest opinion on various occurrences during the battle.

No. 19 From Mr G. J. Pennington of the Treasury
Treasury Chambers, 22 October 1839

ADD MS 34707, FO 147

Sir

I have it in command from the Lords Commissioners of Her Majesty's Treasury to acquaint you, in reply to your letter of 19th September, offering for sale to the public your model of the battle of Waterloo, that my Lords decline complying with your request.[1]

I am, Sir, your obedient servant

G J PENNINGTON

1 His request for Government funds to purchase the model for the nation.

No. 20 From W. Siborne to Major General Sir Henry Hardinge, KCB, Secretary at War[1]
Dublin, 16 September 1841

ADD MS 34707, FO 312ff

Sir,

I take the liberty of submitting the following statement to your consideration.

I need scarcely recall to your recollection that in the year 1830 I was commissioned by the General Commanding-in-Chief to undertake the construction of a model of the battle of Waterloo, his lordship having previously obtained permission [of] your authority, as Secretary at War,[2] for my being reimbursed from time to time for all expenses attending this national work. I entered upon my laborious task, and matters went on smoothly while you, Sir, continued in office, but in 1833 my operations were unexpectedly suspended by the then Secretary at War (Mr Ellice), who intimated to me that the Lords of the Treasury were not disposed to grant any further sum of money for this service, but were willing that the amount already advanced (£380) should be made over to me *if* I thought fit to complete the work on my own account. Upon this understanding, and in consideration of the minutely accurate survey I had made of the field of battle, as also of the extremely valuable information I had succeeded in collecting from numerous eyewitnesses of and participators in, that glorious action, I decided upon continuing the work at my own cost and at my own risk. I need not trouble you with an enumeration of the difficulties I had to encounter, of the expenses I had to incur, or of the endless correspondence I had to maintain; neither will I advert at length to the constant anxiety, the immense labour, and the unremitting perseverance which the fulfilment of such a task entailed upon me. Suffice it to say, the work was at length completed, and for the highly favourable impression it made upon the public, upon the military world, and upon artists generally, I may with the fullest confidence appeal to the numerous and unqualified eulogisms upon it which have emanated from the press. The cost of its construction amounted to £3,000, and yet, notwithstanding its having been visited by so great a number of persons – in London alone by about 100,000 – I have not succeeded in recovering more than a very slight portion of the above outlay.

Whether this has risen from the expensive establishment maintained, from mismanagement, or from the circumstance of my not having been able to devote my personal superintendence to the exhibition, I will not pretend to say, but such, most unfortunately for me, is the result of my labours, in a pecuniary point of view.

The difficulty and expense of transporting the model from place to place, of hiring and fitting up suitable premises for its reception, and of maintaining the number of persons required to be in attendance upon so large a work, are such as to render it by no means profitable as a public exhibition in the hands of a private individual, and I conceive it is only calculated to fulfil the design originally contemplated by Government, of its becoming the property of the nation.

Having been under the necessity of borrowing the money I required for the construction of the model, the yearly interest upon it, and insurance of my life as security, have added materially to my difficulties, and so greatly impoverished my resources, that I have been compelled to subject myself and family to privations which I had never contemplated. To crown all, one of my creditors (who was my agent in London, and whom my friends strongly suspect of designing to get the model into his own hands) will be empowered on the 1st of next December, should I not be prepared to pay him a sum of £500 by that date, and which I shall be utterly unable to do, to give me three months notice of his intention to proceed to a sale of the work, for the purpose of indemnifying himself to that amount; and I have no doubt that as a speculator he will turn it to good account, and thus deprive me of all possibility of retrieving myself, or of obtaining the slightest remuneration for the toil, the expense, the anxiety, as well as injury to my health which I have encountered in consequence of this importunate undertaking.

Under these circumstances, Sir, I appeal to you as a last resource, trusting that your sense of justice will prompt you to take such steps as shall relieve me from my present embarrassment, and entreating you to bear in mind that the work in question originated with the government of which you were a member, and that I was induced by the succeeding government to carry on the model at my own risk, in consequence of the alternative held out of requiring me refund the money previously advanced.[3] I ask for no remuneration either for my seven years labour, or for any ingenuity which the work may be considered to evince, and even should the cost of its construction be deemed too much for its purchase, I would make a great sacrifice rather than allow the model to be seized by the individual to whom I have already referred.

That the model will increase in value in after years, there cannot be the slightest doubt, when we consider how greatly the features of the ground have been altered since 1815; entire fields having been excavated to afford the materials out of which an enormous mound has been erected on the spot by which the Dutch government, thus obliterating a most important portion of the Duke of Wellington's position; several woods, also, having disappeared, and become arable land; and new houses having been raised either in addition to, or in substitution of, former habitations; whereas the model offers a most minute, faithful, and mathematically correct representation of the celebrated field, as it existed at the time, even in its most trivial details.

I think it right to remark that, having about four months since, thoroughly re-painted the model with much brighter colours, I have succeeded in imparting to it a brilliancy of effect which has most materially improved its general appearance; and, in the event of its being purchased for the nation, I shall be most happy still further to embellish it, as also to superintend with the utmost care, the fitting of it up in any room in the British Museum, the Tower, or in such other place as may be appropriated for its reception.

There is another point to which I would wish to allude. I am well aware that in the opinion of some of our highest military authorities, the Prussian troops occupy the prominent a position upon the model, an opinion to which I should be I should be sorry to be so presumptuous as to oppose my own impressions, which may very possibly be erroneous, and the moment the work ceases to be my property, and I am no longer obligated to adhere to those impressions, I shall be most ready and willing to make any alteration that may be suggested in this or in any other respect.[4]

The model is now at Belfast, whence it could be shipped by steamer ship for London.

I have Sir etc.

W SIBORNE

---

1 The Right Honourable Henry Hardinge, KCB, Secretary at War. He had joined the army as an ensign in 1798, serving in the Peninsula. He received a Cross with five bars for Busaco, Albuera, Badajoz, Salamanca, Vittoria (severely wounded), Pyrenees, Nivelle, Nive and Orthes. He was severely wounded when attached to the Prussian army at the battle of Ligny on 16 June 1815, losing his left hand. He became Governor General of India in 1844, was ennobled as Viscount Hardinge of Lahore and King's Newton (Derbyshire) in 1846. He was Commander-in-Chief 1852–56 and became a field marshal in 1855.

2 Hardinge had been Secretary of War between 1828 and 1830 when the project was commissioned. He left the post when the Whig government took power.

3 The prospect that William might be forced to repay the advances already made by government, (although the reasoning for this is unclear as it was merely for payment of legitimate expenditure on an officially sanctioned project) would have been another major factor in his decision to continue the model; this would indicate that he may not be the sole cause of his financial problems.

4 This offer to distort the truth is to be condemned, however it is clear that by this time the huge debts he was accumulating were weighing him down and he was becoming increasingly desperate to unload the model. That a man who had valiantly sought the truth should be forced to such extremities shows the depths of his despair. The model was not purchased at this time and therefore the layout was not altered and the validity of the model was retained.

No. 21 From Mr Sullivan
War Office, 20 November 1841

ADD MS 34707, FO 314ff

Sir,

Your letter of the 16th September last, on the subject of your model of the battle of Waterloo, having been brought under the Secretary of War's consideration, I am directed to acquaint you that Sir Henry Hardinge very much regrets the failure you have experienced in the reimbursement of the expenses incurred in constructing a work of art so interesting to the public, and so creditable to your ability, as that model undoubtedly is.

Sir Henry Hardinge, however, cannot originate any proposal for the purchase of the work by the Government; any measure of that nature appearing to be one which should emanate from the General Commanding-in-Chief, or the Master General of the Ordnance, with a view to placing the model where it may be made applicable to purposes of instruction, at the same time that it remains a record of the battle.

I am Sir etc.

L SULLIVAN

No. 22 From General Sir George Murray[1]

Ordnance Office, 24 November 1841

ADD MS 34707, FO 314ff

My dear Sir,

I am very sorry for all the disappointments, and I may, I believe, add, losses which you have met with in regard to your model of the battle of Waterloo, in the construction of which you have shown so much talent and so much industry.

I do not at present see, however, how I would, as Master General of the Ordnance, originate an application for the purchase of the model at the public expense. It has not any direct connection with the peculiar branch of the service which belongs to this department; and could hardly be considered as being conducive to the instruction of officers of artillery or engineers as such. If it is to be employed as a means of conveying instruction to military men, it must be in the branches of tactical and strategical operations, which are more connected with the department of the Quarter Master General than with the Ordnance.

All I could do would be to support individually as a General officer, the idea of the model being made national property, in the event of the Government asking an opinion from me on the subject.

I remain Sir etc.

G MURRAY

1 General Sir George Murray had been Wellington's Quartermaster General throughout most of the war in Spain and had he not been in America in 1815, he would have sought him again at Waterloo. He served as Master-General of the Ordnance from 1834–5 and again from 1841–6.

No. 23 W. Siborne to the Lord Fitzroy Somerset KCB

Dublin, 27 November 1841

ADD MS 34707, FO 312

My Lord,

I do myself the honour to transmit to your lordship the accompanying copies of a correspondence which I have had with the Secretary at War and the Master General of the Ordnance, relative to the disposal of my model of the battle of Waterloo.

Your lordship will perceive that both those authorities are of opinion that any proposal for the purchase of the above work by the government should emanate from the General Commanding-in-Chief, which circumstance combined with that of his lordship having originally authorised the construction of the model, with, I trust, be deemed to afford sufficient grounds to warrant my requesting you will be pleased to submit the matter for Lord Hill's favourable consideration.

I beg leave at the same time to mention that my pecuniary affairs have become so distressingly embarrassed by the result of my unfortunate undertaking as to render it most desirable that whatever steps Lord Hill may think proper to take in regard to this question, they may be communicated to me as early as may be compatible with his lordship's convenience, so as to enable me to avert, if possible, the impending seizure of the model on the part of certain of my creditors.

I have Sir

W SIBORNE

No. 24 From Lord Vivian[1]

[Indecipherable], 28 November 1841

ADD MS 34707, FO 317

My dear Siborne

You are quite at liberty to keep the map, only take care and do not let it be mislaid, but put it up with the other books you have of mine.

I had some quaint notion that you might have seen the letter but I was not certain. I know I have not read it myself since July 1815 when I returned from Paris in consequence of Lady Vivian's confinement and after I made the corrections which appear on it.

I am sorry to say there are still difficulties in the way of your publication, because from the materials you have collected, you have the means of giving to the world a more honest and a more complete account of the Waterloo campaign than any other was had of any other battle or than any other person ever can have of the great one which was then fought.

You may be assured there cannot *be the slightest question*[2] as to where my brigade bivouacked, and the complete coincidence on the statements of the other officers as to its being near Rossomme only shows how a man writing a history and fancying he has the very best source of facts may be led into error.

I have no doubt that not one of those who corresponded with you on the subject have enquired the name of the hamlet, or knew there was such a place as Hilaincourt. They first saw the observatory, heard the farm of Rossomme was somewhere near it and put it down at once that it was near Rossomme they had passed the night after the battle.

In respect to the model, I will be delighted if your appeal to the corps is of any service to you. Referred to them as you are by the Secretary at War is a point in your favour and he lays high approval of the work in this. But then comes the money, then comes the difficulty of disposing of the model and lastly then comes the D. of Wellington, for without him they will not one of them stir one mite.

Ever my dear Siborne very faithfully yours

H VIVIAN

1 Vivian was created a baron on 19 August 1841.

2 This letter is a good example of how Vivian was quite adamant as to the correctness of his recollections against all others. William does however appear to have been strong enough to stand his own ground and not be swayed heavily by Vivian's forceful personality, strong views or indeed his money.

Appendix A

No. 25 From Lord Fitzroy Somerset
Horseguards, 7 December 1841

ADD MS 34707, FO 320

Sir,

I have had the honour to receive your letter of the 27th ultimo, transmitting copies of your correspondence with the Secretary at War and Master General of the Ordnance relative to the disposal of your model of the Battle of Waterloo, and requesting that I would submit to the General Commanding-in-Chief your earnest hope that he would recommend to the government to purchase it at the public expense.

Having laid your communication before Lord Hill, I am directed to state, that he deeply regrets that a work upon which you have bestowed so much labour and in the execution of which you have displayed so much ability, should have occasioned you an expense which it's subsequent exhibition has not repaid instead of producing as might fairly have anticipated a considerable profit; but he does not feel at liberty to propose to Her Majesty's Ministers to buy it of you

I have the honour to be, Sir, your obedient humble servant

FITZROY SOMERSET

No. 26 William Siborne to Lord Fitzroy Somerset
Dublin, 11 December 1841

ADD MS 34707, FO 322V

My Lord,

I have the honour to acknowledge the receipt of your Lordship's letter of the 7th instant, informing me that the General Commanding-in-Chief does not feel at liberty to propose to Her Majesty's Ministers to purchase my model of the battle of Waterloo as national property.

I think I may be permitted to give expression to the extreme regret which I feel on receiving this intimation of Lord Hill's decision. It is painful to me to reflect that the work that I originally undertook at the instance, and under the authority of His Lordship, upon which I bestowed so many years of [thankless?] labours, and in the execution of which, he has been pleased to remark 'displayed with much ability', should not have proved to be such as would merit His Lordship's recommending the government to purchase it for the nation. I applied my best energies to the laborious task, I deserted all my [other?] prospects to its accomplishment,[1] and endeavoured to the best of my judgement to give a faithful representation of the Battle, such as it was at a certain period of the day; but as, in a complicated work of this nature it is much more probable that I should have erred in many instances than that my design should have been perfectly correct in every particular, I should feel greatly obliged by your informing me whether His Lordship's objections be founded upon any inaccuracy which I may have committed, because, as the model of the field is mathematically true, and such inaccuracy could therefore only occur in the distribution of the figures, and consequently be very easily corrected, I am most desirous of making any alterations which His Lordship or any officers entrusted by him, might consider necessary, with a view to render the representation more faithful, and therefore more deserving of His

Lordship's patronage and support.[2] I still venture to entertain a hope that Lord Hill may be induced, in consideration of the distressful circumstances in which I am placed, to recommend to government the purchase of the work, subject to the fulfilment, on my part, of the condition which I have above suggested, and thus relieve me from the ruinous embarrassment in which I have become involved, by this unfortunate undertaking, and which may yet compel me to ask His Lordship's permission to sell out of the service.[3]

I have Sir…

W SIBORNE

1 This is a tacit agreement by William that his decision to completely immerse himself in this project had severely damaged his prospects for advancement within the army.
2 This is a thinly veiled offer to alter the offending (Prussian) troop dispositions on the model.
3 The sale of his Captain's commission would help pay his debts.

No. 27 Lord Fitzroy Somerset
Horseguards, 24 December 1841

ADD MS 34707, FO 324

Sir,

Having submitted to the General Commanding in Chief your letter of the 11th instant, upon the subject of the purchase of your model, and His Lordship having observed with regret that you still entertain a hope that he may be induced to recommend the purchase of it to government; I am directed to acquaint you, that his decision upon that point as communicated to you in my letter of the 7th instant, must be considered final.

I have the honour to be, Sir, your obedient humble servant,

FITZROY SOMERSET

No. 28 Major Basil Jackson of the Staff Corps[1]
5 January 1846

ADD MS 34708, FO 232

Adverting to the modes[2] which have been suggested of disposing of the Waterloo models, the 'First' is the only one that I think likely to be attended with success.

With regard to the 'Second', I fully concur with all the objections stated. If one third of the required sum could be raised amongst civilians. I have very strong doubts of the possibility of obtaining the remaining two-thirds from the Army.

As regards the 'Third' proposition although a sum of money would undoubtedly be raised in the manner proposed. I greatly question the feasibility of the measure, when the sum required is of such magnitude.

Looking at the 'Fourth' proposal, I should imagine that few, if any, individuals of regiments would come forward with £100.

An idea has occurred to me, with reference to the 3rd mode suggested, viz. that if it were tried, and a considerable sum collected, government might possibly be induced to make up the difference, but in such a view, a vigorous examination into all expenses connected with the models would doubtless be made and no greater sum would be contributed by government than what would barely cover the original cost of the models.

It may be as well for me to give an extract of a letter dated 17th June 1844, with which I was favoured by Mr Alison the historian.[3]

In reference to Captain Siborne's labours, he says, 'I intend in a note (to a new edition of the *History of Europe*) to give the highest praise to his models, which I saw with the utmost delight in this City (Glasgow) some years ago, and to urge the purchase of it, or a similar one on government, as a national monument'

In the failure of other modes of disposing of the models, might it not be advisable to offer them to the government at the lowest possible price.

I do not pretend to be able to form any proper estimate of the value of the models, but it does seem to me that the sums named are beyond what could reasonably be expected, whatever mode of disposing of them might be determined on.

BASIL JACKSON

1 Basil Jackson of the Staff Corps, joined the Military College in 1808 and the army as an ensign in 1811. He served in the Netherlands in 1814–15 and went to St Helena when the island became a prison to Napoleon. He became a Lieutenant Colonel half pay and died in 1889. He was the author of *Notes and Reminiscences of a Staff Officer,* written in 1877 and published in 1903. His earlier articles in the United Services Journal (1830s and 40s) do differ from his later work, thus his *Reminiscences* should be used with caution.

2 The modes are not listed anywhere, but can be generally deduced from the text.

3 Sir Archibald Alison, author of *History of Europe from the Commencement of the French Revolution to the Restoration of the Bourbons,* Edinburgh 1860.

No. 29 From the Chevalier Bunsen[1]

Prussian Legation, 4 Carlton House Terrace, 2 February 1847

ADD MS 34708, FO 263

Chevalier Bunsen presents his compliments to Captain W. Siborne and begs to inform him in answer to his letter of the 16th of September last, respecting the purchase of the model of the battle of Waterloo, which was exhibited at Berlin, by His Majesty the King of Prussia, that he did not fail to recommend it to the Royal Government.

Chevalier Bunsen is now directed to acquaint Captain Siborne that the said government although fully appreciating the praiseworthy undertaking which is already removed from Berlin, has declined to purchase it, not considering it of such an historical interest for His Majesty, as if *that moment* of the battle were represented, when the arrival of the Prussian army contributed to the glory of that day.[2]

1 Christian Charles Josias de Bunsen, Prussian ambassador to Britain (see letters 202–3).

2 This would appear to refer to the second model, which represents the defeat of D'Erlon's corps, as this model toured Germany in 1847–8. This comment could not have been directed against the first model, which was actually criticized by many in Britain for overstating the Prussian involvement in the victory of Waterloo.

APPENDIX B

Letters not printed in full

The following letters are also to be found in the Siborne files, but contain little of interest regarding the battle. I have however listed all of them here, with a brief statement of their contents for reference purposes.

Add Ms 34703 fo 11, is a report of the movements of the King's German Legion throughout the Waterloo campaign by Major Kruse in German. This document does not fall within the remit of this book as it is too large and it is planned to publish this in a separate booklet in the near future.

Add Ms 34703 fo 144, is a letter written in German by Captain C. Muller, featuring a table showing the uniforms of the Hanoverian troops.

Add Ms 34703 fo 180 and fo 324, written by William Siborne to Count Lobau requesting information on his Corps.

Add Ms 34703 fo 197, written by Major General George Cooke, which simply states that he had been wounded and carried from the field before the period alluded to.

Add Ms 34703 fo 207, written by Captain Samson Stawell, 12th Light Dragoons, simply refers Siborne to Batty's history of the campaign for the movements of his regiment.

Add Ms 34703 fo 240, written by Captain James McDonnell of the 2nd Battalion Coldstream Guards, stating that he was unable to furnish any information after such a time.

Add Ms 34703 fo 274, written by Major Robert Henry Dick of the 42nd Regiment, stating that he was wounded on the 18th and was unable to help, but adding that Captain Campbell took command of the regiment as all the senior officers were wounded.

Add Ms 34703 fo 287, written by First Lieutenant George B. Baynes declined to offer any information after such a long period.

Add Ms 34703 fo 319, written by Captain Philip Wodehouse, 15th Hussars, stating that his squadron was detached and he did not see the attack of the Imperial Guard.

Add MS 34703, the letters from Mr Lindsay *fo 129* and General Dalbiac *fo 137* of the Horseguards, are omitted as they merely continue the discussion regarding the proposed subscription and add nothing new.

Add Ms 34704 fo 22, written by First Lieutenant J. Enoch of the 23rd Regiment, stating he was unable to help and referring him to Lieutenant Ellis for information.

Add Ms 34704 fo 30, written by Captain D'Oyly of the 1st Foot Guards, stating he was unable to give any information as he was wounded at about 4 pm.

Add Ms 34704 fo 40, written by Major Percy Drummond, Royal Artillery, who states that he is unable to recollect anything of importance.

Add MS 34704 fo 113, this letter is attributed to Berkeley, but this reference is incorrect, as it is part of a letter previously published in *Waterloo Letters* by Murray.

Add Ms 34704 fo 149, written by William Siborne to Count Lobau requesting information.

Add Ms 34704 fo 179, written by Captain William Marshal of the 79th Highlanders, stating that he was put *hors de combat* on the 16th and so unable to help.

Add Ms 34704 fo 241, written by Lieutenant Colonel George Hartmann of the Hanoverian Artillery Staff, stating that he is unable to furnish any information.

Add Ms 34704 fo 252, written by Major William von Robertson, 1st Line Battalion KGL simply stating that he was wounded before 7 o'clock.

Add Ms 34704 fo 259, written in German by Captain von Gilsa of the 1st Line Battalion KGL simply enclosing a number of documents, here listed under each author's own reference.

Add Ms 34705 fo 32, written by Lieutenant John Winterbottom of the 52nd, simply stating the

correctness of Gawler's account.
Add Ms 34705 fo 39, written in German by Frederick Schnath Adjutant of the 1st Line Battalion KGL (417 in Beamish) stating that he is unable to give any information and refers him to Captain Kuckuck, 3rd Line Battalion KGL (490).
Add Ms 34705 fo 63, written by Captain Charles Frederick Love of the 52nd Regiment, stating that he is unable to forward any information as he had been severely wounded and refers Siborne to Lieutenant Colonel Gawler.
Add Ms 34705 fo 77, written by Ensign the Honourable Edward Stopford of the 3rd Foot Guards, stating that he was unable to furnish any information regarding his Regiment, as he was attached to the Staff of Major General Sir J. Byng, who commanded the 1st Corps, following the wounding of all the senior officers.
Add Ms 34705 fo 111, written by Lieutenant James Nixon of the 1st Foot Guards, simply concurs with the information forwarded by Captain Reeve of his regiment, whose letter is published in this volume (letter 97).
Add Ms 34705 fo 157, written by Ensign Eaton Monins of the 52nd Regiment, states that he was a soldier of a mere six months who did not make any observations of that day, but agreed with Lieutenant Colonel Gawler's account.
Add Ms 34705 fo 196, written by Lieutenant Lord Beaumont Hotham, in which he states that he was in Hougoumont all day and cannot state anything of use.
Add Ms 34705 fo 200, written by Lieutenant John Wildman, 7th Hussars, stating that he was injured and made prisoner on the 17th.
Add Ms 34705 fo 203, written by Lieutenant Donald Chisholm of the 42nd Regiment, stating he was unable to help.
Add Ms 34705 fo 205, written by Major Edward Parkinson of the 33rd Regiment, stating that he was unable to help as he had been wounded.
Add Ms 34705 fo 207, written by Captain Henry Wyndham of the Coldstream Guards, simply states that he was at Hougoumont and was wounded at about the time requested.
Add Ms 34705 fo 225, is recorded in the British Library files as written by Captain Frederick Goulbourn, 13th Light Dragoons, it is however clearly signed Hunter-Blair and is in fact letter 121 published by Siborne in *Waterloo Letters.*
Add Ms 34705 fo 254, written by Lieutenant Henry Hawkins of the 3rd Foot Guards, simply concurring with the letter of Captain Douglas Mercer of his regiment, published in this volume (letter 110).
Add Ms 34705 fo 261, written by Captain William Hewett of the 14th Foot, stating he was unable to give any information.
Add Ms 34705 fo 271, written by Second Lieutenant Darrel Jago of Captain Sandham's Battery, Royal Artillery, simply stating that he was unable to furnish any information.
Add Ms 34705 fo 283, written by Lieutenant Charles Allix, Adjutant of the 1st Foot Guards, simply concurring with the statement of Captain Reeve of his regiment, published in this volume.
Add Ms 34705 fo 285, written by Captain Edward Cheney of the Scots Greys simply concurring with the information sent by fellow officers.
Add Ms 34705 fo 289, is a covering letter written in German by Major F. Jacobi enclosing information regarding the movements of the KGL and Hanoverian troops at Waterloo.
Add Ms 34705 fo 303, written in German and attributed to Prussian Minister of War Schoeler, sending plans back with positions of the Prussian units added. The plan is not present.
Add Ms 34705 fo 310, written by Major George Muttlebury of the 69th Regiment, stating that he was unable to add further to the statement of Lieutenant Colonel Elphinstone, as the latter when drafting his reply had consulted him.
Add Ms 34705 fo 323, Add Ms 34706 fo 439 and Add Ms 34707 fo 494, are all covering letters from Lieutenant Lewis Heise of the KGL Staff, forwarding letters from German officers, which are entered under their own name.
Add Ms 34706 fo 23, is an official history of the Brunswick corps during the Waterloo campaign, written in German by Lieutenant General August von Herzberg. This is a massive document totalling some 10,000 words. This document does not fall within the remit of this book and it is planned to publish it as a separate booklet in the near future.

Add Ms 34706 fo 76, written by Lieutenant Colonel Sir Charles Broke, Permanent Assistant Quartermaster-General, simply apologizes for his inability to give any information, as he was unable to refer to his documents.
Add Ms 34706 fo 280, from the Prussian Minister of War Witzleben in German, thanking Siborne for the plans of the battle of the Boyne and enclosing plans from Wagner, which are not present.
Add Ms 34706 fo 321, is a short covering letter to Mr Lindsay, for the papers sent from the Prussian War Department to Siborne. It is signed by Baron Bülow.
Add Ms 34706 fo 345, written by Colonel Sir John Elley of the Royal Horse Guards, Deputy Adjutant General, who simply wishes Siborne success in his venture.
Add Ms 34706 fo 347, from the Prussian Minister of War Gustav von Rauch in German, forwarding plans and casualty lists from von Plotho's work.
Add MS 34706 fo 431, is a letter attributed to Fraser, this reference is incorrect, as it is actually signed by Lord Saltoun of the Guards and is published in Siborne's *The Waterloo Letters,* number 106. This letter was sent from The Hill, Brampton, which interestingly is the address of Lieutenant Ellis of the 1st Guards, whose letters are quoted within.
Add Ms 34706 fo 459, written by Captain John Gurwood, 10th Hussars, simply states he will try to gain the information requested of him by Sir Hussey Vivian on his return to Apsley House from Paris.
Add Ms 34707 fo 1, written by Lieutenant Robert Law of the 71st Regiment, questions the correct position of the 71st as depicted on the model at the time of the defeat of the French Guard, as when he was wounded at 5pm the 71st were in the centre of the Brigade not the right.
Add Ms 34707 fo 11, written by Lieutenant Colonel Ratcliffe (not at Waterloo) of the 6th Dragoons, forwarding papers from the regiment.
Add Ms 34707 fo 107 & fo 129, written by Lieutenant W. Riach of the 79th Regiment, stating that he had been wounded and carried to Brussels on the 16th.
Add Ms 34707 fo 111 listed correctly by the British Library as by Colonel John E. Jones is merely a short covering letter to a number of artillery returns used in his history.
Add Ms 34707 fo 326 and fo 366, written by Captain T. Wildman, 7th Hussars, Extra Aide de Camp to the Earl of Uxbridge provide no information as he had no clear memories.
Add Ms 34707 fo 416 which is recorded in the British Library catalogue as by Baron Stockman, merely indicates that permission had been granted for Siborne to dedicate the book to Her Majesty Queen Victoria and that she and Prince Albert wished to be subscribers to the same.
Add Ms 34707 fo 434, recorded as Couper, is written by him on behalf of the Duchess of Kent; *Add Ms 34707 fo 440*, recorded as Gillman, is written on behalf of Queen Adelaide; *Add Ms 34707 fo 455* recorded as Knesbech, is written on behalf of the Duke of Cambridge; and *Add Ms 34708 fo 66* by Baron de Brunow all of whom simply wished to subscribe to the book.
Add Ms 34707 fo 493, is correctly recorded as written by Lieutenant Lewis Benne and dated from Hanover on 30 November 1842. It appears that following a copious correspondence between the two, Benne was now being used by Siborne to generate interest in his book in Germany. Benne's brief note indicates his success, as The King of Hanover, The Crown Prince of Hanover and Prince Bernhard of Solms wished to subscribe.
Add Ms 34707 fo 525 listed correctly by the British Library as by Count Revel is merely a short covering letter for a narrative by the Count de Sales.
Add Ms 34707 fo 539, written by Captain Ward on behalf of Captain Sir Henry Hardinge KCB, simply stating that Lord Wellington's dispatch explained the circumstances of the loss of his arm.
Add Ms 34708 fo 64, written by Chevalier Bunsen in French, regretting that he would not be able to take a copy of the book for his library.
Add Ms 34708 fo 88, written by Lieutenant Slayter Smith of the 10th Hussars, merely restating the circumstances of his capture of General Lauriston.
Add Ms 34708 fo 122 from Captain Yorke merely points out a mistake in his duties at Waterloo and *fo 144* from Ensign Leeke of the 52nd regarding the misspelling of his name in the army lists, these were evidently corrected in later editions.
Add Ms 34708 fo 128 from Adjutant General de Rosen of the Swedish Army in French requesting to be added to the list of subscribers for his book.
Add Ms 34708 fo 132 from von Bülow in French stating that the King of Prussia wished to be

placed upon the list of subscribers for his book.
Add Ms 34708 fo 134 from Baron Gersdorff in French stating that the King of Saxony wished to be placed among his list of subscribers for his book.
Add Ms 34708 fo 138 from Madame Bunsen, and *fo 140* from Baron Stockman merely returns thanks for copies of the book.
Add Ms 34708 fo 149 and fo 290 are short notes in French from Frederic Guillaum regarding a copy of the book.
Add Ms 34708 fo 152 from the Reverend Darling, simply documents the services of Lieutenant Colonel Dumaresq.
Add Ms 34708 fo 158, written by Mr A. Maclean pointing out the omission of his brother, Ensign Charles James Maclean in the list of officers with the 79th at Waterloo. This error was corrected in the third edition.
Add Ms 34708 fo 175, written by Lieutenant Colonel B. Des Voeux pointing out the omission of his name from the list of officers of the 11th Light Dragoons in which corps he served as a lieutenant at Waterloo. This was corrected in the third edition.
Add Ms 34708 fo 186, written by Captain J. Ford of the 2nd Life Guards explaining the reasons why regimental records and official returns rarely agreed, either at Waterloo or throughout the Peninsular war. This was published recently in *The Waterloo Journal,* vol. 12, no. 2, of the Association of Friends of the Waterloo committee.
Add Ms 34708 fo 195, written by Captain H. Hill listing the omission of Captain Thomas Gerrard (severely wounded), Captain Henry Grove and Lieutenant and Adjutant Hill in the 23rd Light Dragoons. This was corrected in the third edition.
Add Ms 34708 fo 222 from Captain Ford, simply lists the flags and eagles then held at Chelsea Hospital and the battle honours recorded on them.
Add Ms 34708 fo 239 from Curzon Howe simply declines on Queen Adelaide's behalf, any possibility of her offering a subscription towards the purchase of the models. *fo 256* from Mr Fox Maule offers £5 towards the fund.
Add Ms 34708 fo 237, written by Colonel Bowles on behalf of Prince Albert offering the sum of £100 towards the fund to purchase the models for the nation.
Add Ms 34708 fo 269, is a report of the contribution of the Hanoverian troops throughout the Waterloo campaign. This is a large document written in German comprising some 6,000 words and is outside the remit of this book. It is planned to publish this separately as a booklet in the near future.
Add Ms 34708 fo 291, is merely a covering letter from Prince Count Lowenstein at the Prussian Legation in London forwarding a letter from his Government.
Add Ms 34708 fo 307 from Colonel Shaw Kennedy simply offering his help regarding Quatre Bras.
Add Ms 34708 fo 309, written by Lieutenant Colonel King of the 16th Light Dragoons, the letter simply mentions a very minor change to a previous narrative and states that he became Brigade Major on 19 June.
Add Ms 34708 fo 339, written by First Lieutenant Strangways of Whinyates' Troop R.H.A, the letter simply states that he can add nothing to his previous letters, which I have printed in full.

BIBLIOGRAPHY

A great number of reference books have been utilised in the preparation of this work, many of which I have mentioned in the individual notes. There are however, a few works, which have proven particularly invaluable and which I list here.

Adkin, M. *The Waterloo Comapnion*, Aurum Press, London and Stackpole Books, Pennsylvania, 2001.

Anon. *The Waterloo Medal Roll,* Naval and Military Press, Uckfield, East Sussex, 1992.

Beamish, N.L. *History of the King's German Legion*, Bulmer and Nicol, London, 1832–1937, reprinted Naval and Military Press, Uckfield, East Sussex, 1997.

Dalton, C. *The Waterloo Roll Call,* 2nd edn, Eyre and Spottiswoode, London, 1904, reprinted Arms and Armour Press, London, 1978.

Gurwood, J. *The Duke of Wellington's Despatches, 1799–1818.* Volumes 1–13, John Murrray, London, 1834–1839.

Hamilton-Williams, D. *Waterloo: New Perspectives*, Arms & Armour Press, London, 1993

Hart, H.G. *Annual Army List,* John Murray, London, various years.

Hofschröer, P. *1815 The Waterloo Campaign: The German Victory*, Greenhill Books, London, 1999.

Hofschröer, P. *1815 The Waterloo Campaign: Wellington, his German Allies and the Battles of Ligny and Quatre Bras*, Greenhill Books, London, 1998.

Houssaye, H. *1815 Waterloo*, A. & C. Black, London, 1900.

Lachouque, H. *Waterloo*, Arms and Armour Press, London, 1975.

Mullen, A.L.T. *The Military General Service Roll 1793–1814*, The London Stamp Exchange, London, 1990.

Ropes, J.C. *The Campaign of Waterloo*, Charles Scribners, New York, 1916.

Siborne, H.T. *The Waterloo Letters*, Cassell, London, 1891, reprinted Greenhill Books, London, 1993.

Siborne, W. *History of the Waterloo Campaign*, first published as *History of the War in France and Belgium in 1815*, T. and W. Boone, London, 1848, reprinted Greenhill Books, London, 1990.

INDEX

Name and ranks of writers of letters when at Waterloo

(numbers refer to the letter numbers in this volume)